The AMERICAN HERITAGE®

Children's
Science

Dictionary

HOUGHTON MIFFLIN

ork

Editorial and Production Staff

**Vice President, Publisher of Dictionaries, Director
of Production and Manufacturing Services**
Margery S. Berube

Vice President, Executive Editor
Joseph P. Pickett

Editorial Project Director
David R. Pritchard

Vice President, Managing Editor
Christopher Leonesio

Senior Lexicographer
Benjamin W. Fortson IV

Science Consultants
Rufus Burlingame
Keith Conrad
Jorge José
Allen Kropf

**Production and Manufacturing
Assistant**
Brianne Lutfy

Senior Editor
Steven R. Kleinedler

Administrative Coordinator
Kevin McCarthy

Editors
Hanna Schonthal—*project editor*
Vali Tamm

Database Production Supervisor
Christopher Granniss

Text Design
Edda V. Sigurdardóttir,
Studio Edda

Associate Editors
Matthew Heidenry
Kirsten Patey Hurd

Art and Production Supervisor
Margaret Anne Miles

Pre-Press Development
Pre-Press Company, Inc.
Victory Productions, Inc.

**Production and Manufacturing
Supervisor**
James W. Mitchell

Assistant Editor
Uchenna Ikonné

Library of Congress Cataloging-in-Publication Data

The American heritage children's science dictionary.
     p. cm.
Summary: Introduces the language and concepts of science through alphabetically listed entries with illustrations, "Did You Know" sidebars, and explanatory notes.
   ISBN 0-618-35401-8
   1. Science--Dictionaries, Juvenile. [1. Science--Dictionaries.] I. Title: Children's science dictionary. II. Houghton Mifflin Company.
   Q123.A517 2003
   503--dc21
                                                    2003010476

Manufactured in the United States of America

Visit our Web site: **www.houghtonmifflinbooks.com**

<u>Cover photo:</u>
Getty Images/The Image Bank, Stephen Frink

QWT 10 9 8 7 6 5 4 3 2 1

The AMERICAN HERITAGE®

Children's Science *Dictionary*

Table of Contents

Entries with Notes

Did You Know?

adaptation
air pressure
amino acid
avalanche
blood
cactus
camouflage
carbon
chameleon
charge
comet
computer
condensation
coral
crust
cyanobacteria
desert
direct current
dwarf star
$E = mc^2$
earthworm
effervescence
electromagnetic radiation
enamel
enzyme
evergreen
friction
fruit
glacier
gravity
hail
heart
hibernate
hormone
hurricane
hydra
instinct
intestine
Jupiter
lava
lightning
lungfish

magnetism
mass
measurement
memory
methane
molt
moon
mosquito
nerve
noble gas
nova
nylon
omnivore
ozone
penicillin
plastic
pollination
quicksand
radiocarbon dating
rain forest
regurgitate
relativity
rust
sensor
sleep
sound
steam engine
sublimation
surface tension
tail
telescope
tongue
tornado
trunk
universe
vaccine
velocity
vitamin
warm-blooded
year
zero gravity

Biography

Aristotle
Bell, Alexander Graham
Byron, Augusta Ada
Carver, George Washington
Copernicus, Nicolaus
Cousteau, Jacques Yves
Curie, Marie
Fossey, Dian
Galileo Galilei
Goddard, Robert Hutchings
Harvey, William
Humboldt, Alexander von
Jenner, Edward
Lavoisier, Antoine Laurent
Linnaeus, Carolus
McClintock, Barbara
Pasteur, Louis
Pavlov, Ivan Petrovich
Priestley, Joseph
Richards, Ellen Swallow
Salk, Jonas Edward
Tesla, Nikola
Vesalius, Andreas
Wallace, Alfred Russel
Wegener, Alfred Lothar

Preface

The knowledge of science is really a series of statements that describe what happens in nature. To understand statements like "Matter is made of atoms and molecules," "Each year the Earth makes one orbit around the Sun," and "Living things grow because their cells divide," we must understand the words that are used in them—words like *atom, orbit,* and *cell.*

The American Heritage Children's Science Dictionary can help you understand the basic words that are used in science and the special relationships between them. For instance, matter has three forms: solid, liquid, and gas. To understand what *matter* is, you must know the difference between the three forms. Once you know the difference, you know quite a bit about matter. In this way, learning about words like *solid, liquid,* and *gas* provides the key to greater understanding of the world in general.

This Dictionary contains entry words from many areas of science, areas like astronomy, biology, physics, and chemistry, as well as areas like the environment, the weather, computers, geography, and medicine. Each definition provides you with the most important information for each word in a style that is clear and easy to understand. At some entry words, special Notes add to this information by explaining amazing things that we often take for granted. For instance, if you have seen a compass, you know that its needle points North. But why? It's because the Earth itself is a giant magnet. You can learn about this at the Note for the word *magnetism.* A list of all entries that have Notes is on the previous page.

Science is the story of people searching for knowledge, of people trying to answer questions. What causes things to fall to the Earth? Where does blood go in the body after it has been pumped by the heart? Has the Earth always looked the same, or has it changed? Many of the greatest discoveries were made because people asked questions like these. And many of these people—history's great scientists—are here in this Dictionary. Because of their intelligence and hard work, and often because of their good luck, these thinkers and inventors changed how people look at the world.

We hope that using this Dictionary will change how you look at the world. We hope that it will make you ask questions. This is how science starts—by simple curiosity. And once you start being curious, the discoveries you make may astound you.

—*The Editors*

Parts of the Dictionary

Compare cross-reference shows where to look up a related entry word

guideword

Babbage

entry word a word with one or more definitions

Babbage (BAB-ij), **Charles** Born 1792; died 1871. British inventor who drew up plans for a machine that would perform mathematical calculations. While Babbage never completed his machine, his ideas laid the foundation for the modern computer.

bacteria (bak-TEER-ē-uh) Living things that are made up of single cells, each without a cell nucleus. Bacteria are found in all of the Earth's environments and usually live off other organisms. Some kinds of bacteria cause disease. Bacteria are members of the group of organisms known as **prokaryotes**. *Singular form*: **bacterium** (bak-TEER-ē-uhm).

irregular noun form

bacteriology (bak-teer-ē-OL-uh-jē) The scientific study of bacteria, especially bacteria that cause disease.

badlands An area that has many ridges and gullies. Badlands usually form in dry regions where sudden rains wash away soil and vegetation.

baking soda A white powder that contains sodium and is used to make carbonated drinks and baked goods.

See Table see list of Tables and Charts on page iii

basalt (buh-SAWLT *or* BĀ-sawlt) A common dark-gray rock that forms when magma cools into a solid. Basalt is made mostly of feldspar and minerals rich in iron and magnesium. Most of the ocean bottom is made of basalt covered with sand and mud. ◻ See Table on p. 208.

base **1** A chemical compound that tastes bitter and feels slippery when mixed with water. Bases form salt and water when they come in contact with certain metals and with the chemical compounds known as acids. Baking soda is an example of a base. ◻ Compare **acid**. **2.** A side of a flat shape, such as a triangle. The length of the base can be used to figure out the area of the shape. **3.** A face of a three-dimensional object, such as a pyramid.

beak The hard, projecting part of the mouth in birds. Beaks come in different sizes and shapes, depending on how birds feed. ◻ A beak is also called a *bill*.

Bell, Alexander Graham Born 1847; died 1922. American scientist who invented the telephone in 1876.

Biography

Alexander Graham Bell

Alexander Graham Bell spent many years teaching people who had difficulty hearing. His interest in sound and speech led him to think about devices that could send or record sounds. Besides inventing the telephone, Bell devised an early version of the hearing aid and created one of the first sound recorders.

bill *See* beak.

picture caption explains what the art shows

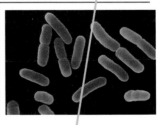

◻ **bacteria**
left to right: *the three shapes of bacteria—sphere, spiral, and rod*

20

See cross-reference shows where to find the definition

Biography see list of Notes on page iv

Did You Know?
see list of Notes
on page iv

boiling point The temperature at which a liquid changes to a gas or vapor. At the boiling point, vapors moving out of the liquid create so much pressure that they form bubbles. The boiling point of water is 212° Fahrenheit (100° Celsius).

Did You Know?
boiling point
You may know that water boils at 212° Fahrenheit or 100° Celsius. But that's only at sea level. If you were to boil water at the top of Mount Everest, it would boil at 159.8° Fahrenheit (71° Celsius). The air pressure up there is much lower, so it takes less heat to make bubbles form in water.

bond An attraction between atoms that holds them together in a molecule or crystal. Bonds are formed when one or more electrons are shared between atoms, or when one atom gives away electrons to another atom.

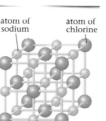

bond

When atoms of sodium and chlorine are joined by bonds, they form molecules of salt (sodium chloride).

bone 1. The hard material that forms the skeleton of most vertebrates. Bone provides protection for organs, such as the brain and heart, and serves as a support for the muscles of the body. Bones are connected to each other by ligaments. 2. One of the parts of the skeleton in vertebrates. The bone of the thigh is called the femur. The bones of the forearm are the radius and ulna.

bone marrow The soft, sponge-like material that fills the center of the bones of

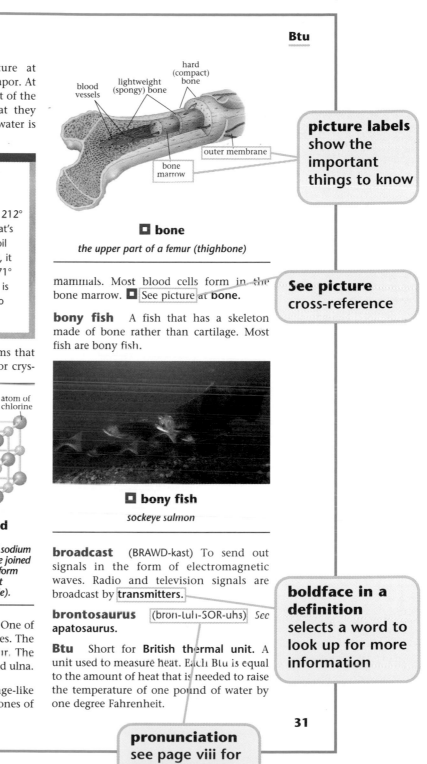

bone

the upper part of a femur (thighbone)

mammals. Most blood cells form in the bone marrow. ☐ See picture at **bone**.

bony fish A fish that has a skeleton made of bone rather than cartilage. Most fish are bony fish.

bony fish

sockeye salmon

broadcast (BRAWD-kast) To send out signals in the form of electromagnetic waves. Radio and television signals are broadcast by **transmitters.**

brontosaurus (bron-tuh-SOR-uhs) *See* **apatosaurus.**

Btu Short for **British thermal unit.** A unit used to measure heat. Each Btu is equal to the amount of heat that is needed to raise the temperature of one pound of water by one degree Fahrenheit.

picture labels
show the important things to know

See picture
cross-reference

boldface in a definition
selects a word to look up for more information

pronunciation
see page viii for pronunciation rules

31

Pronunciation

This Dictionary shows how to say most words that have two or more syllables. It also shows how to say difficult or unusual words that have only one syllable (such as **gneiss**). When a pronunciation is shown, it appears in parentheses following the entry word. The letters and symbols in the pronunciation stand for the sounds in that word. You can see how to pronounce these letters and symbols using the key to the right.

In words with more than one syllable, one of the syllables is usually said with a greater amount of stress. The syllable with the strongest amount of stress is shown by capital letters. For example, at **ligament**, the first syllable has the stress: (LIG-uh-muhnt).

Some words can be pronounced in more than one way, such as **adult**, which can be pronounced as either uh-DUHLT or AD-uhlt. In these cases, both pronunciations are given, with the more common pronunciation shown first. Pronunciations are also given for some plural or singular forms of a word. For example, at **nova**, the plural form **novae** (NŌ-vē) is shown.

Sounds	Sample Words	
Vowels		
a *or* A	rat	(RAT)
ā *or* Ā	rate	(RĀT)
	pay	(PĀ)
ah *or* AH	father	(FAH-*ther*)
aw *or* AW	paw	(PAW)
e *or* E	set	(SET)
ē *or* Ē	seat	(SĒT)
	be	(BĒ)
i *or* I	pit	(PIT)
ī *or* Ī	kite	(KĪT)
o *or* O	pot	(POT)
ō *or* Ō	toe	(TŌ)
	code	(KŌD)
ow *or* OW	cloud	(KLOWD)
	how	(HOW)
oy *or* OY	oil	(OYL)
	boy	(BOY)
o͞o *or* O͞O	blue	(BLO͞O)
	boot	(BO͞OT)
u *or* U	took	(TUK)
	foot	(FUT)
uh *or* UH	cut	(KUHT)
	about	(uh-BOWT)
	action	(AK-shuhn)
Vowels + R		
ar *or* AR	car	(KAR)
air *or* AIR	hair	(HAIR)
er *or* ER	her	(HER)
	better	(BET-er)
	Earth	(ERTH)
eer *or* EER	here	(HEER)
	sphere	(SFEER)
or *or* OR	core	(KOR)
ur *or* UR	pure	(PYUR)
Special Consonants		
th *or* TH	thing	(THING)
th or TH	that	(*THAT*)
	father	(FAH-*ther*)
zh *or* ZH	measure	(MEZH-er)

Aa

aa (AH-ah) A type of lava that has a jagged surface. The rough surface forms as the lava cools and hardens. ◻ See picture at **lava.**

abacus (AB-uh-kuhs) A device that is used for adding and subtracting numbers, made of a frame that is divided into two sections by a bar. Each section has a series of rods with sliding beads.

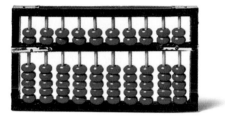

◻ **abacus**

From right to left, the columns of beads stand for ones, tens, hundreds, thousands, and so on. The beads above the middle bar are each worth 5; the beads below it are each worth 1. The beads are added and subtracted by moving them down or up toward the bar.

abalone (ab-uh-LŌ-nē) A mollusk with a large, ear-shaped shell. The shell has a row of holes along the outer edge, and the inside is lined with **mother-of-pearl.**

abdomen (AB-duh-muhn) **1.** The part of the body between the chest and the hips in humans and other vertebrates. The abdomen contains many organs, including the stomach, the intestines, and the liver. **2.** The section of the body farthest from the head of an insect, spider, or other arthropod. ◻ See picture at **insect.**

absolute humidity (AB-suh-lōōt hyōō-MID-i-tē) The actual amount of water vapor that is present in the air. ◻ Compare **relative humidity.**

absolute zero The lowest temperature that can exist. At absolute zero all molecules stop moving, and matter cannot get any colder because its molecules have no more heat to give off. Absolute zero is equal to –459.67° Fahrenheit (–273.15° Celsius).

absorption (ab-SORP-shuhn) **1.** The process of taking in a substance and holding it. When a sponge takes in and holds water, it does so by absorption. Liquids, such as water, can take in and hold gases, such as air, by absorption. **2.** The process of taking in and storing energy, such as radiation, light, or sound. During the day, the Earth takes in and stores heat from the Sun through absorption.

AC *See* **alternating current.**

acceleration (ak-sel-uh-RĀ-shuhn) A continuing change in the speed or direction of a moving object. Acceleration does not just mean going faster and faster; it can mean slowing down as well. An object that moves in a curving path instead of a straight line, even when its speed is constant, is also undergoing acceleration because it is always changing its direction.

acetic acid (uh-SĒ-tik AS-id) A clear, sharp-tasting acid that occurs naturally in vinegar. Acetic acid is used to dissolve other substances and to make rubber and paint.

acid (AS-id) A chemical compound that tastes sour and has a tendency to eat away at other substances. Acids form salts and water when they come in contact with the chemical compounds known as bases. Acids can be weak, like lemon juice and vinegar, or strong, like sulfuric acid and the acids that help us digest food in the stomach. ◻ Compare **base**.

acidic   (uh-SID-ik) Having the properties of an acid.

acid rain   Rain, snow, or other precipitation that has acid mixed in it. Acid rain forms when the gases that are given off by burning fuels, such as coal and gasoline, mix with water vapor in the atmosphere. When acid rain falls to Earth, it poisons things living in rivers and lakes and poisons plants living on land.

◻ **acid rain**

top: *a forest of spruce trees killed by acid rain* bottom: *an evergreen branch* (left) *showing the effects of acid rain and a branch* (right) *that is not affected*

acoustics   (uh-KOO-stiks) The scientific study of sound and how it travels.

acrylic   (uh-KRIL-ik) A man-made plastic used to make paint and fibers that are woven into cloth.

actinides   (AK-ti-nīdz) The chemical elements in the Periodic Table that have atomic numbers from 89 through 103. These elements are all radioactive metals and even-

tually break down into other elements, giving off energy. Uranium and plutonium are actinides. ◻ See Table on pages 178–179.

acute angle   (uh-KYOOT ANG-guhl) An angle that measures between 0° and 90°. ◻ See picture at **angle**.

adaptation   (ad-ap-TĀ-shuhn) A change in an animal or plant that helps it live in a particular environment. Adaptations are the result of **evolution** and can involve changes to a body part or changes in behavior. For example, an elephant's long trunk is an adaptation of its nose that helps the elephant get food and water up to its mouth.

Did You Know?

adaptation
Adaptation is necessary for a species to survive if its surroundings change. The members of a species are all different from each other. If the surroundings change, those members of the species that already have traits that are suited for the new surroundings will live and pass those traits on to their young. After a short time, all the surviving members of the species will have those traits. In that way, a species adapts.

add   To perform addition on two or more numbers.

ADD   *See* **attention deficit disorder**.

addend   (AD-end) A number that is added to another number. In the equation $3 + 2 = 5$, the numbers 3 and 2 are addends.

addiction   (uh-DIK-shuhn) A strong need to use a drug or other harmful substance, such as alcohol. People with addictions are often unable to stop using a substance on their own and need help from a doctor to stop.

addition (uh-DISH-uhn) The process of increasing one number by another in order to figure out the sum of the two numbers.

adenoids (AD-noidz) Small growths of tissue at the back of the throat that can become swollen because of infection. Adenoids can block breathing through the nose when swollen.

adhesion (ad-HĒ-zhuhn) The process of sticking to something. Adhesion is caused by the attraction that molecules of different things sometimes have for each other. Ink sticks to paper because of adhesion.

adhesive (ad-HĒ-siv) A substance, such as glue, that makes things stick together.

adjacent angle (uh-JĀ-suhnt ANG-guhl) Either of two angles that share a side and a common point of origin. ◻ See picture at **angle.**

adolescent (ad-uh-LES-uhnt) A person between childhood and adulthood, usually someone between the ages of 13 and 19. During this period, adolescents become physically mature and undergo emotional changes that help prepare them for the responsibilities of being an adult.

adrenal gland (ad-RĒ-nuhl gland) Either of two glands, one located above each kidney. The adrenal glands produce substances called **hormones.** Adrenaline is one of the hormones produced by the adrenal glands.

adrenaline (uh-DREN-uh-lin) A hormone that is produced by the adrenal glands, which are located on top of the kidneys. Adrenaline is released when a person is afraid, anxious, excited, or angry. Adrenaline is also used as a medicine to make the heart beat faster.

adsorption (ad-SORP-shuhn) The process in which one substance collects on another. In a water filter, particles of pollutants collect on chips of carbon by adsorption.

adult (uh-DUHLT *or* AD-uhlt) An animal or a plant that is fully grown and developed.

aerobic (uh-RŌ-bik) Needing or using oxygen to live. Living things that can exist only in environments that contain oxygen are aerobic. ◻ Compare **anaerobic.**

aerodynamics (air-ō-dī-NAM-iks) The study of the way air moves, especially around moving objects like airplanes.

aeronautics (air-ō-NAW-tiks) The science of designing, building, and flying aircraft.

aerosol (AIR-uh-sahl) A substance that is made of very small particles of a liquid or a solid mixed in a gas. Mist, which is made of very fine drops of water in air, is a naturally occurring aerosol. Paint and hair spray shoot out of spray cans as aerosols.

aerospace engineering (AIR-ō-spās en-juh-NEER-ing) The science of designing and building aircraft and spacecraft.

aftershock (AF-ter-shok) A less powerful earthquake that follows a stronger one, usually in the same place.

agar (Ā-gar) A material that looks like clear jelly and is used to grow bacteria or cells in a laboratory. Agar is made from algae found in the sea, usually seaweed.

Agassiz (AG-uh-sē), **(Jean) Louis (Rodolphe)** Born 1807; died 1873. American scientist who studied rocks and glaciers. He became convinced that parts of the

Earth had once been covered by thick sheets of ice. Later research showed that Agassiz was right and that Europe and North America had in fact experienced an ice age thousands of years ago.

agate (AG-it) A mineral that is a type of quartz. Agates come in a variety of colors and often have stripes or cloudy patterns.

◻ **agate**

agriculture (AG-ri-kuhl-cher) The science of growing crops and raising animals.

AI *See* **artificial intelligence.**

AIDS Short for **acquired immune deficiency syndrome.** A disease that is caused by the virus known as **HIV.** The virus attacks the body's immune system and makes it hard to fight off infections from other germs, such as bacteria. AIDS may be spread when an infected body fluid, such as blood, gets into the body of another person.

aileron (Ā-luh-ron) A small flap on the back edge of the wing of an airplane. The airplane's pilot can move the ailerons up or down to cause the plane to tilt to one side or another.

air The colorless, odorless, tasteless mixture of gases that surrounds the Earth. The two main gases in air are nitrogen and oxygen. Air also contains small amounts of other gases, such as argon, carbon dioxide, neon, and helium.

air bladder An air-filled sac in many fish that helps keep them afloat. Some fish use the air bladder as a source of oxygen. It is also important for hearing and making sounds. ◻ An air bladder is also called a *swim bladder.*

air conditioner A device that cools the air and controls the humidity in a closed area, such as a room or a car. An air conditioner uses a condenser to cool air and force water vapor in the air to condense as drops.

airfoil A part of a vehicle or machine that is shaped so that it will move upward as air flows around it. The air that passes over the airfoil moves faster than the air that passes below it, resulting in greater pressure below than above. Airplane wings are airfoils.

airplane A vehicle that can rise off the ground and fly because of the force of air flowing around its wings. Airplanes move forward because of the power of jet engines or of engines that spin a propeller.

air pressure The force pushing down on the Earth because of the weight of the atmosphere. The air pressure at the surface of the Earth is about 14.7 pounds per square

Did You Know?

air pressure
If you weigh 75 pounds (about 34 kilograms), your skin has a surface area of over $13\frac{1}{2}$ square feet (1.2 square meters). The air is pressing with a force of 14.7 pounds (6.6 kilograms) on each of those inches, which means it's pressing against your whole body with a force of over 28,700 pounds (12,915 kilograms)—nearly $14\frac{1}{2}$ tons! Amazingly, you feel nothing, because your body is actually pushing outward with the same amount of force.

inch (1 kilogram per square centimeter). At the top of high mountains, air pressure is a little less than it is at sea level.

air sac **1.** One of the tiny air-filled sacs in the lungs. Oxygen breathed in by the lungs enters the bloodstream through the air sacs. The air sacs also take up carbon dioxide from the blood. ◻ An air sac is also called an *alveolus.* **2.** An air-filled space that is connected with the lungs in the body of a bird.

albumen (al-BYOO-muhn) The white part of the egg of birds and reptiles. The albumen supplies the growing embryo with water and also acts as a cushion.

alchemy (AL-kuh-mē) An early form of chemistry that was practiced in the Middle Ages. Those who practiced alchemy hoped to change common metals, such as lead, into gold. They also tried to discover a cure for all diseases and to prepare a potion that would allow a person to stay young forever.

alcohol (AL-kuh-hawl) A clear liquid that burns easily and contains carbon, hydrogen, and oxygen. One kind of alcohol is used in medicine to kill germs; another kind is produced naturally by yeast and is part of wine and beer. This kind is also used in certain fuels.

Alexanderson (al-ig-ZAN-der-suhn), **Ernst Frederick Werner** Born 1878; died 1975. American inventor who developed the first practical television system in 1930. He later improved upon his invention when he developed color television in 1955.

algae (AL-jē) A large group of simple living things that grow in water and range in size from single cells to large seaweeds. Algae were once considered to be plants, but they do not have roots, stems, or leaves. They are now considered to be mem-

bers of the group known as **protists.** *Singular form*: **alga** (AL-guh).

algebra (AL-juh-bruh) A type of mathematics that deals with numbers that are known (such as 3), unknown numbers (represented by symbols, such as x), and the relationship between them. To figure out what the value of x is in the equation $x + 2 = 5$, one would have to use the rules of algebra.

algorithm (AL-guh-rith-uhm) A group of rules or procedures for solving a problem in a series of steps. Algorithms are used in mathematics and in computer programs for figuring out solutions.

alien (Ā-lē-uhn) Introduced to a region by humans, either on purpose or by accident. Dandelions, pigeons, and horses are species that are alien to North America but now live naturally throughout the continent. ◻ Compare **endemic, indigenous.**

alimentary canal (al-uh-MEN-tuh-rē kuh-NAL) The tube in the body through which food passes and in which digestion takes place. The alimentary canal includes the esophagus, the stomach, and the small and large intestines.

alkali (AL-kuh-lī) A chemical compound that reacts strongly with an acid and becomes a base when it is mixed with water. An alkali always forms hydroxide ions (molecules made of one atom of hydrogen connected to one atom of oxygen) when it comes into contact with water.

alkali metal One of several soft metals that react easily with other elements. Alkali metals are usually white and burn easily. Sodium and potassium are alkali metals.

alkaline (AL-kuh-lin *or* AL-kuh-līn) Having the chemical properties of an alkali.

alkaline-earth metal   One of a group of metals that react easily with other elements, but not as easily as alkali metals do. Calcium and magnesium are alkaline-earth metals.

allergen   (AL-er-juhn) Something that causes an allergy. Pollen and dust are allergens.

allergy   (AL-er-jē) A condition in which a person is very sensitive to something in the environment, such as pollen or a kind of food. A person with an allergy may sneeze, have trouble breathing, and develop a rash on the skin. Allergies can be mild or so severe that a doctor is needed.

alligator   (AL-i-gā-ter) A large, meat-eating reptile that lives mainly in water and has sharp teeth and powerful jaws. Alligators have a shorter and wider snout than crocodiles, and their teeth do not show when the jaws are closed. There are two species of alligators, one in the southeast United States and one in China.

alloy   (AL-oy) A metal that is made of a mixture of a metal and another chemical element. Steel is an alloy made of iron and carbon. Bronze is an alloy made of copper and tin.

alluvial   (uh-LOO-vē-uhl) Laid down by a stream or other running water. The sand, gravel, and silt found in river deltas are alluvial.

alpha particle   (AL-fuh PAR-ti-kuhl) A particle of matter that is made of two protons and two neutrons. Alpha particles shoot out of the nucleus of some radioactive elements when they break down into smaller elements during the process known as **radioactive decay.** Alpha particles have a positive charge.

alpha ray   A stream of moving alpha particles. Alpha rays can only move across very short distances and can be stopped by something as thin as a piece of paper.

alternate angles   (AWL-ter-nit ANG-guhlz) Two angles that are formed on opposite sides of a line that crosses two other lines. Alternate angles are either both on the inside of the two other lines, or both on the outside of the two other lines, but they are never next to each other. ◻ See picture at **angle.**

alternating current   (AWL-ter-nā-ting KER-uhnt) An electric current in which the direction of the flow of electrons reverses back and forth many times per second. Alternating current is the type of electricity that power stations usually make, because it doesn't lose as much of its power to heat in the wires as direct current does. ◻ Alternating current is called *AC* for short. ◻ Compare **direct current.**

alternator   (AWL-ter-nā-ter) An electric generator that makes an alternating current. An alternator contains two magnets and a coiled wire that rotates between them. As the wire comes close to the positive pole of the magnetic field created by the two magnets, the current flows one way. As the wire comes close to the negative pole, the current flows back the other way.

altimeter   (awl-TIM-uh-ter) An instrument that measures an object's height above sea level. Pilots use altimeters to know how high their airplanes are.

altitude   (AL-ti-tood) **1.** The height of a thing, such as a mountaintop or an airplane, above sea level. **2.** The distance of an object in the sky above the horizon. The position of stars and planets is figured by altitude and **azimuth.**

altocumulus cloud   (al-tō-KYOO-myuh-luhs KLOWD) A gray or white cloud that spreads out in lumpy or broken patches.

Altocumulus clouds form at middle levels of the sky. ◨ See picture at **cloud.**

altostratus cloud (al-tō-STRAT-uhs KLOWD) A flat, gray cloud that spreads in large, smooth sheets or layers. Altostratus clouds form at middle levels of the sky. ◨ See picture at **cloud.**

aluminum (uh-LOO-muh-nuhm) A light, silvery-white chemical element. Aluminum can be easily made into different shapes and is a good conductor of electricity. It is the most common metal in the Earth's crust and is used to make a wide variety of products from soda cans to airplane parts. ◨ See Table on pages 178–179.

Alvarez (AL-vuh-rez), **Luis Walter** Born 1911; died 1988. American scientist who is best known for his studies of the particles that make up atoms. Together with his son, **Walter Alvarez** (born 1940), he also came up with the theory that dinosaurs became extinct because an asteroid collided with the Earth.

alveolus (al-VĒ-uh-luhs) *See* **air sac** (sense 1).

AM *See* **amplitude modulation.**

amber (AM-ber) A clear, brownish-yellow material that is the hardened resin of ancient trees. Amber often contains fossils of insects.

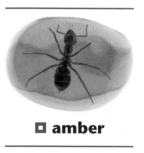
◨ **amber**

amethyst (AM-uh-thist) A purple, transparent form of the mineral quartz. Amethyst gets its color from small amounts of iron inside its crystal structure.

amino acid (uh-MĒ-nō AS-id) A type of chemical compound that proteins are made of. Amino acids are made up mostly of car-

Did You Know?

amino acid

All proteins are made of amino acids, including the proteins that we use to grow and stay healthy. We need about 20 different amino acids, but our bodies can only make about 10 of them. This is one reason why we need to eat lots of different things—to get all the amino acids we need to make proteins.

bon, oxygen, hydrogen, and nitrogen. Some amino acids are made by the body's cells, but others can only be obtained from food.

ammeter (AM-mē-ter) An instrument that measures the strength of an electric current in units called amperes.

ammonia (uh-MŌN-yuh) A clear gas that is lighter than air and has a very strong odor. Ammonia is used as a fertilizer and as a cooling substance in refrigerators. It is made of hydrogen and nitrogen.

◨ **ammonite**

ammonite (AM-uh-nīt) An extinct mollusk that had a spiral-shaped shell. Ammonites are preserved as fossils. Ammonites were especially abundant during the Mesozoic Era.

amoeba (uh-MĒ-buh) A tiny living thing that is made up of a single cell and is only visible with a microscope. Amoebas are constantly changing shape. They are members of the group of organisms known as **protozoans.** *Plural form:* **amoebas** or **amoebae** (uh-MEE-bee).

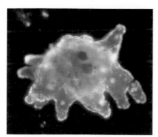

◻ amoeba

an amoeba photographed through a microscope

amorphous (uh-MOR-fuhs) Having atoms that are not arranged in a set pattern. Glass and plastic are amorphous materials.

ampere (AM-peer) A unit used to measure electric current. Electric current is measured by how great a charge passes a given point in a second. The ampere is named after André Marie Ampère.

Ampère (AM-peer *or* ahm-PAIR), **André Marie** Born 1775; died 1836. French scientist who explained the relationship between electricity and magnetic force. Ampère showed how to calculate the strength of a magnetic field that is created by the flow of an electric current.

amphibian (am-FIB-ē-uhn) A cold-blooded animal that has moist skin and no scales. Most amphibians lay eggs in water, and their young breathe with gills before developing lungs and breathing air as adults. Amphibians are vertebrates, and they include frogs, toads, and salamanders.

amplifier (AM-pli-fī-er) An electronic device that increases the strength of a sound or an electric current. Televisions and radios have amplifiers.

amplitude (AM-pli-tōōd) A measure of how high a wave moves, or how far a swing-

◻ amphibian

top: *a northern leopard frog*
bottom: *a tiger salamander*

ing object, such as a pendulum, swings. The amplitude of an ocean wave is the height of the highest part of the wave crest above the level of calm water. The amplitude of a playground swing is the farthest distance the swing moves from its starting position. ◻ See picture at **wave.**

amplitude modulation (AM-pli-tōōd moj-uh-LĀ-shuhn) A method of radio broadcasting that changes the amplitude of radio waves as they are sent out from a **transmitter.** The pattern of different amplitudes represents the different sounds that are being broadcast. Radios change this pattern of amplitudes back into the original sounds, which then come out of the speakers. ◻ Amplitude modulation is called *AM* for short. ◻ Compare **frequency modulation.**

anaerobic (an-uh-RŌ-bik) Able to live or survive without oxygen. Many bacteria are anaerobic. ◻ Compare **aerobic.**

analog (AN-uh-lawg) Using continuously moving parts to show information that is

◻ analog

an analog clock (left) *and a digital watch* (right) *showing hour, minutes, and seconds*

changing. The position of the hands of a clock is an analog representation of time.

analysis (uh-NAL-uh-sis) The careful study of something in order to determine what it is, what its parts are, or how its parts fit together.

anatomy (uh-NAT-uh-mē) The structure of an animal or a plant or of any of its parts.

androgen (AN-druh-juhn) One of the hormones that control physical development in males. Testosterone is an androgen.

◻ anemometer

The three cups (right) *on this anemometer show wind speed. The weathervane* (left) *shows wind direction.*

anemometer (an-uh-MOM-i-ter) An instrument that measures the speed and force of the wind. One type of anemometer is made of plastic cups that are attached to arms that spin around in the wind. The speed with which the cups rotate shows the wind speed.

anemone (a-NEM-uh-nē) *See* **sea anemone.**

anesthesia (an-is-THĒ-zhuh) The use of drugs to cause the body or a part of the body to lose feeling before an operation.

Did You Know?
anesthesia

The word "anesthesia" means "a state of not feeling." The word was invented about 150 years ago, when doctors first used a chemical to make people sleep during an operation. This chemical is called ether. Before then, surgeons were called good surgeons if they could complete an operation very quickly. With anesthesia, there's no need to rush anymore.

angiosperm (AN-jē-uh-sperm) A plant that has flowers and that produces seeds contained in a fruit, pod, or shell. Most living plants are angiosperms. ◻ An an-

Did You Know?
angiosperm

Angiosperms reproduce by means of seeds, but to make seeds, they often need help from animals. For a seed to begin to develop, pollen must first be carried from one flower to another. Sometimes the wind blows pollen to a flower, but often insects and birds carry pollen on their bodies. They pick up the pollen as they feed on nectar at the bottom of one flower and leave some of it behind when they visit another.

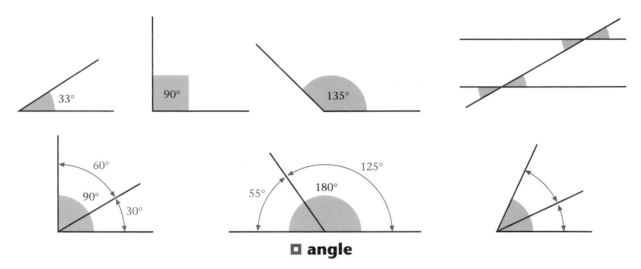

□ **angle**

top row from left to right: *acute angle, right angle, obtuse angle, and two pairs of alternate angles (the outside pair is red, the inside pair is blue)*
bottom row from left to right: *complementary angles, supplementary angles, and adjacent angles*

giosperm is also called a *flowering plant.* □ Compare **gymnosperm.**

angle (ANG-guhl) **1.** The figure that is formed by two lines that start from the same point. **2.** The space between these two lines. Angles are measured in degrees.

angle of incidence The angle at which a wave or a ray of light meets a surface.

angle of refraction The angle at which a wave or a ray of light leaves a surface it has struck.

animal (AN-uh-muhl) A member of a kingdom of living things that are made up of many cells, have the ability to move on their own, and have some kind of digestive system and nervous system. Animals must feed on plants or other animals to survive because they cannot make their own food. All animals develop from embryos, which are formed by the joining of sex cells.

anion (AN-ī-uhn) An atom or a group of atoms that has a negative electric charge. Anions are formed when an atom or group of atoms gains extra electrons.

annual (AN-yōo-uhl) Completing a life cycle in one growing season. Tomatoes and sunflowers are annual plants. Annual plants die at the end of the year, and new plants grow the next year from seeds.

annual ring A growth ring that shows a full year's growth in a woody plant.

anode (AN-ōd) **1.** The negative electrode in an electric cell, such as a battery, that creates its own electricity. The anode attracts positively charged particles in the chemical compounds inside the cell to create the electric current. **2.** The positive electrode in a device that uses a special liquid to bring about chemical reactions. When it is connected to an electric current, the anode attracts negatively charged particles in the liquid. □ Compare **cathode.**

anomaly (uh-NOM-uh-lē) Something that is unusual, irregular, or abnormal.

ant A type of insect that lives in a large, organized group called a **colony,** which is made up of workers, soldiers, and a queen. Ants often tunnel in the ground or in wood. Only males and the queen have wings.

Antarctic Circle (ant-ARK-tik SER-kuhl) The line of latitude that forms the boundary between the South Temperate Zone and the South Frigid Zone. The Antarctic Circle lies south of the equator and has a latitude of 66 degrees, 33 minutes.

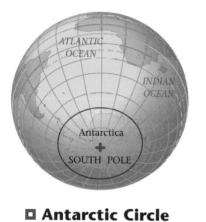

□ **Antarctic Circle**

antenna (an-TEN-uh) **1.** One of two long, thin body parts that are found on the heads of most insects and many other invertebrates, such as crabs and lobsters. Most antennae are used as feelers, but some are sensitive to heat or smell. **2.** A metal device used to send or receive signals, such as radio signals, that are carried by electromagnetic waves. A satellite dish is a large type of antenna. *Plural form*: **antennas** or **antennae** (an-TEN-ē).

□ **antenna**

left: *antennas on a beetle*
right: *a television antenna on a rooftop*

anther (AN-ther) The part of a flower that produces and contains pollen. The anther is at the tip of the **stamen.** □ See picture at **flower.**

anthrax (AN-thraks) A disease that is caused by bacteria and that is usually seen in cows and sheep. It is most often spread to people through the skin, usually by contact with sick animals. In people, anthrax can affect the skin, lungs, or digestive system.

anthropology (an-thrō-POL-uh-jē) The scientific study of humans. Anthropology includes the study of how humans behave and how the first humans developed.

antibiotic (an-ti-bī-OT-ik) A drug used to treat or prevent a disease that is caused by bacteria or other germs that cause disease. Some antibiotics are made in nature by organisms such as molds. Penicillin is a kind of antibiotic.

Did You Know?

antibody
Antibodies are chemicals the body produces to destroy germs and harmful substances that get into the body. When you are immune to a disease, you have antibodies in your blood against it, and your body can produce more of these on short notice. Your body has cells that can remember the antibodies it created to fight against diseases you have had.

antibody (AN-ti-bod-ē) A chemical compound that is made in the body to fight germs, such as bacteria or viruses, that cause disease. Antibodies are made of proteins and circulate around the body in the blood.

anticyclone (an-tē-SĪ-klōn) A large system of winds that rotate around a region of high atmospheric pressure. Winds in an anticyclone spiral out away from the center of the system and often bring clear, dry weather to the region. ◘ Compare **cyclone.**

antigen   (AN-ti-juhn) A substance that causes the body to make antibodies. Antigens are recognized by special cells as not belonging in the body. Bacteria, viruses, and poisons known as toxins are antigens.

antihistamine   (an-tē-HIST-uh-mēn) A drug that relieves the sneezing and itchiness caused by colds or allergies. Antihistamines work by blocking a substance called **histamine,** which the body produces when it has been infected by a virus, for example.

antiseptic   (an-ti-SEP-tik) A substance that kills germs or keeps them from multiplying.

antler   (ANT-ler) A horn-like growth on the head of deer, moose, elk, or other similar animal. Antlers often have one or more branches and usually grow only on males. Antlers are shed and grown back again every year.

anus   (Ā-nuhs) The opening at the lower end of the digestive system through which solid waste leaves the body. ◘ See picture at **digestive system.**

aorta   (ā-OR-tuh) The main artery of the body in mammals. The aorta carries blood from the left side of the heart to all the organs of the body except the lungs.

apatosaurus   (uh-pat-uh-SOR-uhs) A very large dinosaur that walked on four legs and ate plants. It had a long neck and tail and a small head. ◘ The apatosaurus used to be called *brontosaurus.*

ape   A type of large primate that has no tail and lives in the wild only in Africa and Asia. Apes have long arms and broad chests. Chimpanzees, gorillas, and orangutans are apes.

aperture   (AP-er-cher) A hole or an opening. The opening in the lens of a camera that allows light to pass through it is an aperture. ◘ See picture at **camera.**

apex   (Ā-peks) The highest point of a figure or object. The vertex of a triangle is an apex.

aphid   (Ā-fid) A type of insect that feeds by sucking sap from plants. Aphids are small and have soft bodies. They can be destructive to plants and can spread plant diseases.

apogee   (AP-uh-jē) The point in the orbit of an object in space, such as the Moon, where it is farthest from the object it revolves around, such as Earth. ◘ Compare **perigee.**

appendage   (uh-PEN-dij) A part of the body that comes out from another part. The flippers of a seal, the antennas of a crab, and the cilia of a paramecium are all appendages.

appendix   (uh-PEN-diks) A short, narrow pouch that is attached to the large intestine. Although it is part of the **digestive system,** it does not play a part in digestion. The appendix can become infected and have to be removed.

aquarium   (uh-KWAIR-ē-uhm) **1.** A tank or bowl that is filled with water and used for keeping fish or other aquatic animals and plants. **2.** A place where people can see and learn about fish and other aquatic organisms.

aquatic   (uh-KWAT-ik) Living or growing in water. Water lilies are aquatic plants. Shrimp are aquatic animals.

aquifer   (AK-wi-fer) An underground layer of sand, gravel, or rock that collects

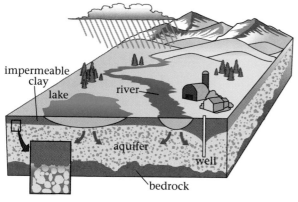

□ aquifer

Water from rain and melting snow collects in rivers and lakes. Some of this water seeps beneath the layer of clay and fills up the tiny spaces between the bits of sand and rock. This wet underground area is called an aquifer.

water and holds it like a sponge. We get much of the water we use by drilling wells into aquifers.

Arabic numeral (AIR-uh-bik NŌŌ-mer-uhl) One of the symbols 0, 1, 2, 3, 4, 5, 6, 7, 8, or 9.

Did You Know?

Arabic numeral

Our numerals 0,1,2,3,4,5,6,7,8,9 were probably invented in India, but then they traveled to the Arabs, who brought them to Europe. That's why we call them "Arabic numerals." Before then, Europe used Roman numerals, like I, V, X, and C. Just try doing multiplication or division with Roman numerals and you'll see how much better Arabic numerals are.

arachnid (uh-RAK-nid) A member of a group of living things that have eight legs, a body divided into two parts, and no wings or antennae. Spiders, mites, scorpions, and ticks are arachnids. Arachnids are members of the group of organisms known as **arthropods**.

arboretum (ar-buh-RĒ-tuhm) A place where different kinds of woody plants, such as trees, are grown for scientists to study and for people to learn about.

arc A curve between two points on the circumference of a circle. **□** See picture at **circle**.

arch A curved structure that is used in building. An arch usually curves upward between two pillars or walls over an open space. Arches are very strong because the curve spreads out the supported weight evenly.

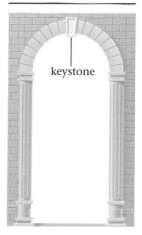

keystone

□ arch

archaeology (ar-kē-OL-uh-je) The scientific study of past human life and culture. Archaeology includes the study of ancient cities and the tools, clothing, and pottery that people made and used.

archaeopteryx (ar-kē-OP-ter-riks) A very early type of bird. Like dinosaurs, it had teeth, claws on the ends of its fingers, and a long bony tail. Like birds, it had wings and feathers.

Archimedes (ar-kuh-MĒ-dēz) Born 287? BC; died 212 BC. Greek mathematician who was an early leader in the study of geometry, physics, and mechanics.

Arctic Circle (ARK-tik SER-kuhl) The line of latitude that forms the boundary between the North Temperate Zone and the North Frigid Zone. The Arctic Circle lies

13

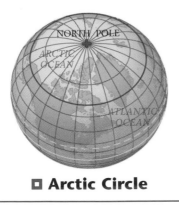

□ **Arctic Circle**

north of the equator and has a latitude of 66 degrees, 33 minutes.

area (AIR-ē-uh) The amount of surface within particular limits. Area is measured in square units of length. The area of a rectangle is equal to its length times its width, so a rectangle that is 4 inches (10 centimeters) long and 7 inches (18 centimeters) wide has an area of 28 square inches (180 square centimeters).

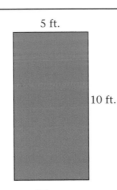

5 ft.

10 ft.

□ **area**

To find the area of a rectangle, multiply length by width. The area of this rectangle is 50 square feet (about 15 square meters).

argon (AR-gon) A chemical element that is one of the noble gases and is found in very small amounts in the Earth's atmosphere. It is used in fluorescent lamps. □ See Table on pages 178–179.

arid (AIR-id) Very dry because of little rainfall. An arid region, such as a desert, does not have enough water for most trees or woody plants to grow.

Aristotle (AIR-is-tot-uhl) Born 384 BC; died 322 BC. Greek philosopher and scientist who emphasized observation and the

Biography

Aristotle

Artistotle thought that the best way to understand the world around him was to look at it. He felt that theory should be based on careful observations and the collection of specimens. His approach to gaining knowledge became the foundation for the scientific method in the Western world.

use of logic as a method of understanding the world.

arithmetic (uh-RITH-muh-tik) The use of addition, subtraction, multiplication, and division to solve mathematical problems.

arithmetic mean (AIR-ith-met-ik MĒN) *See* **average.**

armadillo (ar-muh-DIL-ō) A toothless, insect-eating mammal of South America and the southern part of North America. The body of an armadillo has a hard, scaly, shell-like covering that looks like armor. Armadillos dig burrows and also dig for food.

armature (AR-muh-cher) A coil of wire that rotates in an electric motor or generator. In electric motors, magnets act on the armature to make it move. In generators, magnets act on the armature to make it produce electricity.

artery (AR-ter-ē) A blood vessel that carries blood from the heart to all parts of the body. The walls of arteries are lined with muscle, which helps pump blood through the body. The blood in most arteries contains high levels of oxygen.

arthropod (AR-thruh-pod) A member of a group of animals whose bodies and legs are divided into segments. The skeletons of arthropods are on the outside and are called **exoskeletons.** Arthropods are invertebrates. They include insects, arachnids, and crustaceans, and they make up the largest group of animals in the animal kingdom.

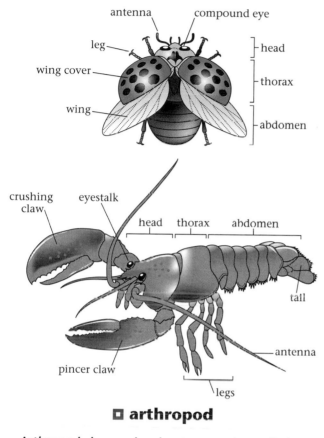

□ **arthropod**

Arthropods have a hard outer covering called the exoskeleton that supports and protects the soft inner body parts. The wing covers of the ladybug (top) protect its fragile wings. A lobster (bottom) is covered with a hard shell that has joints to allow movement.

artificial (ar-tuh-FISH-uhl) Made by humans rather than occurring as part of a natural process or living thing. An artificial sweetener is a chemical compound that is made in a laboratory to taste like sugar but have fewer calories.

artificial intelligence The ability of a computer or other machine to do things that are thought to require human intelli-

gence. Artificial intelligence allows computers to understand spoken language and make decisions based on things they have been programmed to do in the past. □ Artificial intelligence is called *AI* for short.

artificial selection A way of breeding organisms so that certain traits appear from one generation to the next. For example, sheep farmers may use artificial selection to make sure that all their sheep are born with thick, soft wool.

asbestos (as-BEST-tuhs) A grayish mineral that is not affected by heat, fire, or chemical compounds. Asbestos separates into fibers that were once used to make insulation and materials that do not burn except at extremely high temperatures. The fibers are no longer used because they can cause lung disease.

asexual reproduction (ā-SEK-shoo-uhl rē-pruh-DUHK-shuhn) A kind of reproduction in which offspring develop from only one parent, without the joining together of sex cells. Living things that are produced by asexual reproduction are identical to the parent. Bacteria, many plants and fungi, and some invertebrates produce offspring by means of asexual reproduction. □ Compare **sexual reproduction.**

asphalt (AS-fawlt) A thick, sticky, dark-brown mixture of different forms of petroleum, used in paving, roofing, and protecting surfaces from water.

aspirin (AS-per-in *or* AS-prin) A drug that relieves pain or lowers a fever. Aspirin originally came from the bark of willow trees but is now made in laboratories.

asteroid (AS-tuh-roid) One of the millions of rocky objects that orbit the Sun, mostly in the region between Mars and Jupiter. Asteroids are smaller than planets.

They can be as large as several hundred miles across and as small as a speck of dust.

asthenosphere   (as-THEN-uh-sfeer) The upper part of the Earth's mantle. The asthenosphere lies beneath the **lithosphere** and is made of several hundred miles of partially molten rock. ◻ See picture at **plate tectonics.**

asthma   (AZ-muh) A condition in which the air tubes that lead to the lungs become narrow, making it hard to breathe. People who have asthma often cough and sometimes have a tight feeling in the chest. Asthma is usually caused by **allergies.**

astigmatism   (uh-STIG-muh-tiz-uhm) A condition of the eye in which the curve of the cornea or lens is uneven. In astigmatism, light coming into the eye is not focused properly on the retina, causing blurry vision. Astigmatism can be corrected with glasses.

astronaut   (AS-truh-nawt) A person who is trained to travel in a spacecraft or to work in outer space.

astronomy   (uh-STRON-uh-mē) The scientific study of the universe and the objects in it, including stars, planets, and galaxies. People who study astronomy examine not only visible light but also radio waves, x-rays, and other kinds of radiation that come from outside Earth's atmosphere.

astrophysics   (as-trō-FIZ-iks) The scientific study of what happens inside stars and galaxies and how objects in space move in relation to each other.

atmosphere   (AT-muh-sfeer) **1.** The mixture of gases that surrounds the Earth, also known as **air.** The atmosphere forms various layers at different heights above the ground. The air gets thinner as it gets farther away from the Earth until at last the atmosphere disappears into space. **2.** A unit of pressure equal to the pressure of the air at sea level. One atmosphere is equal to about 14.7 pounds per square inch.

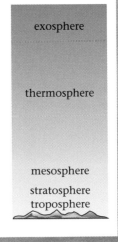
atmospheric pressure   (at-muh-SFEER-ik PRESH-er) Pressure caused by the weight of

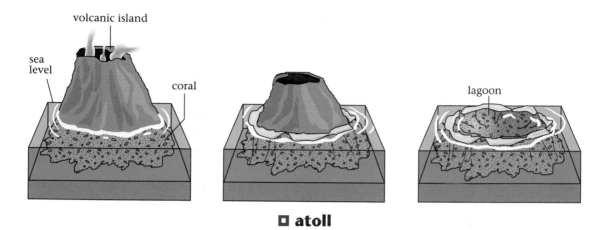

□ atoll

An atoll develops **(from left to right)** *when a volcanic island erodes and a ring of coral grows up around it. The crater of the volcano fills with water, forming a lagoon.*

the air. It is measured in units called atmospheres. The higher you go above the surface of the Earth, the thinner the air gets and the less atmospheric pressure there is.

atoll (AT-awl *or* Ā-tawl) An island that has the shape of a ring and is made of coral. Atolls are surrounded by deep ocean water but have a shallow lagoon at their center.

atom (AT-uhm) The basic structure of a chemical element. Atoms have a nucleus that contains protons and neutrons and is surrounded by electrons that move around it in orbits at high speed. When atoms combine together, they form **molecules.**

— electron

— nucleus (protons and neutrons)

— paths of electrons spinning close to nucleus

— path of electron spinning farther away from nucleus

□ atom

a lithium atom has 3 neutrons, 3 protons, and 3 electrons

atomic bomb (uh-TOM-ik BOM) A very destructive bomb that explodes because of the energy released when the nuclei of radioactive atoms break up in the process known as **fission.** Most atomic bombs use plutonium or a form of uranium as their radioactive material. Billions of nuclei break up in an instant when the bomb is exploded. □ An atomic bomb is also called an *atom bomb.*

atomic number The number of protons in the nucleus of an atom. Each chemical element has a different number of protons in its nucleus. The elements in the Periodic Table are listed according to their atomic numbers, starting with hydrogen at number 1. □ See Table on pages 178–179.

ATP Short for **adenosine triphosphate.** A chemical compound that is found in cells and that is an important source of energy for many cell functions.

atrium (Ā-trē-uhm) A chamber of the heart that receives blood from the veins and pumps it into a ventricle. Mammals, birds, reptiles, and amphibians have two atria; fish have one atrium. *Plural form:* **atria** (Ā-trē-uh) or **atriums.**

attention deficit disorder (uh-TEN-shuhn DEF-uh-sit dis-OR-der) A condition in which a person finds it hard to pay attention and concentrate and tends to act without thinking. Attention deficit disorder interferes with how well a person follows instructions. People with attention deficit disorder sometimes also have **hyperactivity.** ◻ Attention deficit disorder is called *ADD* for short.

attraction (uh-TRAK-shuhn) **1.** The electric or magnetic force that pulls together particles with opposite charges. Protons and electrons are drawn together by attraction. **2.** The force of gravity that causes one object in space to be drawn toward another. The Moon stays in its orbit around the Earth because of the attraction of gravity.

auditory nerve (AW-di-tor-ē NERV) The nerve that carries sound from the ear to the brain.

Audubon (AW-duh-bon), **John James** Born 1785; died 1851. American naturalist and artist who published *The Birds of America,* a collection of life-size paintings of birds found in eastern North America. It is considered a major achievement in the field of ornithology.

aurora (uh-ROR-uh) Bands of colored light that flash and move about in the night sky, especially in the far northern and southern regions of the Earth. The colored light is caused by charged particles from the Sun that excite molecules in the atmosphere.

◻ **John James Audubon**

left: *a photograph of John James Audubon*
right: *Audubon's painting of an American white pelican*

aurora australis (uh-ROR-uh aw-STRĀ-lis) The aurora that appears over southern regions of the Earth. ◻ The aurora australis is also called the *southern lights.*

aurora borealis (uh-ROR-uh bor-ē-AL-is) The aurora that appears over northern regions of the Earth. ◻ The aurora borealis is also called the *northern lights.*

autumn (AW-tuhm) The season of the year between summer and winter. In the Northern Hemisphere, it lasts from the autumnal equinox, in late September, to the winter solstice, in late December.

autumnal equinox (aw-TUHM-nuhl Ē-kwi-noks) The moment of the year when the Sun crosses the equator while moving from north to south. This happens on Septem-

◻ **aurora borealis**

ber 22 or 23. In the Northern Hemisphere, the autumnal equinox marks the beginning of fall. ☐ Compare **vernal equinox.** ☐ See picture at **season.**

Did You Know?

avalanche

Snow avalanches often happen when heavy wet snow falls on top of light fluffy snow, which cannot support the weight of the wet snow above it. Avalanches can roar down a mountainside at speeds of more than 80 miles an hour and knock down trees and houses. Once the snow comes to rest, it hardens up like cement, making it hard to rescue people who have been caught in an avalanche.

avalanche (AV-uh-lanch) The fall or slide of a large mass of snow or rock down the side of a mountain.

average (AV-er-ij) The number that is the result of dividing the sum of a set of numbers by the number of items in the set. If there are three test scores 70, 83, and 90, the average of the scores is their sum (243) divided by the number of scores (3), or 81. ☐ The average is also called the *arithmetic mean.*

aviary (Ā-vē-air-ē) A large cage or other closed-in space for birds, as in a zoo.

axiom (AK-sē-uhm) A statement that is assumed to be true without proof. Axioms are used in mathematics to show that other statements are true or false. An example of an axiom is that for any two points, there is one and only one line that can pass through them.

axis (AK-sis) **1.** An imaginary straight line around which an object turns. For a rotating sphere, such as the Earth, the two ends of the axis are called **poles. 2.** One of the two lines that together make the framework of a graph. One line goes straight up and down, and the other one goes from left to right. Each line is marked at regular distances to show amount, measurement, or other quantity. *Plural form:* **axes** (AK-sēz).

axle (AK-suhl) A bar or rod on which one or more wheels turn. ☐ See picture at **machine.**

axon (AK-son) The long part of a nerve cell that carries information in the form of electric signals.

azimuth (AZ-uh-muhth) The distance of an object in the sky from the northern point on the horizon. The position of stars and planets is figured by azimuth and **altitude.**

Bb

Babbage (BAB-ij), **Charles** Born 1792; died 1871. British inventor who drew up plans for a machine that would perform mathematical calculations. While Babbage never completed his machine, his ideas laid the foundation for the modern computer.

backbone *See* **spine.**

bacteria (bak-TEER-ē-uh) Living things that are made up of single cells, each without a cell nucleus. Bacteria are found in all of the Earth's environments and usually live off other organisms. Some kinds of bacteria cause disease. Bacteria are members of the group of organisms known as **prokaryotes.** *Singular form*: **bacterium** (bak-TEER-ē-uhm).

bacteriology (bak-teer-ē-OL-uh-jē) The scientific study of bacteria, especially bacteria that cause disease.

badlands An area that has many ridges and gullies. Badlands usually form in dry regions where sudden rains wash away soil and vegetation.

baking soda A white powder that contains sodium and is used to make carbonated drinks and baked goods.

Did You Know?

bacteria

Whenever you think you are alone and far from other forms of life, just pick up a little bit of soil in your fingers. In it there are billions of bacteria. Bacteria live all over the Earth—on land, at the bottom of the ocean, even deep in the ice at the North and South Poles. Some kinds of bacteria cause disease, but most do not harm people, and some even live inside us and help us digest food.

balance (BAL-uhns) **1.** A device for weighing objects or amounts. A balance usually has a horizontal bar with a pan hanging at each end. **2.** A steady or stable position. In many animals, the inner ear controls the body's sense of balance. **3.** A condition in which two numbers, amounts, or forces are equal.

baleen (buh-LĒN) A hard, flexible material that hangs in plates from the upper jaw of certain whales. Baleen is used by whales to strain food from seawater.

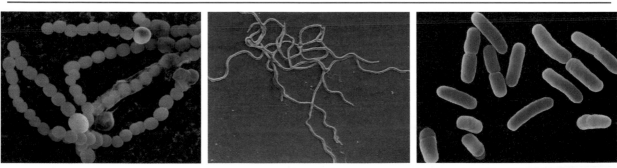

◻ **bacteria**

left to right: *the three shapes of bacteria—sphere, spiral, and rod*

20

outer ring
steel ball
axle
inner ring

□ ball bearing

The ball bearings in a skate wheel allow the wheel to turn freely around the axle with only a small amount of friction.

ball bearing A bearing in a machine in which the moving part slides on loose steel balls in a groove. The balls reduce the amount of friction between moving parts.

bamboo (bam-BOO) A kind of tall, tropical grass that has hollow, wood-like stems divided into segments. Some species of bamboo can grow as tall as 100 feet (30.5 meters) or more.

band A specific range of wavelengths or frequencies in the **electromagnetic spectrum.** Radio waves form one of the bands of the electromagnetic spectrum.

Banneker (BAN-i-ker), **Benjamin** Born 1731; died 1806. American mathematician and astronomer who correctly predicted a solar eclipse in 1789. From 1791 to 1802, Banneker published an almanac every year that contained information about tides and eclipses.

Banting (BAN-ting), **Frederick Grant** Born 1891; died 1941. Canadian scientist who discovered the hormone insulin with Charles Best in 1921. Banting and Best showed that insulin could be used to treat diabetes in humans and animals.

bar graph A graph that uses bars or rectangles to represent amounts. **□** See picture at **graph.**

bark The outer covering of the trunk, branches, and roots of trees. Bark protects the tree from heat, cold, and insects. The inner layer of bark is known as **phloem.**

barnacle (BAR-nuh-kuhl) One of a group of small crustaceans that live in the ocean and attach themselves to underwater objects, such as rocks and the bottoms of ships. Barnacles have hard outer skeletons.

Barnard (BAR-nerd), **Christiaan Neethling** Born 1923; died 2001. South African doctor who performed the first successful transplant of a human heart in 1967.

barometer (buh-ROM-i-ter) An instrument for measuring how high or low the atmospheric pressure is. Barometers are used to make weather forecasts. Because the pressure of the atmosphere grows less with greater height, barometers are also used to find out how high something is above sea level.

barrier island (BAIR-ē-er Ī-luhnd) A long, narrow island that is made of sand and is parallel to the mainland. Barrier islands protect the coast from erosion by waves.

basalt (buh-SAWLT *or* BĀ-sawlt) A common dark-gray rock that forms when magma cools into a solid. Basalt is made mostly of the mineral feldspar and minerals rich in iron and magnesium. Most of the ocean bottom is made of basalt covered with sand and mud. **□** See Table on page 208.

base **1.** A chemical compound that tastes bitter and feels slippery when mixed with water. Bases form salt and water when they come in contact with certain metals and with the chemical compounds known as acids. Baking soda is an example of a base. **□** Compare **acid. 2.** A side of a flat

21

shape, such as a triangle. The length of the base can be used to figure out the area of the shape. **3.** A face of a three-dimensional object, such as a pyramid. The base can be used to figure out the volume of the shape.

basic (BĀ-sik) Having the chemical properties of a base.

basin (BĀ-sin) A region drained by a river and its tributaries. The Amazon River basin includes the Amazon River and all of the streams that empty into it.

bat A small mammal with a body like a mouse and thin, leathery wings. Most bats eat insects or fruit. Bats are active at night and are the only mammals that can fly.

Did You Know?
bat
You might think that sonar is something that humans invented, but nature thought of it millions of years ago. Bats fly through the dark and don't bump into things because they steer using sonar. They send out sounds that bounce off objects and return as echoes, and these echoes tell the bats where the objects are. The objects can be something moving, like flying insects, that the bat can then catch for food.

bathysphere (BATH-i-sfeer) A round structure that was used to study the oceans and deep-sea life. The bathysphere could hold several people and was lowered from a boat by cables. It was replaced by safer vessels that could maneuver on their own.

battery (BAT-uh-rē) A device that changes one form of energy into another. Common household batteries change the energy that

exists in a paste-like mixture of dry chemicals into electric current. Solar batteries change the energy of sunlight into electricity.

Did You Know?
battery
Electricity is made by electrons flowing through a substance. Some substances let electrons flow very easily, and these are used in batteries. Inside the battery, the electrons flow away from the positive end (the cathode) and build up on the negative end (the anode). If you connect a wire to the two ends, the electrons will flow through it in a circuit, leaving the battery from the negative end and flowing back into the positive end.

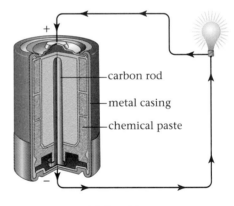

+
carbon rod
metal casing
chemical paste

◻ **battery**

The paste causes electrons to flow from the metal casing through the light bulb to the carbon rod, making the bulb glow.

bay A body of water that is mostly surrounded by land but is also connected to the sea or ocean on one side. A bay is usually smaller than a gulf.

bayou (BĪ-ōo) A slow-moving stream that is connected with a river, lake, or gulf. Bayous have many marshes and are common in the southern United States.

beach The area beside a shore where sand, stones, and gravel are laid down by the action of waves. Beaches usually slope gently toward the body of water they are next to.

beak The hard, projecting part of the mouth in birds. Beaks come in different sizes and shapes, depending on how birds feed and what they eat. ◻ A beak is also called a *bill*.

beaker (BĒ-ker) A wide glass container that is shaped like a cylinder and has a rim with a dip for pouring. It is used in laboratories.

◻ **beaker**

beam A narrow stream of light or of other radiation, such as x-rays or microwaves.

bear A large mammal with a shaggy coat, short tail, and large claws. Bears eat plants and other animals, especially insects and small rodents. Bears walk with the entire lower surface of their foot touching the ground.

bearing A part of a machine that holds a moving part and allows it to move or turn without much friction.

Beaufort scale (BŌ-fert SKĀL) A scale for classifying the force of the wind, ranging from 0 (calm) to 12 (hurricane). The scale was devised in 1805 as a means of describing the effect of different wind velocities on ships at sea.

Becquerel (buh-KREL *or* bek-uh-REL), **Antoine Henri** Born 1852; died 1908. French scientist who discovered that uranium is radioactive in 1896.

bed 1. A layer of sediments or rock that extends over a large area and has other layers below and sometimes above it. 2. The bottom of a body of water, such as a stream.

bedrock The solid rock that lies beneath the soil and other loose material on the Earth's surface.

bee A type of insect that has four wings, a hairy body, and usually a stinger. Bees gather pollen and nectar from flowers for food. Some bees, such as honeybees, live in large organized groups called **colonies,** which are made up of workers, drones, and a queen.

beetle (BĒ-tuhl) A type of insect with hard, shiny front wings that usually cover and protect the hind wings when not in flight. Beetles have mouthparts used for grasping and feeding and jaws that chew.

Did You Know?

beetle
Beetles may be the most successful animal on Earth. There are more species of beetles than any other animal—nearly 300,000 different kinds! Beetles live all over the world in many different environments. They live on the ground, underground, in the water, under bark, and in decaying plants and animals.

behavior (bē-HĀV-yer) 1. The way in which living things act in response to their environment. Changes in the environment, such as those caused by climate or pollution, can lead to changes in the behavior of living things. 2. The way in which something acts or reacts under certain circumstances. Scientists study the behavior of atoms that react with each other.

Bell, Alexander Graham Born 1847; died 1922. American scientist who invented the telephone in 1876.

Biography

Alexander Graham Bell

Alexander Graham Bell spent many years teaching people who had difficulty hearing. His interest in sound and speech led him to think about devices that could send or record sounds. Besides inventing the telephone, Bell devised an early version of the hearing aid and created one of the first sound recorders.

benzene (BEN-zēn) A clear liquid that can catch on fire very easily and that is used to make many products, such as detergents and fuels. A molecule of benzene contains six carbon atoms that are joined together in a ring. Each carbon atom is attached to a hydrogen atom outside the ring.

beriberi (BAIR-ē-BAIR-ē) A disease that is caused by too little vitamin B$_1$ (thiamine) in the diet. Beriberi causes damage to the nerves and blood vessels.

berry (BAIR-ē) **1.** A fruit that has many seeds in a usually soft pulp. Grapes, bananas, tomatoes, and blueberries are known as true berries. **2.** A seed or dried kernel of a plant, such as a grain. Wheat, barley, and coffee have this kind of berry.

beryl (BAIR-uhl) A greenish mineral that usually lets light shine through it. Beryl is found mostly in igneous and metamorphic rocks. Emeralds are a kind of beryl.

Best, Charles Herbert Born 1899; died 1978. Canadian scientist who discovered the hormone insulin with Frederick Banting in 1921.

beta particle (BĀ-tuh PAR-ti-kuhl) An electron that shoots out at very high speed from the atoms of some radioactive elements when they break down into other elements during the process known as **radioactive decay.**

Bhaskara (BAHS-kuh-ruh) Born 1114; died 1185? Indian mathematician who was the first person to show how decimals are used.

biceps (BĪ-seps) The muscle at the front of the upper arm that bends the elbow.

bicuspid (bī-KUHS-pid) *See* **premolar.**

biennial (bī-EN-ē-uhl) Completing a life cycle normally in two growing seasons. Carrots and parsnips are biennial plants.

big bang The powerful explosion of a tiny, very hot object that contained all the matter in the universe. Scientists believe that the big bang was the first thing that happened in the history of the universe, sometime between 12 and 18 billion years ago.

Big Dipper A group of seven stars that form the shape of a dipper or large spoon. Four stars form the bowl of the dipper and three stars form its handle.

bilateral symmetry (bī-LAT-er-uhl SIM-uh-trē) An arrangement of parts in a living thing in which the body is divided into two equal halves. The bodies of most animals, including mammals, fish, birds, and insects, show bilateral symmetry. ◻ Compare **radial symmetry.** ◻ See picture at **symmetry.**

bile A greenish fluid that is produced by the liver. Bile helps the body to digest fats.

bill *See* **beak.**

binary digit (BĪ-nuh-rē DIJ-it) Either of the numbers 0 or 1, used in the binary number system. Binary digits are used by computers for making calculations.

binary number system   A method of writing numbers that uses only zeros and ones. In the binary number system, 1 means 1, 10 means 2, 11 means 3, 100 means 4, 101 means 5, 110 means 6, and so on.

binary star   Two stars that form a pair and revolve around the same central point. Binary stars are held together by gravity and they often look like a single star when seen without a telescope.

binoculars   (buh-NOK-yuh-lerz)   An instrument for seeing things at a distance. It is made of two small telescopes joined together so that both eyes can look through it at once.

biochemistry   (bī-ō-KEM-i-strē) The scientific study of the chemical compounds found in living things and of the role these compounds play in the body.

biodegradable   (bī-ō-di-GRĀ-duh-buhl) Capable of being broken down into simpler parts by natural processes, especially by the action of bacteria. All living things are made up of biodegradable matter that decays after death. Some man-made products, like detergents, can also be biodegradable, while others, such as plastics, are not.

biodiversity   (bī-ō-di-VER-si-tē) The number and variety of plants and animals that are found in an ecosystem.

biology   (bī-OL-uh-jē)   The scientific study of life and of living things. Botany, zoology, and ecology are all branches of biology.

bioluminescent   (bī-ō-loo-muh-NES-uhnt) Giving off light as a result of chemical reactions that take place in the tissues of the body. Some insects, fish, fungi, and bacteria are bioluminescent.

biome   (BĪ-ōm) A large community of plants and animals that exists in a particular region. A biome is defined by its climate, the type of soil it has, and the kinds of plants that grow there. Grassland, tundra, desert, tropical rain forest, and deciduous forests are all biomes.

biotechnology   (bī-ō-tek-NOL-uh-jē) The use of technology to change something found in nature so that it can be of use to humans. Using **genetic engineering** to cre-

□ **biome**

left to right: *three biomes—desert, rain forest, and tundra*

ate cells that fight cancer is one use of biotechnology.

biped (bī-ped) An animal with two feet, such as a bird or human.

bird A warm-blooded, egg-laying animal that has wings, a body covered with feathers, and a beak. The heart of a bird has four sections, called chambers. Birds are vertebrates and range in size from tiny hummingbirds to the ostrich, which can grow to a height of 8 feet (about 2.4 meters).

◻ **bird**

Most birds, like the hummingbird (top), can fly, but some, like the ostrich (bottom), cannot.

bird of prey A large meat-eating bird that hunts its food. Hawks, eagles, falcons, and owls are birds of prey.

bisect (BĪ-sekt) To cut or separate into two equal parts.

bit The smallest unit of information that a computer can recognize. A bit holds one of two possible values, either 0 or 1.

bivalve (BĪ-valv) A mollusk with a shell made up of two halves that open and close as if they were connected by a hinge. Clams and oysters are bivalves. ◻ Compare **univalve.**

Black, Joseph Born 1728; died 1799. Scottish scientist who discovered carbon dioxide in 1756.

Black Death An epidemic of bubonic plague in the 14th century that began in Asia and swept through Europe, where it killed about one-third of the population.

black dwarf star The mass of cold, dense gas that is left after a white dwarf star has cooled and dimmed to the point that it no longer produces light.

black hole An object in outer space that is so dense that its gravity will not let anything escape from it, not even light. Black holes are formed by the collapse of a star in a giant explosion called a **supernova.** ◻ See picture at **star.**

◻ **black hole**

A black hole's powerful gravity pulls matter away from a nearby star. Before disappearing into the black hole, the matter becomes so hot that it shoots out beams of x-rays above and below the swirling disk.

bladder (BLAD-er) A hollow organ that stores urine, which is produced by the kidneys. In mammals, the bladder is connected to each kidney by a long tube called a ureter.

blind spot A small area on the retina of the eye that is not sensitive to light. The optic nerve attaches to the retina in this area.

block and tackle A device used for lifting loads that has a fixed pulley and a movable pulley that are connected by a rope. The rope, which is attached to the load, goes over the fixed pulley, around the movable one, and then back around the fixed one.

blood The fluid that circulates through the body of humans and other vertebrates. Blood is pumped by the heart through the arteries and veins to carry oxygen and nutrients to the cells of the body and to remove their waste products. Blood keeps the body warm and helps keep it disease-free.

Did You Know?

blood

Blood is more than just a red liquid. It is full of cells that are essential to keeping us alive. Red blood cells carry oxygen from the lungs to the body's other cells, and white blood cells help fight off germs. The liquid part of blood contains water, salt, and nutrients that have been soaked up from the stomach and intestines. An adult has between 5 and 6 quarts of blood (between 4 and 6 liters), and nearly 100,000 miles (161,000 kilometers) of blood vessels!

blood cell A cell that is found in blood; a **red blood cell** or **white blood cell**.

blood pressure The pressure of the blood in the blood vessels, especially the arteries, as it circulates through the body. Blood pressure that is too high can cause strain on the heart and other organs.

blood type One of the four main types of human blood: A, B, AB, and O. A person's blood type can be determined by testing for particular substances that are found on red blood cells.

blood vessel A tube in the body that carries blood from one part of the body to another. Arteries, veins, and capillaries are blood vessels.

blubber (BLUHB-er) A thick layer of fat that lies under the skin of whales, seals, and certain other sea mammals. Blubber prevents heat loss and also serves as a source of food energy.

blue-green algae *See* **cyanobacteria.**

blue shift A decrease in the wavelength of radiation given off by an object in outer space as a result of the **Doppler effect.** Objects that are moving toward the Earth appear bluish.

bog An area of wet, spongy ground that is made up mainly of decayed or decaying moss.

Bohr (BOR), **Niels Henrik David** Born 1885; died 1962. Danish scientist who studied the structure of atoms. Bohr discovered that electrons move farther away from the nucleus of an atom when the atom is heated up.

◻ **Niels Bohr**

boil To change from a liquid to a gas or vapor by being heated to the **boiling point.**

boiling point The temperature at which a liquid changes to a gas or vapor. At the boiling point, vapors moving out of the liquid create so

◻ **boil**

a beaker of boiling water

much pressure at the surface that they form bubbles. The boiling point of water is 212° Fahrenheit (100° Celsius).

Did You Know?

boiling point

You may know that water boils at 212° Fahrenheit or 100° Celsius. But that's only at sea level. If you were to boil water at the top of Mount Everest, it would boil at 159.8° Fahrenheit (71° Celsius). The air pressure up there is much lower, so it takes less heat to make bubbles form in water.

---

bond   An attraction between atoms that holds them together in a molecule or crystal. Bonds are formed when one or more electrons are shared between atoms, or when one atom gives away electrons to another atom.

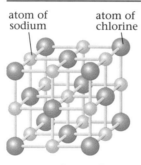

□ **bond**

When atoms of sodium and chlorine are joined by bonds, they form molecules of salt (sodium chloride).

bone   **1.** The hard material that forms the skeleton of most vertebrates. Bone provides protection for organs, such as the brain and heart, and serves as a support for the muscles of the body. Bones are connected to each other by ligaments. **2.** One of the parts of the skeleton in vertebrates. The bone of the thigh is called the femur. The bones of the forearm are the radius and ulna.

bone marrow   The soft, sponge-like material that fills the center of the bones of mammals. Most blood cells form in the bone marrow. □ See picture at **bone.**

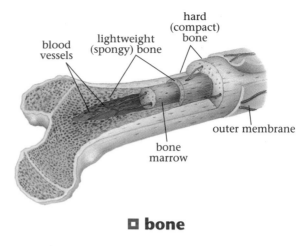

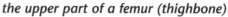

□ **bone**

the upper part of a femur (thighbone)

---

bony fish   A fish that has a skeleton made of bone rather than cartilage. Most fish are bony fish.

□ **bony fish**

sockeye salmon

---

botanical garden   (buh-TAN-i-kuhl GAR-duhn) A place where different kinds of plants are grown for scientists to study and for people to learn about.

botany   (BOT-uh-nē) The scientific study of plants, including their growth, structure, and diseases.

bowels   (BOW-uhlz) The part of the digestive system below the stomach; the intestine.

Boyle   (BOY-uhl), **Robert** Born 1627; died 1691. British scientist who was a pioneer of modern chemistry. Boyle was the first person to explain that all substances are made of chemical elements. Together with Robert Hooke, Boyle conducted experiments on the behavior of gases that led to the discovery of Boyle's law in 1662.

Boyle's law   A scientific law that states that the volume of a given amount of gas depends on the pressure that is put on the gas, as long as the temperature does not change. If the pressure on the gas increases, the gas's volume decreases, and if the pressure decreases, the volume increases. Boyle's law is named after Robert Boyle.

brachiopod   (BRĀ-kē-uh-pod) One of a group of animals that live in the ocean and have shells that resemble those of a clam. Brachiopods are invertebrates. They are attached to a surface by a strong stalk and have hollow tentacles that are used to sweep food into the mouth.

brachiosaurus   (brā-kē-uh-SOR-uhs) An extremely large dinosaur that was one of the biggest animals that ever lived on land. The brachiosaurus was similar to apatosaurus, except that it had longer front legs than back legs, and its nostrils were on the top of its head.

brackish   Containing a mixture of seawater and fresh water. Brackish water is not as salty as seawater, but it is still too salty to drink.

Brahe   (BRAH *or* BRAH-hē), **Tycho** Born 1546; died 1601. Danish scientist who made accurate studies of the planets and stars before the telescope became commonly used. Brahe determined the positions of almost 800 stars. In 1572, he observed the supernova that became known as Tycho's star.

brain   The main part of the nervous system in vertebrates that controls all body activities, such as breathing and walking. In humans, the brain is the center of speech, memory, thought, and feeling. The brain is protected by the bones of the skull and is connected to the spinal cord.

Did You Know?

brain
The adult human brain weighs around 3 pounds and contains about 10 billion nerve cells. Each nerve cell is connected to about 10,000 other nerve cells, meaning there are 100 trillion nerve connections in the brain. The nerve cells are constantly sending signals to each other—a million times more signals per second than the world's fastest computers.

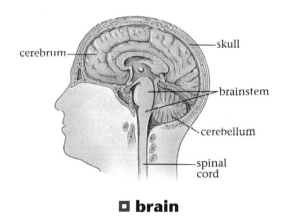

cerebrum — skull — brainstem — cerebellum — spinal cord

☐ **brain**

brainstem   The lower part of the brain in humans and other vertebrates. The brainstem controls automatic body activities, such as breathing and the beating of the heart. The brainstem is connected to the spinal cord. ☐ See picture at **brain**.

bran   The tough outer covering of the seed of grains such as wheat or rye. Bran is high in **fiber** and helps in the digestion of food.

brass   A yellowish alloy of the metals copper and zinc. It usually has twice as much copper as zinc. Brass is strong and easily shaped, and it is not worn away easily.

breast   The part of the body in a female primate that contains glands that produce milk.

breastbone   *See* **sternum.**

breed   **1.** To reproduce by giving birth or hatching. Mosquitoes breed in water. Seals breed on land. **2.** To raise animals or plants, often to produce new or better kinds.

brine   Water that has a large amount of salt. Brine is often used to preserve food.

brittle   (BRIT-uhl) Likely to break, snap, or crack. Chalk is brittle.

broadcast   (BRAWD-kast) To send out signals in the form of electromagnetic waves. Radio and television signals are broadcast by **transmitters.**

broadleaf   (BRAWD-lēf) Having broad leaves rather than needle-like leaves. Deciduous trees are usually broadleaf trees. In tropical regions, most broadleaf trees are evergreen trees. ◻ See picture at **leaf.**

bronchial tube   (BRONG-kē-uhl tōob) A tube that carries air from the windpipe to the lungs. The bronchial tubes get smaller as they get closer to the lungs. ◻ See picture at **respiratory system.**

brontosaurus   (bron-tuh-SOR-uhs) *See* **apatosaurus.**

bronze   A brownish alloy of the metals copper and tin. Bronze is harder than brass and is used to make tools and machine parts.

brown dwarf   An object in outer space that is like a star but does not give off light because it does not have enough mass to produce its own energy.

browser   A computer program that finds and displays information that is on the Internet or another computer network.

Btu   Short for **British thermal unit.** A unit used to measure heat. Each Btu is equal to the amount of heat that is needed to raise the temperature of one pound of water by one degree Fahrenheit.

bubble   (BUHB-uhl) A ball of air or other gas, often with a thin film around it. Bubbles form in boiling water and in soaps or liquids that are shaken.

bubonic plague   (boo-BON-ik PLAG) A usually fatal disease in which a person vomits, has severe diarrhea, and has swollen lumps where the arms and legs join the body. Bubonic plague is carried by fleas that have bitten infected rodents, especially rats. The Black Death of the 14th century was an epidemic of bubonic plague.

bud   **1.** A small swelling on a branch or stem, containing a flower, shoot, or leaves that have not yet developed. **2.** A flower or leaf that has not opened up yet. A small part on a simple living thing, such as a hydra, that can grow into a completely new organism of the same kind.

buffer   (BUHF-er) A substance that prevents a solution from changing when an acid or base is added to it.

bug   A wingless or four-winged insect that has mouthparts used for piercing or sucking. Aphids and lice are examples of an order of insects known as "true bugs."

bulb   A round part of a stem that grows underground and contains the shoot of a new plant. A bulb is surrounded by leaf-like scales that provide nutrients to the new plant. Tulips and onions grow from bulbs.

Bunsen burner (BUHN-suhn BER-ner) A device that provides a flame for heating or burning things in laboratory experiments. It has an upright metal tube connected to a source of gas, with adjustable holes at its base. These holes allow air to enter the tube and mix with the gas in order to make a very hot flame.

◻ Bunsen burner

buoyancy (BOY-uhn-sē) The upward force on an object floating in a liquid or gas. Buoyancy allows a boat to float on water.

burette (byu-RET) A glass tube that has precise markings for measurements and is thinner at the bottom than at the top. Burettes are used in laboratories to pour a measured amount of liquid from one container into another. The liquid comes out through a valve at the bottom.

◻ burette

burn **1.** To be on fire. A substance burns if it is heated up enough to undergo a chemical reaction with oxygen. When a substance burns it usually gives off heat and

light. **2.** An injury that is caused by heat, fire, or a chemical, such as an acid. How bad a burn is depends on how much of the body is affected and how deep the burn is.

bush *See* **shrub.**

butte (BYOOT) A hill with steep, cliff-like sides and a flat top. A butte is smaller than a **mesa.**

◻ butte

Monument Valley, Arizona

butterfly (BUHT-er-flī) An insect with a slender body and four wide, flat wings that are usually brightly colored. Butterflies have

Did You Know?

butterfly

How can you tell a butterfly from a moth? Butterflies are usually active during the day, while moths are active at night. Butterflies hold their wings upright when they are resting, while moths hold their wings out to the sides. Butter-flies tend to have slender bodies and antennae with knobs on the ends. Moths have fatter bodies and hairy antennae without knobs.

antennae with knob-shaped tips. Unlike moths, butterflies are active during the day and hold their wings upright and together when not in flight.

by-product (BĪ-prod-uhkt) Something produced in the process of making something else. When plants produce carbohydrates during photosynthesis, they give off oxygen as a by-product.

Byron (BĪ-ruhn), **Augusta Ada** Born 1815; died 1852. British mathematician who, with Charles Babbage, developed a plan for a mechanical computer. Her detailed description of how the machine could be made to perform specific calculations is considered to be the first computer program.

byte (BĪT) A unit of information that consists of eight **bits** and is used to measure the amount of information in a computer's memory. A byte usually stands for a number or letter. Nowadays, the amount of computer memory is often expressed in terms of megabytes (1,048,576 bytes) or gigabytes (1,073,741,824 bytes).

Biography

Augusta Ada Byron

Augusta Ada Byron is known as the first person to write a computer program. She showed how programs could instruct early computers to do complicated math problems. She also predicted that some day people would use computers to make music and pictures. In the 1970s, computer experts created one of the first languages for writing programs and named it "Ada" in her honor.

Cc

cactus (KAK-tuhs) A type of plant that has thick, usually spiny stems and that grows in hot, dry places. The leaves of a cactus are sharp spines. *Plural form:* **cacti** (KAK-tī).

Did You Know?

cactus

Cacti often look strange, but that's because they're built to hold water. A cactus's body is between 80 and 90 percent water, and its thick walls keep that water from evaporating. Its sharp spines are actually leaves that gather up dew and drip it onto the ground, where the cactus's shallow roots soak it up.

caffeine (ka-FĒN) A bitter chemical compound that is found in tea, coffee, and various plants. Caffeine makes the heart beat faster.

calcification (kal-suh-fi-KĀ-shuhn) The replacement of once living material, especially hard material, with **calcium carbonate.** Calcification happens when an organism that has died becomes a fossil.

calcite (KAL-sīt) A mineral that is usually white, clear, or pale yellow and is made of **calcium carbonate.** Calcite is the main mineral in chalk, limestone, and marble. ◻ See picture at **crystal.**

calcium (KAL-sē-uhm) A chemical element that is a white metal. Calcium is found in bones, teeth, leaves, shells, and limestone. It is necessary for the normal growth of most animals and plants. ◻ See Table on pages 178–179.

calcium carbonate (KAL-sē-uhm CAR-buh-nāt) A white chemical compound that is found in chalk, limestone, marble, and seashells. It is made of calcium, carbon, and oxygen and is used to make toothpaste and white paint.

calculator (KAL-kyōō-lā-ter) A device that solves mathematical problems.

calorie (KAL-uh-rē) A unit used to measure the amount of energy released by food as it is digested in the body.

calyx (KĀ-liks *or* KAL-iks) The sepals of a flower.

cambium (KAM-bē-uhm) A layer of cells in the stems and roots of many plants that forms the plant parts that carry water and nutrients throughout the plant. In woody plants, the cambium forms new layers of wood and bark. ◻ See pictures at **root, stem.**

Cambrian Period (KAM-brē-uhn PEER-ē-uhd) The period of time during the history of the Earth starting about 540 million years ago and ending about 505 million years ago. During the Cambrian Period, the Earth's seas were warm, and deserts covered much of the surface of the land. Marine invertebrates and almost all modern animal groups came into being during this time. ◻ See Table on pages 102–103.

camera (KAM-er-uh) A device for taking photographs or motion pictures. Most cameras consist of a box that has a lens that focuses light so that an image is

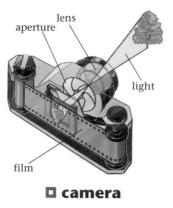

□ **camera**

Light reflecting off a tree passes through the lens, which turns the image upside down and focuses it on the film.

recorded either on film or on a computer chip as digital information.

camouflage (KAM-uh-flawzh) Coloring or body shape that protects an animal by making it look like its surroundings so it can hide from predators or prey.

Did You Know?

camouflage

Camouflage can take many forms. Fawns are spotted in order to blend in with the dappled light of the forest. The bodies of some insects are shaped like sticks or leaves. Fish bellies are white so they look like the surface of the water to predators below.

cancer (KAN-ser) A disease in which the cells in a part of the body become abnormal and multiply without stopping. Treatments for cancer include chemotherapy, radiation, and surgery.

□ **camouflage**

top: *a walking stick on a tree limb*
bottom: *a mantis on a leaf*

canine (KĀ-nīn) **1.** An animal in the family of mammals that is related to the dog. The wolf, fox, and coyote are canines. **2.** One of four sharp, pointed teeth in mammals that are used for cutting and tearing meat. The canines are found behind the **incisors** in most mammals.

canopy (KAN-uh-pē) The highest level in a forest, formed by the leafy tops of the tallest trees. The thickness of the canopy determines how much sunlight gets into the lower levels. In rain forests, the shade produced by the thick canopy helps keep the soil moist.

canyon (KAN-yuhn) A long, narrow valley with steep walls, especially in the western parts of America. Canyons are cut into the land by running water.

capacitor (kuh-PAS-i-ter) A device that is used to store electric charge and to control the flow of electricity through electric circuits. Capacitors are made of two metal plates that collect electric charges and are separated by an **insulator.**

cape A point of land that projects into a body of water.

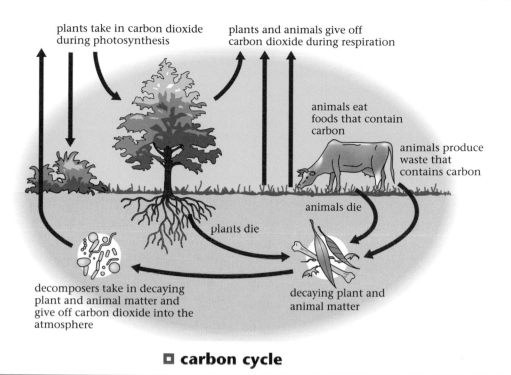

plants take in carbon dioxide during photosynthesis

plants and animals give off carbon dioxide during respiration

animals eat foods that contain carbon

animals produce waste that contains carbon

animals die

plants die

decomposers take in decaying plant and animal matter and give off carbon dioxide into the atmosphere

decaying plant and animal matter

◻ **carbon cycle**

capillary (KAP-uh-lair-ē) A tiny blood vessel that connects the smallest arteries to the smallest veins. Oxygen is delivered to, and carbon dioxide is removed from, the tissues of the body by means of capillaries.

capillary action The movement of a liquid along the surfaces of a solid. Capillary action happens because the molecules of the liquid are attracted to the solid surface and also to each other, pulling one another along. Water moves through the roots of trees or into the pores of a sponge by capillary action.

carbohydrate (kar-bō-HĪ-drāt) A chemical compound that is made in green plants by **photosynthesis** and that is an important source of energy in food. Carbohydrates are made up of carbon, hydrogen, and oxygen. Sugars, starches, and cellulose are all carbohydrates.

carbon (KAR-buhn) A chemical element that is found in all living things and is also part of many rocks, gases, and other nonliving things. Diamonds and graphite are pure forms of carbon, and carbon is also a

major part of coal, petroleum, and natural gas. ◻ See Table on pages 178–179.

Did You Know?

carbon

The chemical element carbon is essential for our lives. It forms part of every molecule that is needed for living things to function, including proteins, fats, and carbohydrates. Many of the chemical compounds that have been made in laboratories and that we use every day also have carbon, such as nylon, polyester, gasoline, and most medicines.

carbon 14 A radioactive form of carbon that has two extra neutrons in its nucleus and is used in **radiocarbon dating.** Carbon 14 is found in all living things. After a plant or animal has died, the amount of carbon 14 that is in it can be measured to figure out how long ago it died.

carbon cycle The process by which carbon is constantly exchanged between living things and the environment. Plants and algae absorb carbon, in the form of carbon dioxide, from the atmosphere during the process known as **photosynthesis.** Carbon enters the food chain and is returned to the atmosphere by the decay of dead animals and plants.

carbon dating   *See* **radiocarbon dating.**

carbon dioxide   (KAR-buhn dī-OK-sīd) A gas that has no color or odor and is produced whenever anything containing carbon, such as wood or gasoline, is burned. It is breathed out of the lungs of animals and taken in by plants for use in **photosynthesis.** Carbon dioxide contains two atoms of oxygen for every atom of carbon; its chemical formula is CO_2.

Carboniferous Period   (kar-buh-NIF-er-uhs PEER-ē-uhd) The period of time during the history of the Earth starting about 360 million years ago and ending about 286 million years ago. During the Carboniferous Period, much of the world's land was covered with swamps. The remains of plants that grew in these swamps later hardened into coal. ◻ See Table on pages 102–103.

carbon monoxide   (KAR-buhn muh-NOK-sīd) A gas that has no color or odor and contains one carbon atom for every atom of oxygen; its chemical formula is CO. Carbon monoxide is very poisonous. It is found in automobile exhaust.

carburetor   (KAR-buh-rā-ter) The part of certain kinds of engines that mixes gasoline with air so that the gasoline will burn properly.

carcinogen   (kar-SIN-uh-juhn) Something that can cause a person to develop cancer. The chemical compounds found in cigarettes are carcinogens.

cardiac   (KAR-dē-ak) Relating to the heart.

cardinal number   (KAR-duh-nuhl NUHM-ber) A number used when counting to indicate a quantity but not a quantity's order in a series. Examples of cardinal numbers include 3, 11, and 412. ◻ Compare **ordinal number.**

cardinal point   One of the four main directions on a compass. The cardinal points are north, south, east, and west.

carnivore   (KAR-nuh-vor) An animal that eats other animals. Carnivores include **predators,** like lions and alligators, and **scavengers,** like hyenas and vultures.

carpel   (KAR-puhl) The part of the pistil of a flower that contains the eggs. A flower can have one carpel or several carpels joined together.

carrier   (KAIR-ē-er) An animal that carries a disease from one organism to another. Mosquitoes are carriers of malaria, for example. In humans and many other animals, carriers have the germs of a disease and can give it to others, but they do not appear to be sick themselves.

Carson   (KAR-suhn), **Rachel Louise** Born 1907; died 1964. American scientist who studied the dangerous effects of pesticides on the environment. Because of her work and the books she wrote, the importance of preserving natural habitats has become much better understood.

Cartesian coordinate system   (kar-TĒ-zhuhn kō-OR-duh-nit SIS-tuhm) A system in mathematics that is used to locate a point in a plane. The point is identified by two numbers that represent its distance from each of two perpendicular lines that cross each other at a point called the **origin.** The lines are called the **x-axis** and the **y-axis.**

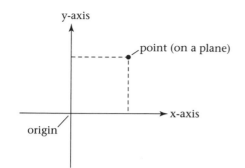

□ **Cartesian coordinate system**

cartilage (KAR-tuhl-ij) The strong, flexible material that is found in the body of many animals. Cartilage lines the surface of the bones in a joint and provides support for the outer ear. In some animals, such as sharks, the entire skeleton is made out of cartilage.

cartilaginous fish (kar-tuh-LAJ-uh-nuhs FISH) A fish that has a skeleton made mainly of cartilage rather than bone. Sharks, rays, and skates are cartilaginous fish.

□ **cartilaginous fish**

a lemon shark

Carver (KAR-ver), **George Washington** Born 1864?; died 1943. American scientist who developed methods to improve agriculture in the United States.

cat A member of a meat-eating group of mammals that includes the domestic cat, lion, tiger, jaguar, lynx, and cheetah. The domestic cat is a common house pet, while all other species live in the wild. All species except the cheetah have claws that can be

Biography

George Washington Carver

George Washington Carver taught farmers in the Southern United States to plant different crops on their land from season to season, so as not to use up all the soil's nutrients. Cotton was the main crop of the South, and when the boll weevil (a kind of destructive beetle) threatened to ruin the cotton harvest, Carver developed hundreds of uses for the peanut, soybean, and sweet potato. As a result, they became important new crops.

completely pulled back into their paws after being exposed.

catalyst (KAT-uh-list) A substance that starts or speeds up a chemical reaction between other substances. Catalysts are not changed by the chemical reactions they are involved in. Certain molecules in saliva are catalysts that help us digest food.

caterpillar (KAT-er-pil-er) The wormlike larva of a butterfly or moth. Caterpillars feed on plants. Their bodies are covered in fine hairs and are often brightly colored.

cathode (KATH-ōd) 1. The positive electrode in an electric cell, such as a battery, that creates its own electricity. The cathode attracts negatively charged particles in the chemical compounds inside the cell to create the electric current. 2. The negative electrode in a device that uses a special liquid to bring about chemical reactions. When it is connected to an electric current, the cathode attracts positively charged particles in the liquid. □ Compare **anode**.

cathode-ray tube   A sealed tube in which electrons are sent in a beam from the negatively charged end to the positively charged end. Cathode ray tubes are used in televisions and computer monitors, in which the screen is the positively charged end of the tube. When the electrons strike the screen, they form an image.

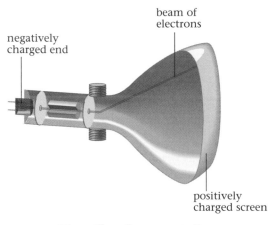

□ **cathode-ray tube**

cation   (KAT-ī-uhn) An atom or a group of atoms that has a positive electric charge. Cations are formed when an atom or group of atoms loses electrons.

CAT scan   Short for **computerized axial tomography.** A three-dimensional x-ray of the inside of a body part, used by doctors to help diagnose a disease. CAT scans are made up of a series of x-rays that are arranged into a single picture by a computer.

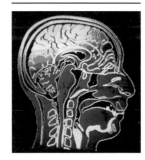

□ **CAT scan**

a CAT scan of a human head

cave   A hollow area in the Earth, having an opening to the outside. Caves are often made by water washing away limestone. Some caves extend for miles beneath the surface of the Earth.

Cavendish   (KAV-uhn-dish), **Henry** Born 1731; died 1810. British scientist who discovered hydrogen in 1766. He also showed that hydrogen was the lightest of all the gases and that water is a chemical compound made of hydrogen and oxygen, not a chemical element.

cavity   (KAV-i-tē) **1.** A hollow area, such as one in a bone. **2.** A hole in a tooth that is caused by decay.

CD   *See* **compact disk.**

CD-ROM   (SĒ-DĒ-RAHM) Short for **compact disk read-only memory.** A compact disk that stores data that cannot be removed, added to, or changed.

celestial   (suh-LES-chuhl) Relating to the sky or outer space. Stars and planets are celestial objects.

cell   **1.** The most basic part of a living thing, made up of a jelly-like substance called cytoplasm that is enclosed by a thin membrane. The cells of plants and many-celled animals have a nucleus, which contains the genes and other structures. The cells of green plants and some algae have chloroplasts, which is where photosynthesis takes place. **2.** *See* **electric cell.**

cell division   The process by which a cell divides into two or more cells. Cells multiply by means of cell division. The most common kind of cell division in humans and other vertebrates is called **mitosis.**

cell membrane   The thin membrane that encloses the contents of a cell. Nutrients and waste materials move into and out of the cell through the cell membrane. □ See picture at **cell.**

cell phone   A phone that sends and receives calls using radio waves. The radio waves are picked up by antennas and sent to other antennas until they reach a station that makes connections to phone lines.

cellulose   (SEL-yuh-lōs) A substance that makes up the cell walls of plants. Cellulose is a kind of **carbohydrate.** It is used to make paper, cloth, plastics, and explosives.

cell wall   The layer on the outside of cells in plants, bacteria, fungi, and many algae. The cell wall gives shape to and pro-

tects the cell. It is made mostly of cellulose. Most animal cells have a cell membrane rather than a cell wall. ◼ See picture at **cell.**

Celsius   (SEL-sē-uhs), **Anders** Born 1701; died 1744. Swedish scientist who in 1742 created the Celsius scale for measuring temperature.

Celsius scale   A temperature scale on which the freezing point of water is 0° and the boiling point of water is 100°. Scientists

A Closer Look

Cell
A cell is the smallest, most basic unit of life. The smallest living things are made up of just one cell. Large animals and plants are often made up of millions or billions of cells. The cells of plants and animals perform many different tasks, but all are made up of the same basic parts: a protective outer membrane or wall, cytoplasm, a nucleus that holds the cell's DNA, and many tiny structures, called organelles, in which the chemical reactions of the body take place.

<u>**animal cell**</u>   <u>**plant cell**</u>

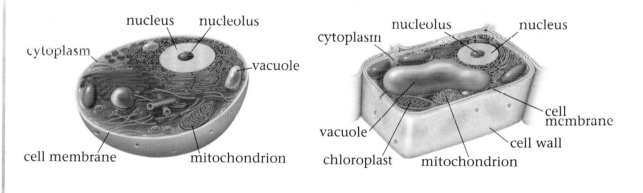

cell division

*Cells must divide for a living thing to grow and stay healthy. In animals, the most common type of cell division is **mitosis**. In mitosis, the chromosomes copy themselves, the nucleus divides, and two new cells are formed.*

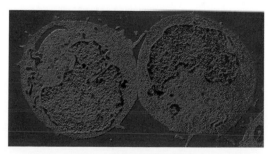

normally use the Celsius scale instead of the **Fahrenheit scale** to measure temperature. The Celsius scale is named after Anders Celsius. ◻ See picture at **temperature.**

cement (si-MENT) A mixture of materials that is made mainly from powdered clay and limestone. When water is added, the mixture forms a paste that becomes hard when it dries. Cement is used for sidewalks and as a building material.

Cenozoic Era (sen-uh-ZŌ-ik EER-uh) The most recent era of geologic time, starting about 65 million years ago and continuing until today. During the Cenozoic Era, the continents took their present form, and many new kinds of mammals and plants developed. ◻ See Table on pages 102–103.

center of gravity The point in an object around which the object's weight is balanced.

center of mass The point in an object that moves or resists being moved as though its entire mass were located in it. It is usually in the same place as the **center of gravity.**

centigrade (SEN-ti-grād) An older name for the Celsius temperature scale.

Did You Know?

centigrade
Because of confusion over the prefix *centi-,* which originally meant 100 but developed the meaning $\frac{1}{100}$, scientists agreed to stop using the word centigrade in 1948. They use the word Celsius instead.

centimeter (SEN-tuh-mē-ter) A unit of length in the metric system equal to $\frac{1}{100}$ of a meter. ◻ See Table on page 148.

centipede (SEN-tuh-pēd) A worm-like animal with a body that is divided into many segments, each with its own pair of legs. The front legs have glands that contain venom and are used to catch prey. Centipedes are members of a group of animals known as **arthropods.**

central nervous system The part of the nervous system in vertebrates that is made up of the brain and spinal cord. The central nervous system receives information from the body and the environment and controls body activities like breathing, walking, and talking. ◻ Compare **peripheral nervous system.**

central processing unit The part of a computer that carries out the instructions that are contained in a computer **program.** It also carries out the instructions that allow information to be sent to and from other computer parts, such as a disk drive and a keyboard. ◻ A central processing unit is called a *CPU* for short.

centrifugal force (sen-TRIF-yuh-guhl FORS) The force that seems to cause an object moving in a circle to break away and fly off in a straight line. Centrifugal force is not a real force, since nothing is pushing the object away from the center of the circle. It is actually an example of inertia, the natural tendency of moving objects to move in a straight line.

centripetal force (sen-TRIP-i-tuhl FORS) The force that causes an object moving in a circle to keep going in a curving path instead of a straight one. Centripetal force pulls the object toward the center of a circle. The Earth's gravity is the centripetal force that keeps the Moon on the circular path of its orbit.

ceramic (suh-RAM-ik) A hard, brittle material made by baking clay at a high tem-

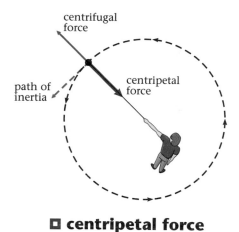

centrifugal force

path of inertia

centripetal force

□ centripetal force

Centripetal force causes the ball being whirled at the end of a string to move in a circle about the person, and not to fly out and away along the path of inertia.

perature. Some ceramics are superconductors, which conduct electric current with little or no resistance.

cereal (SEER-ē-uhl) A plant whose seeds have lots of starch and are used for food. Cereals are actually tall, stiff grasses. Wheat, corn, and rice are cereals.

cerebellum (sair-uh-BEL-uhm) The part of the brain in humans and other vertebrates that controls balance and smooths out body movements. The cerebellum is found at the lower back part of the brain. **□** See picture at **brain.**

cerebral (suh-RĒ-bruhl) Relating to the brain.

cerebrum (suh-RĒ-bruhm) The largest, uppermost part of the brain in humans and other vertebrates. The cerebrum is made up of two halves, called hemispheres. The cerebrum receives information from the rest of the body and controls movement, thought, learning, and memory. **□** See picture at **brain.**

cetacean (si-TĀ-shuhn) A large ocean mammal with a body shaped like a fish except for its flat, horizontal tail and flippers. Unlike seals and walruses, cetaceans never leave the water to come on land. Whales, dolphins, and porpoises are cetaceans.

CFC Short for **chlorofluorocarbon.** A chemical compound that contains carbon and one or more fluorine and chlorine atoms. CFCs were used until recently to make refrigerators and spray cans work. They are now banned because they are very harmful to the Earth's ozone layer.

Chadwick (CHAD-wik), **James** Born 1891; died 1974. British scientist who discovered the neutron in 1932.

chain reaction A kind of nuclear **fission** in which neutrons that are released by the splitting of the nucleus of one atom strike the nuclei of other atoms and cause them to split apart too. This process releases more neutrons that then split other atoms and keep the reaction going. Chain reactions are how nuclear power plants and atomic bombs get their energy.

chalk A soft, white rock made of seashell fossils. Chalk is used to make cement and fertilizers and to add white color to paints and cosmetics. The chalk used in classrooms is an artificial substance that looks and feels like natural chalk.

□ chalk

chalk cliffs in Dorset, England

41

chameleon (kuh-MĒ-lē-uhn) A small lizard that changes color and appears to blend in with its surroundings. Chameleons have large eyes that are able to move separately from each other.

Did You Know?

chameleon
Contrary to what you might have heard, chameleons don't change color because they want to blend in with the background. Sometimes their color changes because the light or the temperature changes. Sometimes it changes because they are angry, frightened, or sick. Sometimes it changes after they have just won a fight.

chaos (KĀ-os) The presence of a pattern when none seems to exist. Chaos describes a whole that is affected by small changes in any of its parts. Weather patterns are studied as examples of chaos; if the weather pattern in one part of the country changes, it will affect the weather pattern of the entire country.

characteristic (kair-uhk-tuh-RIS-tik) Something in the appearance, activity, or behavior of a living thing that is determined by the genes; a trait.

charcoal (CHAR-kōl) A soft, black form of carbon made by heating wood or bone in little or no air. Charcoal burns easily and is used as a fuel for cooking and heating. It is also used in air and water filters because it is able to remove unwanted gases by absorbing them.

charge 1. A property of all particles of matter that causes them to be attracted to or pushed away from other particles. Particles with the same charges drive each other away; particles with opposite charges draw each other together. **Protons** have a positive

Did You Know?

charge
Nature likes things to be electrically balanced or neutral, with equal amounts of positive and negative charges. To achieve this balance, atoms give up or take up electrons, the particles that have negative charge. This giving and taking of electrons is how chemical elements combine to make compounds.

charge, and **electrons** have a negative charge. 2. The amount of electric energy contained in an object, particle, or region of space.

charged Having a positive or negative electrical charge. Electrons are negatively charged. The cathode of a battery is positively charged.

Charles (CHARLZ), **Jacques Alexandre César** Born 1746; died 1823. French scientist who formulated Charles's law in 1787. In 1783 he became the first person to fill a large balloon with hydrogen gas, making it light enough to fly.

Charles's law A scientific law that states that the volume of a given amount of gas depends on its temperature, so long as the pressure remains the same. If the temperature of a gas increases, its volume will increase; if its temperature decreases, its volume will decrease. Charles's law is named after Jacques Alexandre César Charles.

chemical (KEM-i-kuhl) 1. *See* **chemical element**. 2. *See* **chemical compound**.

chemical bond *See* **bond**.

chemical compound A substance made of atoms of two or more chemical elements that are combined in **molecules**.

Water is a chemical compound that has two hydrogen atoms and one oxygen atom in each molecule.

chemical element   A substance that contains only one type of atom and cannot be broken down into simpler substances. Ninety-two elements are known to exist naturally, and another twenty have been created by scientists. All the elements are arranged in the Periodic Table. ◻ See Table on pages 178–179.

chemical formula   A set of symbols and numbers that shows what a chemical compound is made of. The chemical formula for water, H_2O, shows that water is made of two atoms of hydrogen (chemical symbol H) and one atom of oxygen (chemical symbol O).

chemical reaction   A change in the arrangement of the atoms or molecules of two or more substances that come into contact with each other. This rearrangement causes one or more new substances to come into being. During a chemical reaction, the electrons of the substances interact with one another.

chemical symbol   A capital letter, or a capital letter followed by a lower-case letter, that stands for the name of a chemical element. The chemical symbol for carbon is C. The chemical symbol for iron is Fe.

chemistry   (KEM-i-strē) The scientific study of the parts and arrangement of chemical elements and chemical compounds, and of how they react with each other.

chemotherapy   (kē-mō-THAIR-uh-pē) A treatment for cancer in which drugs that are made up of strong chemical compounds are used to kill harmful cells.

chickenpox   (CHIK-uhn-poks) A contagious disease in which a person has fever and an itchy rash on the skin. Chickenpox is caused by a virus.

chimpanzee   (chim-pan-ZĒ) A dark-haired ape of Africa that is smaller than a gorilla, lives mostly in trees, and is highly intelligent. Chimpanzees live in groups and interact with each other in many different ways. They are the closest living relatives of humans.

chip   A complex electric circuit that is etched onto a tiny slice of a material called a **semiconductor.** Chips are used in computers and most electronic devices, such as radios and televisions. A chip may contain millions of tiny switches, capacitors, and other devices. ◻ A chip is also called an *integrated circuit.*

chitin   (KĪ-tuhn) The hard material that makes up the outer skeletons of the invertebrates known as **arthropods,** which include crustaceans and insects. Chitin is a type of carbohydrate. It is also found in the cell walls of some fungi and algae.

chlorinate   (KLOR-uh-nāt) To add chlorine to another substance. Drinking water and water in swimming pools is often chlorinated to kill any germs that might be present.

chlorine   (KLOR-ēn) A greenish-yellow chemical element that exists as a gas and combines with the element sodium to form the salt that is used to season food. By itself, chlorine is very poisonous, but it is added to water in small amounts to kill germs and is also used as a bleach. ◻ See Table on pages 178–179.

chlorophyll   (KLOR-uh-fil) A green pigment that is found in green plants and other living things, such as some bacteria. Chlorophyll helps absorb energy from sunlight. The energy absorbed is then used to make food and produce oxygen during **photosynthesis.**

chloroplast (KLOR-uh-plast) A tiny part of a cell in green plants and some algae. Chloroplasts contain chlorophyll. **Photosynthesis** takes place in the chloroplasts. ◻ See picture at **cell.**

cholera (KOL-er-uh) A disease in which a person has severe diarrhea and vomiting. Cholera is caused by bacteria that live in contaminated food and water.

cholesterol (kuh-LES-tuh-rawl) A fatty substance that is produced by animals and plants and that is important for digestion and normal cell activity. Humans also get cholesterol from eating milk products and meat. Eating too many foods that have a lot of cholesterol may lead to heart disease.

chordate (KOR-dat) One of a group of animals, including all vertebrates, that develop in similar ways during the earliest stages of life. All chordates start out with a long nerve that in some animals develops into the brain and spinal cord.Chordates also have a flexible spine or similar structure and slits that develop into gills in some animals and disappear in others.

chromium (KRO-me-uhm) A chemical element that is a hard, shiny, gray metal and does not rust easily. It is used to make stainless steel and to harden regular steel. ◻ See Table on pages 178–179.

chromosome (KRO-muh-som) A tiny, thread-like structure in each cell of a living thing. Chromosomes carry the genes that pass on hereditary traits, such as eye color or the color of an animal's coat, from parents to offspring.

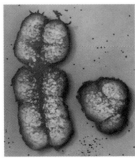

◻ **chromosome**

X-chromosome (left) *and Y-chromosome*

chronometer (kruh-NOM-i-ter) An instrument that measures time very accurately. Chronometers are used in scientific experiments, in ship navigation, and in making observations of objects in space.

chrysalis (KRIS-uh-lis) **1.** A pupa, especially of a moth or butterfly. A chrysalis doesn't move around or eat and is enclosed in a strong case or cocoon. **2.** The case or cocoon of a chrysalis.

cicada (si-KA-duh) An insect with a wide, flat head and transparent wings. Male cicadas make a loud buzzing sound with organs in their abdomens. Cicadas spend two or more years living underground as **nymphs** before emerging to live for a short time in trees as adults.

cilia (SIL-e-uh) Tiny hair-like parts that are found in the cells of some animals and in some one-celled organisms. The paramecium uses cilia to move about. In snails, cilia help move food during digestion. *Singular form*: **cilium** (SIL-e-uhm).

circadian rhythm (sur-KA-de-uhn RI*TH*-uhm) A natural system in living things that controls the timing of daily activities like eating and sleeping.

circle (SER-kuhl) A curve whose points are all on the same plane and at the same distance from a fixed point (the center).

◻ **circle**

circuit (SER-kit) A closed path through which an electric current flows. Circuits have a source of electricity, such as a battery or generator, and a wire that connects the source to a part that uses the electricity, such as a lamp or television. There are two kinds of electrical circuits: **series circuits** and **parallel circuits.**

◻ circuit

Bulbs in a simple circuit (top) and in a parallel circuit (bottom right) shine brightly because each bulb has its own circuit that connects it directly to the battery. Bulbs in a series circuit (bottom left) give off dim light because the electricity has to pass through every bulb in the circuit before returning to the battery.

circuit board   A flat piece of material that has circuits, chips, and other electric parts that are essential to the working of a computer.

circuit breaker   A switch that automatically stops the flow of an electric current through a circuit if the current becomes too strong. Circuit breakers are now used instead of fuses in most buildings to prevent electrical fires and damage to electrical equipment.

circulation   (ser-kyuh-LĀ-shuhn)   The flow of blood in the blood vessels of the body, caused by the pumping of the heart.

circulatory system   (SER-kyuh-luh-tor-ē SIS-tuhm) The system that moves blood through the body, made up of the heart and blood vessels. Blood that is rich in oxygen is pumped by the heart into the arteries,

which carry it to the tissues of the body. Veins carry blood that is low in oxygen back to the heart.

circumference (ser-KUHM-fer-uhns) The line that forms a circle. The length of the circumference of a circle equals 2 times the number pi (π) times the circle's radius (r), or 2πr. ◻ See picture at **circle**.

cirrocumulus cloud (seer-ō-KYOOM-yuh-luhs KLOWD) A thin, white, rippled cloud that often forms in bands or patches. Cirrocumulus clouds form very high in the sky. ◻ See picture at **cloud**.

cirrostratus cloud (seer-ō-STRAT-uhs KLOWD) A thin, hazy cloud very high in the sky that often causes a halo around the Sun. Cirrostratus clouds are made up of tiny crystals of ice. ◻ See picture at **cloud**.

cirrus cloud (SEER-uhs KLOWD) A thin, white cloud that often looks like feathers or streamers. Cirrus clouds form very high in the sky. ◻ See picture at **cloud**.

citric acid (SIT-rik AS-id) A chemical compound that has a sour taste and is found in citrus fruits like oranges and grapefruits. Citric acid is used in medicine and as a flavoring for food.

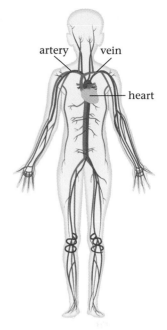

◻ circulatory system

Arteries (red) carry blood that is rich in oxygen from the heart to the tissues of the body. Veins (blue) carry blood that is low in oxygen back to the heart.

45

citrus (SIT-ruhs) A kind of tree or shrub that bears fruit with juicy flesh and a thick rind. Citrus trees and shrubs grow in warm climates around the world. The orange, lemon, and lime are citrus trees.

civil engineering (SIV-uhl en-juh-NEER-ing) The science that deals with designing and building bridges, roads, dams, and other large structures that are used by many people.

clam A mollusk with two shells that open and close as if they were held together by a hinge. Clams have a soft muscle that is used for burrowing in the sand and that is sometimes edible. Some clams live in salt water; others live in fresh water.

class One of the major groups in the classification of living things. A class is below a phylum or division and above an order. ◻ See Table on page 47.

classification (klas-uh-fi-KA-shuhn) The grouping of things into an organized system. For example, the classification of living things is based on how they are alike and how they are related to each other. ◻ See Table on page 47.

clavicle (KLAV-i-kuhl) Either of two slim bones in the upper part of the chest that go from the shoulder to the sternum in the middle of the chest. ◻ The clavicle is also called the *collarbone.* ◻ See picture at **skeleton.**

claw **1.** A sharp, curved nail at the end of a toe of a mammal, reptile, or bird. **2.** A curved part that is used for grabbing or grasping by another kind of animal. The pincers of lobsters and crabs are claws.

clay A sticky material that occurs naturally in the ground and is soft and flexible when wet. Clay is made up of tiny particles of broken-down rock. It hardens when it is heated,

and it is used to make bricks and pottery.

climate (KLĪ-mit) The general or average weather conditions of a particular region, including such things as temperature, rainfall, wind, and seasonal changes. Arizona has a sunny, dry climate for most of the year. The climate in Minnesota is cold and snowy during the winter and warm during the summer.

climatology (KLĪ-muh-TOL-uh-jē) The scientific study of climates, especially in order to understand regional variations and long-term changes in the Earth's climate.

climax community (KLĪ-maks kuh-MYOO-ni-tē) A stable group of plants and animals that live in balance with each other and with their environment. When a climax community is disrupted by something destructive such as fire, some species do not survive, and new ones take their place. The new species compete with each other until a stable climax community is in place again.

cloaca (klō-A-kuh) A hollow part of the body in birds, reptiles, amphibians, some fish, and a few mammals. The cloaca collects fluids and other substances from different parts of the body, such as the intestines, before sending them out of the body.

clone A living thing that is a copy of another. A cell, a group of cells, or a whole organism can be a clone. Scientists make clones of cells to produce natural substances that are normally made by the body and use them to treat disease.

clot A lump that forms when a liquid, such as blood, thickens and sticks together.

cloud **1.** A white or gray mass floating in the atmosphere. Clouds are made up of tiny drops of water or crystals of ice. They can take many different shapes depending on how high above the Earth they form. **2.** A

Classification of Life

Most scientists divide living things into five main groups or **kingdoms**. The five kingdoms are **plants, animals, protists, fungi,** and **prokaryotes.** The scientific word for the system of classifying life is **taxonomy.** This classification system groups living things by how closely they are alike and by which ancestors they have in common. In addition to **kingdom,** the main divisions into which life can be divided are **phylum** (called **division** for plants), **class, order, family, genus,** and **species.** The chart below shows how one species—the gray wolf—is classified in this system.

KINGDOM	PHYLUM	CLASS	ORDER	FAMILY	GENUS	SPECIES
ANIMALS	CHORDATES	MAMMALS	CARNIVORES	DOG	CANIS	CANIS LUPUS

ANIMALS are made up of many cells and are able to move from place to place on their own. They are the only living things with nervous systems or brains. About three-fourths of all life forms are animals.

CHORDATES have a flexible spine or other structure that supports their bodies from the inside. All vertebrates (animals with backbones) are chordates. All chordates also have blood that flows through their bodies in tube-like vessels.

Almost all **MAMMALS** have fur or hair. Mammals nourish their young with milk that is produced in the mammary glands. Mammals are warm-blooded, and all but a few give birth to live young.

CARNIVORES are a specific group of animals that eat only or mostly meat. Most carnivores hunt their prey, though some are also scavengers. Carnivores include the dogs, cats, bears, raccoons, and weasels.

The **DOG FAMILY** includes wolves, coyotes, dingos, domestic dogs, jackals, foxes, and African wild dogs. Most have long, narrow muzzles, sleek bodies, sharp teeth, and long tails.

A **GENUS** is made up of species that are very similar to each other. There are 9 species in the genus *Canis*: 2 species of wolf, 4 species of jackal, the coyote, the dingo, and the domestic dog.

A **SPECIES** includes only a single kind of animal or plant. Members of the same species are able to breed with each other and have offspring. The gray wolf belongs to the species *Canis lupus.*

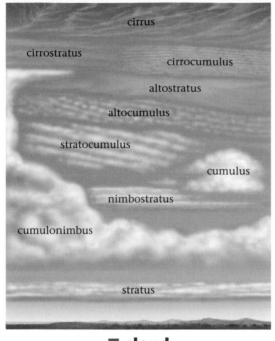

cirrus

cirrostratus

cirrocumulus

altostratus

altocumulus

stratocumulus

cumulus

nimbostratus

cumulonimbus

stratus

◘ cloud

the main types of clouds

mass of particles or gas, such as the collection of gases and dust in a nebula.

coal   A dark solid substance that is made mainly of carbon and is burned as a fuel. Coal forms when large amounts of dead plants are buried under layers of rock. The pressure of the rock layers and the absence of air turn the dead plants into coal.

coast   The edge of the land next to an ocean or sea.

cochlea   (KOK-lē-uh *or* KŌ-klē-uh) A part of the inner ear that is shaped like a spiral and looks likes a snail shell. The cochlea contains the sense organs needed for hearing. ◘ See picture at **ear.**

Cockcroft   (KOK-krawft) **John Douglas** Born 1897; died 1967. British scientist who, with Ernest Walton, performed the first successful splitting of an atom in 1932.

cockroach   (KOK-rōch) A brown or black insect with a flat body and long antennae.

Cockroaches prefer warm, humid climates and are mainly active at night.

cocoon   (kuh-KOON) A silky covering made from strands of material produced by the larva of an insect, such as a butterfly, to protect itself until it becomes an adult. Cocoons are made by an insect before becoming a **pupa.**

coevolution   (kō-ev-uh-LOO-shuhn) The process in which two or more living things in an ecosystem change over time by adapting to changes in each other. The development of plants that depend on insects to feed on nectar and carry pollen from one plant to another is an example of coevolution.

cohesion   (kō-HĒ-zhuhn) The force of attraction that holds the molecules of a substance together. Cohesion is strongest in solids, less strong in liquids, and least strong in gases. Cohesion makes it possible for drops to form from a liquid.

cold-blooded   Having a body temperature that changes with the temperature of the environment. Fish, amphibians, and reptiles are cold-blooded.

cold front   The advancing edge of a mass of cold air that pushes under a mass of warm air. A cold front often brings heavy showers or thunderstorms. ◘ See picture at **front.**

collarbone   (KOL-er-bōn) *See* **clavicle.**

colloid   (KOL-oyd) A mixture in which very small particles of one substance are spread out evenly throughout another substance. Paints, milk, and fog are colloids.

colon   (KŌ-luhn) The longest part of the large intestine, in which solid waste collects before leaving the body as feces.

colony   (KOL-uh-nē) A group of the same kind of animals, plants, or one-celled organisms living or growing together. A colony of ants, for example, is made up of workers, soldiers, and a queen. Bacteria also live in colonies.

color (KUHL-er) The way light of a particular wavelength appears to the eye. The human eye sees light with long wavelengths as red or orange, light with medium wavelengths as yellow or green, and light with short wavelengths as blue or violet. Light of different wavelengths can be mixed together to form all other colors. ◻ See picture on page 50.

color-blind Unable to see the difference between certain colors. People who are color-blind usually cannot tell red from green. ◻ See picture on page 50.

combustion (kuhm-BUHS-chuhn) A chemical reaction in which a substance combines rapidly with oxygen, producing heat and, usually, light.

comet (KOM-it) A mass of ice, frozen

Did You Know?

comet

Although a comet might look like a fuzzy star in the sky, it is not like a star at all. Comets are cold, not hot—astronomers sometimes call them "dirty snowballs"—and they have no light of their own. Instead, they only shine when they come close enough to the Sun for their ice to melt into a cloud of glowing gas and dust.

gases, and dust particles that travels around the Sun in a long path. When a comet comes close to the Sun, it can be seen in the

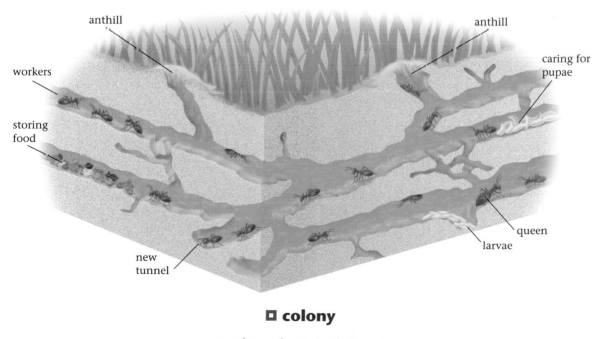

◻ **colony**

a colony of ants in their nest

sky as a bright object with a glowing head and a long, streaming tail.

commensalism (kuh-MEN-suh-liz-uhm) A close relationship between two different kinds of organisms in which one depends on the other but causes it no harm. Commensalism is a kind of **symbiosis**.

common cold (KOM-uhn KŌLD) An infection of the nose and throat that is caused by a virus. Sneezing, coughing, and fever are symptoms of the common cold.

common divisor A number that two or more other numbers can be divided by with a remainder of zero. The number 3 is a common divisor of both 9 and 15.

common multiple A number than can be divided by each of two or more numbers with a remainder of zero. The number

A Closer Look

Color

A ray of sunlight does not seem to have any particular color, but in fact it is made up of all possible colors mixed together. When sunlight passes through a prism, it is bent in such a way that all its different colors are separated and spread out. This band of colors, called the visible spectrum*, is made up of red, orange, yellow, green, blue, and violet.*

*Certain colors, called **primary colors**, can be mixed together to form all other colors. When the colors being mixed are beams of light, the primary colors are red, green, and blue. When the colors being mixed are paints, the primary colors are magenta (purplish red), yellow, and cyan (greenish blue). When two primary colors are mixed equally, they form **secondary colors**. When all three primary colors are mixed equally, as in the center of the diagrams below, they form white for beams of light and black for paints.*

Most people see colors pretty much the same way, but people who are color-blind cannot tell certain colors apart. Most people who are color-blind cannot tell red from green. If you can see a red star in the circle on the right, then you are not color-blind for red.

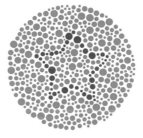

□ **commensalism**

Barnacles make their home on the skin of a gray whale. This helps the barnacles find food and does no harm to the whale.

12 is a common multiple of 2, 3, 4, and 6, because 12 can be divided by each of those numbers evenly.

communicable (kuh-MYOO-ni-kuh-buhl) Able to pass from person to person. Chicken-pox is a communicable disease.

communications satellite (kuh-myoo-ni-KA-shuhnz SAT-uh-līt) A satellite that is put in an orbit around the Earth to relay signals that are sent up from one place on Earth down to another place. Television and telephone signals can be transmitted by a communications satellite. □ See picture at **satellite.**

community (kuh-MYOO-ni-tē) All of the plants and animals that live in a particular place and that depend on each other for survival. A community can be small, such as one in a pond or city park, or it can be large, such as one in a rain forest or ocean.

compact disk (KOM-pakt DISK) A kind of optical disk that holds information, but not as much information as a DVD. Compact disks often contain recorded music. □ A compact disk is called a *CD* for short.

compass (KUHM-puhs) **1.** An instrument that tells you which direction is north. When you know where north is, you can easily find south, east, west, and all the directions in between. A compass is usually made of a magnetic needle that turns freely on an axis until it comes to rest pointing north. **2.** A device that is shaped like an upside-down V and is used for drawing circles and measuring lengths. It is made up of a pair of rigid arms that are hinged together. One of the arms ends in a sharp point, and the other arm holds a pencil.

□ **compass**

complementary angles (kahm-pluh-MEN-tuh-rē ANG-guhlz) Two angles that equal 90° when added together. □ See picture at **angle.**

compost (KOM-pōst) A mixture of rotted plants and food that is used to fertilize soil. Compost is made up of things like leaves, grass clippings, and vegetable peels. Bacteria and other tiny organisms cause these materials to break down into nutrients that help living plants grow better.

compound (KOM-pownd) *See* **chemical compound.**

compound eye An eye that is made up of hundreds or thousands of tiny parts that act like lenses. Each of these parts is sensitive to light and forms part of an image. Compound eyes are common in insects, such as flies, and in crustaceans, such as crabs. □ See picture at **eye.**

compound leaf A leaf that is made up of two or more leaflets on the same stalk. Clover, roses, and walnut trees have compound leaves.

compression (kuhm-PRESH-uhn) A force that shortens or squeezes something, making its volume smaller.

computer (kuhm-PYOO-ter) An electronic device that processes information based on a set of rules that are stored within the device.

Did You Know?

computer
Electronic computers made in the 1940s were large room-sized machines. Today, computers are many times faster even though they are tiny by comparison, thanks to the development of chips. The chips can pack millions of circuits into less space than a fingernail, allowing people to plot courses for spacecraft and play video games at home.

computer science The study of the design and the use of computers, especially in science, business, and the arts.

concave (kon-KĀV) Curved inward, like the inside of a bowl.

concave lens A type of lens that curves inward. When rays of light pass through a concave lens, they spread apart. Concave lenses make things look smaller. ◻ See picture at **lens.**

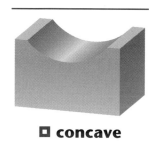
◻ **concave**

concave mirror A mirror that curves inward and directs rays of light toward a point in front of the mirror. Concave mirrors make things look bigger.

concentration (kahn-suhn-TRĀ-shuhn) The amount of a substance that is contained in another substance. A glass of lemonade that contains the juice of one lemon has a lower concentration of lemon juice than a glass of lemonade with the juice of two lemons.

concrete (KON-krēt) A building material that is made of cement, sand, pebbles, and water. Concrete becomes very hard when it dries.

condensation (kon-duhn-SĀ-shuhn) The change of a gas or vapor into a liquid, either by cooling or by being exposed to greater pressure.

Did You Know?

condensation
When water vapor cools high up in the air, it condenses, becoming tiny droplets that form clouds. Closer to the ground, dew forms in the same way. If the air near the ground gets cool enough at night for the water vapor in it to condense, droplets of water appear on the ground, on plants, and on other objects.

condense (kuhn-DENS) To change from a gas or vapor into a liquid. When you blow gently onto a mirror, the water vapor in your warm breath condenses onto the cool glass and forms a mist.

condenser (kuhn-DEN-ser) A device that causes a gas or vapor to turn into a liquid, usually by cooling it. ◻ See pictures at **desalinize, nuclear reactor.**

conduct (kuhn-DUHKT) To let heat, electricity, or sound go through. Copper conducts electricity well. Most metals conduct heat well.

conduction (kuhn-DUHK-shuhn) The movement of heat, electricity, or sound through a solid. A teaspoon in a cup of hot chocolate becomes hot because the heat from the drink moves into the spoon by conduction. An electric current travels from a wall socket, through a wire, and into a lamp by conduction.

conductor   (kuhn-DUK-ter) A material or an object through which heat, electricity, light, or sound can flow easily. Copper is a good conductor of heat and electricity.

cone   **1.** A three-dimensional object that has a flat, round base at one end and tapers to a point at the opposite end. ☐ See picture at **geometry. 2.** A rounded cluster of wood-like scales that grows on pines, spruces, firs, and other **conifers.** Cones are either male or female. The female cones carry the seeds; the male cones produce pollen. **3.** A cone-shaped cell in the retina of the eye of many animals. Cones make vision during daylight hours possible. Cones also permit some animals to see colors. ☐ Compare **rod.**

congenital   (kuhn-JEN-i-tuhl) Present at birth. A baby born with a heart problem has a congenital disorder.

conglomerate   (kuhn-GLOM-uh-rāt) A rock made of pebbles or seashells that are embedded in silt, clay, or a similar material that has hardened over time. ☐ See Table on page 208.

conifer   (KON-uh-fer) A kind of tree or shrub that bears cones. Conifers depend on the wind to spread their pollen from male cones to female cones, where seeds grow. Conifers are usually evergreen and include the pine trees and the fir trees.

conservation   (kon-ser-VĀ-shuhn) The protection and management of the Earth's natural resources, such as forests, mineral deposits, and water, and of the wildlife that depends on them.

constant   (KON-stuhnt) A number, condition, or factor that remains the same. For example, the speed of light in empty space is a constant.

constellation (kon-stuh-LĀ-shuhn) A group of stars that is named after and shaped somewhat like an animal, a person, or an object. There are 88 constellations.

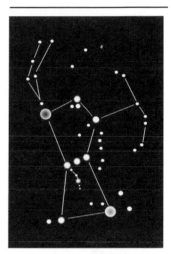

☐ **constellation**

A diagram of the constellation Orion, named after a legendary hunter. The large reddish star is the coolest star in the constellation; the large bluish-white star is the hottest. Orion's "belt" can be seen in the middle of the figure.

constrictor (kuhn-STRIK-ter) A kind of snake that kills prey by coiling around and suffocating it. Boa constrictors, pythons, and anacondas are constrictors.

consumer (kuhn-SOO-mer) A living thing, espe cially an animal, that feeds on other living things in a **food chain.** Consumers include plant-eating animals, called herbivores, and meat-eating animals, called carnivores.

contact   (KON-takt) An area where two pieces of material that are conductors of electricity touch each other to allow an electric current to flow.

contagious   (kuhn-TĀ-juhs) Able to pass from person to person. Colds and many other infections are contagious.

contaminate   (kuhn-TAM-uh-nāt) **1.** To make something impure by mixing it with something harmful or poisonous. When chemical compounds that are used in industry seep into the ground, they can contaminate drinking water. **2.** To cause something to become dangerously radioactive.

continent   (KON-tuh-nuhnt) One of the seven great landmasses of the Earth. The continents are Africa, Antarctica, Asia, Australia, Europe, North America, and South America.

continental divide   (kon-tuh-NEN-tuhl di-VĪD) A region of high ground that separates the rivers flowing in one direction on a continent from the rivers flowing in another direction. In North America, the continental divide is a series of mountain ridges stretching from Alaska to Mexico. On one side of the divide, water flows into the Pacific Ocean; on the other side, water flows into the Atlantic Ocean and the Gulf of Mexico.

continental drift   The slow movement of the Earth's continents toward or away from each other. The continents move a few inches every year, and hundreds of miles over millions of years. Scientists now explain the force behind continental drift through the theory of **plate tectonics.**

continental shelf   The part of the edge of a continent that is covered by shallow ocean water. The continental shelf ends at

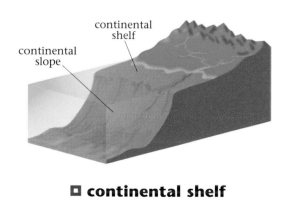

◻ **continental shelf**

the steep slopes that lead to the deep part of the ocean.

contour map   (KON-tur MAP) A map that shows how high land rises above sea level. From the lines on a contour map you can tell where mountains and valleys are located. Each line shows a certain height, and lines that are very close together show that the land there is very steep.

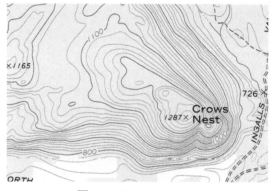

◻ **contour map**

Closely spaced lines (right) show that the land there is steeper than in areas where the lines are farther apart.

contract   (kuhn-TRAKT) To become shorter and thicker. Muscles contract to produce movement. When the biceps in the arm contracts, the elbow bends.

control   (kuhn-TRŌL) A part of a scientific experiment that stays the same while other parts are allowed to change. The control is used as a standard for comparing results.

convection   (kuhn-VEK-shuhn) The movement of heat from one place to another in a liquid or gas by the movement of molecules. In convection, hotter molecules move upward to a cooler area, and cooler molecules move downward. The hotter molecules eventually cool off and move down, so that the liquid or gas starts to flow in a current.

convex (KON-veks) Curving outward, like the outside of a bowl.

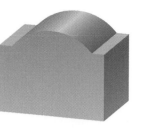

□ convex

convex lens A type of lens that bulges outward. When rays of light pass through a convex lens, they come together. Because convex lenses make things look bigger, they are used in magnifying lenses and in microscopes. **□** See picture at **lens.**

convex mirror A mirror that bulges outward in its center. When light rays hit a convex mirror straight on, they bounce off at wide angles. Convex mirrors give a wide view and make things look smaller.

coordinate (kō-OR-duh-nit) A number or a set of numbers that is used to show the position of a point. One coordinate is needed if the point is on a line, two are needed if the point is in a plane, and three are needed if it is in space.

Copernicus (kuh-PER-nuh-kuhs), **Nicolaus** Born 1473; died 1543. Polish sci-

entist who first put forward the idea that the Earth and other planets revolve around the Sun. Copernicus also showed that the Earth rotates once on its axis every day. His ideas laid the foundation for modern astronomy.

copper (KOP-er) A chemical element that is a reddish-brown metal and is easily shaped. Copper is an excellent conductor of heat and electricity. It is used to make electric wires and water pipes, and it is mixed with other metals to make brass and bronze. **□** See Table on pages 178–179.

Biography

Nicolaus Copernicus

Nicolaus Copernicus was a lawyer and a physician by trade, but he spent his spare time studying astronomy. He observed the movements of the Sun, the Moon, and the planets without the use of a telescope, because the telescope hadn't been invented yet. Still, he was able to work out in full mathematical detail how the Earth and other planets circle the Sun.

Did You Know?

coral

Much of the bright white sand you see on the beaches of tropical islands comes from the skeletons of coral, colorful animals that attach themselves to rocks in shallow ocean waters. Certain kinds of fish eat the coral and spit out the ground-up remains of the coral's hard outer skeletons. Over millions of years, the bits of coral, ground further by the motion of the sea, cover the ocean bottom and are tossed up to cover the island shores.

coral (KOR-uhl) Small sea animals with a soft body, a hard outer skeleton, and tentacles that sting. Coral live in shallow water in large groups called colonies. Coral reefs are formed from the skeletons of these animals.

coral reef A hard underwater mound that is made from the skeletons of millions of kinds of corals. Coral reefs form in warm, shallow seas and provide food and shelter for a wide variety of fish and other animals. ◻ See picture at **reef**.

core   **1.** The hard or stringy middle part of some fruits, such as apples and pears, that contains the seeds. **2.** The part of the Earth that is at its center. The Earth's core is made of iron and nickel and has two sections, one inner and one outer. The inner core is solid and begins at a depth of 3,095 miles (4,983 kilometers); the outer core is liquid and begins at a depth of 1,800 miles (2,898 kilometers). ◻ See picture at **Earth**. **3.** The part of a star that is at its center. The Sun's core is over 2,500 times hotter than its surface. ◻ See picture at **sun**. **4.** The central part of a nuclear reactor where atomic fission occurs.

cork   The light, spongy, outer bark of a kind of oak tree that grows near the Mediterranean Sea. Cork is used for bottle stoppers, insulation, and other products.

cornea   (KOR-nē-uh) The transparent outer covering of the eyeball that covers the pupil and iris. The cornea is a membrane. ◻ See picture at **eye**.

corolla   (kuh-RŌ-luh) The petals of a flower considered as a group. The corolla surrounds the stamens and pistils.

corona   (ku-RŌ-nuh) The outer layer of thin and extremely hot gas that surrounds the Sun and other stars. The corona is only visible during a total eclipse of the Sun. It looks like a halo of white light that extends far out into space.

corpuscle   (KOR-puh-suhl) A small, round structure in the body, especially a blood cell.

corrosion   (kuh-RŌ-shuhn) The breaking down of a material through chemical reac-

◻ **corona**

tions. The most common form of corrosion is rust, which develops when iron combines with oxygen and water.

corundum   (kuh-RUN-duhm) A very hard mineral made mainly of aluminum and oxygen. Rubies and sapphires are types of corundum.

cosmology   (koz-MOL-uh-jē) The scientific study of how the universe began and how it changes. Cosmology is a branch of astronomy.

cosmos   (KOZ-muhs *or* KOZ-mōs) The universe, especially when thought of as an orderly and harmonious whole.

cotyledon   (kot-uhl-ĒD-uhn) A leaf growing from a plant embryo that is contained in a seed. Cotyledons take in and store food for the growing plant. ◻ A cotyledon is also called a *seed leaf*. ◻ See picture at **germination**.

coulomb   (KOO-lom) A unit used to measure electric charge. One coulomb is equal to the quantity of charge that passes a point in an electric circuit in one second when a current of one ampere is flowing through the circuit.

Cousteau   (koo-STŌ), **Jacques Yves** Born 1910; died 1997. French underwater explorer who invented scuba equipment, which allows humans to breathe while underwater.

Biography

Jacques Yves Cousteau

Jacques Cousteau sailed around the world on his ship *Calypso* and explored the ocean. He was one of the first scientists to use underwater photography, and his books, films, and undersea explorations educated the general public about ocean life. His work emphasized the need to protect the oceans and the plants and animals that live underwater.

CPU *See* **central processing unit.**

cranium (KRĀ-nē-uhm) *See* **skull.**

crater (KRĀ-ter) A bowl-shaped hole that is formed after a meteor hits the surface of a planet or after lava flows out from the top of a volcano.

◻ **crater**

Barringer meteor crater, Arizona

crescent moon (KRES-uhnt MOON) The Moon when it appears partly but less than one-half lit. A crescent moon is seen between a new moon and a half moon.

crest The highest part of a wave, such as an ocean wave or a sound wave. ◻ See picture at **wave.**

Cretaceous Period (kri-TĀ-shuhs PEER-ē-uhd) The period of time during the history of the Earth starting about 144 million years ago and ending about 65 million years ago. During the Cretaceous Period, flowering plants developed. The Cretaceous Period ended with the extinction of all dinosaurs and of many other forms of life. ◻ See Table on pages 102–103.

Crick (KRIK), **Francis Henry Compton** Born 1916. British scientist who, with James D. Watson, explained the structure of DNA in 1953. He later discovered how DNA functions in a cell.

crocodile (KROK-uh-dīl) A large, meat-eating reptile that lives mainly in water and has sharp teeth and powerful jaws. Crocodiles have longer and narrower jaws than alligators, and their teeth show when their jaws are closed. Crocodiles live in many tropical parts of the world, including Africa and southeast Asia.

Cro-Magnon (krō-MAG-nuhn) An early form of modern human. Cro-Magnons lived in parts of Europe from about 35,000 to 10,000 years ago. Like Neanderthals they lived in caves, but Cro-Magnons made better stone tools and decorated their cave walls with skilled paintings of animals.

cross-pollination (kraws-pol-uh-NĀ-shuhn) A kind of pollination in which pollen is moved from the stamen of a flower on one plant to the pistil of a flower on another plant. Birds, insects, and wind carry pollen in cross-pollination. ◻ Compare **self-pollination.**

crucible (KROO-suh-buhl) A type of container that can stand a lot of heat and is used to melt metals and other materials.

Did You Know?

crust

Did you know that the Earth's crust beneath the continents is about 22 to 37 miles thick (between 35 and 60 kilometers thick), while the crust beneath the oceans is only about 3 to 6 miles thick (between 5 and 10 kilometers thick)? This is why there are so many more volcanoes on the ocean floor than on the continents: the lava doesn't have to travel as far to get out!

crust   The solid, outermost layer of the Earth. ◻ See picture at **Earth.**

crustacean   (kruh-STĀ-shuhn) A member of a group of living things that live mostly in water and have a hard shell, legs with joints, and a body that is divided into segments. Crabs, lobsters, shrimp, and barnacles are crustaceans. Crustaceans are members of the group of organisms known as **arthropods.**

crystal   (KRIS-tuhl) A solid made of atoms that are arranged in a particular shape, such as a cube or pyramid. The shape is repeated over and over within the solid. Snowflakes and the mineral quartz are examples of substances that form as crystals.

◻ **crystal**

white calcite crystals

cube   **1.** A three-dimensional object that has six equal square faces. ◻ See picture at **geometry. 2.** The result of multiplying a number by itself three times. For example, the number 64 is the cube of 4 because $4 \times 4 \times 4 = 64$. **3.** To multiply a number by itself three times. 5 cubed is $5 \times 5 \times 5$, or 125.

cubic   (KYOO-bik) Relating to a unit of measurement that measures volume. Cubic units, such as a cubic yard and cubic meter, are one unit long, one unit wide, and one unit deep.

cud   Food that has been swallowed by a cow, sheep, or similar animal, and brought up to the mouth again for more chewing. Animals that chew cud are called ruminants.

culture   (KUHL-cher) Living material, such as bacteria or a batch of cells, that is grown in a culture medium so it can be studied or used by scientists.

culture medium   A substance that is used for growing cells or microscopic organisms, such as bacteria, in a laboratory. Agar is a kind of culture medium.

cumulonimbus cloud   (kyoom-yuh-lō-NIM-buhs KLOWD) A very large cloud with a low, dark bottom and a fluffy, white top that rises high into the sky. Cumulonimbus clouds usually produce heavy rains, thunderstorms, or hailstorms. ◻ See picture at **cloud.**

cumulus cloud   (KYOOM-yuh-luhs KLOWD) A white, fluffy cloud that is often flat on the bottom. Cumulus clouds form fairly low in the sky and are usually seen during good weather. ◻ See picture at **cloud.**

Curie   (KYUR-ē *or* kyur-Ē), **Marie** Born 1867; died 1934. French scientist who was a pioneer in the study of radioactivity. With

Biography

Marie Curie

Marie Curie studied at the University of Paris, where she earned degrees in mathematics and physics. She was the first woman in Europe to receive a doctorate in science and the first person to be awarded two Nobel Prizes.

Did You Know?

cyanobacteria

Cyanobacteria is the scientific name for what most people call blue-green algae. Scientists prefer it because the organisms are actually bacteria and not algae, and not all of them are blue or green, either. The Red Sea gets its name from cyanobacteria that turn red when they die. Flamingos get their pink color from eating cyanobacteria that are pink.

her husband, **Pierre Curie** (born 1859; died 1906), she discovered the elements radium and polonium in 1898. She also showed how radioactivity could be used in medicine by designing machines for taking x-rays of wounded soldiers.

current   (KER-uhnt) **1.** *See* **electric current. 2.** A mass of liquid or gas that is in motion. Wind is a current of air. Ocean currents move large amounts of water from one part of the Earth to another.

cursor   (KER-ser) A thin bar, small square, or similar item that appears on a computer screen at the place where a letter, number, or symbol can be added, changed, or removed.

curve   A line or surface that bends in a smooth way and has no angles.

cutaneous   (kyoo-TA-ne-uhs) Relating to the skin.

cuticle   (KYOO-ti-kuhl) **1.** The hard skin around the sides and base of a fingernail or toenail. **2.** The waxy outer layer of plants; the epidermis.

cyanobacteria   (sī-uh-nō-bak-TEER-ē-uh) Bacteria that contain chlorophyll and other pigments and are able to perform photosynthesis. Cyanobacteria are important in the nitrogen cycle because they take nitrogen from the atmosphere and change it into a form that plants can use to grow. Cyanobacteria were once thought to be plants. ◘ Cyanobacteria are also called *blue-green algae*.

cyberspace   (SĪ-ber-spās) The system of computer networks that are connected to each other to allow information to be exchanged online. Communication on the Internet takes place in cyberspace.

cycle   (SĪ-kuhl) A series of events that is repeated over and over again in the same order. The cycle of seasons in temperate climates is made up of spring, summer, winter, and fall.

cyclone   (SĪ-klōn) **1.** A large system of winds that rotate around a region of low atmospheric pressure. Winds in a cyclone spiral in toward the center of the system and often bring rain or snow to the region. ◘ Compare **anticyclone. 2.** A powerful storm with strong, spinning winds, such as a hurricane or tornado.

cyclotron   (SĪ-kluh-tron) A machine that causes particles that are parts of an atom, such as protons and electrons, to move very fast through a spiral-shaped tube. The particles are controlled by magnets and shot into other particles, breaking them apart. Scientists use cyclotrons to find out what particles are made of.

cylinder (SIL-uhn-der) **1.** A three-dimensional object that looks like a tube or pipe. The ends of a cylinder are circles of the same size. ◘ See picture at **geometry. 2.** A hollow chamber that surrounds a piston and the valves that are found inside an engine.

cytology (sī-TOL-uh-jē) The scientific study of cells.

cytoplasm (SĪ-tuh-plaz-uhm) The jelly-like material that the inside of a cell is made of, except for what is inside the nucleus. The cytoplasm contains many tiny structures, such as mitochondria. The cytoplasm of a cell together with the material inside the nucleus is called protoplasm. ◘ See picture at **cell.**

Dd

Dalton (DAWL-tuhn), **John** Born 1766; died 1844. British scientist who was the first person to explain accurately how atoms are put together and how they interact. In 1805, Dalton showed that all matter is made up of combinations of atoms. He also showed that chemical reactions occur when these atoms are combined in different ways.

dam A barrier that is built across a waterway, such as a river, to control the flow of water.

Darwin (DAR-win), **Charles Robert** Born 1809; died 1882. British scientist whose theory of evolution popularized the idea that the variety of life on Earth developed gradually from fewer and simpler forms of life over many millions of years.

data (DĀ-tuh *or* DAT-uh) **1.** Information that is used to make a decision or come to a conclusion. The measurements that are the results of an experiment are considered data. **2.** Information that is in a form that can be processed by a computer.

database (DĀ-tuh-bās *or* DAT-uh-bās) A collection of data that is arranged in a computer so that the data can be easily read, changed, or moved.

Davy (DĀ-vē), **Humphry** Born 1778; died 1829. British scientist who was one of the first people to study the relationship between electricity and chemical reactions. Davy studied many of the chemical elements that were already known in his time, and he discovered new elements, including potassium and sodium.

day The period of time that it takes for a planet to spin around once, completing one rotation on its axis. A day on Earth lasts 24 hours; a day on Jupiter lasts 10 hours.

DC *See* **direct current.**

DDT Short for **dichlorodiphenyltri-chloroethane.** A powerful chemical compound that kills insects and is also poisonous to humans and animals. Farmers used to use DDT on their crops but are no longer allowed to because the chemical is very harmful to the environment.

decay (di-KĀ) **1.** The breaking down of dead plant or animal matter by bacteria or fungi; decomposition. **2.** *See* **radioactive decay. 3.** To be broken down into simpler chemical compounds, especially by bacteria or fungi. **4.** To undergo radioactive decay.

decibel (DES-uh-buhl) A unit used to measure the loudness or strength of a sound. The speaking voice of most people measures between 45 and 75 decibels.

deciduous (di-SIJ-ōō-uhs) Having leaves that fall off at the end of a growing season and then grow back again at the beginning of the next growing season. Most deciduous plants bear flowers and have broad leaves rather than needles. Maples, oaks, and elms are deciduous trees. ◻ Compare **evergreen.**

decimal (DES-uh-muhl) A number that is written using a period called a **decimal point** that separates some of the number's digits from the rest. The first digit to the right of the decimal point shows the number of tenths, the second digit shows the number of hundredths, and so on. For example, 30.456 means 30 and 4 tenths and 5 hundredths and 6 thousandths. Decimals are another way to write **fractions.**

decimal place The position of a digit to the right of the decimal point in a number written as a decimal. In 0.379, for example, 3 is in the first decimal place, representing tenths; 7 is in the second decimal place, representing hundredths; and 9 is in the third decimal place, representing thousandths.

decimal point The period that is used when writing a decimal.

decomposer (dē-kuhm-PŌ-zer) A living thing that feeds on dead plants or animals. Decomposers make important nutrients available to plants and other organisms in an ecosystem. Bacteria and fungi are common decomposers.

decomposition (dē-kom-puh-ZISH-uhn) **1.** The process of decaying or rotting. Decomposition of dead animals and plants is caused by bacteria and fungi that feed on them. **2.** The breaking up of a substance into simpler substances or parts.

deduction (di-DUHK-shuhn) The use of general rules or principles to draw a conclusion or make a calculation. Using a mathematical formula to calculate the volume of air that can be contained in a room is applying deduction. ❑ Compare **induction** (sense 1).

deforestation (dē-for-i-STĀ-shuhn) The cutting down of all or most of the trees in a forest. When trees are removed from a forest, many plants and animals are destroyed too. The deforestation of large areas of tropical rain forest in recent years has led to the extinction of many plant and animal species.

degree (di-GRĒ) **1.** A unit used to measure temperature. The size of a degree can be different on different temperature scales. One degree on the Celsius scale is equal to 1.8 degrees on the Fahrenheit scale. Degrees on the Celsius and Kelvin scales are the same size. **2.** A unit used to measure an angle or an arc of a circle. One degree is $\frac{1}{360}$ of the circumference of a circle. A right angle has 90 degrees. **3.** In geography, a unit used to measure longitude and latitude.

dehydration (dē-hī-DRĀ-shuhn) Severe loss of water, especially from the body. Sweating a lot can cause dehydration.

delta (DEL-tuh) A mass of sediment, especially silt and sand, that is laid down at the mouth of a river. Deltas usually have a triangular shape. They form when a river flows into a body of standing water, such as a sea or lake.

❑ **delta**

satellite photo of the Nile River delta in Egypt

denominator (di-NOM-uh-nā-ter) The number below or to the right of the line in a fraction. The denominator shows the number of equal parts that one whole is divided into. In the fraction $\frac{2}{7}$, 7 is the denominator.

density (DEN-si-tē) A measure of how much matter there is in a certain amount of space. Salt water has a greater density than fresh water.

dentin (DEN-tin) The hard, bony part of a tooth that lies under the enamel. The dentin surrounds the pulp of the tooth.

deposit (di-POZ-it) Solid material left or laid down by a natural process. Deposits include layers of mud left by a stream, piles of stones left by a melting glacier, or a layer of coal formed over many years.

depth The distance of a thing measured from top to bottom or from front to back. Depth is the dimension that distinguishes objects with **volume,** like spheres and cubes, from flat figures like circles and squares.

dermis (DUR-mis) The inner layer of the skin of an animal. The dermis lies under the epidermis and contains nerves and blood vessels. In mammals, sweat glands are found in the dermis.

desalinize (dē-SAL-uh-nīz) To remove salt from something, such as seawater or soil.

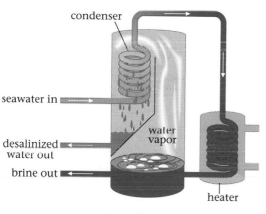

□ **desalinize**

As cold seawater enters the system, it is warmed by water vapors and brought to a boil by a heater. As vapors rise from the boiling water, they are cooled by the condenser and form fresh water, leaving the salty brine behind.

Descartes (dā-KART), **René** Born 1596; died 1650. French philosopher and mathematician who used algebra to solve problems in geometry. Descartes discovered that the position of a point can be described using coordinates. His work led to great advances in mathematics.

desert (DEZ-ert) An area of land that receives very little rain. Few plants and animals live in deserts, which cover about one-fifth of the Earth's surface. A desert is a kind of **biome.**

Did You Know?

desert
We tend to think of deserts as places that are hot and dry, but a place just has to be very dry to be a desert. In fact, Antarctica is the world's biggest desert. In a year, most deserts get only about 10 inches of rain (25 centimeters). Antarctica gets about 2 inches (5 centimeters) of snow a year, which equals less than $\frac{1}{4}$ of an inch of rain (about 0.6 centimeter).

desiccate (DES-i-kāt) To remove the moisture from something or dry it completely.

detergent (dē-TER-juhnt) A cleaning substance that makes it easier for water to get into cloth and carry away bits of grease and dirt. Detergents are similar to soap but are made from petroleum products rather than fats and alkalis.

Devonian Period (di-VŌ-nē-uhn PEER-ē-uhd) The period of time during the history of the Earth starting about 408 million years ago and ending about 360 million years ago. During the Devonian Period, forests, amphibians, and insects first appeared. □ See Table on pages 102–103.

dew   Water droplets that condense from the air onto cool surfaces, such as grass or leaves. Dew usually forms at night, when air near the ground cools and cannot hold as much water vapor as warmer air.

dew point   The temperature at which the surrounding air cannot hold any more water vapor. When the temperature reaches the dew point, the water vapor in the air condenses and forms dew. Air with a great deal of water vapor has a higher dew point than drier, less humid air.

diabetes   (dī-uh-BĒ-tez) A disease in which a person has too much sugar in the blood. In diabetes, the body does not produce enough of a hormone called insulin, which helps the body take up sugar from the blood. If not treated, diabetes can cause damage to nerves and blood vessels.

diagnosis   (dī-uhg-NŌ-sis) The identifying of a disease or injury by a doctor. To make a diagnosis, doctors often examine a person, order tests, and study their results.

diagonal   (dī-AG-uh-nuhl) Slanting from one corner of a four-sided figure, such as a square, to another corner.

diameter   (dī-AM-i-ter) A straight line segment that passes through the center of a circle or sphere from a point on one side to a point on the other side. ◻ See picture at **circle.**

diamond   (DĪ-uh-muhnd) A crystal form of carbon that is the hardest of all minerals. Diamonds are used as gemstones, and also on special tools made to grind or cut hard materials.

diaphragm   (DĪ-uh-fram) A muscle that separates the chest from the abdomen. As the diaphragm contracts and expands, it forces air into and out of the lungs.

diatom   (DĪ-uh-tom) A living thing that is made up of only one cell and that has a hard shell. Diatoms are algae and often live in large, organized groups known as colonies.

◻ **diatom**

a group of diatoms photographed through a microscope

dicotyledon (dī-kot-uhl-Ē-duhn) A flowering plant in which the seed has two **cotyledons,** the leaves have a network of veins, and the flower parts grow in multiples of 4 or 5. Most common garden plants and many trees are dicotyledons. ◻ Dicotyledons are called *dicots* for short. ◻ Compare **monocotyledon.**

diesel engine   (DĒ-zuhl) A type of internal-combustion engine in which the compression of fuel and hot air causes an explosion inside a cylinder. This explosion causes the pistons to move. Diesel engines are usually more efficient than engines that use gasoline.

difference   (DIF-er-uhns) The amount left after subtracting one number from another. In the equation $15 - 10 = 5$, the difference is 5.

diffraction   (di-FRAK-shuhn) The bending of a wave, such as a wave of light, when it goes through a narrow hole or past an edge. The diffraction of white light (light that contains all the colors) breaks it up into the colors of the rainbow.

diffusion   (di-FYOO-zhuhn) **1.** The tendency of two substances that are mixed together to move around until both substances are in all parts of the mixture. When no part of the mixture has more of one substance than any other part, diffusion is complete. When lemon juice is added to a glass of water, the juice mixes with the water by diffusion, until all the liquid tastes like lemon juice. **2.** The movement of light or other radiant energy, such as heat, out from a source into other areas. Light that comes through a window shines on one area most brightly but also makes the whole room brighter by diffusion.

digestion (di-JES-chuhn) The process in which food is broken down into nutrients that are easily taken up and used by the body. Digestion begins when food is taken into the mouth and ends when wastes leave the body.

digestive system (di-JES-tiv SIS-tuhm) The system that breaks down food into nutrients that can be used by the body. The

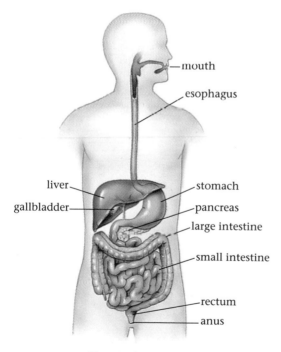

◻ digestive system

Food is broken down in the digestive system to provide the nutrients needed for energy and growth.

digestive system is made up of the mouth, esophagus, stomach, pancreas, gallbladder, liver, small and large intestines, and anus.

digit (DIJ-it) **1.** A finger or toe. Reptiles and many mammals have five digits on each limb. Amphibians and birds usually have four digits. **2.** One of the ten Arabic numerals, 0, 1, 2, 3, 4, 5, 6, 7, 8, or 9.

digital (DIJ-i-tuhl) **1.** Relating to information that can be used by a computer because it is written as a series of 0's and 1's. **2.** Relating to a device, such as a computer, that can read, write, or store information that is written as a series of 0's and 1's. ◻ See picture at **analog.**

dilute (dī-LOOT) To make a substance less concentrated by adding a liquid such as water.

dimension (di-MEN-shuhn) One of the properties that are used to describe a figure or an object in space. The three dimensions are **length, area,** and **volume.** According to Einstein's theory of relativity, there is also a fourth dimension: time.

dinoflagellate (dī-nō-FLAJ-uh-lit) A tiny animal that is made up of only one cell and lives mainly in the ocean. A dinoflagellate moves by means of two whip-like parts called flagella. Dinoflagellates are a main part of plankton and are members of the group of living things known as **protozoans.**

dinosaur (DĪ-nuh-sor) An extinct type of reptile that first appeared about 220 million years ago and died out suddenly about 65 million years ago. Dinosaurs ate both meat and plants, lived mostly on land, and ranged from the size of a small dog to over 90 feet (27 meters) long. Many scientists believe that birds evolved from small, meat-

□ **dinosaur**

left: *a lime-stone fossil of a pterodactyl*
right: *a model of a Tyranno-saurus rex*

eating dinosaurs. This is because fossils of dinosaurs and of early types of birds share many common characteristics.

diode (DĪ-ōd) A device that allows an electric current to flow in one direction only. Diodes can be used to convert alternating current into direct current.

diphtheria (dif-THEER-ē-a *or* dip-THEER-ē-a) A disease in which a person has fever, swollen glands, and a membrane that forms in the throat and makes breathing difficult. Diphtheria is caused by bacteria. It was once a leading cause of death in children.

diplodocus (di-PLOD-uh-kuhs) A very large dinosaur that had an extremely long and thin neck and tail. Diplodocus walked on all fours and grew to nearly 90 feet (27 meters) long.

diploid (DIP-loyd) Having two sets of chromosomes in a cell, one set from the female parent and one set from the male parent. In animals, all cells except sex cells are diploid. □ Compare **haploid.**

direct current (di-REKT KER-uhnt) An electric current in which the electrons flow in one direction only. Batteries use direct current. □ Direct current is called *DC* for short. □ Compare **alternating current.**

Did You Know?

direct current
The electricity that comes from batteries is direct current. It flows out of the battery into your CD player or your flashlight and comes back again in a circuit. Because it loses a lot of its energy by heating up wires, direct current is not used over long distances. The electricity that comes to your house and out of the wall sockets is alternating current, which flows one way and then switches back the other way about 60 times a second.

disease (di-SĒZ) A condition that keeps the body from functioning normally; an illness or sickness.

disk A device that is used to store information that can be read by a computer. Some disks, such as hard disks, store information as magnetic patterns. Other disks, such as compact disks, store it in a pattern of pits and bumps that are read by a laser.

disk drive A computer device that reads data that is stored on a magnetic disk or optical disk. A disk drive can also place data on the disk for storage.

dispersion (di-SPER-zhuhn) The separation of light or other types of radiation into separate parts, usually according to the frequency and wavelength of the waves that it is made of. When a beam of white light (light that contains all the colors) passes through a prism, dispersion causes it to separate into the seven colors of the rainbow.

displacement (dis-PLĀS-muhnt) The amount of fluid that is pushed out of the way when an object floats in the fluid. The amount of water that is pushed out of the way by a person floating in a pool is the displacement. The weight of that water is also known as the displacement.

dissect (di-SEKT *or* DĪ-sekt) To cut apart the tissues of a dead body or a dead animal in order to study them.

dissolve (di-ZOLV) To mix with another substance so that the two substances form a **solution.** Salt dissolves in water, and iron dissolves in acid.

distillation (dis-tuh-LĀ-shuhn) A way of separating one liquid from a mixture of liquids. The mixture is boiled so that the liquid evaporates as a gas into a pipe that takes it to a cooler container, where it condenses back into a liquid. Gasoline is made from petroleum by distillation. Distillation can

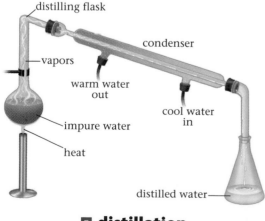

□ **distillation**

also separate pure water from impure water.

divide (di-VĪD) **1.** To perform division on one number by another number. 12 divided by 6 equals 2. **2.** To undergo cell division.

dividend (DIV-i-dend) A number that is divided by another. For example, in the equation 15 ÷ 3 = 5, 15 is the dividend.

division (di-VIZH-uhn) **1.** The mathematical process of finding out how many times one number is contained in another number. **2.** One of the major groups in the classification of plants. A division is below a kingdom and above a class. A division is similar to a **phylum** in the classification of other living things, such as animals and fungi. □ See Table on page 47.

division sign The ÷ sign. It is used to show division, as in 32 ÷ 4 = 8.

divisor (di-VĪ-zer) A number used to divide another. In the equation 15 ÷ 3 = 5, 3 is the divisor.

DNA Short for **deoxyribonucleic acid.** The material that makes up the genes and that is found in all cells. DNA controls the function of all the cells in the body. DNA in the body consists of two thread-like strands that are linked together in the shape of a **double helix.** □ Compare RNA.

□ **DNA**

A strand of DNA is shaped like a twisted ladder. The rungs of the "ladder" are made of four different bases.

DNA fingerprinting The use of DNA to find out the identity of a person or to discover the relationship between different organisms. In DNA fingerprinting, scientists study the patterns of DNA molecules in the genes and compare them.

dog   A member of a meat-eating group of mammals that includes the domestic dog, wolf, fox, jackal, and coyote. The domestic dog is a common house pet, while all other species live in the wild. Unlike cats, almost all dogs have claws that are fully exposed and cannot be pulled back.

dolphin   (DOL-fin) **1.** A sea mammal with flippers, a snout that is shaped like a beak, and cone-shaped teeth. Dolphins are related to whales and porpoises and live mainly in warm waters. They are highly intelligent and communicate with each other by means of high-pitched whistling and squeaking sounds. **2.** A kind of fish that lives in warm ocean waters and has a fin along its back. This type of dolphin is often caught for food.

dominant trait   (DOM-uh-nuhnt TRĀT) A trait that appears in a living thing. A dominant trait is one that appears even if the gene for a trait that is inherited from one parent is different from the gene inherited from the other parent. If you inherit a gene for brown hair from your father and a gene for red hair from your mother, you will have brown hair because brown hair is a dominant trait. ◻ Compare **recessive trait.**

Doppler effect   (DOP-ler i-FEKT) The change in the frequency of sound or light waves that occurs when the source of the sound or light is moving toward or away from a person. In the case of sound, a higher or lower frequency is heard as a higher or lower sound. When a motorcycle is driving toward you, the Doppler effect makes the engine noise sound higher than it does when the motorcycle is driving away from you.

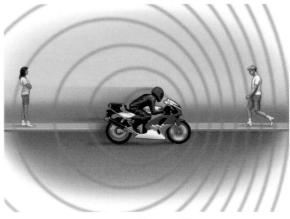

◻ **Doppler effect**

Sound waves from the motorcycle's engine are shown in orange. As the motorcycle speeds forward, the waves are pushed closer together in front to make higher frequencies. They are also pulled farther apart behind to make lower frequencies.

dormant   (DOR-muhnt) Not active for a period of time. Animals in hibernation are dormant. A dormant volcano is one that is not erupting but that could still erupt at some time.

dorsal   (DOR-suhl) Located on the back of an animal. Many fish, such as sharks, have dorsal fins.

double bond   (DUHB-uhl BOND) A type of chemical bond between two atoms in which each atom shares two electrons with the other.

double helix   The shape of a DNA molecule. A double helix resembles a ladder that has been twisted into a spiral. ◻ See picture at **DNA.**

download   To copy or move data from one computer on a network to another.

drag   The force that slows an object's movement through a fluid such as air or water. A person with a parachute falls slowly because of the drag of the air.

□ drag

A parachute increases drag on the shuttle.

dragonfly (DRAG-uhn-flī) An insect with a slender body and two pairs of wings that have many veins. Dragonflies hold their wings out to the side when not in flight.

drone A male bee, especially a honeybee whose only function is to fertilize the queen. Drones have no stingers, do no work, and do not produce honey.

drought (DROWT) A long, dry period in which there is unusually low rainfall. Crops and wildlife often suffer during a drought because they can't get enough water.

drug A substance that is taken into or put on the body because it can kill germs or change how the body works. Drugs are prescribed by doctors to treat or prevent illness. Drugs that affect the nervous system can cause addiction.

dry cell An electric cell, such as a flashlight battery, in which the chemical compounds that produce the current are made of a paste so that they cannot spill from their container.

dry ice The chemical compound carbon dioxide in solid form. Dry ice can change from a solid to a gas without first passing through a liquid stage by the process known as **sublimation**. It is used to keep things cold.

duck-billed dinosaur A medium-sized or large dinosaur that ate plants and had a mouth shaped like a duck's bill. Duck-billed dinosaurs walked on their back two legs, had small front legs, and had many rough teeth for grinding tough food.

duct A tube or passage through which something flows. In the body, ducts provide a passageway for the flow of fluids produced by glands. Tears, which are made by glands near the eyes, pass through tear ducts before leaving the body.

ductile (DUK-tuhl) Easily molded or shaped without breaking into pieces. When they are heated, ductile materials, such as gold, can be easily drawn out into thin wires. □ Compare **brittle**.

dune A hill or ridge of sand that is heaped up by the wind. Dunes can move by

□ dune

the movement of their individual grains of sand, but they usually keep the same shape overall.

DVD   A kind of compact disk that holds a great amount of information. DVDs can store both sound and pictures and are used for showing movies.

dwarf star   A small star that has a low mass and that gives off an average or below average amount of light. The Sun is a dwarf star.

dynamic   (dī-NAM-ik) Relating to objects or systems that are always moving or changing. The exchange of carbon between the atmosphere and living things is dynamic because it is a cycle that doesn't end. ◻ Compare **static.**

dynamite   (DY-nuh-mīt) A powerful explosive used in blasting and mining. Dynamite is usually made of a mixture of the chemical compound nitroglycerin and other nitrogen compounds.

dynamo   (DĪ-nuh-mō) *See* **generator.**

Did You Know?

dwarf star
Don't be fooled by its name. Dwarf stars may be small when compared to bigger stars, but even a dwarf star is quite large. Our Sun is a dwarf star— and it's more than 100 times larger than the Earth! Unlike other dwarf stars, brown dwarf stars don't have enough mass to make their own energy, and they never quite become true stars.

dysentery   (DIS-uhn-tair-ē) A disease in which a person has severe diarrhea. Dysentery is caused by bacteria or parasites and spreads when a person comes into contact with contaminated food, water, or other substance.

dyslexia   (dis-LEK-sē-uh) A learning disability that interferes with a person's ability to read and understand written words and numbers.

Ee

E = mc² A formula that shows that the energy contained in an object (E) is equal to its mass (m) multiplied twice by the speed of light (c). The formula means that even small amounts of matter can contain large amounts of energy. The formula was created by Albert Einstein as part of his theory of **relativity.**

Did You Know?

E = mc²

Einstein's famous equation shows how matter and energy are related. Because it takes a lot of energy to hold the parts of an atom together, a lot of energy is released when an atom breaks apart. This energy is what powers nuclear reactors.

ear The organ of hearing. In humans and many other animals, the ear is made up of three parts: the **inner ear,** the **middle ear,** and the **outer ear.** The ear also helps living things keep their balance.

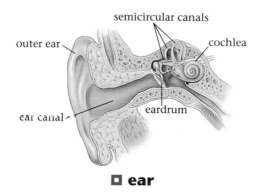

◻ ear

eardrum The thin, oval membrane that separates the middle ear from the outer ear. The eardrum vibrates when sound waves strike it, and these vibrations are then sent to the three small bones of the middle ear. ◻ See picture at **ear.**

Earth The planet on which humans live. Earth is the third planet from the Sun and is the fifth largest planet in the Solar System. It is the only planet on which water exists in liquid form. ◻ See Table on pages 184–185.

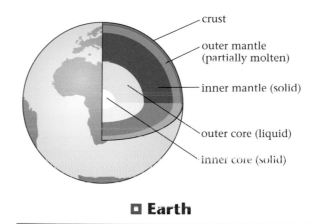

crust

outer mantle (partially molten)

inner mantle (solid)

outer core (liquid)

inner core (solid)

◻ Earth

earthquake A sudden movement of the Earth's crust. Earthquakes usually occur

◻ earthquake

In an earthquake, one section of the Earth's crust moves in relation to another section along the line of a fault. Earthquakes can cause serious damage to buildings and roads.

along cracks in the crust known as faults. They also happen in areas where large sections of the outer part of the Earth, known as plates, rub against each other.

earth science   A science that studies the Earth or its oceans, atmosphere, and history. Geology, oceanography, and meteorology are earth sciences.

earthworm   A worm with a body that is divided into ring-shaped segments. Earthworms burrow into soil, making tunnels that let in air and water and make it easier for plants to grow.

Did You Know?

earthworm

Earthworms may be small, but they can do a lot. Each year, in a single acre of land, earthworms move 18 tons of soil as they tunnel up and down. Their tunnels allow air and water to enter the soil, and they loosen the soil to make it easier for plants to send down roots.
Earthworms also eat and digest soil, and their own wastes provide nourishment for plants and other living things.

east   The direction in which the Sun rises.

Eastern Hemisphere   The half of the Earth that includes Europe, Africa, Asia, and Australia.

ebb tide   The period between high tide and low tide when water is flowing away from the shore. ◻ Compare **flood tide**.

echinoderm   (i-KĪ-nuh-derm) A sea animal with a hard outer skin that is usually covered with spines. Echinoderms are invertebrates with internal skeletons and parts that branch out evenly from the center of the body. Starfish, sea urchins, and sand dollars are echinoderms.

echo   (EK-ō) A sound that is heard more than once because its sound waves bounce off a surface or an object and come back to where they were first heard.

echolocation   (ek-ō-lō-KĀ-shuhn) A system in some animals, such as bats and dolphins, for locating objects using sound waves. The high-pitched sounds made by these animals echo as they bounce off objects. Animals use echolocation to avoid dangers or to hone in on a target.

eclipse   (i-KLIPS) The partial or total blocking of light from one object by another object in outer space. During an eclipse, one object passes in between two other objects. In an eclipse of the Sun, the Moon passes between the Sun and the Earth.

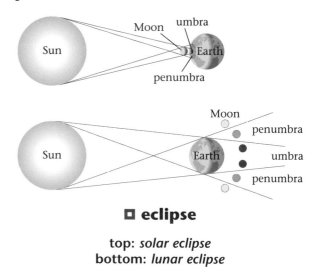

◻ **eclipse**

top: *solar eclipse*
bottom: *lunar eclipse*

ecology   (ē-KOL-uh-jē) The scientific study of the relationships between living things and their environments.

◻ ecosystem

Living things adapt to the conditions around them, as in this pond. The pond, together with the life forms that it supports and the surrounding environment, make up one ecosystem.

ecosystem   (Ē-kō-sis-tuhm) All the living things in a community and the environment in which they live. An ecosystem includes **producers, consumers,** and **decomposers** and may be as small as a pond or as large as a rain forest. Climate, the kind of soil, and the main sources of energy are all part of an ecosystem.

Eddington   (ED-ing-tuhn), **Arthur Stanley** Born 1882; died 1944. British scientist who studied the formation, structure, and movement of stars. Eddington was one of the first scientists to promote the theory of relativity that was first introduced by Albert Einstein. He is one of the founders of modern astrophysics.

eddy   (ED-dē) A current, such as a water current or an air current, that moves in a direction that is different from that of the main current. Eddies often move in circular patterns.

Edison   (ED-i-suhn), **Thomas Alva** Born 1847; died 1931. American scientist who

Biography

Thomas Alva Edison

Thomas Edison is probably best known for inventing the incandescent lamp in 1879, but he patented more than 1,000 other inventions in his lifetime. These include the microphone (1877) and the phonograph (1878). Edison also designed and built the first electric power plant, and he developed the technology that made talking movies possible.

was one of the most productive inventors in history.

eel   A long, slippery fish with a snake-like body but no scales. Eels usually migrate from fresh water to salt water to lay their eggs.

effervescence (ef-er-VES-uhns) The formation of bubbles in a liquid when gas escapes from it.

Did You Know?

effervescence

A liquid can have effervescence for several reasons. Soft drinks have bubbles because carbon dioxide gas was put into the liquid under pressure. When you open a container with a soft drink in it, the pressure is released, and the gas comes out as bubbles. Effervescence also happens if a chemical reaction like fermentation creates gas in a liquid. This is where the bubbles in champagne come from.

---

egg 1. The sex cell of female animals. An egg that has been fertilized by a male sex cell, or sperm, can grow into a new animal. In mammals and other vertebrates, eggs are contained in the **ovary. 2.** The round or oval structure that is laid by a female animal, such as a bird, fish, insect, or reptile. An egg is surrounded by a shell or membrane. After an egg is fertilized, a young animal starts to develop inside it. **3.** The female

sex cell of plants, algae, and some fungi. In some plants, such as flowering plants, eggs are fertilized in the part of the plant ovary called an **ovule** before growing into seeds.

egg case A capsule that is made by certain animals, such as insects, spiders, and mollusks, and contains eggs. Egg cases look like cocoons and protect the developing eggs.

egg tooth A small, sharp structure on the beak of some baby birds and reptiles that is used to break through the shell of the egg during hatching. The egg tooth later falls off.

Ehrlich (AIR-lik), **Paul** Born 1854; died 1915. German scientist who was a pioneer in the study of blood and the immune system. In 1900, he was the first to describe how antibodies are made in the body and how they act with other substances to fight germs that cause disease.

Einstein (ĪN-stīn), **Albert** Born 1879; died 1955. German-born American scientist whose theories

◻ **Albert Einstein**

◻ **egg**

left to right: *American robin eggs in a nest, hognose snake eggs hatching, and silk moth eggs attached to leaves*

changed the way scientists understand space and time. Einstein formulated the theory of **relativity.** He explained that light was made not just of waves but of particles. He also developed a new way of understanding gravity.

elastic   (i-LAS-tik) Capable of returning to the original shape and size after having been stretched, squeezed, or bent. Rubber bands are elastic.

electric   (i-LEK-trik) Relating to, producing, or operated by electricity.

electrical engineering   (i-LEK-tri-kuhl en-juh-NEER-ing) The scientific study of the design, building, and uses of electric systems.

electric cell   A device that can turn a form of energy into electricity. Solar cells are electric cells that turn sunlight into electricity. Electric cells in car batteries convert the energy that is stored as bonds in chemical compounds into electricity.

electric current   The flow of electricity through a material known as a **conductor.** Electric current can flow in one direction only, or it can flow forwards and backwards. Electric current is usually measured in amperes.

electricity   (i-lek-TRIS-i-tē) A form of energy produced by particles that have **charge,** especially electrons. Electricity can flow in an electric current, or it can be static.

electrode   (i-LEK-trōd) A piece of metal or carbon through which an electric current can enter or leave an electric device. Batteries have two electrodes, positive and negative.

electrolysis   (i-lek-TROL-i-sis) The process of passing an electric current through a solution in order to cause a change in the chemical compounds that make up the solution. Hydrogen and oxygen can be separated out from water by electrolysis.

electrolyte   (i-LEK-truh-līt) A substance that can conduct electricity in a solution. An electrolyte's atoms get their electric charge by adding or giving up electrons. The movement of these charged atoms, called **ions,** carries the electric current.

electromagnet   (i-lek-trō-MAG-nit) A magnet that gets its force of attraction from an electric current. Electromagnets are made of a coil of wire wrapped around a piece of iron. When an electric current runs through the wire the iron becomes a magnet; when the current stops, the magnetism goes away.

electromagnetic force   (i-lek-trō-mag-NET-ik FORS) The forces of attraction and repulsion that electric fields have for each other and that magnetic fields have for each other. The areas of the fields with opposite electric charges or different magnetic poles attract each other. The areas with the same electric charges or the same magnetic poles push each other apart.

electromagnetic radiation   Energy that moves in the form of magnetic and electric waves. Electromagnetic radiation

Did You Know?
electromagnetic radiation
Light waves, x-rays, and radio waves are all the same thing, in a way. They are all kinds of electromagnetic radiation. The only difference between them is in their wavelengths—how long their waves are—and in their frequencies—the number of waves that pass a particular point in a second.

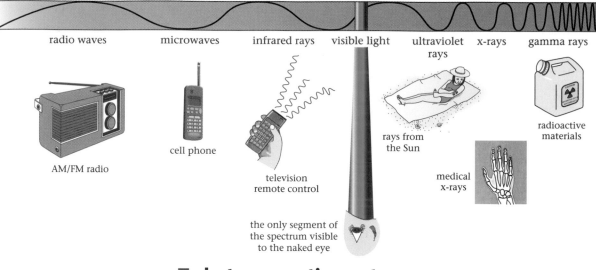

radio waves · microwaves · infrared rays · visible light · ultraviolet rays · x-rays · gamma rays

AM/FM radio

cell phone

television remote control

rays from the Sun

medical x-rays

radioactive materials

the only segment of the spectrum visible to the naked eye

◻ electromagnetic spectrum

consists of particles of energy called **photons.** Visible light, x-rays, and microwaves are all forms of electromagnetic radiation.

electromagnetic spectrum All the different kinds of electromagnetic radiation. The electromagnetic spectrum is arranged according to the wavelengths of each kind of radiation. At one end are the waves with the shortest wavelengths, known as gamma rays; at the other end are the waves with the longest wavelengths, known as radio waves.

electromagnetic wave A wave of energy that is made of electric and magnetic fields that swing back and forth together as they travel forward. Radio waves, light waves, and x-rays are electromagnetic waves.

electromagnetism (i-lek-trō-MAG-ni-tiz-uhm) Magnetism that is produced by electric charges that are moving, as when electrons move through a wire in an electric circuit.

electromotive force (i-lek-trō-MŌ-tiv FORS) The force that makes electrons move to produce an electric current. Electromotive force is supplied by a power source, such as a battery or generator. It is measured in volts. ◻ Electromotive force is also called *voltage.*

electron (i-LEK-tron) The particle in an atom that has a negative electric charge and revolves around the nucleus in an orbit. Atoms combine to make molecules by sharing electrons.

electronics (i-lek-TRON-iks) The science that deals with electrons and with devices and systems that operate by using electrons. Electronics has led to the development of radio, TV, flights in space, and computers.

electron microscope A very powerful microscope that uses a beam of electrons, instead of light, to magnify objects that are too small to be seen with an ordinary microscope. As the electrons hit the object being viewed, other electrons are knocked loose from its surface. Those electrons are then picked up by a device that turns them into a black-and-white image.

electroplating (i-LEK-trō-plā-ting) The process of coating one metal with another by electrolysis. Electroplating is used for protecting or decorating metal surfaces.

element (EL-uh-muhnt) *See* **chemical element.**

elevation (el-uh-VĀ-shuhn) The height of a point on the Earth's surface above sea level. The elevation of the highest point on Earth, the top of Mount Everest, is 29,035 feet (8,850 meters) above sea level.

ellipse (i-LIPS) A curved shape that looks like an oval or a circle that is flattened at opposite ends. ◻ See picture at **geometry.**

El Niño (el NĒN-yō) A period during which the surface water of the eastern Pacific Ocean becomes warmer than usual. The warmer water has fewer nutrients, causing fish and plankton to die because of lack of food. El Niño also causes heavy rains in South America and drought in Australia and Indonesia. ◻ Compare **La Niña.**

e-mail (Ē-māl) **1.** A system of sending and getting messages and documents over a computer network. **2.** A message or document that is sent by using this system.

embryo (EM-brē-ō) **1.** An animal in the earliest stages of growth, just after an egg has been fertilized. **2.** A plant in the earliest stages of growth, when it is contained within a seed.

emerald (EM-er-uhld) A transparent, green form of the mineral beryl. It is valued as a gem.

emission (i-MISH-uhn) Energy or matter that is released from something. Rays of light from the Sun and exhaust from a car's engine are both emissions.

empirical (em-PEER-i-kuhl) Based on observation, usually as part of an experiment, rather than on thought alone.

empty set (EMP-tē SET) The set that has no members. A set consisting of the number

0 is not empty because it has one member: {0}. The empty set is written { } or ∅.

emulsion (i-MUL-shuhn) A mixture of two liquids in which tiny droplets of the first liquid are mixed throughout the second. Oils can be mixed with water to form emulsions like paint.

enamel (i-NAM-uhl) The hard, white substance that covers the part of the tooth that sticks out from the gums.

Did You Know?

enamel
Enamel is the hardest substance that your body produces. The hardest enamel is on the biting edges of your front teeth, which is nearly as hard as the blade of a knife or a piece of glass.

endangered species (en-DĀN-jerd SPĒ-shēz) A plant or animal that is found in such small numbers that it is in danger of becoming extinct, usually because its habitat is being destroyed. Ginkgo trees, chimpanzees, and blue whales are endangered species.

endemic (en-DEM-ik) Native to a certain region and not occurring naturally anywhere else. Kangaroos and wombats are endemic to Australia and its surrounding islands. ◻ Compare **alien, indigenous.**

endocrine system (EN-duh-krin SIS-tuhm) A group of glands in the body that produce substances called **hormones.** The thyroid, ovary, and pancreas are all glands of the endocrine system.

endoskeleton (en-dō-SKEL-i-tuhn) A skeleton in an animal that is located inside the body. The endoskeletons of most vertebrates, including humans, are made of bone. Some invertebrates, such as sponges, have endoskeletons made of other firm materials. ◻ Compare **exoskeleton.**

energy (EN-er-jē) The ability to do work, such as the ability to move an object by pushing on it. Energy can exist in many forms, including motion, heat, and electricity. Energy cannot be created or destroyed, but it can be changed from one form to another.

engine (EN-jin) A machine that turns energy into motion. Engines get their energy from a source of heat, such as a burning fuel.

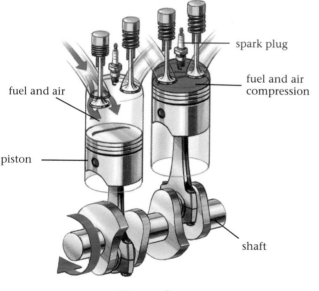

spark plug

fuel and air compression

fuel and air

piston

shaft

◻ **engine**

Fuel and air mix in a cylinder and are lit by a spark from the spark plug. The explosion causes the piston to move up and down. The piston's movement causes a shaft to turn, which provides motion to parts such as wheels or gears.

engineering (en-juh-NEER-ing) The use of science to design and build structures and machines. Engineering is necessary for safe bridges, roads, and buildings and for reliable cars, trains, and airplanes.

entomology (en-tuh-MOL-uh-jē) The scientific study of insects.

environment (en-VĪ-ruhn-muhnt) The surroundings and conditions that determine how living things grow and develop. Soil, air, water, climate, plant life, and animal life are all part of an environment. To survive, living things often have to adjust to changes in their environments.

enzyme (EN-zīm) A molecule that helps start or speed up chemical reactions by acting as a **catalyst.** Enzymes are proteins and are found in the cells of all plants and animals. They play a part in all body activities, such as digestion and respiration.

Did You Know?

enzyme
Your body has hundreds of enzymes, each one made for one specific purpose. Your stomach has one enzyme for breaking down proteins in food, another for breaking down fats, and another for breaking down carbohydrates. Inside your cells, enzymes are used to make and repair DNA and to build proteins.

Eocene Epoch (Ē-uh-sēn EP-uhk) The period of time during the history of the Earth starting about 58 million years ago and ending about 37 million years ago. During the Eocene Epoch, the Earth's climate was warm, and most of the larger groups of mammals we know today first appeared. ◻ See Table on pages 102–103.

eon (Ē-on) The longest division of time in the history of the Earth. There are two eons in the history of the Earth: the **Precambrian Eon** and the **Phanerozoic Eon.**

epicenter (EP-i-sen-ter) The point on the Earth's surface that is directly above the place where an earthquake first starts.

epidemic (ep-i-DEM-ik) An outbreak of a contagious disease that spreads quickly and affects many people.

epidermis (ep-i-DER-mis) **1.** The outer layer of the skin of an animal. The epidermis helps protect against the Sun's rays and keeps out germs that cause infection. Hair and feathers grow from the epidermis. **2.** The outer layer of cells of the stems, roots, and leaves of a plant. The epidermis protects plants from water loss and disease.

epiphyte (EP-uh-fīt) A plant that grows on another plant, which gives it support. Epiphytes get moisture and nutrients from the air or from water that collects on the supporting plant. Many mosses and orchids are epiphytes.

epoch (EP-uhk) The shortest division of time in the history of the Earth. The most recent part of the Earth's history is divided into epochs.

epoxy (i-POK-sē) A very sticky substance that is made in a laboratory and is barely affected by other chemical compounds. Epoxies are used to make strong glue and paints that do not chip or peel.

equal (Ē-kwuhl) Being exactly the same in amount or measurement. 5 + 7 is equal to 12. The lengths of the four sides of a square are equal.

equal sign The = sign. It comes between two sides of an equation to show that the two sides are equal, as in 2 + 4 = 6.

equation (i-KWĀ-zhuhn) A written statement that shows that two quantities are equal. An equation is made up of two parts that are joined by an equal sign. For example, 2 + 3 + 5 = 10 is an equation.

equator (i-KWĀ-ter) **1.** The imaginary line that forms a circle around the middle of the Earth halfway between the North and South Poles. The equator divides the Earth into the Northern Hemisphere and the Southern Hemisphere. **2.** A similar circle on the surface of an object in outer space, such as the Sun.

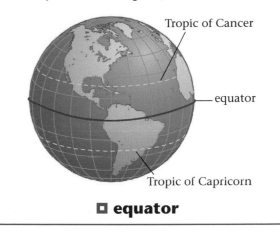

Tropic of Cancer
equator
Tropic of Capricorn

□ **equator**

equidistant (ē-kwi-DIS-tuhnt) Equally distant. If three people are all standing in different places 15 feet away from a tree, they are equidistant from the tree.

equilateral triangle (e-kwuh-LAT-er-uhl TRI-ang-guhl) A triangle whose sides are all the same length. □ See picture at **triangle**.

equilibrium (ē-kwi-LIB-rē-uhm) A state of balance between opposite forces or different substances. An object that is in equilibrium is either at rest or moving at a constant speed in a straight line.

equinox (Ē-kwi-noks) Either of the two times during the year when the Sun is directly above the equator and daylight and night are the same length. The two equinoxes are known as the **vernal equinox** and the **autumnal equinox**. □ See picture at **season**.

era (EER-uh) A division of time in the history of the Earth that is shorter than an eon and longer than a period. The Mesozoic Era, for example, is part of the Phanerozoic Eon, and includes the Triassic Period, the Jurassic Period, and the Cretaceous Period.

❑ **erosion**

tree roots exposed and damaged by erosion

Eratosthenes (air-uh-TOS-thuh-nēz) Lived in the third century BC. Greek mathematician who was the first person to estimate the circumference of the Earth with accuracy. He also calculated how far the Earth is from the Sun and how far the Earth is from the Moon.

erosion (i-RŌ-zhuhn) The gradual wearing away of the surface of land by water, wind, or a glacier. Erosion usually moves the loosened material, such as rocks and soil, from one place to another. Erosion can be very damaging to the habitats of wildlife and to land used for farming.

erupt (i-RUPT) **1.** To release lava, gas, ash, or hot water into the atmosphere or onto the Earth's surface. Active volcanoes are ones that continue to erupt. **2.** To shoot a spray of steam and hot water into the air. Some geysers erupt several times a day.

escape velocity (i-SKĀP vuh-LOS-i-tē) The speed at which an object, such as a rocket, must travel in order to escape from a planet's pull of gravity. The escape velocity for a rocket traveling into space from Earth is 7 miles (11 kilometers) per second.

esophagus (i-SOF-uh-guhs) The tube that carries food from the mouth to the stomach. ❑ See picture at **digestive system.**

Espy (ES-pē), **James Pollard** Born 1785; died 1860. American scientist who explained the role heat plays in the formation of clouds and storms. He also used the telegraph for collecting and transmitting weather information, which led to the practice of weather forecasting that is common today.

estivate (ES-tuh-vāt) To pass the summer in a state of inactivity that is similar to sleep. Animals that estivate usually live in hot climates. When they estivate, they are protected from the heat and dryness of the summer months. Some snails estivate. ❑ Compare **hibernate.**

estrogen (ES-truh-juhn) A hormone that controls the growth and development of the reproductive system in female vertebrates.

estrus (ES-truhs) A period of time in which female mammals are ready to mate. In some mammals, such as deer, estrus occurs once a year. In other mammals, such as mice, it occurs many times a year. ◘ Estrus is also called *heat*.

estuary (ES-choo-air-ē) The wide lower end of a river where it flows into the sea. The water in estuaries is a mixture of fresh water and salt water.

ether (Ē-ther) A strong-smelling liquid that evaporates easily and was once used to make people sleep during surgery.

Euclid (YOO-klid) Lived in the third century BC. Greek mathematician who wrote books on geometry that were used continuously until the 19th century. Euclid also came up with basic rules that are used for solving mathematical problems.

euglena (yoo-GLĒ-nuh) A living thing that has only one cell and lives in fresh water. Euglenas have a long tail called a flagellum and often have chlorophyll, like many plants. Euglenas belong to the group of living things called **protozoans.**

eukaryote (yoo-KAIR-ē-ōt) A member of a large group of living things that are made up of one or more cells, each having a cell nucleus. All organisms except bacteria are eukaryotes. ◘ Compare **prokaryote.**

eustachian tube (yoo-STĀ-shuhn TOOB) A thin tube that connects the middle ear with the throat. The eustachian tube helps keep air pressure equal on both sides of the eardrum.

evaporation (i-vap-uh-RĀ-shuhn) The change of a liquid into a vapor when the liquid is below its boiling point. Puddles dry up and disappear because of evaporation.

evening star (ĒV-ning STAR) A planet, not a star, that can be seen in the west just after sunset. The evening star is usually Venus or Mercury.

even number (Ē-vuhn NUHM-ber) A number that can be divided by 2 with a remainder of 0. Examples of even numbers include 12 and 876. ◘ Compare **odd number.**

evergreen (EV-er-grēn) Having green leaves or needles all year. Evergreen trees and shrubs in colder climates usually have needles, while evergreen plants in warmer climates often have broad leaves. Pines, firs, and palms are evergreen trees. ◘ Compare **deciduous.**

Did You Know?

evergreen

It is not true that evergreen trees never lose their leaves. In fact, they lose them all the time. If you look on the ground underneath an evergreen tree, you will see lots of dead leaves, such as the needles of a pine tree. The needles fall off one by one throughout the year, rather than all at once.

evolution (ev-uh-LOO-shuhn) The gradual change that takes place in living things over long periods of time. New species come into being from earlier life forms through evolution. Evolution is based on the idea of **natural selection,** which says that only living things that are best able to survive in a particular environment live long enough to reproduce.

evolve (i-VOLV) To change or develop as part of the natural process of evolution. Scientists believe that birds evolved from a group of dinosaurs.

excrete   (ik-SKRĒT) To get rid of waste materials from the cells or from the body. Humans and other vertebrates excrete urine, feces, and carbon dioxide.

exhale   (eks-HĀL) To breathe out.

exhaust   (ig-ZAWST) The gases that are given off by an engine when fuel is burned.

exoskeleton   (ek-sō-SKEL-i-tuhn) A hard covering on the body of an animal, such as an insect or a crustacean. Exoskeletons provide support and protection for the soft inside body parts and are usually made of a hard material called **chitin**. Only invertebrates have exoskeletons. ◻ Compare **endoskeleton**.

exosphere   (EK-sō-sfeer) The upper part of the thermosphere, forming the outermost region of the Earth's atmosphere. The air in the exosphere gets thinner and thinner until the lightest particles, such as hydrogen atoms, begin to escape Earth's gravity.

expand   (ik-SPAND) To become larger in size, volume, or amount. Gases expand in volume when they are heated.

experiment   (ik-SPAIR-uh-muhnt) A test that is done by scientists to find out whether an idea or **hypothesis** is true. Experiments usually involve careful measurements and the use of laboratory equipment. Designing and performing an experiment is an important step in the **scientific method**.

explosion   (ik-SPLŌ-zhuhn) A powerful bursting caused by energy that is released very quickly. Explosions can be caused by the violent reaction of chemical compounds, by nuclear reactions, or by the sudden escape of gases that have been trapped under pressure.

exponent   (EK-spō-nuhnt) A number that shows how many times a number is multipied by itself. The exponent usually appears in a smaller size and to the right and above the other number. For example, 3 is the exponent in 5^3 = 125, which is another way of saying $5 \times 5 \times 5$ = 125.

extinct   (ik-STINGKT) **1.** No longer existing or living. Plants and animals may become extinct because of changes in climate, destruction of their habitat, natural disasters, or disease. **2.** No longer active or burning. An extinct volcano is not able to erupt any more.

extraterrestrial   (ek-struh-tuh-RES-trē-uhl) Coming from, located, or happening outside the Earth or its atmosphere.

eye   **1.** The organ of sight. In humans and many other animals, the eye is shaped like a ball with fluid inside. Light enters the eye through the cornea and passes through the pupil to the lens, which focuses images on the retina. **2.** A small, hard spot on a potato from which another potato plant can grow. **3.** The calm area at the center of a hurricane.

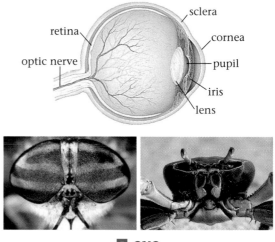

◻ **eye**

human eye (top); compound eye of a horsefly (bottom left); eyestalks of a land crab (bottom right)

eyepiece The part of a viewing instrument that is closest to the eye of the user. Eyepieces hold a lens or a group of lenses and can often be removed and changed. Telescopes and microscopes have eyepieces.

eyespot **1.** An area or a cell in some living things that is sensitive to light. Eyespots are found in many one-celled organisms. **2.** A round mark that looks like an eye, as on the tail feather of a peacock.

eyestalk A long, thin body part with a compound eye on its tip. Eyestalks are found on crustaceans, such as crabs and lobsters. ◻ See picture at **eye.**

Ff

factor (FAK-ter) A number that can be multiplied by another number to reach a specific number. For example, 2 and 3 are both factors of 6, because 2 × 3 = 6.

Fahrenheit (FAIR-uhn-hīt), **Gabriel Daniel** Born 1686; died 1736. German scientist who invented the mercury thermometer in 1714. The Fahrenheit temperature scale was created in 1724.

Fahrenheit scale A temperature scale on which the freezing point of water is 32° and the boiling point of water is 212°. The Fahrenheit scale is the one used by most people in the United States. Scientists around the world use the **Celsius scale** instead of the Fahrenheit scale. The Fahrenheit scale is named after Gabriel Daniel Fahrenheit. ◻ See picture at **temperature.**

fall The season of autumn.

fallout The particles that fall from the sky after the explosion of a nuclear weapon. Most fallout is poisonous because of its **radioactivity.**

family (FAM-uh-lē) One of the major groups in the classification of living things. A family is below an order and above a genus. ◻ See Table on page 47.

fang A long sharp tooth or similar body part that some animals have for seizing prey. The fangs of some animals, such as snakes and spiders, contain venom.

Faraday (FAIR-uh-dā), **Michael** Born 1791; died 1867. British scientist who studied the connection between electricity and magnetism. In 1831 he invented the first electric generator and transformer, making it possible for electricity to be used as a source of power for machines.

farsighted (FAR-sī-tid) Able to see distant objects more easily than nearby objects. In farsighted people, light that enters the eye is focused behind the retina instead of right on it. ◻ Compare **nearsighted.**

fat An oily substance that is produced by plants and animals and that serves as a source of energy. In mammals, fat lying under the skin and around the organs prevents the loss of heat and provides protection. Fats are made mostly of **fatty acids.**

fatty acid (FAT-ē AS-id) A kind of acid that is found mainly in animal and vegetable fats and oils. The molecules of fatty acids are made up of long chains of carbon atoms connected to hydrogen atoms.

fault A long crack in a rock along which the two sides of the rock slide past each other, pull away from each other, or push against each other. Earthquakes often happen where there are faults.

◻ **fault**

along a fault line in southern California

fauna (FAW-nuh) The animals of a paticular region or time period. The fauna of tropical regions include many animals that are not found in cold regions. Prehistoric fauna include the dinosaurs and saber-toothed tiger. ◻ Compare **flora.**

feather (FE*TH*-er) A light, flat structure that grows out of the skin of birds. A feather has a narrow, hollow shaft from which smaller branches stick out. Feathers are made of keratin and help keep birds from losing heat.

□ feather

Down feathers (top left) *prevent heat loss. Contour feathers* (top right) *have a hollow shaft and cover most of a bird's body. Tail feathers* (bottom left) *help in balance and steering. Flight feathers* (bottom right) *are large and stiff.*

feces (FĒ-sēz) The solid waste material that is produced by the digestion of food and that leaves the body through the anus.

feedback (FĒD-bak) A part of the **output** of a system or process that returns to become part of the **input**. Sound that comes out of a speaker and is picked up by a microphone and returned to the amplifier is a form of feedback.

feeler (FĒ-ler) A slender body part that is used for touching or sensing. Insects' antennas are feelers.

feldspar (FELD-spar) A mineral that makes up more than 60 percent of the Earth's crust. Feldspar occurs in many varieties, but all feldspar is made mainly of aluminum, silicon, and oxygen. The pink and white flecks in granite consist mostly of feldspar.

female (FĒ-māl) **1.** Belonging to the sex that can produce eggs or give birth to young. **2.** Being a plant, flower, or flower part that can produce seeds. **3.** A female animal, plant, flower, or flower part.

femur (FĒ-mer) The long bone of the thigh. **□** See picture at **skeleton.**

fermentation (fer-men-TĀ-shuhn) The breaking down of larger chemical compounds into simpler substances when no oxygen is present. Fermentation produces energy and occurs especially in muscle cells, as well as in plants and some bacteria. Yeast turns sugars into alcohol and carbon dioxide by fermentation.

Fermi (FER-mē), **Enrico** Born 1901; died 1954. Italian-born American scientist who brought about the first man-made nuclear reaction in 1942 and helped to develop the atomic bomb.

fern A kind of plant that usually has feathery leaves with many leaflets. Ferns do not have seeds and reproduce by means of **spores.**

□ fern

clusters of spores on the underside of a fern

fertile (FER-tuhl) **1.** Able to produce offspring, seeds, or fruit. **2.** Fertilized by a male sex cell. A fertile egg can grow into a new organism. **3.** Rich in nutrients. Fertile soil is good for growing crops and plants.

fertilization (fer-tuhl-i-ZĀ-shuhn) The process in which a female sex cell and a male sex cell join together to produce a new organism. In mammals, fertilization takes place inside the body of the female. In fish, eggs are fertilized in the water.

fertilize (FER-tuh-līz) **1.** To unite with a female sex cell to form a new organism. In plants, pollen fertilizes the egg in an ovary to form a seed. **2.** To make soil good for growing plants and crops by adding materials that are rich in nutrients.

fertilizer (FER-tuh-lī-zer) A substance that is added to the soil so that plants or crops will grow better. Manure is a kind of fertilizer.

fetus (FĒ-tuhs) The young of a mammal before it is born.

fever (FĒ-ver) A body temperature that is higher than normal. Fever is usually a sign that the body is fighting an infection.

fiber (FĪ-ber) **1.** A long, thread-like piece of natural or artificial material, such as cotton or nylon. **2.** The parts of a grain, fruit, or vegetable that cannot be broken down into simpler substances by the body. Fiber contains **cellulose** and helps in the digestion of food. **3.** A long cell with thick walls that gives support to plant tissue.

fiberglass (FĪ-ber-glas) A material made up of very thin fibers of glass. The fibers are very strong when woven together, and they can be shaped for use in automobile bodies and boat hulls. In loose, fluffy form, the fibers are used as building insulation.

fiber optics The use of thin tubes or fibers of glass or plastic to carry light from one place to another. Fiber optics allows light to be transmitted around curves, and it allows information to be transmitted as pulses of light. Doctors use fiber optics to look at the inside of the body, and communications companies use fiber optics to send long-distance telephone calls.

Fibonacci (fē-buh-NAH-chē), **Leonardo** Born 1170?; died 1250? Italian mathematician who published a book in 1202 that popularized the decimal system used today.

fibrin (FĪ-brin) A molecule that helps stop bleeding by causing blood clots to form. Fibrin is made of protein.

fibula (FIB-yuh-luh) The smaller of the two bones of the lower leg. ◻ See picture at **skeleton.**

field The area in which a force, such as magnetism or gravity, has an effect. Iron filings that fall within the magnetic field around a magnet will be pulled toward the magnet.

figure (FIG-yer) A distinct shape or outline. Squares, circles, and rectangles are figures.

filament (FIL-uh-muhnt) **1.** A thin thread, wire, or fiber. **2.** A thin wire that is enclosed in the bulb of an incandescent lamp and gives off light when an electric current is passed through it. **3.** The stalk of a stamen in a flower. The filament supports the anther. ◻ See picture at **flower.**

film A very thin covering or coating. Soap often forms a film on the surface of water.

filter (FIL-ter) **1.** A material or device that has tiny holes. Solid particles in a liquid or gas can be removed by passing the liquid or gas through a filter. **2.** A sheet of material that changes the colors of light passing through it by blocking certain light waves and letting others pass through.

◻ filter

a liquid mixture being poured into a beaker through filter paper

fin   One of the thin, flat parts that stick out from the body of fish and some other water animals, such as dolphins and whales. Fins are used for steering, moving forward, and balancing in the water.

finite   (FĪ-nīt) Having a limit. The set of even numbers between 1 and 20 is finite.

fir   A tall, evergreen tree that has cones and short, flat needles. Firs usually grow in colder climates and are related to the pines.

fire   The flame, light, and heat that are given off when something is burning. Fire is a chemical reaction that happens when a substance combines with oxygen very quickly.

fish   A cold-blooded animal that lives in water and uses gills for taking in oxygen. Most fish are covered with scales and have fins. Fish are vertebrates with skeletons made either of bone or cartilage. The three types of fish are **bony fish, cartilaginous fish,** and **jawless fish.**

fission   (FISH-uhn) **1.** The splitting of the nucleus of an atom into two or more nuclei. The splitting may occur because the nucleus has so many neutrons that it falls apart or because a free-moving neutron has smashed into the nucleus, breaking it apart. Fission releases one or more neutrons and energy in the form of **radiation. 2.** The splitting of a cell into two new cells. Fission is a kind of **reproduction.** Bacteria reproduce by means of fission.

fissure   (FISH-er) A long, narrow crack in a rock or cliff. If water that has dissolved minerals in it passes through a fissure, the fissure may eventually become filled with minerals.

fixed star   A star that is so far away from the Earth that it appears not to change positions, but to stay "fixed" in one place. Its movements can be measured only by precise observations over long periods of time. Sirius is a fixed star.

fjord   (FYORD) A narrow body of sea water that stretches inland between steep slopes of a mountainous coast. Most fjords are valleys formed by glaciers.

flagellum   (fluh-JEL-uhm) A slender tail or part that is attached to some one-celled living things. When the flagellum whips back and forth, the cell moves. *Plural form:* **flagella** (fluh-JEL-uh).

flame   The hot, visible, and often bright gases given off by a fire.

flammable   (FLAM-uh-buhl) Easy to set fire to and able to burn very quickly.

flask   A round, glass container with a long neck, used in laboratories.

flea   A very small insect that sucks blood from humans and other animals. Fleas have no wings and move about by jumping with their powerful hind legs.

Fleming   (FLEM-ing), **Alexander** Born 1881; died 1955. Scottish scientist who discovered penicillin in 1928.

flint   A very hard, gray or black sedimentary rock that makes sparks when it is struck

◻ floe

with steel. Flint is made of very small crystals of quartz.

flipper   (FLIP-er) A wide, flat limb that is used for swimming. Flippers are found on water animals such as whales, seals, and sea turtles.

float   To be in the air, in a liquid, or on the surface of a liquid without sinking.

floe   A sheet of ice floating in the ocean.

floodplain   Flat land that lies on either side of a river. A floodplain is made up of sediments such as sand, silt, and clay that are left by a river when it floods.

flood tide   The period between low tide and high tide when water flows toward the shore. ◻ Compare **ebb tide.**

floppy disk   (FLOP-ē DISK) A flexible plastic disk used for storing data. Floppy disks are coated with magnetic material and covered by protective jackets. Floppy disks can be used to move information from one computer to another.

flora   (FLOR-uh) The plants of a particular region or time period. The flora of tropical regions include many plants that are not found in cold regions. ◻ Compare **fauna.**

flower   The part of a flowering plant that contains the organs of reproduction and is able to produce seeds. Flowers of some plants have either male or female organs of reproduction. Other flowers

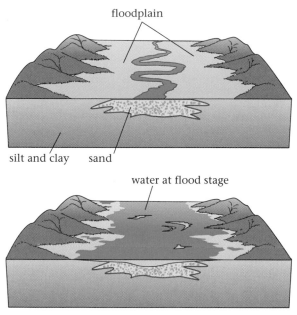

◻ floodplain

The top diagram shows a river at normal level. In the bottom diagram, the river has flooded and spread to low-lying areas on either side of the river, known as the floodplain.

contain both types of organs. The female organ of reproduction is the pistil, and the male organ of reproduction is the stamen.

flowering plant   *See* **angiosperm.**

flu   *See* **influenza.**

fluid   (FLŌO-id) A substance, such as air or water, in which the atoms or molecules

can freely move past one another. Fluids flow easily and take on the shape of their containers. All liquids and gases are fluids.

fluid ounce   A unit of volume used to measure liquids, equal to $\frac{1}{16}$ of a pint. ■ See Table on page 148.

fluorescent   (flu-RES-uhnt) Giving off light when exposed to a form of electro-

A Closer Look

Flower

Flowers contain the male and female parts (organs of reproduction) of a flowering plant. Most flowers, like the lily shown here, have both male and female parts on the same flower. Other plants have separate male flowers and female flowers on the same plant. Still others have separate male plants and female plants. The **stamen,** *or male organ, releases pollen at its tip. The pollen is carried to the female organ, or* **pistil,** *by wind or by an animal, such as a bee or bird.*

stigma — pistil (female)
style —
petal
stamen (male) [anther filament]
ovary
ovules

Flowers may be large, as in the lily and clematis, or small, as in wild-rye flowers. Clover has groups of flowers arranged in clusters. Some trees, such as the alder, produce blossoms in long clusters called catkins. *The sausage-shaped part of another flower type—the cattail—is actually a tightly packed group of female flowers. The male flowers grow at the tip, or "tail."*

clematis

wild-rye

white clover

alder

cattail

magnetic radiation, such as visible light or x-rays. Fluorescent substances stop being fluorescent once the electromagnetic radiation is removed. ◘ Compare **phosphorescent**.

fluorescent lamp A lamp that produces light when electricity is connected to a glass bulb or tube that contains a mixture of gases. The gas atoms give off ultraviolet rays that then light up a special coating on the inside of the glass. ◘ Compare **incandescent lamp**.

fluoridate (FLUR-i-dāt) To add fluorine or fluoride to another substance, especially drinking water. Only very tiny amounts of fluoride are needed to fluoridate water so that it helps prevent tooth decay.

fluoride (FLUR-īd *or* FLOR-īd) A compound made of fluorine and another element. Fluorides are used in dentistry to harden teeth, and they are added to drinking water to help prevent cavities.

fluorine (FLUR-ēn) A chemical element that is a poisonous, pale-yellow gas. Fluorine reacts easily with other elements to form compounds, such as fluorides. ◘ See Table on pages 178–179.

flux 1. A substance that can be added to another substance, such as a metal, to make it melt more easily. 2. *See* **magnetic flux**.

fly A type of insect that has one pair of wings and large compound eyes. Houseflies and mosquitoes are flies.

FM *See* **frequency modulation**.

foam Small, frothy bubbles that form in a liquid or on its surface. Chemical reactions or shaking can cause foam to form.

focal length (FO-kuhl LENGKTH) The distance from the surface of a lens or mirror to the point where the light rays come together to form a clear image (the point of focus).

focus (FO-kuhs) 1. The point where rays of light come together or begin to spread apart after they pass through a lens. 2. The degree of clearness that an image has when it strikes the back of the eye or when it is recorded by an instrument, such as a camera. 3. The place or point where an earthquake starts. The focus of an earthquake is usually located underground.

fog Tiny drops of water floating in the air close to the surface of the Earth. Fog is actually a cloud that has formed near the ground. Fog makes it difficult to see very far and can make it dangerous to operate cars, airplanes, or other vehicles.

fold A bend in a layer of rock. Folds form in rocks when the rocks are squeezed by the forces of **plate tectonics**.

◘ **fold**

folds in a rock wall at a gorge in western Australia

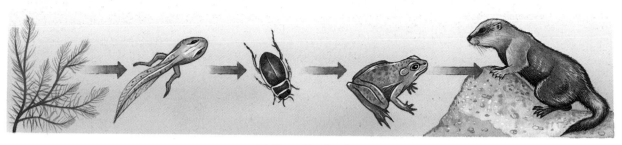

□ food chain

A typical food chain in a water community: A plant is eaten by tadpoles, a great diving beetle eats tadpoles, a bullfrog eats great diving beetles, and a river otter eats frogs.

follicle (FOL-i-kuhl) A small, protective sac in the body. Hair grows from follicles in skin.

food chain A series of plants and animals in which each kind is a source of food for the next in the series. In a typical food chain, plants use the Sun's energy as a source of food and are then eaten by one kind of animal, which is in turn eaten by another kind of animal.

food web A group of food chains that are connected to each other in various ways within an **ecosystem.** The relationships between the members of a food web are more complicated than in a food chain. Some animals eat both plants and animals, so they play a more complex role in the web.

fool's gold A mineral, especially pyrite, that is sometimes mistaken for gold.

foot A unit of length equal to $\frac{1}{3}$ of a yard or 12 inches. □ See Table on page 148.

foot-pound A unit used to measure work. One foot-pound is equal to the work or energy needed to lift a one-pound weight a distance of one foot against the force of gravity.

force Something that causes an object to move, change its shape, or change its speed or direction if it is moving. One force can be canceled by another.

forest (FOR-ist) A thick growth of trees that covers a large area. Forests are found in all regions of the Earth except where it is extremely cold or dry. □ A forest is also called a *woodland.*

formaldehyde (for-MAL-duh-hīd) A colorless gas that has a sharp smell. When mixed with water, it forms a solution that is used to preserve specimens of plants and animals. Formaldehyde is also used in making plastics.

formation (for-MA-shuhn) A long layer of sediments or rocks that look alike and were formed at the same time.

formula (FOR-myuh-luh) **1.** A set of symbols that shows what a chemical compound is made up of. A formula lists the elements in the compound and shows how many atoms of each element there are. In the formula for water, which is H_2O, H_2 means there are two atoms of hydrogen, and O means there is one atom of oxygen. **2.** A set of symbols that expresses a way of figuring something out in mathematics. The formula for figuring out the area of a rectangle is $a = lw$, which means area (a) is equal to length (l) times width (w).

Biography

Dian Fossey

Before Dian Fossey went to Africa, gorillas were thought to be ferocious and violent. Fossey spent 18 years making close observations of these animals in the wild. When one of the gorillas touched her on the hand, it was the first time that a human was known to have made friendly contact with a gorilla. Fossey showed that gorillas are peaceful and that they need to be protected.

□ **fossil**

top: *fossil of a fern from the Pennsylvanian Period*
bottom: *fossil of a group of bony fish from the Eocene Epoch*

Fossey (FOS-ē), **Dian** Born 1932; died 1985. American scientist who studied mountain gorillas in Rwanda.

fossil (FOS-uhl) The hardened remains or traces of a plant or animal that lived long ago. Fossils are often found in **sedimentary rocks.**

fossil fuel A source of energy that was formed millions of years ago from the remains of plants and animals. Oil, natural gas, and coal are fossil fuels.

fossilize (FOS-uh-līz) To change into a fossil. Plants and animals usually become fossilized when layers of sediment gradually harden around them after they die.

Foucault (foo-KŌ), **Jean Bernard Léon** Born 1819; died 1868. French scientist who measured the velocity of light and proved that light moves more slowly in water than in air. He built the first gyroscope in 1852, a year after he made his famous pendulum, known as the Foucault pendulum.

Foucault pendulum A pendulum that was made by Jean Foucault in 1851 to show that the Earth is rotating. As the pendulum swings back and forth in a straight line, the mark it traces on the ground shifts as the Earth rotates.

fractal (FRAK-tuhl) A figure or pattern that appears again and again inside a larger pattern that is exactly like it. The patterns in snowflakes are fractals.

fraction (FRAK-shuhn) A number that compares part of an object or a set with the whole. A fraction is written with a line separating the part from the whole. The fraction $\frac{1}{2}$ means that there is 1 part of a whole that consists of 2 equal parts, or that 1 is being divided by 2.

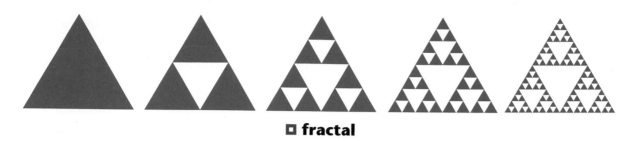

□ **fractal**

The pattern in these fractals is based on a single triangle. From left to right, each figure repeats the preceding pattern three times at a smaller size to make a new design using exactly the same pattern.

fracture (FRAK-cher) A break or crack, especially in a bone.

Franklin (FRANGK-lin), **Benjamin** Born 1706; died 1790. American scientist and public official who discovered that lightning is a source of electricity. He also repeated the experiments of other scientists and developed uses for scientific ideas in everyday life. Some of his inventions include the lightning rod and a stove that was widely used for indoor heating.

Franklin, Rosalind Born 1920; died 1958. British scientist who used x-rays to study DNA molecules. Her research helped lead to the discovery of the structure of DNA.

freeze To change from a liquid to a solid by cooling to the **freezing point.** Water becomes ice when it freezes.

freeze-dry To preserve something, especially food, by freezing it quickly and then putting it in a container and removing all the air from it.

freezing point The temperature at which a liquid becomes a solid. The freezing point of the liquid form of a substance is the same as the **melting point** of its solid form. The freezing point of water is 32° Fahrenheit (0° Celsius), and the freezing point of liquid nitrogen is –345.75° Fahrenheit (–209.89° Celsius).

frequency (FRĒ-kwuhn-sē) A measure of how often an action or movement is repeated within a certain amount of time. The movement of **waves** is measured in terms of frequency. The frequency of radio waves is the number of times per second that the waves pass a particular point.

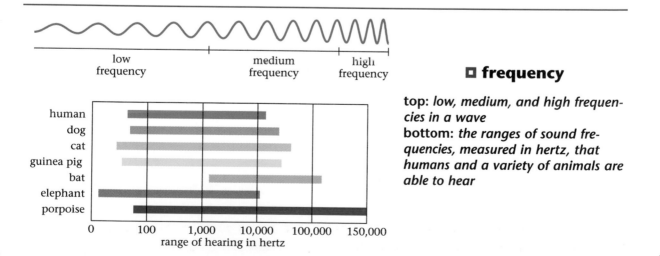

□ **frequency**

top: *low, medium, and high frequencies in a wave*
bottom: *the ranges of sound frequencies, measured in hertz, that humans and a variety of animals are able to hear*

frequency modulation (FRĒ-kwuhn-sē moj-uh-LĀ-shuhn) A method of radio broadcasting that changes the frequency of the radio waves in order to make different sounds come out of the radio's speakers. Frequency modulation lessens the amount of **static** that is heard on the radio. ◻ Frequency modulation is called *FM* for short. ◻ Compare **amplitude modulation**.

freshwater (FRESH-wah-ter) Containing water that is not salty. Rivers and lakes are freshwater bodies that are fed mainly by rain and melting snow.

friction (FRIK-shuhn) The resistance to movement that occurs when two objects are in contact. Friction slows down a ball that is rolling on grass. It also causes the blade of a saw that is cutting wood to get hot. There is less friction between smooth surfaces than between rough surfaces.

◻ **friction**

The ball on the left keeps rolling because the smooth sidewalk does not cause much friction. On the right the ball slows down quickly because of friction from the rough grass.

Frigid Zone (FRIJ-id zōn) Either of two regions of the Earth that are farthest away from the equator: the **North Frigid Zone** and the **South Frigid Zone**. The Frigid Zones have cold weather all year, and a mass of permanent ice covers the area around the poles.

Did You Know?
friction
When something rubs against something else, some of its energy is changed from motion to heat. The rubbing is called friction. Friction is bad for machines because when machine parts rub together, they lose energy that should be doing work and start to get hot. But friction can also be good. Asteroids entering the Earth's atmosphere get hot from rubbing against air molecules and usually burn up before they hit the ground.

frog A type of amphibian that has smooth, moist skin, webbed feet, long hind legs used for leaping, and no tail when fully grown. Frogs mostly live in or around water, but some species, such as tree frogs, live on land.

front The boundary between two large air masses that have different temperatures. Fronts are named after the air mass that is moving into the region where the other mass already is. For example, a mass of warm air that is moving into a mass of cold air is called a warm front.

frost Tiny ice crystals that form in a layer on the surface of something, such as grass or a window. Frost is formed when water vapor in the air condenses at a temperature below freezing.

frostbite Damage to a part of the body that is caused by extreme cold. Frostbite results from the gradual loss of proper blood flow.

fructose (FRUHK-tōs) A sugar found in honey, many fruits, and some vegetables. Fructose is similar to glucose and is an important source of energy found in food.

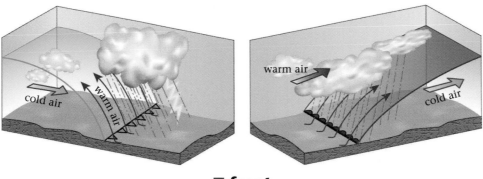

□ front

In a cold front (left), a mass of cold air moves into a mass of warm air, pushing the warm air up. In a warm front (right), a mass of warm air rises over a mass of cold air.

fruit   The part of a flowering plant that contains the seeds. A fruit is the ripe ovary of a flower. Berries, grains, nuts, and pods are fruits.

Did You Know?

fruit

We think of a fruit as a plant part that we eat for snacks or dessert because it is sweet, but scientifically speaking, a fruit is the part of a flowering plant that contains seeds. It may or may not taste sweet.
In this sense, tomatoes, peppers, and cucumbers are fruits, just as apples and strawberries are.

fruiting body   A part in a living thing, especially a fungus, that produces tiny **spores**, the structures that some living things use to reproduce. In fungi, such as mushrooms, the fruiting body is the part that is visible to the eye.

fuel   **1.** A substance that can be burned to produce energy. Coal, wood, and gas are fuels. **2.** A radioactive substance, especially a form of uranium, that is used to produce energy in a nuclear reactor.

fuel cell   A device that uses a chemical reaction to make electricity. Fuel cells are used in space shuttles, where they create electricity by combining hydrogen gas with oxygen.

fuel rod   A metal tube containing a radioactive substance that is used to produce energy in a nuclear reactor.

fulcrum   (FUL-kruhm) The point or support on which a lever turns. The fulcrum of

□ fulcrum

top: *A seesaw with children of equal weight at the same distance from the fulcrum will balance.*
bottom: *When one weight moves closer to the fulcrum, that end of the seesaw will rise.*

a seesaw is the base on which the seesaw moves up and down.

full moon   The Moon when it is appears as a fully lit disk. A full moon happens when the Moon and Sun are on opposite sides of the Earth, and the Moon is not in the Earth's shadow. ◻ See picture at **moon**.

Fulton   (FUL-tuhn), **Robert** Born 1765; died 1815. American inventor who in 1807 developed a boat powered by a steam engine that became widely used throughout the United States.

fume   Smoke, vapor, or gas, especially if irritating, harmful, or smelly.

fungus   (FUHNG-guhs) A member of a kingdom of living things that produce off-spring by means of **spores**. Most fungi get their nutrients by feeding off other living organisms or dead plants and animals. Mushrooms, molds, yeasts, and mildews are all fungi. *Plural form:* **fungi** (FUN-jī *or* FUNG-gī).

fuse   **1.** A safety device that protects an electric circuit from becoming overloaded. Fuses contain a length of thin wire that melts and causes an interruption in the circuit if too much current flows through it. Fuses have largely been replaced by **circuit**

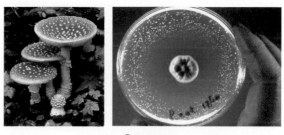

◻ **fungus**

left: *poisonous amanita mushrooms*
right: *mold growing in a petri dish*

breakers. **2.** Something that sets off an explosive charge. A fuse can be a cord or strand of soft fibers that is lighted at one end to carry a flame to the explosive. It can also be a mechanical device attached to the explosive.

fusion   (FYOO-zhuhn) **1.** The joining together of the nuclei of two different atoms resulting in the formation of a new atom and the release of **energy.** The new atom has more protons and neutrons than the first two atoms. Fusion takes place when atoms are heated to very high temperatures, making them move so fast that they crash into each other and unite. Stars produce their heat and light through fusion. **2.** A mixture or blend of two materials, such as plastics or metals, that is made by melting. Bronze is a fusion that is made by melting copper and tin.

Gg

Gabor (GAH-bor *or* guh-BOR), **Dennis** Born 1900; died 1979. Hungarian-born British scientist who invented the technique for making holograms in 1947.

galaxy (GAL-uhk-sē) A huge mass of stars, gas, and dust clouds that exists in one area of space. The Earth and the Solar System are located in the Milky Way galaxy. Scientists think that there may be as many as 100 billion galaxies in the universe.

Galen (GĀ-luhn) Born 130? AD; died 200? AD. Greek doctor who described the parts and functions of the human body, based mostly on knowledge that he gained from dissecting animals. Galen's work greatly influenced European medicine until the 17th century.

galena (guh-LĒ-nuh) A gray, shiny mineral that looks like metal and is made of lead and sulfur.

Galileo Galilei (gal-uh-LĀ-ō gal-uh-LĀ) Born 1564; died 1642. Italian scientist who was the first person to use a telescope to study the stars and planets. He discovered

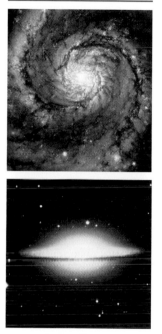

□ **galaxy**

The Whirlpool (top) and Sombrero (bottom) galaxies are both shaped like a spiral. The Sombrero galaxy is seen from the side.

Biography

Galileo Galilei

When Galileo Galilei heard about an instrument invented in Norway that made distant things appear closer, he quickly went to work to create his own telescope, using lenses that were made for reading glasses. He realized that the telescope could be made stronger if he changed the shape of the lenses. His improvement on the telescope allowed him to discover the moons of Jupiter.

that the Earth's Moon reflects the Sun's light, that Jupiter has moons, and that Venus has phases like those of Earth's Moon.

gallbladder (GAWL-blad-er) A small sac in the body that stores **bile**. The gallbladder is located below the liver and releases bile into the small intestine during digestion.

gallon (GAL-uhn) A unit of volume used for measuring liquids, equal to 4 quarts (3.79 liters). □ See Table on page 148.

galvanize (GAL-vuh-nīz) To coat iron or steel with a thin layer of zinc so that it does not rust. Metal is usually galvanized by the process called **electrolysis.**

gamete (GAM-ēt) *See* **sex cell.**

gamma ray (GAM-uh rā) A stream of electromagnetic radiation that is similar to x-rays but has shorter wavelengths. Gamma rays are given off by radioactive materials during **radioactive decay.**

garnet (GAR-nit) A deep red mineral that has a glassy appearance and is found especially in metamorphic rocks.

gas **1.** One of the three basic forms of matter. The molecules of a gas are constantly moving about. For this reason, a gas has no set shape or volume and will spread out to fill any space that is available. **2.** *See* **gasoline.**

gaseous (GAS-ē-uhs *or* GASH-uhs) Relating to or being a gas.

gas exchange The exchange of gases, especially oxygen and carbon dioxide, between a living thing and its environment. Gas exchange in green plants takes place during **photosynthesis.** In humans and other animals, gas exchange takes place during **respiration.**

gasoline (GAS-uh-lēn) A mixture of liquids made from petroleum. Because gasoline burns very easily, it is used as a fuel for engines. ◻ Gasoline is called *gas* for short.

gastric (GAS-trik) Relating to the stomach.

gastropod (GAS-truh-pod) A type of mollusk that has a head with eyes and feelers and a muscle under its body that it moves with. Most gastropods, such as snails, have shells, while some, such as slugs, do not. Gastropods live both on land and in the water.

gauge (GĀJ) An instrument that is used to measure or keep track of a quantity. A car has gauges that show the car's speed and the temperature of the engine.

Gay-Lussac (gā-luh-SAK), **Joseph Louis** Born 1778; died 1850. French scientist who studied gases. In 1808, he developed a for-

mula that explains how gases behave when they combine with each other. This formula is now known as Gay-Lussac's law.

gear A wheel with bumps called teeth around its rim. The teeth of one gear fit into the spaces between the teeth of another gear, so that when the first gear turns, it causes the second to turn also. The gear is a simple machine. ◻ See picture at **machine.**

Geiger (GĪ-ger), **Hans Wilhelm** Born 1882; died 1945. German scientist who invented devices that detect radiation, including the Geiger counter in 1908.

Geiger counter An instrument that detects and measures radioactivity, such as x-rays or gamma rays. The Geiger counter is named after Hans Wilhelm Geiger.

gelatin (JEL-uh-tuhn) A substance that is made by boiling a mixture of water and the skin, bones, and tendons of animals. When the mixture cools, it forms a jelly that can be used in foods, medicines, and glues.

Gell-Mann (GEL-MAN), **Murray** Born 1929. American scientist who helped classify the particles that make up the parts of an atom. In 1964, Gell-Mann also came up with the idea of the particles known as quarks.

gene A tiny part of a chromosome, made up of molecules of **DNA.** Traits are passed from parent to offspring through the genes. The shape of a plant leaf, the color of an animal's coat, and the texture of a person's hair are all determined by genes.

generation (jen-er-Ā-shuhn) A group of plants, animals, or cells of the same kind that are born around the same time. Parents and their offspring are two different generations.

generator (JEN-uh-rā-ter) A machine that uses moving parts to make electricity. Generators make an electric current by spinning a coiled electric wire between the two poles

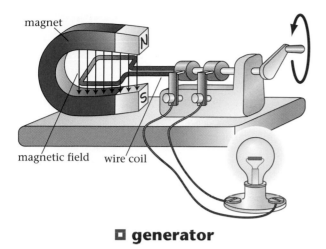

□ generator

of a magnet. When the wire spins inside the magnetic field created by the magnet, an electric current flows through it. **□** A generator is also called a *dynamo*.

gene-splicing   (JĒN-splī-sing) The joining together of genes or pieces of genes that are then placed inside a cell or virus. The genes used in gene-splicing may come from different organisms. Gene-splicing is used in **genetic engineering**.

genetic code   (juh-NET-ik KŌD) The arrangement of the smaller molecules that make up the large molecules of DNA and RNA. The genetic code determines the type and action of each cell in the body.

genetic engineering   The science of changing the genes in the cells of a living thing. Scientists use genetic engineering to control the traits produced by genes. Scientists also use it to make natural substances, such as hormones, that can be used to fight disease.

genetics   (juh-NET-iks) The scientific study of how traits are passed from parents to offspring. Genetics is a branch of biology.

genitals   (JEN-i-tuhlz) The external organs of mating and reproduction in male and female animals.

genome   (JĒ-nōm) All the genes that are contained in the chromosomes of a living thing.

genus   (JĒ-nuhs) One of the major groups in the classification of living things, made up of a group of species that are similar to each other. A genus is below a family and above a species. *Plural form*: **genera** (JEN-er-uh). **□** See Table on page 47.

geocentric   (jē-ō-SEN-trik) Having the Earth as the center. In ancient and medieval times, people thought the universe was geocentric. **□** Compare **heliocentric**.

geode   (JĒ-ōd) A hollow, rounded rock that is lined on the inside with crystals.

□ geode

geodesic dome
(jē-uh-DES-ik DŌM *or* jē-uh-DĒ-sik DŌM) A structure that has the overall shape of a dome or the upper part of a sphere but is made up of many triangular sections that fit together.

□ geodesic dome

geographic north   (JĒ-uh-graf-ik NORTH) *See* **true north**.

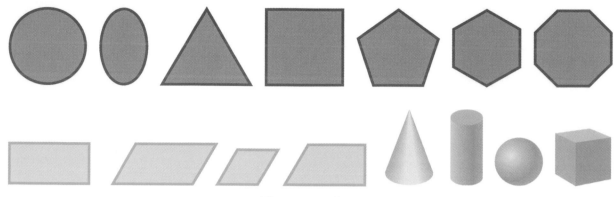

◻ geometry

top row from left to right: *circle, ellipse, equilateral triangle, square, pentagon, hexagon, and octagon*
bottom row from left to right: *rectangle, parallelogram, rhombus, trapezoid, cone, cylinder, sphere, and cube*

geography (jē-OG-ruh-fē) The scientific study of the Earth's surface. Geography includes the study of land features, climates, and natural resources.

geologic time (jē-uh-LOJ-ik TĪM) The period of time that covers the history of the Earth, from the time it formed, about 4.6 billion years ago, until today. ◻ See Table on pages 102–103.

geology (jē-OL-uh-jē) The scientific study of the history and materials of the Earth. Geology includes the study of rocks, minerals, and land features, and of the changes these have undergone over billions of years.

geomagnetism (jē-ō-MAG-ni-tiz-uhm) The magnetism of the Earth. The Earth gets most of its geomagnetism from the movement of the molten material in the outer part of its core.

geometry (jē-OM-uh-trē) The study of points, lines, planes, surfaces, angles, and solids. Geometry is a branch of mathematics.

geothermal (jē-ō-THER-muhl) Made hot by the heat that is contained in rocks below the Earth's surface. The water in hot springs and geysers is geothermal.

germ A microscopic organism or structure that causes disease. Bacteria and viruses are germs.

German measles (JUR-muhn MĒ-zuhlz) A contagious disease in which a person has fever and a rash on the skin. German measles can be dangerous if caught by a pregnant woman because it can harm the developing baby. ◻ German measles is also called *rubella*.

germ cell An egg or sperm; a sex cell.

germination (jer-muh-NĀ-shuhn) The sprouting of a seed, spore, or bud. Germina-

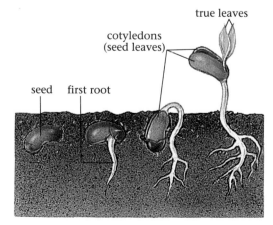

◻ germination

germination of a bean seed

tion usually takes place in the spring, when climate and soil are warm and moist.

gestation (je-STĀ-shuhn) The period of time that an animal spends inside its mother's body before being born. Gestation in humans is about nine months.

geyser (GĪ-zer) A natural hot spring that regularly shoots a spray of steam and hot water into the air. The water is heated when it comes into contact with hot rock or steam underground. Old Faithful, one of more than 200 geysers in Yellowstone National Park, erupts on average every 65 minutes to heights of 150 feet (about 46 meters).

□ **geyser**

Old Faithful geyser in Yellowstone National Park, Wyoming

g-force A force that is caused by acceleration. An acceleration that causes a g-force equal to that of the force of gravity is referred to as 1-G. Jet pilots often experience 3-Gs or 4-Gs when they make a turn.

giant star (JĪ-uhnt STAR) A star that has become very large and very bright because of the enormous heat in its center. Stars become giant stars near the end of their existence.

gibbous moon (GIB uhs MOON) The Moon when it appears more than half lit but less than fully lit. A gibbous moon happens between a full moon and a half moon.

gigabyte (GIG-uh-bīt) A unit of information that can be stored in a computer memory and is equal to 1,024 megabytes or 1,073,741,824 bytes. The number

1,073,741,824 is equal to 2 multiplied by 2 thirty times.

Gilbert (GIL-bert), **William** Born 1544; died 1603. English scientist who was the first person to study and explain the concepts of electricity and magnetism in depth. In 1600, he wrote the first major scientific book published in England. In it, he introduced the words *electricity* and *magnetic pole*.

gill The organ that is used for breathing by many animals that live in water, such as fish and tadpoles. Gills are made up of membranes and small blood vessels. Oxygen in the water passes through the gills into the blood, and carbon dioxide in the blood passes through the gills into the water.

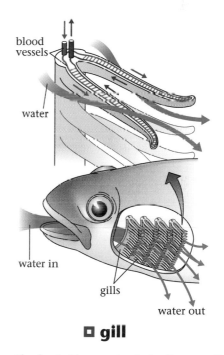

□ **gill**

Fish breathe by taking water into the mouth and passing it through gills on each side of the head. Blood in the gills picks up oxygen as the water flows through.

gizzard (GIZ-erd) A pouch behind the stomach in birds. It has a thick lining and often contains swallowed sand or grit, which helps to break food into small pieces.

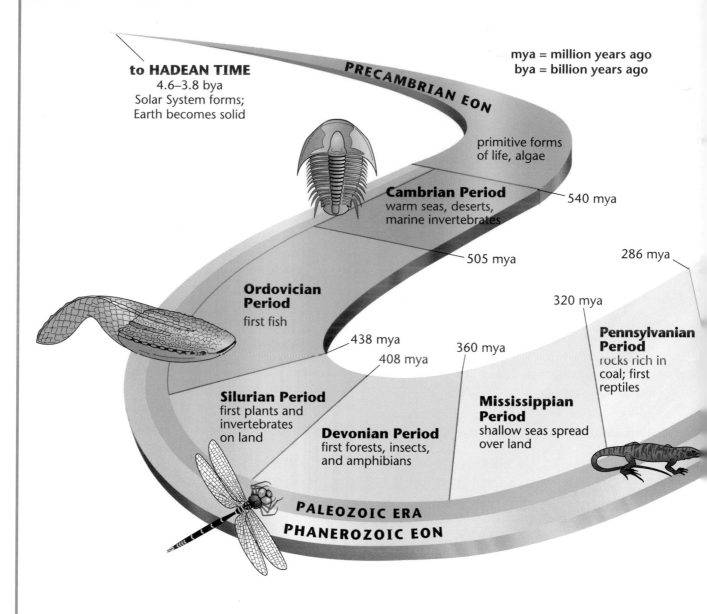

to HADEAN TIME
4.6–3.8 bya
Solar System forms;
Earth becomes solid

mya = million years ago
bya = billion years ago

PRECAMBRIAN EON

primitive forms
of life, algae

Cambrian Period
warm seas, deserts,
marine invertebrates

540 mya

505 mya

286 mya

Ordovician
Period
first fish

320 mya

Pennsylvanian
Period
rocks rich in
coal; first
reptiles

438 mya

408 mya

360 mya

Silurian Period
first plants and
invertebrates
on land

Devonian Period
first forests, insects,
and amphibians

Mississippian
Period
shallow seas spread
over land

PALEOZOIC ERA
PHANEROZOIC EON

The Earth is about 4.6 billion years old. During the first 800 million years of the Earth's history (Hadean Time), the Solar System was still forming and the Earth was becoming solid. During the next 3.8 billion years, the oceans formed, the continents took shape, and an amazing variety of life forms appeared on Earth, including bacteria, algae, plants, and animals. Through the years, many species died out and many new ones evolved to take their place.

To help them study the Earth's history, scientists have divided the past 3.8 billion years into **eons, eras, periods,** and **epochs,** just as a year is divided into months, weeks, days, and hours to help us keep track of time. Eons are the longest divisions of time, and epochs are the shortest.

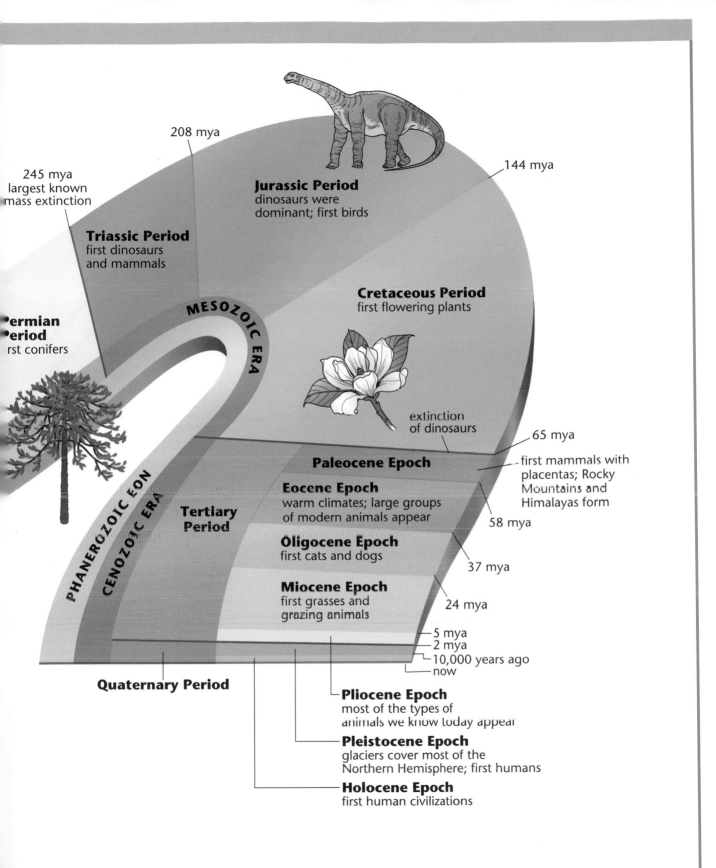

245 mya
largest known
mass extinction

208 mya

144 mya

Jurassic Period
dinosaurs were
dominant; first birds

Triassic Period
first dinosaurs
and mammals

Cretaceous Period
first flowering plants

MESOZOIC ERA

**Permian
Period**
first conifers

extinction
of dinosaurs

65 mya

PHANEROZOIC EON

CENOZOIC ERA

Paleocene Epoch

first mammals with
placentas; Rocky
Mountains and
Himalayas form

Eocene Epoch
warm climates; large groups
of modern animals appear

58 mya

**Tertiary
Period**

Oligocene Epoch
first cats and dogs

37 mya

Miocene Epoch
first grasses and
grazing animals

24 mya

5 mya
2 mya
10,000 years ago
now

Quaternary Period

Pliocene Epoch
most of the types of
animals we know today appear

Pleistocene Epoch
glaciers cover most of the
Northern Hemisphere; first humans

Holocene Epoch
first human civilizations

glacier (GLĀ-sher) A large mass of ice flowing very slowly through a valley or spreading outward from a central point. Glaciers form over many years from packed snow in areas where snow piles up faster than it melts. A glacier is always moving.

Did You Know?

glacier
During the last Ice Age, some 10,000 years ago, much of North America was covered by glaciers that were over a mile thick. South America, by contrast, did not get covered by glaciers except in the Andes mountains.

gland An organ in the body of an animal that produces a particular substance and releases it into the blood or into a duct. The thyroid and pituitary glands produce **hormones.** Glands in the mouth produce saliva.

glass A hard substance that lets light through and breaks easily. Glass is made by melting sand with lime or sodium carbonate.

Global Positioning System (GLŌ-buhl puh-ZISH-uh-ning SIS-tuhm) A system that shows the exact position of objects on Earth by displaying their latitude and longitude on a computer screen. The instruments in the Global Positioning Systems get their information by exchanging signals with satellites in orbit around the Earth. ◻ Global Positioning System is called *GPS* for short.

global warming A rise in the average temperature of the Earth's atmosphere. Many scientists believe that global warming is caused by the release of **greenhouse gases.** Global warming is believed to be capable of causing major changes in weather patterns.

glucose (GLŌŌ-kōs) A sugar that all animals need in their diet in order to live. Glucose is produced by **photosynthesis** and is found in all plants.

glue A thick, sticky substance that can be used to join things together. Glue is made of gelatin, epoxy, or other substances.

glycerin (GLIS-er-in) *See* **glycerol.**

glycerol (GLIS-er-awl) A sweet liquid that is made from animal fats and oils. Glycerol is similar to syrup and is used as a sweetener and in making soaps and explosives. ◻ Glycerol is also called *glycerin.*

gneiss (NĪS) A rock with light and dark layers that are often folded into curves. It is made mainly of the minerals quartz and feldspar. Gneiss forms when rocks such as granite are under great pressure from surrounding rocks. ◻ See Table on page 208.

Goddard (GOD-erd), **Robert Hutchings** Born 1882; died 1945. American sci-

Biography

Robert Hutchings Goddard
There was no such thing as a rocket when Robert Goddard was a boy. But that did not stop him from being fascinated with the idea of space flight. Using mathematics, Goddard showed how rockets could be powered, and he also predicted that someday a rocket would be sent to the Moon. Today's rockets are based on Goddard's ideas.

entist who was one of the first people to propose that rockets could be used to travel into space. In 1926, he built the first successful rocket to get its energy from a liquid fuel.

Goeppert-Mayer (GUHP-urt-MĀ-er), **Maria** Born 1906; died 1972. German-born American scientist who explained why some atoms are likely to break down into other types of atoms while others are not. She was the first to figure out that this had to do with the arrangement of protons and neutrons in the nucleus of an atom.

gold A shiny, yellow chemical element that is the most easily shaped of all metals. Gold is a good conductor of heat and electricity and does not rust easily. It is used to make jewelry. ◻ See Table on pages 178–179.

gonad (GŌ-nad) An organ in the body that produces sex cells. Ovaries and testes are gonads.

Goodall (GUD-awl), **Jane** Born 1934. British zoologist whose study of the lives and habitat of chimpanzees has greatly increased understanding of primate behavior. She founded a research center in Tanzania in 1960, and she has been a leader in conservation efforts around the world.

◻ **Jane Goodall**

googol (GŌŌ-gawl) The number that is written as 1 followed by 100 zeros.

Gorgas (GOR-guhs), **William Crawford**

Born 1854; died 1920. American army surgeon who stopped the spread of yellow fever in Cuba and Panama between 1898 and 1913 by destroying mosquitoes in the area.

gorge A deep, narrow canyon with very steep sides. A gorge often has a stream that flows through it.

gorilla (guh-RIL-uh) The largest and most powerful of the apes, found in the forests and mountains of central Africa. Gorillas have a heavy body with dark hair, live on the ground, and feed mostly on leaves and stems.

GPS See **Global Positioning System.**

gradient (GRĀ-dē-uhnt) **1.** The amount that something slopes up or down. The higher the gradient is, the steeper the slope is. **2.** The rate at which temperature or pressure changes over a distance. A swimming pool with a high temperature gradient has a big difference in temperature between the water near the surface and the water near the bottom.

◻ **gradient**

The gradient on the left side of the hill is gentle enough for trees to take root. Trees cannot grow on the steeper gradient on the right.

graduated (GRAJ-ōō-ā-tid) Marked with a series of short lines that are at equal

105

distance from each other in order to measure length, volume, or temperature. Rulers and thermometers are graduated instruments.

graft **1.** A plant part, such as a stem with a bud, that is joined to the stem or root of another plant so that the two grow together as a single plant. Grafts are used to create new or healthier plants without having to grow the plant from a seed. **2.** The moving of a body tissue, such as skin or bone, from one part to another. Doctors sometimes use grafts of healthy skin to cover severe burns and allow them to heal.

◻ graft

A stem with buds from one plant is cut so that it fits tightly into a stem with roots from another plant. When joined, the two plants will grow together to make a new plant.

grain **1.** A small, hard seed, especially of wheat, corn, or rice. **2.** A small particle of something, such as salt, pollen, or sand.

gram A unit of mass or weight in the metric system, equal to $\frac{1}{1000}$ of a kilogram. ◻ See Table on page 148.

granite (GRAN-it) A common rock that is made of the minerals quartz, feldspar, and mica, and usually has a pink or gray color. It is formed underground in pools of magma that become solid when they cool. ◻ See Table on page 208.

graph A diagram that shows how one group of quantities relates to another. Graphs usually have lines, bars, or shaded areas that show how a quantity in one group depends on or changes with another.

graphite (GRAF-īt) A dark or black form of carbon in which the carbon atoms are joined together in sheets. The sheets slide off each other easily when graphite touches something, leaving a mark. For this reason, graphite is used in pencils and paints.

grass A kind of plant with narrow leaves, hollow stems, and clusters of small flowers. Grasses include many plants that are grown as food or for grazing. Wheat, rice, barley, sugar cane, and bamboo are grasses. ◻ See picture at **leaf.**

grassland A large area of mostly flat land that is covered with grasses and has few

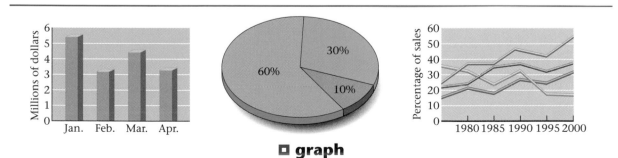

◻ graph

left to right: *a bar graph, a pie chart, and a line graph*

trees. Prairies, steppes, and savannas are examples of grasslands. A grassland is a kind of **biome.**

gravitation   (grav-i-TĀ-shuhn) The force of attraction that causes objects to be drawn toward each other simply because they have mass. The more mass the objects have and the closer together they are, the stronger the gravitation between them is.

gravity   (GRAV-i-tē) An invisible force that pulls all objects toward each other. The more mass the objects have and the closer together they are, the stronger this force is. The gravity of the Earth pulls all objects toward the Earth's center.

Did You Know?

gravity
The force of gravity depends on the amount of mass in an object. The Moon has much less mass than the Earth, and you would weigh six times less on the Moon than you do on Earth. The large planet Jupiter has more mass than the Earth, and on it you would weigh two and one-half times what you weigh on Earth.

greenhouse effect   The trapping of the Sun's heat in the Earth's atmosphere. The greenhouse effect is caused by the presence of greenhouse gases in the atmosphere. Many scientists believe it is the main cause of **global warming.** ◻ See picture on page 108.

greenhouse gas   A gas in the atmosphere that makes the greenhouse effect worse. Carbon dioxide, water vapor, and methane are greenhouse gases.

Greenwich Time   (GREN-ich TĪM) *See* **universal time.**

ground   **1.** The solid surface of the Earth. **2.** A connection that is made between an electric wire and the Earth so that electric currents that are too strong can be sent away before damaging the circuits.

groundwater   (GROWND-wah-ter) Water that collects underground from rainfall and melting snow and ice. The water fills the small empty spaces in soil and rocks and flows toward a lower point, such as a stream or river. Groundwater can be brought up to the surface for drinking water through wells.

group   One of the columns of chemical elements in the Periodic Table. Elements in the same group behave in similar ways in chemical reactions. ◻ See Table on pages 178–179.

growth   **1.** The process of growing, especially in size or amount. Growth in living things may stop in adulthood, as in the case of humans, or it may continue throughout life, as in most plants. Growth in living things is caused by an increase in the number of cells. **2.** Something that grows. A wart is a growth on the skin.

growth ring   A layer of wood that forms in a plant during one period of growth. Growth rings can be seen when a tree is cut crosswise. Growth rings usually take a full year to form, but changes in the environment can cause a plant to produce more than one growth ring in a year.

◻ **growth ring**

grub   A beetle or other insect that has hatched from an egg but is not fully grown. Grubs look like small worms.

guano (GWAH-nō) A substance that is made up mostly of the wastes of sea birds or bats. Guano is used as a fertilizer.

guard cell A cell that controls the opening and closing of the small pores, called stomata, on the surface of a leaf. Guard cells allow gases and water vapor to pass into and out of a plant. ◘ See picture at **stoma.**

gulf A large body of ocean water that is partly surrounded by land. A gulf is usually larger than a **bay.**

Gulf Stream A warm ocean current in the Atlantic Ocean that is found off the eastern coast of North America. The Gulf Stream flows northward and eastward from the Gulf of Mexico. Part of the current continues across the Atlantic to warm the coast of northwest Europe.

gully (GUHL-ē) A ditch or channel that is cut into the Earth by flowing water. Gullies are usually dry except after periods of heavy rainfall or after the melting of snow or ice.

A Closer Look

Greenhouse Effect

A greenhouse is designed to trap the Sun's energy. Sunlight can go through the greenhouse's glass roof, but the heat given off by the soil can't go back out through the glass, so it stays inside and warms the air.

*A similar process takes place on the Earth as a whole, where the atmosphere acts like a glass roof. Sunlight comes through the atmosphere, warming the soil and the oceans on the Earth. The Earth then gives off heat, sending it back up into the atmosphere. Although some of this heat does manage to pass back out into space, much of it is trapped by water vapor, carbon dioxide, and other gases in the atmosphere that absorb it. For this reason, these gases are known as **greenhouse gases,** and the whole process is called the **greenhouse effect.***

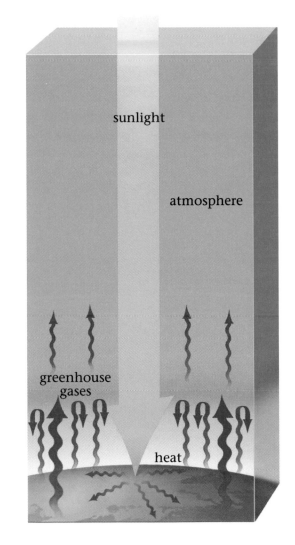

sunlight

atmosphere

greenhouse gases

heat

gum　**1.** A thick, sticky juice that is produced by some plants and trees. Gum dissolves in water and hardens when it is exposed to air. Gum is used to make glue and rubber. **2.** The firm flesh that surrounds and supports the teeth.

gut　The tube in the body of an invertebrate that is used for digestion.

gymnosperm　(JIM-nuh-sperm) A plant that produces seeds that are not contained in a fruit, pod, or hard outer shell. Most gymnosperms have **cones**. The seeds of gymnosperms grow underneath the scales of female cones. ◻ Compare **angiosperm**.

gypsum　(JIP-suhm) A soft mineral made of calcium and phosphate. Gypsum is clear or white. It is used to make plaster of Paris, wall boards, cement, and fertilizers.

gyroscope　(JĪ-ruh-skōp) An instrument that is made of a disk or wheel that spins about an axis like a top. The axis stays in one place, no matter how the thing that holds it turns or twists. Gyroscopes are used to keep boats and airplanes on their courses and to keep spacecraft in the right position.

Hh

habitat (HAB-i-tat) The area in which an animal or plant normally lives, such as a rain forest, a pond, or a coral reef. A particular habitat is often home to many different plants and animals. Cactus, lizards, scorpions, and many insects can live in a desert habitat.

Hadean Time (hā-DĒ-uhn TĪM) The period of time during the history of the Earth starting about 4.6 billion years ago and ending about 3.8 billion years ago. During the Hadean Time, the Solar System was forming, and the Earth was becoming solid. ◻ See Table on pages 102–103.

Hahn (HAHN), **Otto** Born 1879; died 1968. German scientist who studied radioactive elements and helped discover several new ones. His work on uranium led to the discovery of nuclear fission.

hail Water that falls to the Earth as small, rough balls of ice and hard snow. Hail usually falls during thunderstorms and can be very damaging to crops. It is a form of **precipitation.**

Did You Know?

hail
Hail forms when raindrops are blown up and down within a cloud. The drops pass repeatedly through layers of warm and freezing air and collect coatings of ice until they are too heavy for the winds to keep them from falling. If you cut a very large hailstone in half, you will see it has layers like an onion.

hair **1.** One of the thin strands that grow from the skin of humans and other mammals. Hair provides protection against the cold in most mammals. **2.** A thin strand found on other animals, especially insects.

half-life The length of time needed for half of an amount of a radioactive element to decay. If the half-life of an element is 4 minutes long and you start with 100 grams of it, only 50 grams of it will be left after 4 minutes, and the other 50 grams will have decayed into another element. After another 4 minutes, only 25 grams will be left.

halite (HAL-īt *or* HĀ-līt) A white or clear mineral that is made of sodium chloride. Halite is found on land where lakes have dried out. Halite is used as table salt.

Halley (HAL-ē), **Edmund** Born 1656; died 1742. English astronomer best known for his study of comets. Halley figured out the orbit of a comet that had appeared in 1531, 1607, and 1682, and he accurately determined that it would return in 1758. This comet is now named for him.

Halley's comet (HAL-ēz KOM-it *or* HĀ-lēz KOM-it) A comet that is very bright and that takes 76 years to make one complete orbit around the Sun. Halley's comet was last seen in 1986, and it is named after Edmund Halley.

◻ **Halley's comet**

halo (HĀ-lō) A hazy ring of whitish or rainbow-colored light in the sky around the

Sun or Moon. It is caused when light rays are bent by ice crystals floating high in the sky.

hamstrings The group of muscles at the back of the thigh that bends the knee.

haploid (HAP-loyd) Having only a single set of chromosomes in a cell. In animals, only the sex cells are haploid. ◻ Compare **diploid.**

hard disk A rigid magnetic disk that is part of a computer and is used for storing information.

hard drive A disk drive that reads data that is stored on **hard disks.**

hardness (HARD-nis) A measure of how easily a mineral can be scratched. Hardness is measured on the **Mohs scale.**

hardware The pieces of equipment that make up a computer system. Hardware includes computer chips, disk drives, monitors, cables, modems, speakers, and printers. ◻ Compare **software.**

hard water Water that has a lot of salts dissolved in it. Hard water makes it difficult for soap to form lather. ◻ Compare **soft water.**

Harvey (HAR-vē), **William** Born 1578; died 1657. English doctor who was the first person to demonstrate how the heart works and how blood circulates through the human body (1628).

Hawking (HAW-king), **Stephen William** Born 1942. British scientist known for his study of black holes and the origin of the universe, especially the big bang theory.

◻ **Stephen Hawking**

hay fever An allergy to pollen that causes sneezing, itching, and watery eyes. Hay fever is caused by the pollens of many different plants, especially ragweed and certain trees and grasses.

hazardous waste (HAZ-er-duhs) Poisonous material that is left over from human activity. Hazardous waste can be harmful to health and to the environment if it is not stored properly. Radioactive material left over from nuclear power plants is an example of hazardous waste.

heart The organ that pumps blood through the body. The hearts of humans

Biography

William Harvey

Before William Harvey, no one understood that blood actually circulates through the body. Harvey showed that the heart is a pump that forces blood around the body and back to the heart. Although it took many years for his ideas to be accepted, they eventually led others to carry out important research on circulation and the heart.

Did You Know?

heart

If your pulse is 70 beats a minute, your heart beats 4,200 times per hour. That means 100,800 beats per day, 36,792,000 beats per year, and nearly 3 billion beats if you live to be 80. Over that time, your heart moves enough blood to fill more than 1,000,000 barrels.

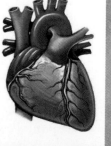

and other mammals are made of muscle and have four main parts or chambers.

heart attack   A sudden stop in the normal working of the heart. Heart attacks are usually caused by a blockage in an artery that carries blood to the heart muscle.

heat   **1.** A form of energy that is caused by the motion of molecules. Heat moves from hotter things to colder things until everything has the same level of energy. The amount of heat contained by a substance depends on how much of the substance there is. **2.** *See* **estrus.**

heat exchanger   A device that transfers heat from one object to another. A car radiator is a heat exchanger. It transfers the heat in a liquid that has circulated through the engine to the air so that the engine does not get too hot and melt.

height   The distance above a level, such as the distance from sea level to the top of a mountain.

heliocentric   (hē-lē-ō-SEN-trik) Having the Sun as the center. The Solar System is heliocentric. ◻ Compare **geocentric.**

heliotropism (hē-lē-OT-ruh-piz-uhm) The growth or turning of a plant toward the Sun.

helium   (HĒ-lē-uhm) A chemical element that is one of the noble gases and is one of the most abundant

◻ **heliotropism**

a field of sunflowers all facing toward the Sun

gases inside stars. Helium is found in natural gas and in small amounts in the Earth's atmosphere. It is one of the lightest elements, and because it does not catch fire easily, it is used as a gas in balloons and blimps. ◻ See Table on pages 178–179.

helix   (HĒ-liks) A three-dimensional spiral curve. A helix can be imagined as winding around a cylinder or cone.

Helmholtz   (HELM-hōlts),   **Hermann Ludwig Ferdinand von** Born 1821; died 1894. German scientist who, in 1847, helped formulate the law of conservation of energy. Helmholtz also studied the senses of hearing and vision. In 1851, he invented an instrument for examining the inner parts of the eye.

hematite   (HĒ-muh-tīt) A reddish or silvery mineral made of iron and oxygen. Hematite is used as a source of iron.

hemisphere   (HEM-i-sfeer) **1.** One half of a sphere. **2.** Either of the halves of the Earth, as divided by the equator or a meridian. **3.** Either of the two halves of the upper part of the brain in humans and other animals.

hemoglobin   (HĒ-muh-glō-bin) A protein in the blood that contains iron and carries molecules of oxygen from the lungs to the tissues of the body. Hemoglobin is found in red blood cells and gives them their red color.

herb   **1.** A type of plant that has no wood in its trunk, stem, or roots. Herbs reproduce by means of seeds and often die at the end of the growing season. **2.** A plant that is used to make medicines. **3.** A plant with a distinct smell or taste that is used to flavor food. Basil and oregano are herbs.

herbicide   (HER-bi-sīd *or* UR-bi-sīd) A chemical compound that is used to kill unwanted plants, such as weeds.

herbivore   (HUR-bi-vor *or* UR-bi-vor) An animal that eats plants. Herbivores include insects and large mammals, such as elephants. Hoofed mammals, like deer and pigs, are all herbivores.

hereditary (huh-RED-i-tair-ē) Passed from parent to offspring through the **genes.** Height is usually a hereditary trait.

heredity (huh-RED-i-tē) The passing of traits from parents to offspring through the **genes.** The appearance, size, and shape of all living things depends on heredity.

hermaphrodite (her-MAF-ruh-dīt) A plant or animal that has both male and female organs of reproduction. Earthworms and most flowering plants are hermaphrodites.

Hero (HĒ-rō) Lived in the first century AD. Greek mathematician who invented machines that were powered by water and steam. He also developed a formula for determining the area of a triangle.

herpetology (her-pi-TOL-uh-jē) The scientific study of reptiles and amphibians.

Herschel (HER-shuhl), **William** Born 1738; died 1822. British astronomer who discovered the planet Uranus in 1781. Herschel also identified more than 800 binary stars and 2,500 nebulae.

hertz A unit used to measure the frequency of vibrations and waves. One hertz is equal to one cycle per second. Radio waves are usually measured in megahertz, or millions of hertz.

hexagon (HEK-suh-gon) A flat shape that has six sides. ◻ See picture at **geometry.**

hibernate (HĪ-ber-nāt) To pass the winter in a state of inactivity that is similar to sleep. Animals that hibernate usually live in cold climates. When they hibernate, they are protected from cold and need very little food. ◻ Compare **estivate.**

Did You Know?

hibernate

When amphibians and reptiles hibernate, they are barely alive. Their hearts are barely beating, and their blood is close to freezing. Mammals that hibernate lie in burrows or caves in what looks like deep sleep, but most of them wake up from time to time to roll over and even have a snack, before going back to bed until spring.

hiccups (HIK-uhps) Sudden, quick breaths that are immediately cut off by a closing of the throat. Hiccups are caused by automatic contracting of the diaphragm, the muscle that separates the chest from the belly.

high-tension wire (HĪ-TEN-shuhn wīr) A wire that carries electricity at a high voltage. High-tension wires are used to carry electricity over long distances.

high tide The time when the tide reaches its highest level on the shore. High tide happens twice each day.

Hipparchus (hi-PAR-kuhs) Lived in the second century BC. Greek astronomer who made the first known chart of the stars and planets. Hipparchus calculated the sizes of the Sun and the Moon, and he determined the positions of 850 stars. His observations formed the basis of Ptolemy's model of the universe with Earth at its center.

Hippocrates (hi-POK-ruh-tēz) Born 460? BC; died 377? BC. Greek doctor who took the first steps to make medicine scientific. He and his followers worked to distinguish medicine from superstition by basing their treatment of illness on close observation and logic.

histamine (HIS-tuh-mēn) A chemical compound that is released into the blood during an allergy or when the body is fighting an infection. Histamine causes the itching, sneezing, and hives that are seen in allergies.

histology (hi-STOL-uh-jē) The scientific study of the body tissues that make up living things. In histology, plant and animal tissues are studied under a microscope.

HIV Short for **human immunodeficiency virus.** The virus that causes **AIDS.**

hive A natural or man-made home for bees.

hives Itchy bumps on the skin that are often caused by an allergy, such as an allergy to a particular food.

Hodgkin (HOJ-kin), **Dorothy Mary Crowfoot** Born 1910; died 1994. British scientist who used x-rays to analyze the structure of complex molecules including penicillin, insulin, and vitamin B$_{12}$.

Holmes (HŌMZ), **Arthur** Born 1890; died 1965. British scientist who developed a way to determine how old rocks are by measuring the amount of radioactive material they contain.

Holocene Epoch (HOL-uh-sēn EP-uhk or HŌ-luh-sēn EP-uhk) The period of time during the history of the Earth starting about 10,000 years ago and going all the way up to today. During the Holocene Epoch, human civilizations developed. ◻ The Holocene Epoch is also called the *Recent.* ◻ See Table on pages 102–103.

hologram (HOL-uh-gram or HŌ-luh-gram) A three-dimensional image of an object. Holograms are made by shining laser beams onto mirrors that are placed around the object, and then projecting the reflected light onto a special type of photographic paper.

hominid (HOM-uh-nid) A member of the human species or of certain earlier species that are related to humans. Hominids stand upright, walk on two feet, and have larger brains than other primates, such as chimpanzees and gorillas. All hominids except humans are now extinct.

homogenize (huh-MOJ-uh-nīz) To make a liquid mixture the same throughout by spreading tiny droplets of one substance in another. Milk is homogenized so that the cream does not rise to the top.

Homo sapiens (HŌ-mō SĀ-pē-uhnz) The species name of the modern form of humans. Scientists believe that modern humans evolved in Africa more than 100,000 years ago. All people living today belong to the species *Homo sapiens.*

hoof A hard, thick covering of the toes of certain mammals. Like the fingernails and toenails of humans, hooves are made of **keratin.** Mammals with hooves are called **ungulates.** *Plural form:* **hooves.**

Hooke (HUK), **Robert** Born 1635; died 1703. English scientist who studied plant tissues and fossils under microscopes. Hooke invented the word *cell* to describe the structures he observed. Together with Robert Boyle, he conducted experiments on the behavior of gases that led to the discovery of Boyle's law in 1662.

Hooke's law A scientific law that states that the degree to which an elastic material stretches depends on the amount of force applied to it. The more force that is applied, the more the material will stretch. Hooke's law is named after Robert Hooke.

horizon (huh-RĪ-zuhn) The line along which the Earth and the sky appear to meet. The horizon often looks flat, but it is actually slightly curved because the Earth is a sphere with a round surface.

hormone (HOR-mōn) A chemical compound that is produced in a gland and then carried to another part of the body by the blood. Hormones control many important body activities, such as growth. Hormones act by causing and adjusting chemical reactions in the body.

horn A hard growth on the head of a hoofed mammal. The horns of cows, sheep, and goats grow in pairs, are never shed, and are made of bone covered by **keratin.** The horns of animals like the giraffe and rhinoceros are shed every year.

horsepower (HORS-pow-er) A unit used to measure the power of engines and motors. One horsepower is equal to the power needed to lift 550 pounds one foot in one second. Scientists now use the watt instead of horsepower to measure engine power.

horseshoe crab A type of invertebrate that lives in the ocean and has a large, round shell that covers the body and a stiff, pointed tail. Horseshoe crabs are not true crabs but belong to a different group of arthropods that is quite ancient.

horticulture (HOR-ti-kuhl-cher) The sci-ence of growing fruits, vegetables, and decorative flowers, shrubs, and trees.

host A living thing or cell that serves as a home or a source of food for another living thing. A cat can be host to fleas that feed on its blood. A cell can be host to a virus.

hot spot A volcano that gets its magma from very deep areas in the Earth. The magma forms from the heat that is produced by pockets of radioactive chemical elements deep inside the Earth. The volcanoes of the Hawaiian Islands are hot spots. ◻ See picture at **plate tectonics.**

hot spring A spring of warm water. Hot springs are heated by the Earth's internal heat. The temperature of water in hot springs is usually higher than that of the human body.

hovercraft (HUHV-er-kraft) A kind of vehicle that creates a small cushion of air underneath it so it can move with less friction. Hovercraft are driven by propellers and can travel on land or on the water.

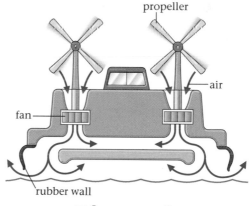

◻ **hovercraft**

Powerful fans suck air into the hovercraft, creating a cushion of air between it and the water. A flexible rubber wall holds the air in. The propellers push the hovercraft forward.

Hubble (HUB-uhl), **Edwin Powell** Born 1889; died 1953. American astronomer who showed that there are galaxies beyond our own and that they are constantly moving outwards from ours. Hubble's discovery proved that the universe is expanding. He also developed the methods that are used today to measure the age and size of the universe.

Hubble Space Telescope   A satellite that orbits the Earth and carries a very powerful telescope for observing objects throughout the universe. The Hubble Space Telescope goes around the Earth every 97 minutes. It has taken hundreds of thousands of pictures of objects in outer space.

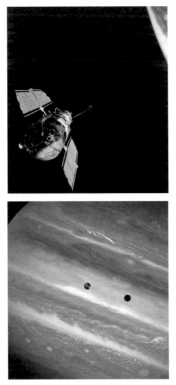

□ **Hubble Space Telescope**

top: *the Hubble Space Telescope in orbit*
bottom: *close-up photograph of the planet Jupiter and its moon Io, taken by the Hubble Space Telescope on April 20, 1999*

hue   (HYŌO) The quality of colors that is described by words such as red, yellow, green, and blue. Two things can have the same hue (red or blue, for example), but one can be brighter or paler than the other. Hue is determined by the **wavelength** of the color.

human   (HYŌO-muhn) **1.** A member of the species *Homo sapiens*; a human being. **2.** A member of one of the extinct species of earlier primates that are closely related to *Homo sapiens,* such as a Cro-Magnon or a Neanderthal.

Human Genome Project   A research project that studies and tries to identify all of the genes in humans. The Human Genome Project began in the United States in 1990. Scientists from all over the world can get information about human DNA from the project's computer database.

Biography

Alexander von Humboldt
Alexander von Humboldt quickly became bored studying the plants of his native Germany and decided to travel in order to find new specimens. He became one of the earliest scientific explorers of the Amazon region of South America, where he studied the plants, animals, and landscape, and created maps of his travels. He was also the first to study the electric eel, as he found many of them in the swamps of South America.

Humboldt   (HUHM-bōlt), **(Friedrich Heinrich) Alexander von** Born 1769; died 1859. German scientist and writer who went on scientific expeditions in South America, Asia, and Europe. Humboldt's writings about his journeys contributed greatly to the study of geography and meteorology.

humerus   (HYŌO-mer-uhs) The long bone of the upper arm. □ See picture at **skeleton.**

humid (HYOO-mid) Having a large amount of moisture, especially in the form of water vapor. Humid air feels damp and sticky. Warm regions usually have humid climates because warm air can hold more moisture than cool air.

humidifier (hyoo-MID-uh-fī-er) A device that increases the humidity in a closed area, such as a room or greenhouse. A humidifier uses an absorbent material to slowly take up water from a basin. A fan then blows air through the moist material and releases its moisture.

humidity (hyoo-MID-i-tē) Moisture in the air. When one measures the humidity of the air one can measure the **relative humidity** or the **absolute humidity.**

humus (HYOO-muhs) Dark soil that is formed from the decay of dead plants and animals. Humus contains nutrients that help plants to grow. Humus holds moisture well and does not dry out easily.

Did You Know?

hurricane
Hurricanes are giant storms with powerful winds that move in a circle. The circle can be as wide as 500 miles (805 kilometers) across, and the winds can reach speeds as high as 190 miles (306 kilometers) per hour. Hurricanes start out over the ocean in warm weather, and lose some of their force when they come over colder water or land.

hurricane (HER-i-kān) A powerful tropical storm with heavy rains and winds of more than 74 miles (119 kilometers) per hour. The winds rotate around an area of calm known as the eye. Hurricanes begin in trop-

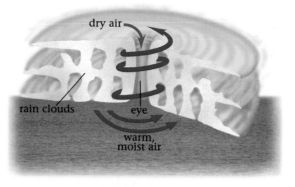

□ hurricane

In a hurricane, warm, moist air rises from the surface of the ocean and circles around a central point called the eye. As the winds get faster, they make tunnels through the thick clouds. Dry air above the storm sinks down into the eye and keeps it free of clouds.

ical parts of the Atlantic Ocean and move generally northward.

husk The dry outer covering of seeds or fruits, such as a nut or an ear of corn.

Hutton (HUHT-uhn), **James** Born 1726; died 1797. Scottish scientist who is considered the founder of modern geology. He formed the theory that the history of the Earth can be explained by observing the geological processes that are still happening today.

□ James Hutton

Huygens (HĪ-guhnz *or* HOI-guhnz), **Christiaan** Born 1629; died 1695. Dutch scientist who invented a way to make better lenses for telescopes. Using these improved lenses, he discovered Saturn's fourth satellite (1655) and its rings (1659).

hybrid (HĪ-brid) A plant or animal that has parents of different species or varieties. A mule is a hybrid because it is the offspring of a male donkey and a female horse. Hybrid animals are usually unable to reproduce.

hydra (HĪ-druh) A small animal that is related to the jellyfish. Hydras have long bodies shaped like tubes with tentacles at one end.

Did You Know?

hydra

Imagine a very small jellyfish turned upside down, stretched out a bit, and attached to a surface such as a rock or a plant. That's basically a hydra. Although a hydra doesn't look much like a jellyfish, its body plan is the same.

hydraulic (hī-DRAW-lik) Relating to a machine that works by the pressure of water or another liquid, such as oil. Hydraulic lifts are used in car garages to raise cars by pumping oil into a large cylinder that carries the weight of the car.

hydrocarbon (hī-druh-KAR-buhn) A chemical compound that contains only carbon and hydrogen. There are many different types of hydrocarbons. Each type is different from the others in the amount of carbon and hydrogen it has, and in the arrangement of its molecules. Hydrocarbons are used for fuels, to make plastic, and to make many other products, including crayons. Methane and benzene are hydrocarbons.

hydrochloric acid (hī-druh-KLOR-ik AS-id) A very strong, poisonous acid with a sharp odor. It is used to clean metal. Small amounts of hydrochloric acid are also made by the stomachs of animals to break down food.

hydrofoil (HĪ-druh-foyl) A boat that has a wing-like structure on its bottom that pushes the boat partly or mostly out of the water. Because so little of the hydrofoil's bottom is touching the water, it can move very fast.

hydrogen (HĪ-druh-juhn) A chemical element that exists freely on Earth as a gas and is combined with oxygen in water. Hydrogen is the lightest and most common element in the universe. It burns easily and occurs in many important chemical compounds. ◻ See Table on pages 178–179.

hydrogen bomb An extremely destructive bomb that gets its explosive power by turning hydrogen atoms into helium atoms, through the process knows as **fusion**. A hydrogen bomb is much more powerful than an atomic bomb.

hydrogen peroxide A clear, dense liquid that is mixed with water for use as an antiseptic and a bleach. Each molecule of hydrogen peroxide has two atoms of hydrogen and two atoms of oxygen.

hydrologic cycle (hī-druh-LOJ-ik SĪ-kuhl) *See* **water cycle.**

hydrometer (hī-DROM-i-ter) An instrument that measures how dense a liquid is compared to water. A hydrometer has a tube with a heavy glass bulb at the bottom that lets the tube stand upright when it is placed in a liquid. The lower the tube sinks into the liquid, the less dense the liquid is.

hydroponics (hī-druh-PON-iks) The growing of plants in water rather than in soil. In hydroponics, plant roots take in nutrients that have been added to the water.

hydrothermal (hī-druh-THER-muhl) Relating to hot water, especially water that is heated by the Earth's internal heat. Hydrothermal energy, for example, is power that is produced using the Earth's hot water.

hygiene (HĪ-jēn) A practice or condition that promotes good health. Washing the hands before eating is good hygiene.

hyperactivity (hī-per-ak-TIV-i-tē) A level of activity or excitement that is higher than that of most people. Hyperactivity may affect how well a person can pay attention or follow instructions.

hypotenuse (hī-POT-uh-noōs) The longest side of a right triangle. The hypotenuse is always opposite the right angle.

hypothalamus (hī-pō-THAL-uh-muhs) A small part of the brain that controls body temperature, sleep, hunger, and thirst. The hypothalamus also directs the production of important hormones, especially hormones that control the body's growth.

hypothermia (hī-puh-THER-mē-uh) Body temperature that is very low, caused by being exposed to cold for long periods.

hypothesis (hī-POTH-i-sis) A statement that explains a set of facts and can be tested to determine if it is false or not accurate. Scientists test a hypothesis by making observations and performing experiments. Making a hypothesis is an important step in the **scientific method.**

Ii

ice Water frozen solid, normally at or below a temperature of 32° Fahrenheit (0° Celsius).

ice age One of several periods during which glaciers covered a large part of the Earth.

Did You Know?

ice age

The last ice age ended about 10,000 years ago. During this time, huge sheets of ice over a mile thick covered much of North America, Greenland, northern Europe, and northern Russia. Over thousands of years, these massive glaciers wore down mountains, ground up huge rocks, and made deep gouges in the Earth's surface that often became lakes after the ice melted.

iceberg A very large mass of ice that is floating in the ocean. Icebergs are pieces of a glacier that have broken off. Most of an iceberg is below the water, and only about one-ninth of it is above the surface.

□ **iceberg**

icecap A sheet of ice and snow that covers a large area year-round. An icecap that is about 665,000 square miles (1,729,000 square kilometers) covers most of the island of Greenland. The icecaps covering the North and South Poles are called **polar caps**.

ichthyology (ik-thē-OL-uh-jē) The scientific study of fish.

ichthyosaurus (ik-thē-uh-SOR-uhs) A sea reptile that lived during the time of the dinosaurs and is now extinct. It looked like a dolphin and had a long beak, four flippers, and a tail with a large fin.

igneous rock (IG-nē-uhs ROK) A rock that is formed by the cooling and hardening of magma or lava. Basalt and granite are igneous rocks. □ See Table on page 208.

imago (i-MĀ-gō) An insect in its final adult stage after metamorphosis.

immune system (i-MYOON SIS-tuhm) The parts of the body that act together to protect the body against infection or disease. White blood cells and antibodies, which attack and weaken germs, are parts of the immune system that circulate in the blood. The skin, which acts as a barrier to germs, is also part of the immune system.

immunity (i-MYOO-ni-tē) The ability of the body to resist disease or infection. Immunity to a particular germ can be provided by the body's own immune system or by vaccines.

immunization (im-yuh-ni-ZĀ-shuhn) **1.** The production of immunity to a particular disease. Immunization is usually brought about by **vaccination. 2.** A vaccine for a particular disease.

impedance (im-PĒD-uhns) A measure of how much an electric circuit will slow an alternating current that flows through it. Impedance is measured in ohms.

impermeable (im-PER-mē-uh-buhl) Not allowing a liquid or gas to pass through. Plastic sheeting is impermeable to rain.

improper fraction (im-PROP-er FRAK-shuhn) A fraction in which the numerator is greater than or equal to the denominator, such as $\frac{3}{2}$. ☐ Compare **proper fraction.**

impulse (IM-puhls) **1.** A sudden, short burst of electric current that flows in one direction. **2.** An electric signal that travels along a nerve. Impulses carry signals toward the brain or toward a part of the body, such as a muscle.

incandescent lamp (in-kan-DES-uhnt LAMP) A lamp that produces light by connecting an electric current to a very thin wire inside a glass bulb. The current causes the wire to become hot enough to glow. ☐ Compare **fluorescent lamp.**

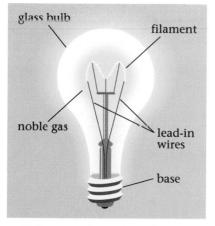

☐ incandescent lamp

In an incandescent lamp, a thin wire (the filament) in the glass bulb is heated by an electric current until it glows. A noble gas protects the filament from burning.

inch A unit of length equal to $\frac{1}{12}$ of a foot. ☐ See Table on page 148.

incisor (in-SĪ-zer) A tooth with a sharp edge, located between the canines. Incisors are used for cutting or gnawing food. Mammals have eight incisors, four on top and four on the bottom.

inclined plane (IN-klīnd PLĀN) A surface, such as a ramp, that is set at an angle so as to make it easy to slide or roll an object up or down it. Inclined planes are considered simple machines because it takes less force to move an object up the plane than to lift it. ☐ See picture at **machine.**

incubator (IN-kyuh-bā-ter) A device in which the flow of air, temperature, and light can be controlled. Babies who are born earlier than normal are often placed in incubators for protection. Incubators are also used in laboratories to grow cells.

indicator (IN-di-kā-ter) A chemical compound that changes color when it is exposed to other chemicals or to certain conditions. Indicators are used to test for the presence of chemical elements. An indicator in **litmus paper** is what makes the paper change color when it is exposed to acids or bases.

indicator species A plant or animal whose well-being is a sign of the overall health of its ecosystem. The presence or absence of an indicator species shows whether important changes have taken place in that environment. Trout need clear, cold, running water to live, so when they disappear from a stream it probably means that the water has become too warm or polluted.

indigenous (in-DIJ-uh-nuhs) Native to a certain region. Species can be indigenous to more than one region. The wolf is indigenous to both North America and Europe. ☐ Compare **alien, endemic.**

induction (in-DUK-shuhn) **1.** The use of specific facts or observations to draw general rules or principles. If you observe hundreds of examples in which a chemical compound kills plants, you might conclude by induction that the compound kills all plants. ◻ Compare **deduction. 2.** The process of making an electric current flow through a material, such as a copper wire, by putting it close to a magnet or to a material that already has an electric current running through it. **3.** *See* **magnetic induction.**

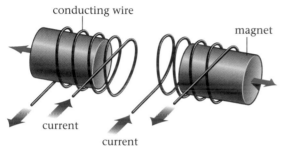

◻ **induction**

When a magnet is passed through a coil of wire that can conduct electricity, it produces an electric current. The direction of the flow of the current depends on the direction in which the magnet moves. In the wire on the left, the current flows from right to left. In the wire on the right, the current flows from left to right.

induction coil A device that changes a low-voltage direct current into a high-voltage alternating current. Induction coils are used in car engines and in devices that ignite oil furnaces. An induction coil is a kind of **transformer.**

inert (in-URT) Not able to react with other chemical elements. Noble gases, such as helium and argon, are almost always inert.

inert gas *See* **noble gas.**

inertia (in-UR-shuh) The tendency of an object that is not moving to stay still, or of an object that is moving to keep moving in a straight line at the same speed, unless a force is applied to it. The greater the **mass** of an object is, the more inertia it has.

infection (in-FEK-shuhn) The invasion of the body or a part of the body by germs that cause disease, such as bacteria, viruses, or fungi.

infectious disease (in-FEK-shuhs di-ZĒZ) A disease caused by infection, such as by bacteria or viruses, that can be spread from person to person.

infertile (in-FER-tuhl) **1.** Not able to produce offspring, seeds, or fruit. **2.** Low in nutrients. Crops and plants do not grow well in infertile soil.

infinite (IN-fuh-nit) Not having an end or limit. There is an infinite number of integers greater than 1.

inflammable (in-FLAM-uh-buhl) Able to catch fire easily.

inflammation (in-fluh-MĀ-shuhn) The swelling, pain, and rise in temperature that is caused by injury or infection.

influenza (in-floo-EN-zuh) A contagious disease in which there is fever, coughing and sneezing, and muscle pain. Influenza is caused by a virus and often occurs in **epidemics.** ◻ Influenza is called the *flu* for short.

information science (in-fer-MĀ-shuhn SĪ-uhns) The study of how to collect, organize, store, and retrieve recorded knowledge, especially by using computers.

infrared light (in-fruh-RED LĪT) Electromagnetic radiation that is invisible and has wavelengths that are longer than those of visible light but shorter than those of microwaves. All objects absorb and give off infrared light.

ingest   (in-JEST) To take in food, nutrients, or other substances, especially for digestion. Snakes ingest small animals. Some cells in the body ingest harmful bacteria.

inhale   (in-HĀL) To breathe in.

inheritance   (in-HAIR-i-tuhns) The process by which traits pass from parents to offspring through the genes; heredity.

ink   A dark liquid that is squirted out by animals like the octopus and squid to confuse predators.

innate   (i-NĀT) Inherited through the genes rather than learned. The flight of migratory birds to warmer climates during the winter is an example of innate behavior.

inner ear   The innermost part of the ear, containing the cochlea and semicircular canals. The inner ear receives sound vibrations and sends them to the brain. The inner ear also helps humans and many other animals keep their sense of balance.

inoculation   (i-nok-yuh-LĀ-shuhn) *See* **vaccination.**

inorganic   (in-or-GAN-ik) **1.** Not having to do with living things or with any of the substances that are made by living things. **2.** Relating to a chemical compound that does not contain any carbon atoms attached to hydrogen atoms. Salt (NaCl) and ammonia (NH$_3$) are inorganic compounds. ◻ Compare **organic.**

input   (IN-puht) **1.** The energy, power, or work that is put into a system or device. Battery-operated radios get their input from the batteries. **2.** Information that is entered into a computer.

insect   (IN-sekt) A type of small animal that has six legs and a body that is divided into three parts. More than 600,000 species of insect are known, including flies, bees, grasshoppers, cockroaches, beetles, butterflies, and ants. Insects are members of the group of animals known as **arthropods.**

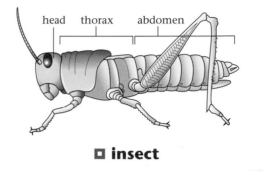

head   thorax   abdomen

◻ **insect**

insecticide   (in-SEK-ti-sīd) A chemical compound that is used to kill insects.

insectivore   (in-SEK-tuh-vor) An animal or plant that eats insects. The anteater and the Venus flytrap are insectivores.

insoluble   (in-SOL-yuh-buhl) Not able to be dissolved in a particular substance. Many rocks and metals are insoluble in water, though they can be dissolved in other substances.

instinct   (IN-stingkt) A way of behaving that is natural and automatic rather than

Did You Know?

instinct
Different birds build different kinds of nests—some in tree branches, some on the ground, some hanging down, some made from mud. They are not taught how to build their nests, but instead do it by instinct, which they inherit from their parents. Lots of animal behavior is caused by instinct, such as the spawning of fish and the gathering of food by insects.

learned. Animals use instinct to mate and defend territory.

insulation (in-suh-LĀ-shuhn) A material that blocks or slows down heat, electricity, or sound. The walls of houses are lined with insulation to limit heat loss. Electric cords on appliances are covered with insulation to prevent shock.

insulator (IN-suh-lā-ter) A material that blocks or slows down the passage of sound, heat, or electricity. Rubber is a good insulator of electricity.

insulin (IN-suh-lin) A hormone that helps the body take up sugar from the blood. Insulin is produced in the pancreas. It can also be made in a laboratory and used to treat disease, especially **diabetes.**

integer (IN-tuh-jer) A positive or negative whole number or zero. The numbers 4, –876, and 5,280 are all integers.

integrated circuit (IN-ti-grā-tid SUR-kuht) *See* **chip.**

intelligence (in-TEL-uh-juhns) The ability to learn from experience and remember what has been learned. Many animals, such as primates and whales, show high levels of intelligence. Tests that measure a person's knowledge, memory, and ability to reason are sometimes used to determine human intelligence.

interference (in-ter-FEER-uhns) **1.** The wave that forms when two or more waves come together. When two pebbles are thrown into a pond, their waves radiate out until they meet and make a third wave. That third wave is the interference. **2.** The interruption of or changing of a radio or television broadcast signal by other signals.

intergalactic (in-ter-guh-LAK-tik) Existing or happening between galaxies.

internal-combustion engine (in-TER-nuhl-kuhm-BUHS-chuhn EN-jin) A type of engine in which the fuel is burned inside the engine itself rather than in an outside furnace or burner. Gasoline and diesel engines are internal-combustion engines; a steam engine is not.

International Date Line (in-ter-NASH-uh-nuhl DĀT LĪN) An imaginary line that runs north and south through the Pacific Ocean roughly at a longitude of 180°. The International Date Line marks the beginning of each new day. When it is Saturday to the west of the line, it is Friday to the east of it.

International System The formal name for the most modern version of the **metric system,** used by scientists all over the world to perform experiments and measure results.

Internet (IN-ter-net) The network that connects computers around the world. People all over the world are able to send and receive information over the Internet because of a special set of rules that control the way that information travels.

interplanetary (in-ter-PLAN-i-tair-ē) Existing or happening between planets. A satellite that is launched from the Earth to orbit Mercury travels through interplanetary space.

intersection (IN-ter-sek-shuhn) **1.** The point or set of points where one line, surface, or solid crosses another. **2.** The set that contains only those elements shared by two or more sets. The intersection of the sets {3,4,5,6} and {4,6,8,10} is the set {4,6}.

interstellar (in-ter-STEL-er) Existing or happening between the stars. Particles of dust and gas drift in interstellar space.

Did You Know?

intestine

The intestine is the longest organ in your body. In an adult, the small intestine is about 22 feet long (6.7 meters), and the large intestine is over 5 feet long (1.5 meters). So when you grow up, you'll have 9 yards (8.2 meters) of intestine inside you! It needs to be that long so that it can absorb as many nutrients from food as it can.

intestine   (in-TES-tin) The part of the digestive system that is shaped like a hollow tube and goes from the stomach to the anus. In the intestine, digestion of food is completed, and nutrients and water are absorbed into the body. The intestine is made up of the **small intestine** and **large intestine.**

invertebrate   (in-VER-tuh-brāt) An animal that has no backbone. Most animals are invertebrates. Sponges, corals, jellyfish, starfish, earthworms, and insects are all invertebrates. ◻ Compare **vertebrate.**

iodine   (Ī-ō-dīn) A chemical element that is shiny, grayish-black, and poisonous. Iodine is found in very small amounts in most of nature, but in seaweed it is found in large amounts. Compounds made with iodine are used in medicine and dyes. ◻ See Table on pages 178–179.

ion   (Ī-uhn) An atom or a group of atoms that has an electric charge. Positive ions, or **cations,** are formed by the loss of electrons. Negative ions, or **anions,** are formed by the gain of electrons.

ionize   (Ī-uh-nīz) **1.** To change the electric charge of an atom by adding or removing an electron. When an electron is added, the atom becomes negatively charged. When an electron is removed, the atom becomes positively charged. **2.** To form ions in a substance. Lightning ionizes the air around it.

ionosphere   (Ī-ON-uh-sfeer) A region of the Earth's upper atmosphere in which atoms are ionized by the sunlight that passes through it. When radio waves are sent up from the Earth and hit the ionosphere, they bounce back down instead of continuing into space. By bouncing their signals off the ionosphere, radio stations can broadcast for long distances over the Earth's curved surface.

iris   (Ī-ris) The colored part of the eye around the pupil. The iris is a muscle that controls how much light gets into the eye through the pupil.

iron   (Ī-ern) A chemical element that is a silvery-white, hard metal. Iron can be magnetized and is used to make steel and other

◻ **invertebrate**

left to right: *jellyfish, snail, and earthworm*

alloys that are important in construction. Iron in red blood cells helps carry oxygen in the blood. ◻ See Table on pages 178–179.

irradiate (i-RĀ-dē-āt) To expose something to radiation in order to bring about a change in it. Meat that is sold as food is often irradiated with gamma rays to kill bacteria.

irrational number (i-RASH-uh-nuhl NUHM-ber) A real number that cannot be expressed as a fraction. Irrational numbers, when they are written as decimals, have an endless number of digits to the right of the decimal point that do not repeat in any pattern. Pi and the square root of two are irrational numbers.

isobar (Ī-sō-bar) A line drawn on a weather map connecting places that have the same atmospheric pressure.

isosceles triangle (ī-SOS-uh-lēz TRĪ-ang-guhl) A triangle that has two sides with the same length. ◻ See picture at **triangle**.

isotherm (Ī-sō-therm) A line drawn on a weather map connecting places that have the same average temperature.

isotope (Ī-suh-tōp) An atom that has a different number of neutrons in its nucleus from other atoms of the same element. Isotopes are indicated by a number that shows the total number of protons and neutrons. The number of protons in an isotope is always the same. Carbon 12 has six protons and six neutrons; carbon 14 has six protons and eight neutrons.

ivory (Ī-vuh-rē) The hard, smooth, yellowish-white substance that forms the teeth and tusks of some animals, such as the tusks of elephants and walruses.

Jj

jaundice (JAWN-dis) An abnormal yellowish coloring of the skin and the whites of the eyes. Jaundice is usually caused by a disease of the liver that interferes with the way **bile** is produced.

jaw **1.** Either of two parts in humans and other vertebrates that provide shape and support for the mouth, hold the teeth, and are used for biting and chewing. The lower, movable part of the jaw is called the **mandible. 2.** A part in invertebrates, such as the pincers of spiders or mites, that is used for grasping food.

jawless fish A type of fish that has no jaw and looks like an eel. Jawless fish are a very ancient group of fish. Lampreys and hagfish are jawless fish.

□ **jawless fish**

hagfish

jellyfish (JEL-ē-fish) A type of water animal with a soft body that is shaped like an umbrella or bell. The mouth of a jellyfish is surrounded by stinging tentacles that are used to catch prey. Jellyfish are related to the corals and hydras.

Jenner (JEN-er), **Edward** Born 1749; died 1823. British doctor who discovered in the late 18th century that vaccines can be used to prevent specific diseases.

Biography

Edward Jenner

In the late 18th century, Edward Jenner showed that people who were exposed to a small dose of cowpox (a skin disease of cows) did not catch smallpox. Jenner figured that getting cowpox somehow gave people immunity to smallpox. This discovery led to the first effective vaccination program and laid the foundation for today's understanding of how the immune system works.

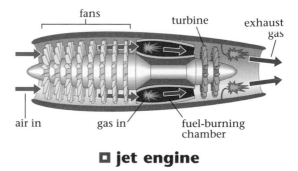

jet engine An engine that creates forward power by pushing out hot gases behind it. Jet engines produce the hot gases by burning fuel in a special chamber.

□ **jet engine**

jet propulsion **1.** The force provided by a jet engine in driving an aircraft or other

127

vehicle forward. **2.** The forward force created by the pushing of a gas or liquid backward. Squids and octopuses move through the ocean by jet propulsion as they take in water and then quickly push it out behind them.

jet stream   A strong wind that blows in a narrow path around the Earth high above the ground. Jet streams blow from west to east at altitudes of 6 to 10 miles (10 to 19 kilometers) above sea level.

joint   A body part that is formed by the coming together of two or more bones. Joints are held together by **ligaments**. The elbow and knee are joints.

Joliot-Curie   (zhaw-lyō-kyur-Ē), **Irène** Born 1897; died 1956. French scientist who worked with her husband, **Frédéric Joliot-Curie** (born 1900; died 1958), to create the first artificial radioactive isotope. They also contributed to the development of nuclear reactors.

joule   (JŌOL) A unit used to measure energy or work. One joule is equal to the work done when a force of one newton acts over a distance of one meter. The joule is named after James Prescott Joule.

Joule, James Prescott Born 1818; died 1889. British scientist whose experiments proved that energy is never destroyed but may be converted from one form into another.

jugular vein   (JUHG-yuh-ler VĀN) Either of two large veins, each on one side of the neck. The jugular veins carry blood from the head and neck back to the heart.

jungle   (JUHNG-guhl) An area of thick forest that is found in tropical regions. Jungles have hot, humid climates, are overgrown with trees, bushes, and vines, and are home to a wide variety of living things.

Did You Know?

Jupiter

Jupiter isn't only the largest planet in the Solar System—it also could have become a star, only it didn't quite make it as one.

Like the Sun and other stars, Jupiter is not solid, but a giant ball of gas. It gives off more than twice as much heat as it gets from the Sun, but it does not have enough mass to create the energy needed to glow like a star.

Jupiter   (JŌOpi-ter) The planet that is fifth in distance from the Sun. Jupiter is the largest planet in the Solar System and has the shortest day, lasting less than ten hours. ❑ See Table on pages 184–185.

Jurassic Period   (ju-RAS-ik PEER-ē-uhd) The period of time during the history of the Earth starting about 208 million years ago and ending about 144 million years ago. During the Jurassic Period, dinosaurs were the dominant life on land, and the earliest birds appeared. ❑ See Table on pages 102–103.

❑ **juvenile**

Juvenile and adult emperor penguins. The juvenile's body is covered with soft down.

juvenile   (JŌO-vuh-nīl) An animal or plant that is not fully grown or developed.

Kk

kangaroo (kang-guh-ROO) A mammal that lives in Australia and has large hind legs that are good for jumping. Female kangaroos have a pouch in which the young grow after being born. Kangaroos are members of the group of mammals known as **marsupials.**

kelp A type of large, brown seaweed that is found in colder ocean regions. Some species of kelp can grow to over 200 feet (61 meters) long.

kelvin (KEL-vin) One of the units of the Kelvin scale. A kelvin is equal in amount to a degree on the Celsius scale.

Kelvin First Baron. Title of **William Thomson.** Born 1824; died 1907. British scientist who studied heat and electricity and invented the Kelvin scale in 1848.

Kelvin scale A temperature scale that starts at the lowest temperature possible, absolute zero (-273.15°C). On the Kelvin scale, water freezes at 273.15 K and boils at 373.15 K. The Kelvin scale was named for its inventor, Lord Kelvin. ◘ See picture at **temperature.**

Kepler (KEP-ler), **Johannes** Born 1571; died 1630. German astronomer who demonstrated that the orbits of the Earth and the other planets around the Sun are in the shape of an ellipse.

keratin (KAIR-uh-tin) A tough protein that forms the main part of hair, nails, horns, feathers, and hooves. Keratin also makes up the outer layer of skin in humans and many other animals.

kerosene (KAIR-uh-sēn) A light-colored oil that is made from petroleum. Kerosene burns easily and is used as a fuel for lamps, heaters, furnaces, and jet engines.

keyboard A set of buttons pressed by the fingers in order to operate a computer. Most keys are marked with a letter, number, or symbol, and are used to enter that letter, number, or symbol as a piece of data into the computer. Other keys do not enter data but do other things, such as making lowercase letters become uppercase or making lines of text move up or down on the screen.

keystone The middle stone at the top of an arch. The keystone holds or locks the other stones together in the rest of the arch. ◘ See picture at **arch.**

kidney (KID-nē) Either of two organs in humans and other vertebrates that separate waste materials from the blood in the form of urine. The kidneys control the amount of water in the body. Each kidney is attached to the bladder by a long tube called a ureter.

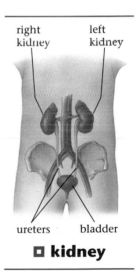

right kidney   left kidney

ureters   bladder

◘ **kidney**

kilobyte (KIL-uh-bīt) A unit of information that can be stored in a computer memory and is equal to 1,024 bytes. The number 1,024 is equal to 2 multiplied by 2 ten times.

kilogram (KIL-uh-gram) The basic unit of mass in the metric system, equal to 1,000 grams or 2.2 pounds. ◘ See Table on page 148.

kilometer (ki-LOM-i-ter *or* KIL-uh-mē-ter) A unit of length in the metric system, equal to 1,000 meters (0.62 mile). ◻ See Table on page 148.

kilowatt (KIL-uh-waht) A unit of power equal to 1,000 watts.

kinetic energy (ki-NET-ik EN-er-jē) The energy that an object has as a result of being in motion. The amount of kinetic energy an object has depends on the mass and velocity of the object. ◻ Compare **potential energy**.

kingdom (KING-duhm) One of the major groups in the classification of living things. A kingdom is the highest classification into which organisms are grouped. Life is divided into five kingdoms: prokaryotes, protists, fungi, plants, and animals. ◻ See Table on page 47.

Koch (KAWK), **Robert** Born 1843; died 1910. German scientist who found that specific diseases are caused by specific bacteria.

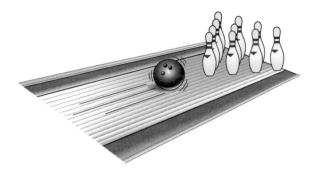

◻ **kinetic energy**

The bowling ball has kinetic energy because it is moving. When it hits the pins, it will pass some of its energy to them.

He identified the bacteria that cause anthrax, tuberculosis, and cholera.

Krebs (KREBZ), **Hans Adolf** Born 1900; died 1981. German-born British scientist who showed how cells in the bodies of living things store energy and make food.

Kuiper belt (KĪ-per BELT) A region in the outer Solar System that contains thousands of small, icy objects.

Ll

laboratory   (LAB-ruh-tor-ē) A room or building that is used for doing scientific research or running scientific experiments.

lactation   (lak-TĀ-shuhn) The production of milk in a female mammal after she has given birth.

lactic acid   (LAK-tik AS-id) An acid that is created when milk sours or when fermentation takes place in the juices of certain fruits. It is also created by muscles during exercise and can cause cramps.

lactose   (LAK-tōs) A sugar that is found in milk. People who have trouble with the digestion of milk lack the enzyme that is needed to break down lactose.

lagoon   (luh-GOON) A shallow body of salt water that is separated from the sea by a narrow strip of land or by a coral reef.

□ lagoon

an atoll in the Pacific Ocean

lake   A large body of fresh or salt water that is surrounded by land.

landfill   An area of land where garbage and trash are buried between layers of dirt. Landfills often have sheets of plastic that are placed around the garbage so that the surrounding land is not polluted.

landmass   A large, continuous area of land, such as a continent or a very large island.

landslide   A mass of soil and rock that slides down a steep slope.

Landsteiner   (LAHND-stī-ner), **Karl** Born 1868; died 1943. American scientist who discovered that human blood falls into one of four different groups: A, B, AB, or O.

La Niña   (lah NĒN-yah) A period during which the surface water of the eastern Pacific Ocean becomes cooler than usual. The cooler water brings drought to South America and heavy rains to Australia and Indonesia. **□** Compare **El Niño**.

lanthanides   (LAN-thuh-nīdz) The chemical elements in the Periodic Table that have an atomic number between 57 and 71. These elements are all shiny metals and burn easily. **□** The lanthanides are also called *rare-earth elements*. **□** See Table on pages 178–179.

large intestine   The wide, lower part of the intestine, in which water is absorbed from food during digestion. The large intestine is found between the small intestine and the anus. **□** See picture at **digestive system**.

larva   (LAR-vuh) An animal in an early stage of development that looks very different from its adult stage. Tadpoles are the larvae of frogs, and caterpillars are the larvae of moths and butterflies. *Plural form:* **larvae** (LAR-vē) or **larvas**.

larynx (LAIR-ingks) The upper part of the trachea or windpipe. The vocal cords are found in the larynx. ◻ The larynx is also called the *voice box*. ◻ See picture at **respiratory system.**

laser (LĀ-zer) A device that sends out a very narrow and intense beam of light. Lasers work by adding energy to the atoms of a substance that is contained inside them. The color of laser light depends on how much energy is added to the atoms. Lasers are used for many purposes, including cutting hard substances, copying or printing documents, and performing some types of surgery.

◻ laser

a laser being used to cut steel

latitude (LAT-i-tood) Distance that is measured as you travel north or south on the surface of the Earth. Latitude is measured in degrees from the equator, which has a latitude of 0°. If you know both the longitude and latitude of a place, you can find its exact location on the Earth's surface. ◻ Compare **longitude.**

lattice (LAT-is) A set of points that forms the outline of a pattern or shape. The molecules of crystals in minerals are arranged in a lattice.

lava (LAH-vuh) Hot, molten rock that flows out from a volcano or from a crack in the Earth's surface.

Did You Know?

lava

Lava is hot. At temperatures of 1300° to 2200° Fahrenheit (700° to 1200° Celsius), it is hot enough to set a house on fire from a distance. Sometimes lava flows fast, and sometimes very slowly, depending on its density. Lava flows usually start out at a rate as slow as 6 miles (10 kilometers) per hour, but once they have found a good pathway they can move as fast as 35 to 40 miles (55 to 65 kilometers) per hour.

Lavoisier (lah-vwah-ZYĀ), **Antoine Laurent** Born 1743; died 1794. French scientist who wrote the first chemistry textbook in 1789. By repeating the experiments of Joseph Priestley, Lavoisier showed that air is a mixture of gases, including the gas he named *oxygen.*

law A statement that describes something that always works in the same way under the same set of conditions. Laws in nature describe relationships and events that do not vary. The Moon orbits around Earth and water flows downhill because of the laws of gravity.

law of conservation of energy A law in physics that states that energy can neither be created nor destroyed, just changed from one form to another.

law of conservation of mass A law in physics that states that matter can nei-

Biography

Antoine Laurent Lavoisier

In his book *Elementary Treatise of Chemistry,* Antoine Lavoisier collected, organized, and expanded upon everything that was known about chemistry in his time. He showed the difference between chemical elements and chemical compounds, and he introduced the system for naming chemical compounds that is used today.

ther be created nor destroyed, just changed from one form of mass into another form, or from mass into energy.

LCD Short for **liquid-crystal display.** A screen used in many digital devices to display numbers or images. It is made with a special substance that is like a liquid but has crystals that can twist to reflect light or allow light to pass through. LCDs have the advantages of being very thin and of not using much electricity.

leach To cause certain materials to pass out of a substance when a liquid passes through it. Heavy rains can leach minerals out of rock and soil.

lead (LED) A chemical element that is a heavy, bluish-gray metal. Lead is easily shaped and, unlike most metals, it is a poor conductor of electricity. Because lead is poisonous, it is no longer used to make pipes and paints. ☐ See Table on pages 178–179.

leaf A usually flat, green plant part that grows on a stem or stalk. Leaves take in carbon dioxide from the air and absorb energy from sunlight to make food through the process of **photosynthesis.** Leaves that are made up of several leaflets are called compound leaves.

A Closer Look

Leaf

*Leaves take energy from sunlight and use it to make food through the process of **photosynthesis.** The shape of leaves depends on the climate and habitat in which a plant grows. Broad leaves, such as maple leaves, are suited to wetter climates. Their large surface makes maximum use of sunlight for photosynthesis. The smaller surfaces of needle-shaped leaves prevent water from being lost through evaporation. In dry desert climates, where water is scarce, water vapor in the air condenses on the spines of a cactus and then drips to the ground, where it is taken up by the roots.*

| **broadleaf** *maple* | **grass** *field grass* | **needle** *pine* | **spine** *cactus* |

leaflet (LĒ-flit) A small or young leaf. The parts or divisions of a compound leaf are leaflets.

Leakey (LĒ-kē), **Louis** Born 1903; died 1972. British scientist who, with his wife, **Mary Leakey** (born 1913; died 1996), discovered fossils of early humans in Tanzania in 1959. These fossils, which are estimated to be almost 2 million years old, proved that humans had existed for much longer than was previously believed, and that they had evolved in Africa rather than in Asia.

learning disability A condition that interferes with a person's ability to learn. Learning disabilities may affect how well a person can pay attention, follow instructions, or understand written words or numbers.

Leavitt (LEV-it), **Henrietta Swan** Born 1868; died 1921. American astronomer who discovered four novae and over 2,400 variable stars. She also developed a mathematical formula to calculate the distance from the Earth to various stars.

leech A type of worm that lives in water and sucks blood from other animals. Leeches are related to earthworms. One kind of leech is used in medicine to help wounds heal.

Leeuwenhoek (LĀ-vuhn-huk), **Anton van** Born 1632; died 1723. Dutch scientist who pioneered the use of microscopes in scientific research. In 1674, using simple microscopes that he built himself, he was the first person to observe and describe bacteria and protozoa. He also studied yeasts, red blood cells, and blood capillaries.

legume (LEG-yoŏm) A type of plant with seeds that grow inside pods. Legumes get some of their nutrients from nitrifying bacteria on their roots. Beans, peas, and peanuts are legumes.

length The distance of a thing measured from one end to the other end.

Lenoir (le-NWAR), **Jean-Joseph-Étienne** Born 1822; died 1900. French inventor who designed and assembled the first practical internal-combustion engine in 1859.

lens **1.** A piece of glass or plastic that is shaped in such a way as to form an image. Lenses work either by bringing together or spreading apart light rays that pass through them. **2.** The clear part of the eye that lies behind the iris. The lens focuses light onto the retina to form images. ◻ See picture at **eye.**

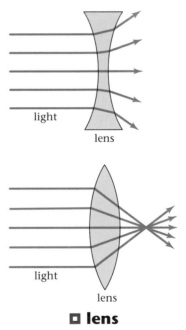

light
lens

light
lens

◻ **lens**

top: *As light rays pass through a concave lens they spread apart.*
bottom: *As light rays pass through a convex lens they come together.*

Leonardo da Vinci (lē-uh-NAR-dō duh VIN-chē) Born 1452; died 1519. Italian scientist, inventor, and artist who had interests in a wide range of areas. He drew plans for the first helicopter, para-

■ **Leonardo da Vinci**

Leonardo da Vinci made many drawings of flying machines, including one that looked like a helicopter (right).

chute, and bicycle, devices that were not built until centuries after his death.

leukemia   (loo-KĒ-mē-uh) A type of cancer in which white blood cells multiply out of control in the blood and bone marrow. Leukemia is often treated with chemotherapy.

lever   (LEV-er) A simple machine made of a bar that pivots on a fixed support called the **fulcrum**. Levers are used to transmit force or move heavy objects. The crowbar and seesaw are kinds of levers. ■ See picture at **machine**.

lichen   (LĪ-kuhn) A living thing that is made up of algae and a fungus living and growing together in a relationship known as **symbiosis**. The algae supply nutrients to the fungus by means of photosynthesis, and the fungus provides shade and moisture to the algae. Lichens often form a scaly growth on rocks and trees.

life   **1.** The quality that sets apart living things from nonliving things, such as rocks or metals. A living thing that is able to grow, respond to the environment, and reproduce is said to have life. **2.** All of the living things of a particular kind or in a particular area. The plant life in a tropical rain forest includes hundreds of different types of trees.

life cycle   The series of changes, or stages, in the life of a plant or animal between the time that it reproduces to the time that its offspring become adults and are able to reproduce.

life science   A science that studies living things, the environments they are found in, and their behavior. Biology, ecology, and genetics are life sciences. ■ Compare **physical science**.

lift   A force that pushes an object upward against the pull of gravity. Lift can be creat-

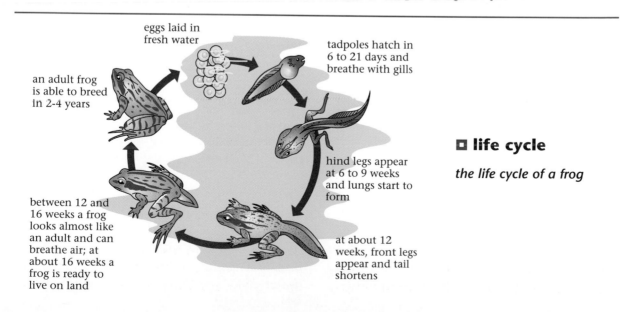

eggs laid in fresh water

tadpoles hatch in 6 to 21 days and breathe with gills

an adult frog is able to breed in 2-4 years

hind legs appear at 6 to 9 weeks and lungs start to form

between 12 and 16 weeks a frog looks almost like an adult and can breathe air; at about 16 weeks a frog is ready to live on land

at about 12 weeks, front legs appear and tail shortens

■ **life cycle**

the life cycle of a frog

ed by a gas that weighs less than air, such as helium in a balloon. It can also be created when the air pressure above an object is less than the air pressure below it, as when an airplane wing moves through the air.

ligament   (LIG-uh-muhnt) A tough band of body tissue that connects two bones or holds an organ in place.

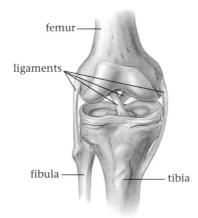

femur
ligaments
fibula   tibia

□ **ligament**

The ligaments of a human knee joint connect the bones of the upper and lower leg and help keep the joint stable.

light   **1.** A form of electromagnetic radiation that can be seen by the human eye. It is made up of electromagnetic waves that travel at a speed of about 186,282 miles (299,728 kilometers) per second. **2.** A form of electromagnetic radiation, such as infrared light and ultraviolet light, that cannot be seen by the human eye.

light bulb   The part of an electric lamp that gives off light. The bulb of an **incandescent lamp** contains a thin wire inside a rounded piece of glass. The bulb of a **fluorescent lamp** is a glass tube that contains a mixture of gases and has no wire inside.

lightning   (LĪT-ning) A flash of light in the sky caused by a sudden flow of electricity between two clouds or between a cloud and

Did You Know?

lightning

Lightning is a gigantic electric spark. The spark travels at over 130,000 miles (209,300 kilometers) per hour and heats the air around it to over 50,000° Fahrenheit (27,760° Celsius), which is several times hotter than the surface of the Sun! The great heat causes the air to glow white-hot and expand very fast, so fast that it causes a loud bang, which we hear as thunder.

the ground. The flash of light heats the air and usually causes thunder. Lightning usually appears as a jagged streak or a bright sheet.

lightning rod   A metal rod that protects a building or another structure from lightning. A lightning rod conducts lightning along a heavy wire and into the ground.

light-year   The distance that light travels in a vacuum in one year. A light-year is equal to about 5.88 trillion miles (9.48 trillion kilometers).

lignin   (LIG-nin) A chemical compound that is found in woody plants. Lignin binds to fibers made of cellulose and strengthens the cell walls of plants.

lime   A white, lumpy powder that contains calcium combined with oxygen. Lime is made by heating things that are rich in calcium, like limestone, bones, or shells. It is used to make glass, paper, steel, and other materials.

limestone   A rock that is made mainly of calcite, especially from seashells. Limestones can have many colors but are usually white, gray, or black. They form on the ocean floor. ◻ See Table on page 208.

line   A figure that consists of a point and all the points going away from it in two exactly opposite directions. The intersection of two planes is a line.

linear accelerator   (LIN-ē-er ak-SEL-uh-rā-ter) A machine that causes particles of an atom, such as protons and electrons, to move very fast through a straight tube and smash into other particles, breaking them apart. The movement of the particles is controlled by impulses from electric fields that change back and forth between positive and negative charges. Scientists use linear accelerators to find out what the particles are made of.

line graph   A graph that uses lines to represent amounts. The lines are drawn from left to right, and often go up and down to represent increases and decreases in whatever is being measured. ◻ See picture at **graph.**

line segment   The part of a line that lies between two points on the line.

lines of force   Lines that show how the force of an electric or magnetic field is working. Iron filings placed close to a magnet will rearrange themselves along the magnet's lines of force.

Linnaeus   (li-NĒ-uhs or li-NĀ-uhs), **Carolus** Born 1707; died 1778. Swedish scientist who was the first to give scientific names to plants (1753) and animals (1758).

lipid   (LIP-id) A fatty substance that is found in living things and that is an important source of food energy. Oils, fats, and waxes are lipids.

Biography

Carolus Linnaeus

Methods for classifying plants and animals had existed as early as the fourth century BC, but the system we use today to classify living things was invented in 1735 by Carolus Linnaeus. The names in Linnaeus's system are in Latin and are made up of two parts: the genus and the species. The system is now used to show how different organisms are related to each other through evolution.

liquefy   (LIK-wuh-fī) To turn into a liquid. The flame of a burning candle liquefies the wax around it.

liquid   (LIK-wid) One of the three basic forms of matter. Liquids are made up of molecules that can move short distances. Unlike solids, liquids do not have a set shape and take on the shape of the container they are in. Unlike gases, liquids have a set volume.

Lister   (LIS-ter), **Joseph** Born 1827; died 1912. British doctor who introduced the use of antiseptics in surgery in 1865. Lister emphasized the importance of keeping wounds clean and of sterilizing surgical instruments to prevent infection. Lister was influenced by Pasteur's theories on germs and disease.

liter   (LĒ-ter) The basic unit of volume in the metric system, equal to about 1.06 quarts. ◻ See Table on page 148.

lithosphere   (LITH-uh-sfeer) The outer part of the Earth, including the crust and upper mantle. It is about 62 miles (100 kilometers) thick. ◻ See picture at **plate tectonics.**

litmus paper (LIT-muhs PĀ-per) A strip of specially treated paper that changes to red when it touches an **acid** and to blue when it touches a **base**. Litmus paper is used to determine if a liquid is an acid or a base.

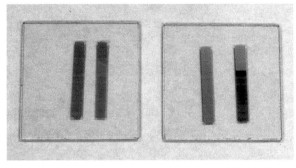

□ **litmus paper**

Blue litmus paper turns red in acid (left). *Red litmus paper turns blue in a base* (right).

Little Dipper (LIT-uhl DIP-er) A group of seven stars that form the outline of a dipper, or a large spoon. Four stars form the bowl of the dipper and three stars form its handle. Polaris, or the North Star, is on the end of the handle.

littoral (LIT-er-uhl) The area of land between the limits of high and low tides. During high tide, the littoral is covered with seawater. During low tide, the water has receded and the littoral is solid ground.

liver (LIV-er) A large organ in the abdomen of humans and other vertebrates. The liver makes bile, which helps the body absorb food during digestion. The liver also stores sugars and vitamins, removes waste materials and poisons from the blood, and helps keep a steady amount of blood in the body.

lizard (LIZ-erd) A type of reptile that has a slender body with a long tail and usually walks on four legs. Unlike most other reptiles, lizards usually have movable eyelids. Iguanas and chameleons are lizards.

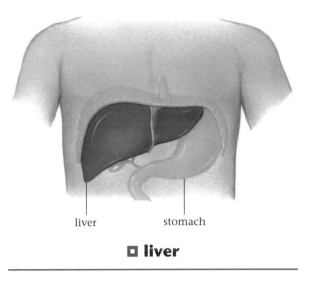

liver   stomach

□ **liver**

load 1. The resistance that a machine must overcome in order to work. 2. The amount of power that is supplied by a generator or power plant.

loam Soil that is made up of sand, clay, and **silt**. Loam also contains dead plant matter that has been broken down into simpler chemical compounds. Loam is good for growing plants because it holds water and has lots of nutrients.

locomotion (lō-kuh-MŌ-shuhn) Movement from one place to another. Animals often use limbs, wings, or other appendages for locomotion. One-celled animals, such as some bacteria, often have a whiplike part called a flagellum that is used for locomotion.

lodestone (LŌD-stōn) A piece of the mineral magnetite that acts like a magnet.

logic (LOJ-ic) The use of strict rules of reasoning to show whether a statement is true or false.

longitude (LON-ji-tood) Distance that is measured as you travel east or west on the surface of the Earth. Longitude is measured in degrees east or west from the prime meridian, which has a longitude of 0°. If you know both the longitude and latitude

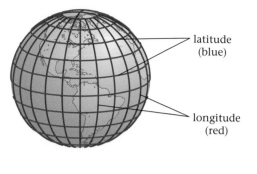

latitude
(blue)

longitude
(red)

◻ **longitude**

of a place, you can find its exact location on the Earth's surface. ◻ Compare **latitude**.

long ton　*See* **ton** (sense 2).

loran　(LOR-an) A system used to determine a boat's position at sea. Loran measures the amount of time it takes for radio signals to be exchanged between it and two or more radios that are on land.

loudspeaker　(LOWD-spē-ker) A device that changes an electric signal into sound and makes the sound louder.

louse　A small, wingless insect that often lives on the bodies of other animals, including humans. The mouthparts of lice are made for biting or sucking, and they often feed on blood. *Plural form:* **lice**.

lowest common denominator　The lowest number that the denominators of two or more fractions will make when they are multiplied together. Finding the lowest common denominator makes it easier to add or subtract fractions. The lowest common denominator of $\frac{1}{3}$ and $\frac{3}{4}$ is 12.

low tide　The time when the tide reaches its lowest level on the shore. Low tide happens twice each day.

luminescent　(loo-muh-NES-uhnt) Giving off light because of the action of chemical compounds rather than heat. Fireflies are luminescent insects.

lunar　(LOO-ner) Relating to the Moon.

lunar eclipse　An eclipse of the Moon that happens when the Sun, Earth, and Moon are positioned so that the Earth is between the Moon and the Sun.

lung　Either of two large organs in the chest that are the main organs of **respiration** in humans and other vertebrates that breathe air. Oxygen that is breathed in is taken up by the blood that flows through the lungs. Carbon dioxide is released from the blood into the lungs and then breathed out. ◻ See picture at **respiratory system**.

lungfish　A type of fish that has organs like lungs for breathing air. Lungfish also have gills like other fish.

Did You Know?
lungfish
Lungfish belong to an important group of fish that arose hundreds of millions of years ago. These fish developed fins that had a muscular middle part, and one group also developed lungs. They were able to crawl onto land and breathe air. Eventually, the fins of some developed into legs, and in this way the first true land animals evolved.

luster　(LUHS-ter) The shine on the surface of a mineral. Luster is important in describing different kinds of minerals. Luster can be metallic, glassy, pearly, or dull.

Lyell　(LĪ-uhl), **Charles** Born 1797; died 1875. Scottish scientist who studied the history of the Earth and made many contributions to our understanding of fossils. His book, *Principles of Geology* (1830–1833), helped popularize the field of geology.

Lyme disease   A disease caused by bacteria that enter the body through the bite of a deer tick. Lyme disease often starts with a rash in the area of the bite, followed by fever, tiredness, and pain in the joints.

lymph   (LIMF) A clear liquid that carries nutrients to the tissues of the body and contains many white blood cells, which help the body fight infection. Lymph forms from liquid that leaks out of capillaries, the smallest blood vessels in the **circulatory system.**

lymphatic system   (lim-FAT-ik SIS-tuhm) A network of tissues and small tubes that helps keep the amount of fluid in the body steady. When a part of the body has too much fluid, the lymphatic system drains the fluid and returns it to the blood. The fluid carried by the lymphatic system is called **lymph** and contains white blood cells that help fight disease.

lymphocyte   (LIM-fuh-sīt) A kind of white blood cell that is found in the lymphatic system. Some lymphocytes produce **antibodies,** which fight germs that have entered the body.

Mm

machine (muh-SHĒN) A device that performs a task by doing work. Machines perform tasks either by applying a force to something or by changing the direction of a force that is already being applied. Machines can be simple, like the lever and pulley, or they can be more complicated, like the washing machine and automobile. ◻ See picture on page 142.

Mach number (MAHK NUHM-ber) The ratio of the speed of an object to the speed of sound in air. An aircraft that flies through the air at twice the speed of sound (about 1,300 miles or 2,100 kilometers per hour) has a Mach number of 2.

macroclimate (MAK-rō-klī-mit) The climate of a large geographic area. The United States has several different macroclimates. The states in the northwest are generally cool and rainy, the southwest states are hot and dry, and the southeast states are hot and humid. ◻ Compare **microclimate**.

macrophage (MAK-ruh-fāj) A kind of white blood cell that is found in the blood. Macrophages fight infection by taking in germs, such as bacteria and viruses, and destroying them.

mad cow disease A disease of cattle, in which the brain is gradually destroyed and the animal dies. A form of mad cow disease that affects humans may be caused by eating infected beef.

Magellanic Clouds (maj-uh-LAN-ik KLOWDZ) Two small galaxies that are the galaxies closest to the Milky Way. The Magellanic Clouds are faintly visible in the night sky of the Southern Hemisphere.

maggot (MAG-uht) The larva of a type of fly, often found in decayed animal and plant matter. Maggots look like small white worms.

magma (MAG-muh) The hot, liquid rock that is formed under the Earth's crust. Magma can either cool underground, or it can flow out as lava if it reaches the Earth's surface. Magma turns into igneous rock when it cools.

magnesium (mag-NĒ-zē-uhm) A chemical element that is a silvery-white metal that gives off an intense white flame when it burns. Magnesium is very light and is often added to aluminum or other metals to make airplane parts. It is also used in fireworks. ◻ See Table on pages 178–179.

magnet (MAG-nit) A rock, piece of metal, or other object that attracts iron, steel, and some other metals and alloys. Magnets have two magnetic poles, called north and south.

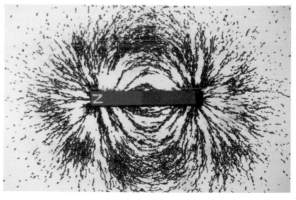

◻ **magnet**

Tiny iron filings show the lines of force in the magnetic field surrounding a bar magnet.

magnetic (mag-NET-ik) Having the properties of a magnet. A magnetic substance or object attracts iron and steel.

Machines

*Machines make it easier for us to do work. There are three basic simple machines: the **inclined plane**, the **lever**, and the **pulley**. Four others—the **wedge**, the **screw**, the **wheel and axle**, and the **gear**—are variations of these. More complicated machines, such as washing machines and cars, are based on the same ideas as simple machines but have more parts and use fuel and electricity as sources of power.*

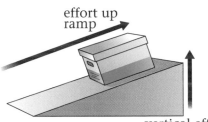

inclined plane

Pushing a load up a gentle slope is easier than lifting it up directly.

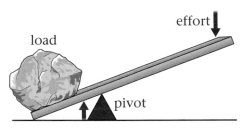

lever

Pushing down on the long lever is easier than lifting the load directly.

pulley

Pulling down on a pulley is easier than lifting a load directly.

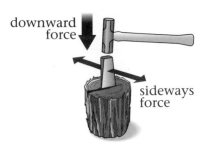

wedge

The two sides of the wedge push the downward force of the hammer outward, making it easier to split the block of wood.

screw

Turning a screw into an object is easier than pushing it in directly.

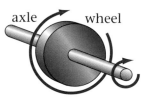

wheel and axle

Turning the axle a short distance moves the wheel a greater distance, therefore making it go farther.

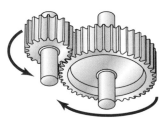

gear

Turning the smaller wheel's axle a short distance causes the larger wheel to turn a greater distance.

magnetic disk   A device in a computer, such as a hard disk, that stores information as patterns of magnetism.

magnetic field   The area around a magnet in which objects can be affected by the force of the magnet.

magnetic induction   The creation of magnetism in a substance by placing it in a magnetic field.

magnetic north   The direction from any point on the Earth toward the north magnetic pole. This is the direction to which the magnetic needle of a compass points. ◻ Compare **true north.**

magnetic pole   1. Either of two opposite areas of a magnet where the magnetic field is strongest. They are called the **north pole** and the **south pole.** When two magnets are placed near each other, the opposite poles attract each other while the same poles force each other away. 2. Either of two points on the Earth's surface where the Earth's magnetic field is strongest. The north and south magnetic poles are located near to but not exactly at the North and South Poles. Unlike the North and South Poles, the magnetic poles change position slightly over long periods of time.

magnetism   (MAG-ni-tiz-uhm) The force produced by a magnetic field. Magnetism can cause certain materials, like iron and steel, to be attracted to a magnet, or it can cause two magnets to attract or repel each other, depending on which way their poles line up.

magnetite   (MAG-ni-tīt) A naturally magnetic mineral made of iron, magnesium, and oxygen. Magnetite is brown or black and is found in many different types of rocks. It is an important source of iron.

magnetize   (MAG-ni-tīz) To cause an

Did You Know?

magnetism
Why does a compass point north? Because the Earth itself is a giant magnet with its own huge magnetic field. The field causes the molecules in the metal arrow of the compass to line up with its own lines of magnetic force, which run from north to south, and the compass needle swings toward north and stays there.

object to become magnetic. A nail can be magnetized by wrapping it in a wire and connecting the wire to a battery.

magnetometer   (mag-ni-TOM-i-ter) An instrument for measuring the strength and direction of a magnetic field. Scientists use magnetometers to study the Earth's magnetic field.

magnification   (mag-nuh-fi-KĀ-shuhn) A number that shows how many times larger an object looks than it really is. An object seen through a microscope with a magnification of 50 appears to be 50 times larger than it is.

magnifying glass   (MAG-nuh-fī-ing GLAS) A lens that makes objects look larger than they really are. A magnifying glass has a **convex lens.**

magnitude   (MAG-ni-tood) The strength or power of something, such as the brightness of a star or the amount of energy released by an earthquake.

Maiman   (MĀ-muhn), **Theodore Harold** Born 1927. American scientist who invented the first working laser in 1960.

malaria   (muh-LAIR-ē-uh) A disease that is caused by a parasite that enters the body through the bite of a mosquito. A person with malaria has attacks of chills, fever, and sweating that happen over and over again. Malaria is most often seen in tropical climates.

male **1.** Belonging to the sex that can fertilize eggs and father young. **2.** Being a plant, flower, or flower part, especially a stamen or anther, that produces cells that can fertilize an egg in an ovary to produce seeds. **3.** A male animal, plant, flower, or flower part.

malleable (MAL-ē-uh-buhl) Capable of being shaped or formed, especially by pressure or hammering. Gold, silver, and copper are all malleable metals and are often shaped into coins or jewelry.

malnutrition (mal-nōō-TRISH-uhn) A condition that is caused by having too little food to eat or by eating food that does not have enough nutrients.

mammal (MAM-uhl) A warm-blooded animal whose young feed on milk that is produced by the mother's mammary glands. Mammals are vertebrates, almost always give birth to live young, and are usually covered with hair or fur.

mammary gland (MAM-uh-rē gland) A gland in a female mammal that produces milk.

mammoth (MAM-uhth) A large, extinct elephant that lived in the Northern Hemisphere during the Ice Age. Mammoths were covered with thick hair and had long tusks that curved upward.

manatee (MAN-uh-tē) A water mammal that is found in rivers and bays along the tropical Atlantic Ocean. Manatees have flippers that are shaped like paddles and are more closely related to elephants than they are to dolphins or whales. Manatees are plant-eaters.

mandible (MAN-duh-buhl) **1.** The lower part of the jaw in humans and other vertebrates. ◻ See picture at **skeleton. 2.** One of the mouthparts of an insect or other arthropod. The mandible is shaped like a pincer and used for grasping and grinding food.

manganese (MANG-guh-nēz) A chemical element that is a grayish-white metal. Although manganese is easily broken into pieces, it can be combined with other elements to form strong, hard alloys. ◻ See Table on pages 178–179.

manometer (muh-NOM-i-ter) An instrument that measures the pressure of liquids and gases.

mantle (MAN-tuhl) **1.** The layer of the Earth between the crust and the core. The mantle has an upper part that is partially molten and a lower part that is solid. The lava that flows from volcanoes comes from the upper mantle. ◻ See picture at **Earth. 2.** The soft layer of tissue that makes up the

◻ **mammal**

top: *female mandrill with young*
bottom: *female manatee nursing young*

outer layer of the body of many mollusks, such as clams. The mantle produces the material that forms the shell.

manure (muh-NOO-er) Animal wastes that are added to soil as a **fertilizer.** Manure is usually made from the wastes of horses, cows, and chickens.

map A drawing or chart of an area of the Earth's surface. Maps can show physical features such as mountains and rivers, or they can show features like cities and highways.

marble (MAR-buhl) A rock that is made mainly of the minerals calcite and dolomite. It is usually white or gray, but often also has marks of other colors. Marble is the metamorphic rock that forms when limestone is exposed to heat and pressure from the Earth's crust. ◻ See Table on page 208.

Marconi (mar-KO-ne), **Guglielmo** Born 1874; died 1937. Italian scientist who built the first practical antenna. In 1901, Marconi successfully sent signals in Morse code across the Atlantic Ocean. Soon after his experiment, people started to use radio waves regularly for communication across distances.

mare (MAH-rā) One of the large dark areas on the Moon or on Mars or other planets.

marine (muh-REN) Living in or near the sea. Seals, plankton, and seaweed are examples of marine life.

marine biology The scientific study of life in and around the oceans.

marrow (MAIR-ō) See **bone marrow.**

Mars The planet that is fourth in distance from the Sun. Mars is the third smallest planet in the Solar System and, similar to Earth, it has seasons that change. ◻ See Table on pages 184–185.

marsh An area of low-lying wet land.

Grasses and reeds are the main plants that grow in a marsh. Freshwater marshes are common at the mouths of rivers. Saltwater marshes are formed by the flow of ocean tides.

marsupial (mar-SOO-pē-uhl) A type of mammal in which the young finish growing and developing outside the mother's body, attached to her nipple. The females usually have pouches in which the young are carried. Kangaroos, koalas, and opossums are marsupials.

◻ **marsupial**

female red kangaroo with young

maser (MĀ-zer) A device that sends out microwaves. Masers add energy to atoms in much the same way as lasers, but they send out microwaves instead of visible light. They are used to strengthen weak radio signals.

mass The amount of matter contained in an object. Mass is a measure of an object's **inertia** or resistance to being moved.

Did You Know?

mass

Mass is how much matter an object has, so it always stays the same. Weight, though, is a measure of gravity's pull on an object, so it is different depending on where the object is. On the moon, you would weigh one-sixth what you weigh on Earth, and in space you would weigh nothing at all, but in all cases your mass would still be the same.

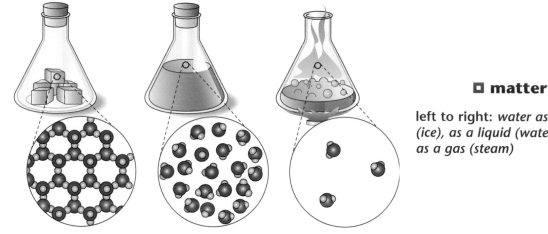

□ matter

left to right: *water as a solid (ice), as a liquid (water), and as a gas (steam)*

mass number The total number of protons and neutrons in the nucleus of an atom. For example, nitrogen has 7 protons and 7 neutrons in its nucleus, giving it a mass number of 14.

mastodon (MAS-tuh-don) A large, extinct mammal that looked like an elephant. Some mastodons had two pairs of tusks, one growing from the upper jaw and one growing from the lower.

mathematician (math-uh-muh-TISH-uhn) A person who is an expert in mathematics.

mathematics (math-uh-MAT-iks) The study of the measurement and relationships of quantities, using numbers and symbols.

matrix (MĀ-triks) **1.** A substance that contains another substance or has something embedded in it. Some fossils are embedded in a matrix of sediments that make up a rock. **2.** A group of items, such as numbers, arranged in columns and rows.

matter (MAT-er) Something that occupies space, has mass, and exists as a solid, liquid, or gas.

maximum (MAK-suh-muhm) The highest possible number, measure, quantity, or degree.

Maxwell (MAKS-wel), **James Clerk** Born 1831; died 1879. Scottish scientist who studied electricity and magnetism. After noting that electromagnetic waves move at the same speed as light, he showed that light itself is an electromagnetic wave. Maxwell also studied color and produced the first color photograph in 1861.

McClintock (muh-KLIN-tuhk), **Barbara** Born 1902; died 1992. American scientist who proved that genes can change position on chromosomes.

Biography

Barbara McClintock

Barbara McClintock spent her life studying corn plants, trying to understand their genes. She found that the genes for specific traits, such as kernel color, did not stay in the same place on the chromosomes, as scientists thought. She received a Nobel Prize for her studies in 1983.

mean A number that is midway in value between other numbers; the average.

measles (MĒ-zuhlz) A disease that is caused by a virus and gives a person a fever and a rash. The rash first appears on the face and then spreads to other parts of the body. Measles is very contagious.

measurement (MEZH-er-muhnt) A way of determining the amount, size, or volume of something. Accurate measurement requires the use of units that have a set value, such as pounds, inches, grams, or liters. The **metric system** is the system of measurement used by scientists the world over to perform experiments and compare results. ◻ See Table on page 148.

Did You Know?

measurement

It used to be that units of measurement were different in different places. This was a problem for science because a scientist using one system of measurement would not be understood by a scientist using another system. This is why the metric system was invented: its units are the same and have the same meaning everywhere in the world.

---

mechanical engineering (mi-KAN-i-kuhl en-juh-NEER-ing) The science that deals with how to design, make, and use machines.

mechanics (mik-KAN-iks) The scientific study of the motion of objects and of how objects react to forces. Mechanics is a branch of physics.

median (MĒ-dē-uhn) **1.** The middle number in a sequence of numbers listed from smallest to largest if there is an odd number of numbers. In the sequence 3, 4, 14, 35, 280, the median is 14. **2.** The average of the two middle numbers of a sequence of numbers listed from smallest to largest if there is an even number of numbers. In the sequence 4, 8, 10, 56, the median is 9 (the average of 8 and 10).

medicine (MED-i-sin) **1.** The scientific study of identifying, preventing, and treating disease and injury. **2.** A substance that is used to treat or prevent a disease.

medium (MĒ-dē-uhm) **1.** *See* **culture medium. 2.** A substance that energy travels through, especially in waves. Sound waves travel through the medium of air before striking our eardrums.

megabyte (MEG-uh-bīt) A unit of information that can be stored in a computer memory and is equal to 1,024 kilobytes or 1,048,576 bytes. The number 1,048,576 is equal to 2 multiplied by 2 twenty times.

meiosis (mī-Ō-sis) A kind of cell division that produces sex cells, each with half the number of chromosomes as the original cell. Meiosis allows an egg and sperm to combine during **fertilization** to make a new organism with a full set of chromosomes.

melanin (MEL-uh-nin) A dark chemical compound that gives color to the skin, hair, scales, feathers, and eyes of animals. It provides protection against the sun's rays by absorbing ultraviolet light. Melanin is a **pigment.**

melt To change from a solid to a liquid by being heated to the **melting point.**

meltdown Severe overheating of a nuclear reactor core that causes the core to melt and radiation to escape.

melting point The temperature at which a solid becomes a liquid. The melting point of the solid form of a substance is the same as the **freezing point** of its liquid form. The melting point of ice is 32° Fahrenheit (0° Celsius); the melting point of iron is 2,797° Fahrenheit (1,535° Celsius).

membrane (MEM-brān) **1.** A thin layer of tissue that covers a surface or divides a space in the body of a plant or animal.

Measurement

The Metric System

The metric system is the system of weights and measures used by scientists all over the world because it provides the most precise measurements. The basic units of the metric system are the **meter**, the **kilogram**, and the **liter**. Larger or smaller units are formed by adding a prefix to the basic units and multiplying them by the number the prefix stands for. The most common prefixes are **kilo-** (1,000), **centi-** ($\frac{1}{100}$), and **milli-** ($\frac{1}{1000}$). Thus a **kilogram** is 1,000 grams, and a **centimeter** is $\frac{1}{100}$ of a meter.

Length	Weight or Mass	Volume
1 centimeter = 10 millimeters 1 meter = 100 centimeters 1 kilometer = 1,000 meters	1 gram = 100 centigrams 1 kilogram = 1,000 grams 1 metric ton = 1,000 kilograms	1 centiliter=10 milliliters 1 liter = 100 centiliters 1 kiloliter = 1,000 liters

The United States Customary System

In the United States, the Customary System is widely used, although the metric system is used by scientists and throughout most of the world. The basic units of the Customary System are the **yard**, the **pound**, and the **gallon**.

Length	Weight or Mass	Volume
1 foot = 12 inches 1 yard = 3 feet 1 mile = 5,280 feet	1 pound = 16 ounces 1 ton (short) = 2,000 pounds	1 cup = 8 fluid ounces 1 pint = 2 cups 1 quart = 2 pints 1 gallon = 4 quarts

Converting from the United States Customary System to the Metric System

Length	Weight or Mass	Volume
1 inch = 2.54 centimeters 1 foot = 0.305 meter 1 yard = 0.91 meter 1 mile = 1.61 kilometers	1 ounce = 28.35 grams 1 pound = 453.6 grams 1 ton (short) = 0.91 metric ton	1 fluid ounce = 29.57 milliliters 1 cup = 0.24 liter 1 pint = 0.47 liter 1 quart = 0.95 liter 1 gallon = 3.79 liters

Converting from the Metric System to the United States Customary System

Length	Weight or Mass	Volume
1 centimeter = 0.39 inch 1 meter = 3.28 feet 1 kilometer = 0.62 mile	1 gram = 0.035 ounce 1 kilogram = 2.2 pounds 1 metric ton = 1.1 tons (short)	1 liter = 1.06 quarts or 0.26 gallon

Converting Temperature between Fahrenheit (F) and Celsius (C)

Fahrenheit to Celsius = (degrees Fahrenheit – 32) x $\frac{5}{9}$

For example, to convert 77° Fahrenheit to Celsius: $(77°F - 32) \times \frac{5}{9} = 25°C$

Celsius to Fahrenheit = (degrees Celsius x $\frac{9}{5}$) + 32

For example, to convert 25° Celsius to Fahrenheit: $(25°C \times \frac{9}{5}) + 32 = 77°F$

Membranes line the inside of the mouth and nose. The eardrum, which separates the middle ear from the outer ear, is a membrane. **2.** *See* **cell membrane. 3.** A thin sheet of material that blocks some substances and allows others to pass through.

memory (MEM-uh-rē) **1.** The ability to remember something that happened in the past or something that has been learned. **2.** The part of a computer where data is stored. A computer has memory in its chips and in storage devices such as hard drives. **3.** The capacity of a computer to store information. Computer memory is usually measured in bytes, kilobytes, megabytes, or gigabytes.

Did You Know?

memory
We remember different things in different ways. Some things, like our friends' faces and multiplication tables, go into long-term memory, and we remember them for a long time. Other things, like the thousands of little things that happen to us every day, go into short-term memory, and we remember them for only a few days.

Mendel (MEN-duhl), **Gregor Johann** Born 1822; died 1884. Austrian scientist who studied heredity in plants. His ideas were ignored during his lifetime, but they have since formed the basis of modern genetics.

Mendeleev (men-duh-LĀ-uhf), **Dmitri Ivanovich** Born 1834; died 1907. Russian

□ Dmitri Mendeleev

scientist who invented the Periodic Table of the elements in 1869.

menstrual cycle (MEN-strōō-uhl SĪ-kuhl) The series of changes that take place in the body of a woman or girl from one period of menstruation to the next. An egg can be fertilized during the menstrual cycle. The menstrual cycle takes about a month to complete.

menstruation (men-strōō-Ā-shuhn) The monthly flow of blood from the uterus that marks the beginning of the **menstrual cycle.** Eggs that have not been fertilized leave the body by means of menstruation.

menu (MEN-yōō) A list of choices for making a computer do something. For example, to copy highlighted text, you could select "copy" from the onscreen menu.

mercury (MER-kyuh-rē) A chemical element that is a silvery-white metal and is a liquid at room temperature. Mercury is poisonous and is used to make pesticides. Until recently, mercury was also used as the fluid in thermometers. **□** See Table on pages 178–179.

Mercury The planet that is closest to the Sun. Mercury is the second smallest planet in the Solar System and has a rocky surface covered with mountains and craters. It has the shortest year, lasting 88 days. **□** See Table on pages 184–185.

meridian (muh-RID-ē-uhn) An imaginary line on the Earth's surface that runs from the North Pole to the South Pole. Meridians are used to measure **longitude.** All the places on the same meridian have the same longitude.

mesa (MĀ-suh) An area of high land with a flat top and two or more steep, cliff-like sides. Mesas are larger than buttes and smaller than plateaus. They are common in the southwest United States.

Mesolithic Period (mez-uh-LITH-ik PEER-ē-uhd) The middle period of the Stone Age, between the **Paleolithic Period** and the **Neolithic Period.** The Mesolithic Period began at different times in different parts of the world, between about 40,000 to 10,000 years ago. During this period, humans developed sharper and better stone tools, and they began to settle in permanent communities.

mesosphere (MEZ-uh-sfeer) The layer of the Earth's atmosphere lying above the stratosphere and below the thermosphere.

Mesozoic Era (mez-uh-ZŌ-ik EER-uh) The era of geologic time starting about 245 million years ago and ending about 65 million years ago. Early during the Mesozoic Era dinosaurs first appeared, and at its end they became extinct. Flowering plants also developed during the Mesozoic Era. ◻ See Table on pages 102–103.

metabolism (mi-TAB-uh-liz-uhm) The chemical reactions that take place in cells and allow living things to grow, function, and repair damaged body tissues. The chemical reactions in metabolism change food into energy.

metal (MET-uhl) One of a large group of chemical elements that heat and electricity can easily move through. Metals are usually shiny and can usually be molded or shaped without breaking into pieces. Iron, gold, copper, lead, and magnesium are metals.

metallurgy (MET-uhl-er-jē) The science of removing metals from the rocks in which they are found. Metallurgy also studies how to make metals pure.

metamorphic rock (met-uh-MOR-fik ROK) A rock formed from an older rock that has been changed because of heat or pressure in the Earth's crust. Metamorphic rocks often have folded layers, and they sometimes have pockets of precious minerals. Gneiss and marble are metamorphic rocks. ◻ See Table on page 208.

metamorphosis (met-uh-MOR-fuh-sis) A complete change in the appearance or form of an animal during its development into an adult. The change of a maggot into a fly, or of a tadpole into a frog, are both types of metamorphosis. The young of such animals are called **larvae.**

◻ **metamorphosis**

the development of a monarch butterfly from egg to larva (caterpillar) to pupa (cocoon) to imago (adult)

meteor (MĒ-tē-er) A bright streak of light that flashes in the night sky when a rocky object enters the Earth's atmosphere. Friction with the air causes the object to heat up and glow. Most meteors burn up before reaching the Earth's surface. ◻ Meteors are also called *shooting stars.*

meteorite (MĒ-tē-uh-rīt) A meteor that reaches the Earth's surface.

meteoroid (MĒ-tē-uh-roid) A small object that is made up of rock or metal and travels in outer space. Most meteoroids are no bigger than a pebble. When a meteoroid enters the Earth atmosphere, it is called a **meteor.**

meteorology (mē-tē-uh-ROL-uh-jē) The scientific study of the Earth's atmosphere and weather patterns.

meter (MĒ-ter) The basic unit of length in the metric system, equal to about 39.37 inches. ◻ See Table on page 148.

methane (METH-ān) A gas that burns easily and is the most important chemical compound in natural gas. Methane is produced by the decay of plants and animals. It is the simplest of the chemical compounds known as **hydrocarbons.**

Did You Know?

methane

We get methane by drilling under the ground, but methane doesn't just occur on Earth. It is one of the main gases in the atmosphere of that great gas planet Jupiter. And methane is common on Neptune, where the temperature is so cold (–373° Fahrenheit or –225° Celsius) that it freezes solid.

metric system (MET-rik SIS-tuhm) A system of measuring in which the meter, the kilogram, and the liter are the basic units. The metric system is used in most countries of the world. ◻ See Table on page 148.

metric ton A unit of weight equal to 1,000 kilograms or 2,205 pounds. ◻ See Table on page 148.

mica (MĪ-kuh) A mineral that is made of thin, shiny sheets that split apart easily. Mica occurs in different colors and is common in igneous and metamorphic rocks. It is mostly made of aluminum, silica, and oxygen.

microbe (MĪ-krōb) A microscopic organism that can cause infection or disease.

microbiology (mī-krō-bī-OL-uh-jē) The scientific study of microscopic organisms.

microclimate (MĪ-krō-klī-mit) The climate of a small, specific place within a larger area. An area as small as a hill or a city park can have several different microclimates. Microclimates depend on many factors, such as sunlight, shade, wind, temperature, and humidity. ◻ Compare **macroclimate.**

micrometer (mī-KROM-uh-ter) **1.** *See* **micron. 2.** A device for measuring very small distances, angles, or objects.

micron (MĪ-kron) A unit of length in the metric system equal to one millionth ($\frac{1}{1,000,000}$) of a meter. ◻ A micron is also called a *micrometer.*

microorganism (mī-krō-OR-guh-niz-uhm) A living thing that can be seen only with the aid of a microscope. Bacteria and protozoans are microorganisms.

microphone (MĪ-kruh-fōn) A device that turns sounds into electric impulses. Microphones are used with recording devices to record sounds and with amplifiers to make sounds louder.

microscope (MĪ-kruh-skōp) An instrument that makes very small objects appear

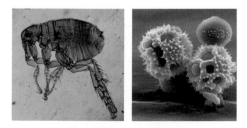

◻ **microscope**

left: *a flea photographed through a microscope* right: *dandelion pollen (larger) and horse-chestnut pollen photographed through a scanning electron microscope*

larger. Optical microscopes use a combination of lenses to focus visible light. Other kinds of microscopes, such as the electron microscope, use other forms of energy besides visible light to make things look larger.

microscopic (mī-kruh-SKOP-ik) Too small to be seen by the eye without the aid of a microscope. Amoebas are microscopic organisms.

microwave (MĪ-krō-wāv) A wave of electromagnetic radiation that has wavelengths that are shorter than radio waves but longer than infrared light. Microwaves are used to cook food in microwave ovens, to transmit cell-phone calls, to broadcast radio and television signals, and to detect objects by radar.

middle ear (MID-uhl EER) The part of the ear that contains the eardrum and three small bones that send sound vibrations to the inner ear.

midnight sun (MID-nīt SUHN) The Sun as seen at midnight during the summer in the North and South Polar regions. Although the Sun does not set during this period, it never gets high in the sky. Instead, it makes a complete circle in the sky just above the horizon.

Did You Know?

midnight sun
Because the Earth's axis is tilted, the polar regions are pointed toward the Sun during the summer and away from the Sun during the winter. This means that during the summer the Sun shines all day long on one of the polar regions. At the other polar region, where it is winter, the Sun does not shine at all.

mid-ocean ridge (MID-ō-shuhn RIJ) An underwater mountain range that extends through the North and South Atlantic Oceans, the Indian Ocean, and the South Pacific Ocean. A mid-ocean ridge has a crack called a **rift valley** at its center. Magma flows out of the crack and then cools and hardens into part of the mountain range.

migratory (MĪ-gruh-tor-ē) Traveling from one place to another at regular times of the year, often over long distances. Salmon, whales, and swallows are all migratory animals.

mildew (MIL-doo) A kind of fungus that forms a white or grayish coating on surfaces like plant leaves, cloth, or leather. Mildews usually grow in warm, damp conditions.

mile A unit of length equal to 5,280 feet or 1,760 yards. ◻ See Table on page 148.

milk A white liquid that is produced by female mammals for feeding their young. Milk is produced by the mammary glands. It contains proteins, fats, vitamins, minerals, and sugars.

Milky Way (MIL-kē WĀ) The galaxy that contains the Solar System. The Milky Way is shaped like a ball that has curved

◻ **Milky Way**

The Milky Way photographed through a telescope. The pink area (right) is a nebula.

arms, so that from outer space it would look like a spinning pinwheel. It is visible from Earth as a broad band of faint light in the night sky.

milligram (MIL-i-gram) A unit of mass or weight in the metric system equal to $\frac{1}{1,000}$ of a gram.

milliliter (MIL-uh-lē-ter) A unit of fluid volume or capacity in the metric system equal to $\frac{1}{1,000}$ of a liter. ◻ See Table on page 148.

millimeter (MIL-uh-mē-ter) A unit of length in the metric system equal to $\frac{1}{1,000}$ of a meter. ◻ See Table on page 148.

millipede (MIL-uh-pēd) A worm-like animal with a body that is divided into many narrow segments, most of which have two pairs of legs. Millipedes feed on plants, and, unlike centipedes, do not have glands with venom in their front legs. Millipedes are members of a group of animals known as **arthropods**.

mimicry (MIM-i-krē) The ability of a

living thing to look like another living thing or like its surroundings. Viceroy butterflies use mimicry to avoid getting eaten by birds because they look like monarch butterflies, which taste bad. By looking like bees or wasps, some insects use mimicry as protection against predators.

mineral (MIN-er-uhl) One of many different solid chemical compounds that are found in rocks and soil and are sometimes dissolved in water. Each mineral has a specific mix of chemical elements and a specific structure. Quartz, mica, and feldspar are minerals.

mineralogy (min-uh-ROL-uh-jē) The scientific study of minerals, which chemical compounds they are made of, and where they are likely to be found.

minimum (MIN-uh-muhm) The lowest possible number or measure.

minuend (MIN-yoo-end) A number that another number is subtracted from. In the equation $100 - 23 = 77$, the minuend is 100.

minus sign (MĪ-nuhs sīn) **1.** The – sign. It is used to show subtraction, as in $9 - 5 = 4$. It is also used to show that a number is negative (less than zero), as in –10. **2.** The – sign, used to show that an atom, molecule, or substance has more electrons than protons, and therefore has a negative charge.

◻ **mimicry**

The wings of the viceroy butterfly (top) look like those of the foul-tasting monarch butterfly.

◻ **mineral**

left to right: *barite, blue azurite combined with green malachite, and pyrite (fool's gold)*

minute (MIN-it) **1.** A unit of time equal to $\frac{1}{60}$ of an hour or 60 seconds. **2.** In geography, a unit used to measure longitude and latitude that is equal to $\frac{1}{60}$ of a degree.

Miocene Epoch (MĪ-uh-sēn EP-uhk) The period of time during the history of the Earth starting about 24 million years ago and ending about 5 million years ago. During the Miocene Epoch, grasses and grazing mammals first appeared. ◻ See Table on pages 102–103.

mirage (mi-RAHZH) An optical illusion in which something that is not really there appears in the distance. Mirages are often false images of water or upside-down reflections of objects that are much farther away than they appear. Mirages are caused by the bending of light after it enters a low layer of hot air.

◻ mirage

The mirage on this desert highway makes it look like it is flooded with water.

mirror (MIR-er) A surface, such as glass coated with a metal, that reflects light. Mirrors are used in science in many ways. They gather light in reflecting telescopes, direct light in making holograms, and help increase the strength of light in lasers.

Mississippian Period (mis-i-SIP-ē-uhn PEER-ē-uhd) The period of time during the history of the Earth starting about 360 million years ago and ending about 320 million years ago. During the Mississippian Period, shallow seas spread over land areas. ◻ See Table on pages 102–103.

mist A mass of tiny drops of water or another liquid in the air.

mite A tiny animal that is related to the tick. Mites often live as **parasites** on other animals or plants. Mites, like ticks and spiders, are members of the group of animals known as **arachnids.**

mitochondria (mī-tuh-KON-drē-uh) The tiny parts of a cell that change food into energy for use in the growth and functioning of a living thing. Mitochondria are found in all cells except bacteria. *Singular form*: **mitochondrion** (mī-tuh-KAHN-dre-uhn). ◻ See picture at **cell.**

mitosis (mī-TŌ-sis) A kind of cell division in which a cell splits into two identical cells. In mitosis, the number of chromosomes doubles, and each new cell receives the same number and type of chromosomes as the original cell. All of the body's cells divide by mitosis except for the sex cells. ◻ See picture at **cell.**

mixture (MIKS-cher) A combination of two substances in which the atoms or molecules of the two substances are spread around in a single mass but do not join up with one another. The substances in a mixture easily separate from each other. The sugar in a mixture of sugar and water will settle to the bottom of the container if the container is left undisturbed for a while.

mode The value that occurs the most in a set of data. In the set {25, 40, 72, 64, 40, 10}, the mode is 40.

modem (MŌ-duhm) A device for sending and receiving computer data over telephone wires. Modems send data in digital form by changing the data into pulses of electricity. The pulses are then changed back into data by the modem at the other end.

modulate   (MOJ-uh-lāt) To change or vary radio waves so they can carry different kinds of sounds for broadcasting.

Mohs   (MŌZ), **Friedrich** Born 1773; died 1839. German scientist who developed the Mohs scale in 1812.

Mohs scale   A scale used to measure and compare the hardness of minerals based on how easy it is to scratch them. There are ten minerals on this scale, ranging from talc, the softest (measuring 1 on the scale), to diamond, the hardest (measuring 10 on the scale).

molar   (MŌ-ler) A tooth with a broad upper surface, found at the back of the jaws. Molars are used for grinding or chewing food. Most adult mammals have 12 molars, 6 on top and 6 on the bottom.

mold   A kind of fungus that forms a fuzzy coating on the surface of damp or decaying materials. Molds can cause foods to spoil. Some molds make substances that kill bacteria and have been used to make **penicillin** and other medicines.

molecule   (MOL-i-kyool) A group of two or more atoms that are joined together by sharing electrons in a chemical bond. Molecules can have only two atoms or can combine thousands of atoms into complex chemical compounds.

mollusk   (MOL-uhsk) A type of animal that has a soft body and usually lives inside a hard shell. Most mollusks live in water. Snails, slugs, oysters, clams, scallops, octopuses, and squids are all mollusks. Mollusks are invertebrates.

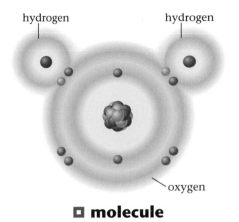

hydrogen   hydrogen

oxygen

❑ **molecule**

Two atoms of hydrogen and one atom of oxygen join together to form a molecule of water. The hydrogen atoms share their electrons (yellow) with the oxygen atom. The oxygen atom shares two of its electrons (blue) with the hydrogen atoms.

molt   To shed an outer covering, such as skin or feathers, so it can be replaced by a new one. Many snakes, birds, and insects molt.

Did You Know?

molt

Not all animals molt for the same reason. Some, like insects, crabs, and snakes, molt because they keep growing and can't fit into their old skins or shells anymore, and need to grow new ones from time to time. Others, like birds, molt because they grow a different covering for the cold season or for attracting a mate in the spring.

molten   (MŌL-tuhn) Melted by heat. The Earth's liquid outer core is made of molten iron and nickel.

momentum   (mō-MEN-tuhm) A quantity that describes moving objects and is equal to the object's **mass** times its **velocity**. The more mass an object has, and the faster it is moving, the more momentum it has.

moneran (muh-NEER-uhn) *See* **prokaryote.**

monitor (MON-i-ter) A device that gets video signals from a computer and displays information or images on a screen.

monkey (MUHNG-kē) A type of primate that is of medium size, has a narrow chest, and often has a long tail. Most monkeys live in warm forests. Baboons, mandrills, and marmosets are monkeys.

monocotyledon (mon-uh-kot-uh-LĒ-duhn) A flowering plant in which the seed has one **cotyledon,** the leaves have parallel veins, and the flower parts grow in multiples of 3. Grasses, palms, and lilies are monocotyledons. ◻ Monocotyledons are called *monocots* for short. ◻ Compare **dicotyledon.**

monosodium glutamate (mon-uh-SŌ-dē-uhm GLOO-tuh-māt) A kind of salt that forms crystals and is used to flavor food. Parmesan cheese, tomatoes, and seaweed contain monosodium glutamate. ◻ Monosodium glutamate is called *MSG* for short.

monotreme (MON-uh-trēm) A type of mammal that lays eggs. The females provide milk directly through the skin to their young. The platypus is a monotreme.

monsoon (mon-SOON) **1.** A wind that blows in the opposite direction during the summer than it does during the winter. Monsoons are caused by seasonal changes in temperature. **2.** The rainy summer season in southern Asia that is brought by the monsoon.

month One of the twelve periods that make up a year. Months are based on the amount of time that it takes for the Moon to make one complete revolution around the Earth.

moon **1.** The round object that moves around the Earth at a distance of about 240,000 miles (386,000 kilometers). The Moon is about one-fourth the size of the Earth and can be seen because it reflects the Sun's light. It takes 29 days, 12 hours, and 44 minutes for the Moon to make a complete orbit of the Earth. ◻ Earth's Moon is usually spelled with a capital *M.* **2.** A round object that moves around a planet other than the Earth. Saturn has at least 30 moons.

Did You Know?

moon
Earth's Moon is basically a big chunk of stone, but other moons in the Solar System are very different.

Io, one of Jupiter's moons, is covered with huge, erupting volcanoes. Another of Jupiter's moons, Europa, is a big frozen ball of muddy water.

Morgan (MOR-guhn), **Thomas Hunt** Born 1866; died 1945. American biologist who studied the genetics of fruit flies. Morgan's experiments showed the importance of genes in passing on traits from one generation to the next.

morning star (MOR-ning STAR) A planet, not a star, that can be seen in the east just before or at sunrise. The morning star is usually Venus or Mercury.

morphing (MOR-fing) The changing of one computer image into another. In morphing, the first image gradually disappears as the second image takes its place. Morphing is used to create special effects in movies.

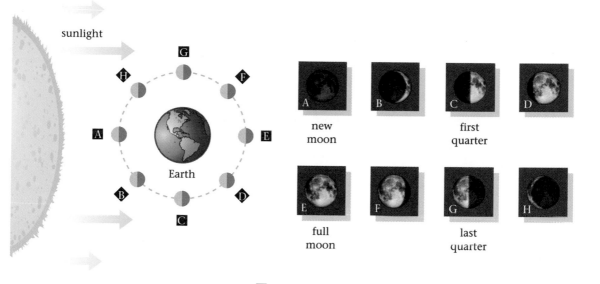

□ moon

Half of the Moon is always in sunlight, as seen on the left. The relative positions of Earth, the Moon, and the Sun determine how much of the lighted half can be seen from Earth, as seen on the right. These forms in which the Moon appears are known as phases.

Morse, Samuel Finley Breese Born 1791; died 1872. American inventor who developed the telegraph in 1854 and developed Morse code for sending messages by it.

Morse code A system for sending messages in which the letters of the alphabet and numbers are represented by combinations of short and long sounds or beams of light called dots and dashes. The Morse code was first used to send and receive messages by **telegraph.** The Morse code is named after Samuel Morse.

mosquito (muh-SKĒ-tō) A type of winged insect that is related to the fly. Female mosquitoes suck blood for food and may carry diseases, such as malaria.

A	B	C	D
E	F	G	H
I	J	K	L
M	N	O	P
Q	R	S	T
U	V	W	X
Y		Z	

□ Morse code

Did You Know?

mosquito

Mosquito bites itch because we're allergic to chemical compounds in the mosquitoes' saliva. Some of those chemicals are proteins that keep blood from forming clots, so that the mosquito can feed more easily. A few people, though, have little or no allergic reaction to mosquito saliva, meaning they can get bitten without itching afterwards.

moss A kind of small green plant that grows in clusters in moist, shady areas, usually on the ground, on rocks, or on tree trunks. Mosses do not have flowers, seeds, xylem, or phloem.

□ **moss**

moss growing on tree trunks

moth An insect that resembles a butterfly but has a thicker body and smaller, less brightly colored wings. Moths have featherlike antennae. Unlike butterflies, moths are active at night and hold their wings out to the side when not in flight.

motherboard (MUH*TH*-er-bord) The main circuit board of a computer. The motherboard usually has the central processing unit, memory, and circuits that control the disk drives, keyboard, monitor, mouse, and other devices that are used with the computer.

mother-of-pearl The hard, smooth, pearly layer on the inside of certain seashells, such as abalones and some oysters. It is used to make buttons and jewelry.

motile (MŌ-tīl) Able to move by itself. Amoebas and most other protozoans are motile.

motor (MŌ-ter) A machine that uses energy, such as electricity or heat from a burning fuel, to cause something to move. Electric motors run fans and pumps.

mountain (MOWN-tuhn) An area of land that rises sharply to great heights. Mountains can form as single peaks or as part of a long chain, either by the formation of volcanoes or by the collision of two plates through the forces of **plate tectonics.** The tallest mountain in the world is Mount Everest, which rises 29,000 feet above sea level.

mouse **1.** A type of small rodent that usually has a pointed snout, round ears, and a long thin tail. Some kinds of mice build nests in or near where people live because there is food nearby. Scientists also use mice for laboratory experiments. **2.** A device that is connected to a computer and that is moved on a flat surface to position the cursor on the computer screen. A mouse has one or more buttons. Clicking a button causes the computer do something.

mouth **1.** The opening of the body through which animals take in food and air. Human mouths have teeth, lips, and a tongue, which help us eat and speak. **2.** The part of a stream or river that empties into a larger body of water. **3.** A natural opening, as in a harbor, cave, canyon, or volcano.

mouthpart One of the parts around the mouth of an insect, spider, or other arthropod that are used for feeding. Mouthparts grow in pairs.

MRI Short for **magnetic resonance imaging.** The use of a strong magnetic field and radio waves to produce a detailed picture of the inside of the body. In MRI, the body is placed inside a magnetic field, radio waves are applied to a body part, and the body part then produces energy in response. A computer measures the kind and amount of energy that is produced and changes it into an image that can be studied by a doctor.

MSG *See* **monosodium glutamate.**

mucous membrane (MYOO-kuhs MEM-brān) A membrane that lines the surface of a body part or passage. Mucous membranes produce **mucus,** which helps fight infections. The mouth, nose, lungs, stomach, and intestines are lined with mucous membranes.

mucus (MYOO-kuhs) A thick, slippery substance that covers and protects a part of the body, such as the inside of the mouth and nose.

mulch A material that is placed around growing plants to protect them against cold or to keep the soil moist. Leaves, straw, and wood chips can be used for mulch.

multicellular (muhl-ti-SEL-yuh-ler) Made of many cells. All living things in the kingdoms of plants and animals are multicellular. ◻ Compare **unicellular.**

multiple (MUHL-tuh-puhl) A number that may be divided by another number without any amount left over. For example, 4, 10, and 32 are multiples of 2.

multiplicand (muhl-tuh-pli-KAND) A number that is to be multiplied by another number. In the equation $7 \times 3 = 21$, the multiplicand is 7.

multiplication (muhl-tuh-pli-KĀ-shuhn) A mathematical operation that is a short way of adding a certain number to itself the number of times indicated by a second number. For example, the equation $3 \times 4 = 12$ is the same as $3 + 3 + 3 + 3 = 12$.

multiplication sign The $\times$ sign. It is used to show multiplication, as in the equation $8 \times 4 = 32$.

multiplier (MUHL-ti-pli-er) The number by which another number is to be multiplied. In the equation $5 \times 8 = 40$, the multiplier is 8.

multiply (MUHL-tuh-plī) **1.** To perform multiplication on two numbers. **2.** To increase in number, especially by reproducing. Bacteria can multiply inside the cells of humans and cause disease.

mumps A disease that is caused by a virus, in which the glands at the back of the jaw become painful and swollen. Mumps is very contagious.

muscle (MUHS-uhl) A part of the body that can shorten or contract to produce movement. In humans and other vertebrates, muscles that are attached to the bones of the skeleton can be moved at will. The muscles of the heart and other organs contract automatically.

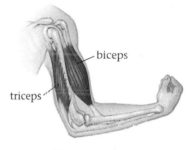

◻ **muscle**

When the biceps contracts to bend the elbow, the triceps relaxes. When the triceps contracts to straighten the elbow, the biceps relaxes.

mushroom (MUHSH-room) A type of fast-growing fungus with a stalk that is topped by a soft cap, often in the shape of an umbrella. Some mushrooms are edible, but others are poisonous.

mushroom cloud A cloud of smoke that is shaped like a mushroom, especially one caused by an atomic bomb.

mutant (MYOO-tuhnt) Something, such as a trait determined by the genes, that is caused by a **mutation.**

mutation (myoo-TĀ-shuhn) A change in the genes of an organism. Mutations that are passed through the genes from one generation to the next can be harmful or can improve the ability of a living thing to survive. A mutation that benefits one member of a species may become a trait shared by all members through the process of **natural selection.**

mutualism (MYOO-choo-uh-liz-uhm) A close relationship between two different kinds of organisms in which each organism is helped and neither is harmed. Mutualism is a kind of **symbiosis.**

mycelium (mī-SĒ-lē-uhm) The soft mass of thin tubes that make up the part of a fungus that grows, usually in something else, such as soil or a tree trunk. The mycelium usually can't be seen, but it produces the parts of a fungus, such as the stalk and cap of a mushroom, that are easy to see.

◻ **mutualism**

Tickbirds ride on a rhino's back and eat the ticks that bother it. Both animals are helped by this relationship.

mycology (mī-KOL-uh-jē) The scientific study of fungi, including mushrooms.

myopia (mī-Ō-pē-uh) The condition of being **nearsighted.** Myopia can be corrected with glasses.

Nn

nail   The thin, hard covering at the end of a finger or toe. Nails are made of keratin. The claws of a cat and the hooves of a horse are nails.

naked eye   (NĀ-kid Ī) The human eye by itself, without the aid of an optical instrument such as a microscope or telescope.

NASA   Short for **National Aeronautics and Space Administration.** A government agency that was started in 1958. Scientists at NASA are involved in the research and exploration of outer space.

nasal   (NĀ-zuhl) Relating to the nose.

native   (NĀ-tiv) Living or growing naturally in a certain region. Plants and animals that are native to a region developed in that area without the assistance of humans.

natural gas   (NACH-er-uhl GAS) A mixture of gases that occurs naturally beneath the Earth's surface, often near petroleum. Natural gas is used as a fuel, especially to heat buildings. Natural gas is made mostly of methane, but it also contains propane and other gases in smaller amounts.

natural history   The scientific study of living things and objects that are found in nature and of how they change over time. Natural history includes the sciences of zoology, mineralogy, geology, and paleontology.

naturalist   (NACH-er-uh-list) A person who specializes in natural history, especially in the study of plants and animals in their natural surroundings.

natural number   A positive integer.

natural resource   Any part of the Earth or its atmosphere that is necessary or useful to humans. Forests, mineral deposits, and fresh water are natural resources.

natural science   A science that studies the laws and physical objects of nature. Biology, chemistry, and physics are natural sciences.

natural selection   The basic principle that only those living things that are best suited to living in a particular environment live long enough to produce offspring. The individual plants and animals that reproduce themselves pass their genes to their young, giving them a better chance of survival. Natural selection forms the basis of **evolution.**

nature   (NĀ-cher) The world and all of the naturally occurring life forms, objects, and events that are part of it.

nautilus   (NAWT-uhl-uhs) A mollusk that lives in tropical seas and has a spiral shell and many compartments. The nautilus is related to the squids and octopuses.

Neanderthal   (nē-AN-der-thawl *or* nē-AN-der-tawl) An extinct variety of human that lived in Europe, Africa, and Asia until about 30,000 years ago. Neanderthals usually lived in caves, made stone tools, and were the earliest humans known to bury their dead.

neap tide   (NĒP tīd) A tide in which the difference between high and low tide is the least. Neap tides happen twice a month when the positions of the Earth, Sun, and Moon cause the pull of gravity on the

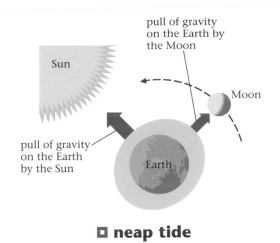

□ neap tide

Neap tides occur when the Sun, Moon, and Earth are not all lined up. When this happens, the pull of gravity on the Earth and its waters comes from two different directions and is less strong.

Earth's ocean to be weakest. □ Compare **spring tide.**

nearsighted (NEER-sī-tid) Able to see nearby objects more easily than distant objects. In nearsighted people, light that enters the eye is focused in front of the retina instead of right on it. □ Compare **farsighted.**

nebula (NEB-yuh-luh) A large cloud of gas and dust in outer space. Nebulae pro-

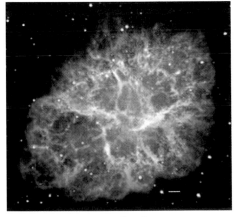

□ nebula

The Crab Nebula is named for its round, crablike shape.

vide the material from which stars form. They appear as a bright patch of light in the night sky when they give off their own light or reflect the light of nearby stars. *Plural form:* **nebulae** (NEB-yuh-lē) or **nebulas.** □ See picture at **star.**

nebular hypothesis (NEB-yuh-ler hī-POTH-i-sis) An explanation of how the Solar System began. According to the nebular hypothesis, a spinning cloud of gas and dust cooled and drew together and then flattened into a disk shape with a bulge in the middle. The matter in the disk turned into the planets, their moons, asteroids, and comets, while the great mass at the center became the Sun.

nectar (NEK-ter) A sweet liquid that is made by flowers. Insects and birds use nectar as food, and bees use nectar to make honey.

needle (NĒ-duhl) A narrow, stiff leaf that is found on fir and pine trees and other conifers. □ See picture at **leaf.**

negative (NEG-uh-tiv) **1.** Less than zero. The minus sign is used to show that a number is negative, such as –2 and $-\frac{3}{8}$. **2.** Having the charge of an electron. The symbol for a negative charge is a minus sign. □ Compare **positive.**

Neolithic Period (nē-uh-LITH-ik PEER-ē-uhd) The final period of the Stone Age that began around 10,000 years ago in the Middle East. This period ended when humans began to use metal tools. During the Neolithic Period, humans began to farm, to develop crafts such as pottery and weaving, and to use polished stone tools.

neon (NĒ-on) A chemical element that is a noble gas and is found in small amounts in the atmosphere. When electricity passes through a tube of neon gas, as in neon signs, it glows reddish-orange. Neon is also used for refrigeration. ◻ See Table on pages 178–179.

Neptune (NEP-tōōn) The planet that is eighth in distance from the Sun. Neptune is the fourth largest planet in the Solar System. It has long, powerful storms. ◻ See Table on pages 184–185.

nerve A bundle of cells, called **nerve cells,** that carries signals in the form of electric impulses between parts of the body and the brain and spinal cord. The nervous system is made up of nerves.

◻ **neon**

a neon sign

Did You Know?

nerve

The nerves are the electrical wires of the nervous system. Some of the signals that they carry travel very fast, while others are slower. The fastest ones are signals that move the muscles. They travel along special super-fast nerve fibers up to 390 feet (119 meters) per second! Signals that carry information about what you touch aren't so fast. They move about 250 feet (76 meters) per second. Signals that carry information about pain are the slowest, traveling at a poky 2 feet (0.6 meter) per second.

nerve cell A cell of the nervous system. Nerve cells send and receive signals in the form of electric impulses from other nerve cells. A bundle of nerve cells is called a

nerve. ◻ A nerve cell is also called a *neuron.*

nervous system (NER-vuhs SIS-tuhm) The system in the body that is made up of the brain, the spinal cord, and all of the nerves in the body. The nervous system allows living things to respond to changes in the environment. Breathing, heartbeat, digestion, movement, thinking, and speech are all controlled by the nervous system.

nest A shelter or container made by an animal, especially one used to lay eggs or raise young in. Birds, mice, squirrels, fish, and many insects make nests.

network (NET-werk) **1.** A structure that has the pattern of a net. Capillaries form networks throughout the body. **2.** A system of computers that are linked together in order to share information.

neuron (NUR-on) *See* **nerve cell.**

neutral (NŌŌ-truhl) Being neither an acid nor a base. Water is a neutral chemical compound.

neutron (NŌŌ-tron) One of the particles that make up an atom. Along with protons, neutrons make up the atom's nucleus. Neutrons have no electric charge.

neutron star An object in space made of a very dense mass of neutrons. Neutron stars form near the end of a star's existence, when the star's core collapses in a giant explosion called a **supernova.** Neutron stars are usually less than 16 miles (26 kilometers) across, extremely small compared with most other stars. ◻ See picture at **star.**

new moon The Moon when it is not visible or when it is visible only as a thin crescent. ◻ See picture at **moon.**

newton (NŌŌ-tuhn) A unit used to measure force. One newton is equal to the

163

force needed to make an object that weighs 1 kilogram (2.2 pounds) undergo acceleration at a rate of 1 meter (3.3 feet) per second per second. The newton is named after Isaac Newton.

Newton, Isaac

□ **Isaac Newton**

Born 1642; died 1727. English scientist who made revolutionary discoveries in mathematics, physics, optics, and astronomy. Newton explained how gravitation works, demonstrated that white light contains all the colors of the spectrum, and developed new forms of mathematics. In 1668 he invented the first reflecting telescope.

niche (NITCH *or* NĒSH) The environment and conditions that a particular kind of living thing needs to survive. A plant or animal's niche includes a place to live, along with enough food and protection from predators or other dangers. Each kind of living thing has its own niche within an ecosystem.

nickel (NIK-uhl) A chemical element that is a silvery, hard, and easily shaped metal. Nickel does not rust easily, and it is used to make alloys such as stainless steel. □ See Table on pages 178–179.

nicotine (NIK-uh-tēn) A poisonous chemical compound that is found in the tobacco plant. It is the chemical in cigarette smoke that causes **addiction.**

nimbostratus cloud (nim-bō-STRAT-uhs KLOWD) A low, gray, dark cloud that covers the whole sky. Nimbostratus clouds usually produce steady rain, sleet, or snow. □ See picture at **cloud.**

nimbus cloud (NIM-buhs KLOWD) A cloud that produces rain.

nipple (NIP-uhl) The small, central part of the mammary gland. In female mammals, milk is released through the nipple.

nitrate (NĪ-trāt) A chemical compound that contains a nitrogen atom attached to three oxygen atoms. Nitrates are very important nutrients for plants.

nitrifying bacteria (NĪ-truh-fī-ing bak-TEER-ē-uh) Bacteria that take in nitrogen from the air that is mixed in soil and use the nitrogen to make chemical compounds that plants use as food. Nitrifying bacteria are an important part of the **nitrogen cycle.**

nitrogen (NĪ-truh-juhn) A chemical element that is a gas with no color or odor. Nitrogen makes up about four-fifths of the Earth's atmosphere, and it is essential for life because it is a part of all proteins. Nitrogen is used to make ammonia, TNT, and fertilizers. □ See Table on pages 178–179.

nitrogen cycle The process that allows nitrogen to move from the environment into living things and then go back into the environment. Nitrogen in the atmosphere is taken in by bacteria in the soil to make chemical compounds that plants take up as nutrients. Animals take in this nitrogen when they eat the plants, and when the animals die, bacteria feeding on their decaying bodies release the nitrogen back into the atmosphere as a gas.

nitrogen fixation The process that allows nitrogen in the air to become absorbed by plants. Bacteria in the soil take up the nitrogen gas and use it to make chemical compounds that plants can take in through their roots as nutrients.

nitroglycerin (nī-trō-GLIS-er-in) A thick liquid that explodes easily. It is used to

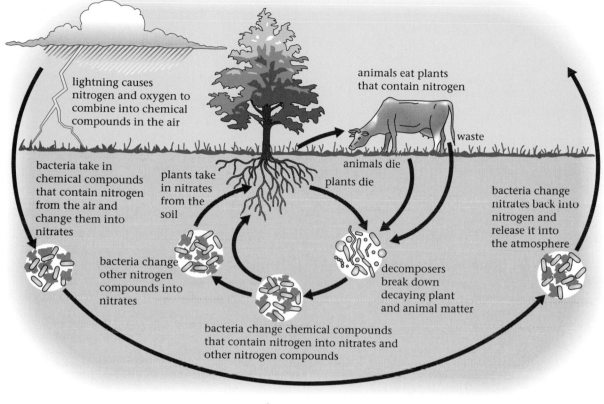

□ nitrogen cycle

make dynamite and as a drug in medicine to treat heart disease.

Nobel (nō-BEL), **Alfred** Born 1833; died 1896. Swedish scientist who invented dynamite in 1866. When he died, he left his fortune to create a prize which is named for him. The Nobel Prize is awarded every year for scientific achievements in physics, physiology and medicine, and chemistry.

noble gas (NŌ-buhl GAS) One of the six gases that almost never react with other chemical elements. The noble gases are helium, neon, argon, krypton, xenon, and radon. They appear in the column of the Periodic Table that is farthest to the right.
□ Noble gases are also called *inert gases*.
□ See Table on pages 178–179.

nocturnal (nok-TER-nuhl) Most active at night. Owls, bats, and mice are nocturnal.

nonmetal (non-MET-uhl) One of a group of chemical elements that do not conduct heat or electricity well. Carbon, oxygen, silicon, and sulfur are nonmetals.

nonrenewable (non-ri-NOO-uh-buhl) Relating to a natural resource, such as oil or

Did You Know?
noble gas
Why are the noble gases noble? The word noble refers to dukes, earls, counts, and other wealthy people that belong to the court of a king or queen. They don't spend much time with common folk. In the same way, noble gases do not combine with other chemical elements.

iron ore, that cannot be replaced once it has been used. ☐ Compare **renewable**.

north   The direction to your right when you face a sunset.

Northern Hemisphere   The half of the Earth that is north of the equator.

northern lights   *See* **aurora borealis**.

North Frigid Zone   The region of the Earth that extends from the Arctic Circle to the North Pole. ☐ See picture at **zone**.

North Pole   The most northern point of the Earth. The North Pole is the northern end of the axis on which the Earth rotates. It is located in the Arctic Ocean. ☐ See picture at **Arctic Circle**.

North Star   A bright star at the end of the handle of the Little Dipper. The North Star is used to show which direction is north because it remains in nearly the same place in the sky above the North Pole. ☐ The North Star is also called *Polaris*.

North Temperate Zone   The region of the Earth that is located between the Arctic Circle and the Tropic of Cancer. ☐ See picture at **zone**.

nose   The part of the head that contains the nostrils and the organs of smell. Air is breathed in and out through the nose. The nose is part of the respiratory system.

nova   (NŌ-vuh) A star that explodes and becomes very bright. Because a nova only explodes at its surface, it returns to its original brightness over a period of weeks to years. *Plural form*: **novae** (NŌ-vē) or **novas**.

nuclear   (NOO-klē-er) **1.** Relating to the nucleus of a cell. **2.** Relating to the nucleus of an atom. **3.** Using energy that comes from the nuclei of atoms.

Did You Know?

nova

The word *nova* means "new." A nova is thus a "new star," one that wasn't seen in the heavens before it exploded and suddenly became very bright. Some novas are so bright they can be seen during the day.

---

nuclear energy   Energy that comes from the nuclei of atoms when they are split apart in **fission** or joined together with other nuclei in **fusion**.

nuclear power   Electricity that is produced by a nuclear reactor. The heat from the nuclear reactor is used to heat water into steam. The steam is then used to turn turbines that drive generators to produce electricity.

nuclear reaction   A process that brings about a change in the mass or energy of the nucleus of an atom. Fusion, fission, and radioactive decay are nuclear reactions.

nuclear reactor   A device in which the nuclei of atoms break up under controlled conditions to produce heat for generating electricity. The nuclei split, or undergo **fission**, in a series of events called a **chain reaction**.

nuclear weapon   A weapon that gets its destructive power from the energy released when the nuclei of atoms that are loaded into it split up or join together. Atomic bombs and hydrogen bombs are nuclear weapons.

nucleolus   (noo-KLĒ-uh-luhs) A tiny round part in the nucleus of a cell. The nucleolus contains and stores RNA. ☐ See picture at **cell**.

nucleus   (NOO-klē-uhs) **1.** The central

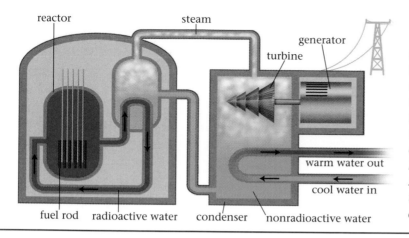

☐ nuclear reactor

Radioactive atoms stored in fuel rods split apart in a chain reaction that releases enormous amounts of energy. The energy heats the radioactive water, which in turn causes nonradioactive water in a second loop to heat up into steam. The steam drives a turbine that turns a generator, producing electricity.

part of an atom that contains most of its mass. The nuclei of all atoms except hydrogen contain both protons and neutrons; the nucleus of hydrogen contains only one proton. Electrons move at high speed around the nucleus. ☐ See picture at **atom. 2.** The part of a cell that contains the chromosomes and controls the growth, reproduction, and metabolism of the cell. A nucleus that is set off from the rest of the cell by a membrane is found in almost all plant and animal cells. Bacteria do not have nuclei. ☐ See picture at **cell.** *Plural form:* **nuclei** (NOO-klē-ī).

number (NUHM-ber) One of a series of symbols that occur in order and are used for counting. Numbers other than zero can be positive or negative.

numeral (NOO-mer-uhl) A symbol or mark that is used to represent a number.

numerator (NOO-mer-ā-ter) The number above or to the left of the line in a fraction. The lower number (the **denominator**) shows the total number of equal parts that the whole is divided into, and the numerator shows how many of those parts there are. In the fraction $\frac{2}{7}$, 2 is the numerator.

nutrient (NOO-trē-uhnt) A substance, such as protein or a mineral, that living things need for proper growth and good health. Plants get minerals and other nutri-

ents from the soil. Animals get nutrients from the foods they eat.

nutrition (noo-TRISH-uhn) The process by which a living thing takes in food and makes use of nutrients.

nylon (NĪ-lon) A strong, flexible substance that can be made into fibers, sheets, or bristles, and is used to make fabrics and plastics. Nylon is made in a laboratory or factory.

Did You Know?

nylon

Nylon was the first fiber that scientists created in the laboratory. It was actually invented by accident when a scientist pulled a heated rod out of a jar that contained a mixture of chemicals, and the mixture stretched. The scientists realized that it would be a good substitute for silk.

nymph (NIMF) An early stage in the development of an insect that does not become a pupa during its life cycle. Nymphs usually look like adults but are smaller, do not have full-grown wings, and cannot reproduce. Nymphs molt several times as they grow. The young of crickets, cockroaches, and termites are nymphs.

Oo

oasis (ō-Ā-sis) An area in a desert where there is enough water for plants to grow. An oasis forms when groundwater lies close enough to the surface to form a spring or to be reached by wells. *Plural form*: **oases** (ō-Ā-sēz).

objective lens (uhb-JEK-tiv LENS) The lens that is closest to the object being viewed with an instrument such as a telescope or a microscope.

observation (ob-zer-VĀ-shuhn) The act of watching something closely and recording how it behaves or changes under certain conditions. Observation is an important step in the **scientific method.**

observatory (uhb-ZERV-uh-tor-ē) A building that is specially designed and equipped for observing things, such as the weather or objects in outer space.

□ observatory

Mount Haleakala on the island of Maui, Hawaii

obsidian (uhb-SID-ē-uhn) An igneous rock that is made of shiny black glass. Obsidian forms from lava that cools so quickly that minerals do not have a chance to form within it. □ See Table on page 208.

obtuse angle (ob-TOOS ANG-guhl) An angle that measures between 90° and 180°. □ See picture at **angle.**

ocean (Ō-shuhn) **1.** The body of salt water that covers about 72 percent of the Earth's surface. **2.** One of the four main divisions of this body of water, made up of the Atlantic, Pacific, Indian, and Arctic Oceans. The Pacific Ocean is by far the world's largest ocean. It covers 70 million square miles, which is larger than the world's entire land area.

oceanography (ō-shuh-NOG-ruh-fē) The scientific study and exploration of the ocean and of the plants and animals that live in it.

octagon (OK-tuh-gon) A flat shape that has eight sides. □ See picture at **geometry.**

octahedron (ok-tuh-HĒ-druhn) A three-dimensional object that has eight faces, each one a triangle.

octopus (OK-tuh-puhs) A type of mollusk that has a soft, rounded body with eight tentacles and large eyes. The tentacles of the octopus have two rows of suckers that are used for holding on to things. Octopuses are considered to be the most intelligent of the invertebrates. *Plural form*: **octopuses** or **octopi** (OK-tuh-pī).

odd number A number that is the number 1 or that has a remainder of 1 when it is divided by 2, such as 17, 65, or –103.

Oersted (UR-sted), **Hans Christian** Born 1777; died 1851. Danish scientist who founded the scientific study of electromagnetism in 1819 when he observed that electric current produces a magnetic force. He also discovered the element aluminum.

offspring   The young of a living thing, especially a plant or animal.

ohm   (ŌM) A unit used to measure the **resistance** of an object to the flow of electricity. The ohm is named after Georg Simon Ohm.

Ohm, Georg Simon Born 1789; died 1854. German scientist who discovered the relationship between voltage, current, and resistance in an electric circuit. His discovery is now known as Ohm's law.

Ohm's law   A scientific law that states that the amount of **current** in an electric circuit is equal to the **voltage** divided by the **resistance** of the conducting material. The amount of current increases as the voltage increases, but it decreases as the resistance increases. Ohm's law is named after Georg Simon Ohm.

Oligocene Epoch   (OL-i-gō-sēn EP-uhk) The period of time during the history of the Earth starting about 37 million years ago and ending about 24 million years ago. During the Oligocene Epoch, the groups of mammals we know today, including the cats and dogs, first appeared. ◻ See Table on pages 102–103.

Did You Know?

omnivore
Humans aren't the only animals that can eat anything—so can dogs, bears, and crows. It pays to be an omnivore, because if you are willing to eat anything, you are more likely to find something to eat than if you eat only plants or other animals.

---

omnivore   (OM-nuh-vor) An animal that feeds on both plants and animals. Many mammals and birds are omnivores.

Oort cloud   (ORT klowd) A group of more than 100 billion comets that makes up the outer edge of the Solar System. The Oort cloud surrounds the planets and the region of icy objects known as the **Kuiper belt.**

opaque   (ō-PĀK) Not letting light pass through. Metals and many minerals are opaque. Most glass is not opaque.

operating system   (OP-uh-rā-ting SIS-tuhm) The software on a computer that controls the computer's hardware, allowing a person to use the computer and run programs.

Oppenheimer   (OP-uhn-hī-mer), **J(ulius) Robert** Born 1902; died 1967. American scientist who helped to develop the first atomic bomb between 1942 and 1945.

opposable thumb   (uh-PO-zuh-buhl THUHM) A thumb that can move across the palm to touch the tips of the other fingers. An opposable thumb allows an animal to grasp and handle objects easily. Only primates have opposable thumbs.

optical   (OP-ti-kuhl) **1.** Relating to sight. **2.** Designed to assist sight. Microscopes and telescopes are optical instruments.

optical disk   A disk that is coated with plastic and is used for storing information that can be read by a computer. The surface of an optical disk has tiny pits etched into it, and these pits stand for the binary digits 0 and 1. A laser reads the pits and changes their data into electric impulses. CDs and DVDs are optical disks.

optical fiber   A thin tube or fiber of bendable glass or plastic that can carry light from one place to another. Optical fibers are used by doctors to see the inside of the body and by telephone companies to send signals in the form of pulses of light.

optic nerve (OP-tik NERV) The nerve that carries visual information from the retina of the eye to the brain.

optics (OP-tiks) The scientific study of light and vision.

oral (OR-uhl) Relating to the mouth.

orbit (OR-bit) **1.** The path of an object as it circles around another object in outer space. The Earth makes an orbit around the Sun. **2.** The path of an electron around the nucleus of an atom. **3.** To move in a path around another object. Satellites orbit the Earth. Electrons orbit the nucleus of an atom.

order (OR-der) One of the major groups in the classification of living things. An order is below a class and above a family. ◘ See Table on page 47.

ordinal number (OR-duh-nuhl NUHM-ber) A number, such as 3rd, 11th, or 412th, used in counting to indicate position in a series. ◘ Compare **cardinal number.**

Ordovician Period (or-duh-VISH-uhn PEER-ē-uhd) The period of time during the history of the Earth starting about 505 million years ago and ending about 438 million years ago. During the Ordovician Period, the first types of fish appeared. ◘ See Table on pages 102–103.

ore A rock or other solid material that contains a mineral or a metal that can be separated from it.

organ (OR-guhn) A part of a living thing that has a particular function. The eyes, ears, lungs, heart, and kidneys are organs in mammals. The roots, stems, and leaves are the organs in many plants.

organelle (or-guh-NEL) One of the tiny parts or structures that are found inside a cell and that act in a particular way. Nuclei, chloroplasts, and mitochondria are organelles. Almost all plant and animal cells have organelles.

organic (or-GAN-ik) **1.** Relating to living things or to any of the substances that are made by living things. **2.** Relating to chemical compounds that contain carbon and hydrogen. ◘ Compare **inorganic. 3.** Grown using only fertilizers or pesticides that are made of ingredients found in nature.

organism (OR-guh-niz-uhm) A single form of life, such as a plant, animal, or fungus, that is able to grow and reproduce. An organism may be made up of only one cell, such as a bacterium, or many cells, such as a plant or animal.

origin (OR-uh-jin) The point at which the x-axis and the y-axis cross each other in a Cartesian coordinate system. ◘ See picture at **Cartesian coordinate system.**

ornithology (or-nuh-THOL-uh-jē) The scientific study of birds.

oscillation (os-uh-LĀ-shuhn) A steady, backward and forward motion across a central point.

oscilloscope (uh-SIL-i-skōp) An electronic instrument that is used to measure the strength of electric signals. It displays the electric signals as waves on a screen.

osmosis (oz-MŌ-sis) The movement of a dissolved substance, such as salt dissolved in water, through a membrane. Osmosis happens when the membrane separates two different solutions and one of the solutions contains a higher concentration of the dissolved substance than the other. The dissolved substance moves from the side with

☐ **oscillation**

*The oscillation of the clock's pendulum takes it from point **a** to point **b** and back to **a**. The dotted red line in the middle shows the position of the pendulum at rest.*

the higher concentration to the side with the lower concentration, until both sides have the same concentration of the dissolved substance.

ounce 1. A unit of weight equal to $\frac{1}{16}$ of a pound. 2. *See* **fluid ounce.** ☐ See Table on page 148.

outcrop An area where the rock that makes up the Earth's crust is visible and not covered with soil.

outer ear The part of the ear on the outside of the body, made mostly of cartilage. The outer ear contains the passage that leads to the eardrum. The outer ear gathers sound waves and sends them to the eardrum, where they are transmitted to the inner ear. ☐ See picture at **ear.**

output 1. The energy, power, or work produced by a system or device, such as an engine. 2. The information that a computer produces after **input** has been entered into it.

ovary (Ō-vuh-rē) 1. The part in female animals that produces **eggs.** Most verte-

brates have two ovaries, one on each side of the body. 2. The part in a flowering plant that contains **ovules** and ripens into a fruit after **fertilization.** The ovary is found at the base of the **pistil.** ☐ See picture at **flower.**

ovipositor (ō-vuh-POZ-i-ter) A tube in many female insects that sticks out from the end of the abdomen. The ovipositor is used to lay eggs.

ovulation (ov-yuh-LĀ-shuhn) The release of a fully developed egg from the ovary of a female animal. Ovulation usually takes place halfway through the menstrual cycle and is controlled by hormones. An egg can be fertilized by a male sex cell around the time of ovulation.

ovule (Ō-vyōol *or* OV-yōol) A small part in a plant that contains an egg and becomes a seed after **fertilization.** ☐ See picture at **flower.**

ovum (Ō-vuhm) The female sex cell of an animal or plant; an egg. *Plural form:* **ova** (Ō-vuh).

oxidation (ok-si-DĀ-shuhn) 1. The combination of a chemical element or a chemical compound with oxygen. Rust comes from the oxidation of iron. 2. A chemical reaction in which an atom loses electrons. ☐ Compare **reduction.**

oxide (OK-sīd) A chemical compound that has oxygen and another element or group of elements. Water (H_2O) is an oxide.

oxidize (OK-si-dīz) 1. To combine with oxygen. When iron oxidizes, it turns to rust. 2. To lose one or more electrons in a chemical reaction.

oxygen (OK-si-jen) A chemical element that is a colorless, odorless gas and that makes up about one-fifth of the Earth's atmosphere. Oxygen is the most common element in the Earth's crust, and it combines with other elements to form water, carbon dioxide, and iron ore. Oxygen is needed for plants and animals to live, and it is required for the process of **combustion**. ☐ See Table on pages 178–179.

Did You Know?

ozone

The chemical compound ozone is both good and bad for life on Earth. High up in the atmosphere, ozone collects in the ozone layer, which protects the Earth from the harmful effects of the Sun's radiation. But ozone can damage the lungs when it is breathed in, and it is considered to be a pollutant when found in the air near the ground.

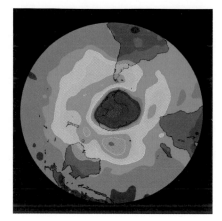

☐ ozone

A satellite picture of ozone levels over the Southern Hemisphere. The different colors show different amounts of ozone. The gray color in the middle shows an ozone "hole," a place where the ozone layer is very thin.

ozone   (Ō-zōn) A poisonous form of oxygen that is produced naturally in the atmosphere by sunlight or lightning. Ozone is often present in smog that forms from car and truck exhaust. It is also made in factories for use as a bleach and in killing germs in drinking water.

ozone layer   A region of the upper atmosphere that has a high amount of ozone. The ozone layer blocks much of the Sun's most harmful radiation.

Pp

pachyderm (PAK-i-derm) A large mammal with thick skin, such as the elephant, rhinoceros, or hippopotamus.

pahoehoe (puh-HOY-hoy) A type of lava that has a smooth, swirled surface. The swirled surface forms as the lava cools and hardens. ◻ See Table on page 208. ◻ See picture at **lava.**

palate (PAL-it) The roof of the mouth in humans and other vertebrates. The palate separates the mouth from the nose. It is made up of two parts, a bony hard palate in front and a movable soft palate in the back.

Paleocene Epoch (PĀ-lē-uh-sēn EP-uhk) The period of time during the history of the Earth starting about 65 million years ago and ending about 58 million years ago. During the Paleocene Epoch, mammals that have a placenta first appeared. The Rocky Mountains and the Himalayas also formed during the Paleocene Epoch. ◻ See Table on pages 102–103.

Paleolithic Period (pā-lē-uh-LITH-ik PEER-ē-uhd) The earliest period of the Stone Age that began about 2 million years ago. The Paleolithic Period ended at different times in different parts of the world, between about 40,000 and 10,000 years ago. During this period, humans first used tools, like choppers and scrapers, made of chipped stone.

paleontology (pā-lē-on-TOL-uh-jē) The scientific study of life in the past, especially through the study of **fossils.**

Paleozoic Era (pā-lē-uh-ZŌ-ik EER-uh) The era of geologic time starting about 540 million years ago and ending about 245 million years ago. During the Paleozoic Era, sea-dwelling invertebrates, fish and reptiles, and land plants first appeared. ◻ See Table on pages 102–103.

palm A kind of evergreen tree that is found in tropical or subtropical regions. Palms usually have a branchless trunk with a group of large, feathery or fan-shaped leaves at the top.

pampa (PAM-puh) A large, treeless grassland of southern South America.

pancreas (PANG-krē-uhs) A gland behind the stomach in humans and other vertebrates. The pancreas produces insulin, a hormone that helps the body absorb sugar from the blood. The pancreas also produces fluids that are important in digestion. ◻ See picture at **digestive system.**

Pangaea (pan-JĒ-uh) A very large continent that is thought to have existed around 250 million years ago. Scientists believe that all of the land on Earth at this time was joined together in the single continent of Pangaea. According to the theory of **plate tectonics,** Pangaea later broke up into the continents we know today.

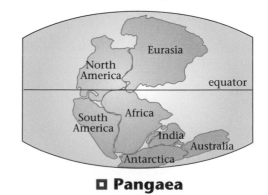

◻ **Pangaea**

paraffin (PAIR-uh-fin) A white or colorless substance that is like wax. Paraffin is used to make candles and to seal jars. Paraffin is made from petroleum and burns easily.

parallel (PAIR-uh-lel) **1.** Relating to lines or surfaces that are separated from each other by the same distance everywhere. A floor is parallel to a ceiling. **2.** An imaginary line that circles the Earth's surface and runs parallel to the equator. Parallels are used to measure **latitude**.

parallel circuit An electric circuit in which the source of electricity is connected directly to two or more devices that each have their own wire running off the main circuit. If the flow of current to one of the devices gets interrupted, that device will stop working. The other devices will still work, however, because they continue to get electricity. ◻ Compare **series circuit**. ◻ See picture at **circuit**.

parallelogram (pair-uh-LEL-uh-gram) A four-sided figure having opposite sides that are parallel to each other. ◻ See picture at **geometry**.

paralysis (puh-RAL-uh-sis) Loss of the ability to move. Paralysis is caused by damage to nerves from a disease or injury.

paramecium (pair-uh-MĒ-sē-uhm) A living thing that is made up of only one cell and is found in fresh water. A paramecium is usually oval in shape and moves by means of cilia. Paramecia are members of the group of organisms known as **protozoans**. *Plural form*: **paramecia** (pair-uh-MĒ-sē-uh) or **parameciums**.

parasite (PAIR-uh-sīt) A living thing that can only exist on or in a different kind of living thing, called the **host**. Parasites rely on their hosts for food and are usually harmful to them. Lice, ticks, and fleas are

◻ **parasite**

top: *a tick on human skin*
bottom: *mistletoe growing on a tree branch*

parasites of humans and other mammals.

parasitism (PAIR-uh-si-tiz-uhm) A close relationship between two different kinds of organisms in which one is helped and the other is usually harmed. A tick that burrows into the skin of a mammal is an example of parasitism because the tick feeds on the mammal's blood and sometimes passes disease to it. Parasitism is a kind of **symbiosis**.

parsec (PAR-sek) A unit of length equal to 3.26 light-years. Scientists use parsecs to measure the distance between objects in outer space.

particle (PAR-ti-kuhl) **1.** A very small piece of matter, such as a speck of dust. **2.** One of the tiny parts that make up atoms. Electrons, protons, and neutrons are particles. **3.** A tiny packet of energy, such as a photon.

particle accelerator A machine used to study the particles that make up atoms and their nuclei. Particle accelerators work by causing particles such as protons to move at extremely high speeds through a long tube until they smash into a nucleus and break it apart.

pascal (pa-SKAL *or* pah-SKAHL) A unit used to measure pressure. One pascal is equal to one newton per square meter. The pascal is named after Blaise Pascal.

Pascal, Blaise Born 1623; died 1662. French mathematician who in 1642 invented the first mechanical calculator. In 1654, he helped develop the first theory of probability.

Pascal's law A scientific law that states that when something pushes on a liquid or gas, the pressure is the same on every part of the liquid or gas. This is because the molecules of liquids and gases are able to move easily, spreading out the pressure among all the molecules. Pascal's law is named after Blaise Pascal.

Pasteur (pas-TER), **Louis** Born 1822; died 1895. French scientist who discovered that germs cause diseases. Pasteur also developed methods to combat them.

pasteurization (pas-cher-i-ZĀ-shuhn) A process that kills germs in liquids, making them safe to drink. The liquid, such as milk, is heated up high enough to kill the germs without boiling it or changing the chemical compounds that it is made of.

pathogen (PATH-uh-juhn) Something that causes disease or infection. Bacteria and viruses are pathogens.

pathology (puh-THOL-uh-jē) The scientific study of the causes, signs, and results of disease.

Pauling (PAW-ling), **Linus Carl** Born 1901; died 1994. American scientist who studied the structure of molecules and chemical bonds.

Pavlov (PAV-lawv *or* PAV-lawf), **Ivan Petrovich** 1849–1936. Russian scientist who was among the first people to study how the repetition of events can affect animal behavior.

Biography

Louis Pasteur

Louis Pasteur did not accept what other scientists believed—that diseases arose from inside the human body without any outside cause. He demonstrated that tiny germs traveled through the air and entered the body, causing various diseases. He spent the rest of his life working  to identify the germs that cause specific diseases and developing treatments, such as vaccines, to prevent them.

Biography

Ivan Petrovich Pavlov

Ivan Petrovich Pavlov's work was influential in the field of psychology. He showed that if a bell is rung whenever food is given to a dog, the dog will eventually produce saliva in its mouth whenever it hears the bell, even if the dog is not offered any food. The dog associates the sound of the bell with the taste and smell of food. This is known as a conditioned response.

PC *See* **personal computer.**

peak **1.** The highest part of a wave. **2.** The highest part of a mountain.

pearl A smooth, shiny, round growth inside the shells of oysters and some other mollusks. Pearls form as a covering around a small object, such as a grain of sand, that gets caught between the mollusk's body and its shell.

peat Partly decayed plant matter that is found in bogs. Peat consists mainly of decayed mosses. Peat is burned as fuel and is also used as a fertilizer.

pectin (PEK-tin) A substance that is found in ripe fruit and can be used to make jellies and jelly-like substances.

pelvis (PEL-vis) The part of the skeleton that joins the spine with the legs. The pelvis is shaped like a bowl and contains the intestines, bladder, and organs of reproduction. ☐ See picture at **skeleton.**

pendulum (PEN-juh-luhm) An object that is hung so that it can swing back and forth under the influence of gravity. Many older clocks have pendulums to keep them moving at a steady rate.

penicillin (pen-i-SIL-in) An antibiotic that is made from a kind of mold. Penicillin is used to treat or prevent infection by different types of bacteria.

peninsula (puh-NIN-syuh-luh) An area of land that projects into a body of water. Three sides of a peninsula are bordered by water, and the fourth side is connected with a larger landmass. Florida and Italy are peninsulas.

☐ **peninsula**

satellite view of the Italian peninsula

penis (PĒ-nis) The male organ of reproduction in mammals and some reptiles and birds. Urine and semen leave the body through the penis.

Pennsylvanian Period (pen-suhl-VĀN-yuhn PEER-ē-uhd) The period of time during the history of the Earth starting about 320 million years ago and ending about 286 million years ago. During the Pennsylvanian Period, rocks that are rich in coal formed, and the first reptiles appeared. ☐ See Table on pages 102–103.

pentagon (PEN-tuh-gon) A flat shape that has five sides. ☐ See picture at **geometry.**

penumbra (pi-NUHM-bruh) A partial shadow. The lighter, outer part of the shadow that is cast by the Moon onto the Earth during a solar eclipse is the penumbra. ☐ Compare **umbra.** ☐ See picture at **eclipse.**

Did You Know?

penicillin

In 1928, Alexander Fleming discovered penicillin completely by accident. During his experiments with bacteria, Fleming noticed that a group of bacteria stopped growing soon after it had been contaminated with the common bread mold (known as *Penicillium*). Fleming's discovery of the bacteria-killing substance made by the mold started the search for other natural substances that kill bacteria.

pepsin (PEP-sin) An enzyme in the stomach that breaks down proteins, such as those found in meat, cheese, and seeds, during digestion.

percent (per-SENT) One part in a hundred. For example, 62 percent (also written 62%) means 62 parts out of 100.

perennial (puh-REN-ē-uhl) Living for three or more years. Strawberries and irises are perennial plants.

perigee (PAIR-uh-jē) The point in the orbit of an object in space, such as the Moon, where it is closest to the object it revolves around, such as Earth. ☐ Compare **apogee.**

perimeter (puh-RIM-i-ter) The distance around the outside of an area or a flat figure. The perimeter of a circle is its circumference. The perimeter of a polygon, such as a square, is the sum of the lengths of its sides.

period (PEER-ē-uhd) **1.** A division of time in the history of the Earth, longer than an epoch and shorter than an era. The Quaternary Period includes the Pleistocene Epoch and the Holocene Epoch. The Quaternary Period and the Tertiary Period together make up the Cenozoic Era. ☐ See Table on pages 102–103. **2.** The amount of time it takes for something that regularly happens again and again to be repeated. The time it takes for a pendulum to swing forward and then come back to its starting point is its period. **3.** One of the horizontal rows in the **Periodic Table.** The atoms in each period have the same number of layers in which their electrons move around their nucleus. ☐ See Table on pages 178–179. **4.** An occurrence of menstruation.

Periodic Table (peer-ē-OD-ik TĀ-buhl) A table that arranges all the chemical ele-

ments in rows called **periods,** and columns called **groups.** Elements are placed in a particular period depending on the number of layers their electrons are in as they move around the nucleus. Elements are placed in a particular group depending on the number of electrons that are available to make bonds with other elements. ☐ See Table on pages 178–179.

peripheral nervous system (puh-RIF-er-uhl NER-vuhs SIS-tuhm) The part of the nervous system that connects the brain and spinal cord with the rest of the body. The nerves of the peripheral nervous system run from the spinal cord to the trunk and limbs of the body. ☐ Compare **central nervous system.**

periscope (PAIR-i-skōp) An instrument that allows objects that are not in the direct line of sight to be seen. Periscopes do this by having mirrors or prisms positioned at angles in a long tube. Periscopes are used on submarines to see above water.

peristalsis (pair-i-STAWL-sis) The wave-like movement of the muscles of the digestive system. In peristalsis, food is pushed from the esophagus into the stomach and then to the intestines. Peristalsis ends when wastes leave the body.

permafrost (PER-muh-frawst) A layer of ground that is permanently frozen. Permafrost is found below the topsoil of most of the land in the **Frigid Zones.** It can reach a depth of almost one mile (1.61 kilometers).

permeable (PER-mē-uh-buhl) Allowing the passage of ions or molecules. Cell membranes are usually permeable to water molecules.

Permian Period (PER-mē-uhn PEER-ē-uhd) The period of time during the history of the Earth starting about 286 million years

1	— atomic number
H	— symbol
Hydrogen	— name

The Periodic Table is an arrangement of the chemical elements. The elements are arranged in rows, or **Periods**, and columns, or **Groups**, based on their structure and the way they combine with other elements. For each element, three pieces of information are given: the name of the element, its chemical symbol, and the number of protons in its nucleus. For example, the element in Group 2, Period 4, is called *calcium*, has the symbol Ca, and has 20 protons in its nucleus. Each element box is also color-coded. For example, all the elements that are noble gases (Group 18) are shown in light green.

	Group 1	Group 2	Group 3	Group 4	Group 5	Group 6	Group 7	Group 8
Period 1	1 **H** Hydrogen							
Period 2	3 **Li** Lithium	4 **Be** Beryllium						
Period 3	11 **Na** Sodium	12 **Mg** Magnesium						
Period 4	19 **K** Potassium	20 **Ca** Calcium	21 **Sc** Scandium	22 **Ti** Titanium	23 **V** Vanadium	24 **Cr** Chromium	25 **Mn** Manganese	26 **Fe** Iron
Period 5	37 **Rb** Rubidium	38 **Sr** Strontium	39 **Y** Yttrium	40 **Zr** Zirconium	41 **Nb** Niobium	42 **Mo** Molybdenum	43 **Tc** Technetium	44 **Ru** Ruthenium
Period 6	55 **Cs** Cesium	56 **Ba** Barium	57–71* Lanthanides	72 **Hf** Hafnium	73 **Ta** Tantalum	74 **W** Tungsten	75 **Re** Rhenium	76 **Os** Osmium
Period 7	87 **Fr** Francium	88 **Ra** Radium	89–103** Actinides	104 **Rf** Rutherfordium	105 **Db** Dubnium	106 **Sg** Seaborgium	107 **Bh** Bohrium	108 **Hs** Hassium

*LANTHANIDES	57 **La** Lanthanum	58 **Ce** Cerium	59 **Pr** Praseodymium	60 **Nd** Neodymium	61 **Pm** Promethium	62 **Sm** Samarium
**ACTINIDES	89 **Ac** Actinium	90 **Th** Thorium	91 **Pa** Protactinium	92 **U** Uranium	93 **Np** Neptunium	94 **Pu** Plutonium

Alkali metals | Alkaline-earth metals | Other metals | Nonmetals | Noble gases

The two rows of elements at the bottom of the table are called the **lanthanides** and the **actinides**. The chemical elements in these rows are supposed to fit into Periods 6 and 7, but are set aside because they all combine with other elements in a similar way to the elements in Group 3 and would stretch out the table too much if they were put in their proper place.

Group 13	Group 14	Group 15	Group 16	Group 17	Group 18
					2 He Helium
5 B Boron	6 C Carbon	7 N Nitrogen	8 O Oxygen	9 F Fluorine	10 Ne Neon

Group 9	Group 10	Group 11	Group 12	13 Al Aluminum	14 Si Silicon	15 P Phosphorus	16 S Sulfur	17 Cl Chlorine	18 Ar Argon
27 Co Cobalt	28 Ni Nickel	29 Cu Copper	30 Zn Zinc	31 Ga Gallium	32 Ge Germanium	33 As Arsenic	34 Se Selenium	35 Br Bromine	36 Kr Krypton
45 Rh Rhodium	46 Pd Palladium	47 Ag Silver	48 Cd Cadmium	49 In Indium	50 Sn Tin	51 Sb Antimony	52 Te Tellurium	53 I Iodine	54 Xe Xenon
77 Ir Iridium	78 Pt Platinum	79 Au Gold	80 Hg Mercury	81 Tl Thallium	82 Pb Lead	83 Bi Bismuth	84 Po Polonium	85 At Astatine	86 Rn Radon
109 Mt Meitnerium	110†	111†	112†						

† These elements have only recently been discovered and have not been named yet.

63 Eu Europium	64 Gd Gadolinium	65 Tb Terbium	66 Dy Dysprosium	67 Ho Holmium	68 Er Erbium	69 Tm Thulium	70 Yb Ytterbium	71 Lu Lutetium
95 Am Americium	96 Cm Curium	97 Bk Berkelium	98 Cf Californium	99 Es Einsteinium	100 Fm Fermium	101 Md Mendelevium	102 No Nobelium	103 Lr Lawrencium

ago and ending about 245 million years ago. During the Permian Period, conifers first appeared, and the number of different kinds of reptiles increased. At the end of the Permian Period many of the animals and plants that had been living on Earth up until that point died out. ◻ See Table on pages 102–103.

perpendicular (per-puhn-DIK-yuh-ler) Crossing at or forming a right angle. A wall is perpendicular to the floor and to the ceiling.

personal computer (PER-suh-nuhl kuhm-PYOO-ter) A computer that is designed to be used by one person or family. ◻ A personal computer is called a *PC* for short.

perspiration (per-spuh-RA-shuhn) *See* **sweat.**

pertussis (per-TUHS-is) *See* **whooping cough.**

pesticide (PES-ti-sīd) A chemical compound that is used to kill harmful insects, plants, or other living things. The use of pesticides is regulated by the government because pesticides are poisonous and can be harmful to the environment and to humans.

petal (PET-uhl) One of the often brightly colored parts of a flower that surround the organs of reproduction. ◻ See picture at **flower.**

petri dish (PĒ-trē dish) A shallow, round dish with a loose cover, used to grow cells or tiny organisms in a laboratory.

petrified (PET-ruh-fīd) Changed into minerals and hardened into rock. Plant and animal parts, such as wood and bone, become petrified when water that contains minerals gets into them and leaves the min-

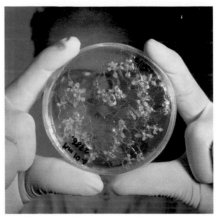

◻ **petri dish**

seedlings growing in a petri dish

erals. The minerals take the place of material that has decayed.

petrochemical (pet-rō-KEM-i-kuhl) A chemical compound that is made from petroleum or natural gas. Ammonia, gasoline, and kerosene are important petrochemicals. Petrochemicals are used to make plastics, explosives, fertilizers, and many other products.

petroleum (puh-TRŌ-lē-uhm) A thick liquid mixture of different chemical compounds that is found where large numbers of dead plants and animals were covered by dirt and rock millions of years ago. Petroleum is black or yellowish and is mainly found below ground. Petroleum is used to make gasoline, oils, plastics, and many other products.

pH (PĒ-ĀCH) A measure of how acidic or basic a solution is. The pH is a number between 0 and 14, where 0 is the most acid and 14 the most basic. Neutral solutions, like pure water, have a pH of 7.

Phanerozoic Eon (fan-er-uh-ZO-ik Ē-on) The period of geologic time starting about 540 million years ago and continuing all the way up to today. The Phanerozoic Eon includes the Paleozoic Era, the Mesozoic Era, and the Cenozoic Era. Almost all the types of animals and plants we know of first developed during the Phanerozoic Eon. ◻ See Table on pages 102–103.

pharynx (FAIR-ingks) The passageway that leads from the nose and mouth to the larynx (voice box) and esophagus.

phase **1.** One of the ways that the moon appears depending on how much of its sunlit surface is visible. The phases of the Moon change because the Moon orbits the Earth. The **full moon** and **new moon** are two phases of the moon. **2.** A condition in which two or more waves are in step with each other. Two waves are said to be in phase when their peaks and troughs line up.

pheromone (FEER-uh-mōn) A chemical compound made by one animal that affects the behavior of other animals of the same kind. Many animals attract mates or mark their territory by means of pheromones.

phlegm (FLEM) Mucus that is produced by the organs of the respiratory system, especially the lungs.

phloem (FLŌ-uhm) A tissue in plants that moves food from the leaves to other parts of the plant. ◻ Compare **xylem.** ◻ See pictures at **root, stem.**

phosphate (FOS-fāt) A chemical compound that contains a phosphorus atom attached to four oxygen atoms. Phosphates are important nutrients for plants.

phosphor (FOS-fer) A substance that can give off visible light after it has absorbed some form of radiation like x-rays or ultraviolet light. The insides of television screens and fluorescent lamp tubes are coated with phosphors.

phosphorescent (fos-fuh-RES-uhnt) Giving off light as a result of having been struck by electromagnetic radiation, such as visible light or x-rays. Unlike fluorescent substances, phosphorescent substances continue to give off light for a short while after the source of radiation has been removed. ◻ Compare **fluorescent.**

phosphorus (FOS-fer-uhs) A chemical element that burns very easily. Phosphorus is an important part of the structure of plant and animal cells, and it helps to build teeth and bones. Phosphorus is used to make matches, fireworks, and fertilizers. ◻ See Table on pages 178–179.

photon (FŌ-ton) The particle of energy that makes up light and other forms of **electromagnetic radiation.** A beam of light is a stream of photons.

photosphere (FŌ-tuh-sfeer) The thin layer of gas that is the visible surface of the Sun or another star. ◻ See picture at **sun.**

photosynthesis (fō-tō-SIN-thi-sis) The process that allows green plants and some

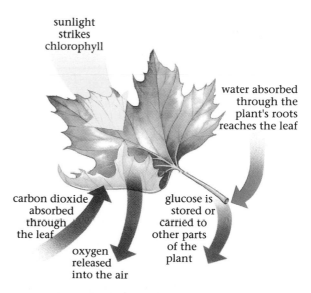

sunlight strikes chlorophyll

water absorbed through the plant's roots reaches the leaf

carbon dioxide absorbed through the leaf

glucose is stored or carried to other parts of the plant

oxygen released into the air

◻ **photosynthesis**

Sunlight provides the energy for a chemical reaction in which water combines with carbon dioxide to make sugar (glucose) and oxygen.

algae and bacteria to make sugars from water, carbon dioxide, and sunlight. The plants and other organisms use the sugars as food and release oxygen into the air as a waste product.

phototropism (fō-TOT-ruh-piz-uhm) The growth or turning of a plant toward or away from light.

photovoltaic cell (fō-tō-vol-TĀ-ik) *See* solar cell.

phylum (FĪ-luhm) One of the major groups in the classification of living things. A phylum is below a kingdom and above a class. *Plural form:* **phyla** (FĪ-luh). ◘ See Table on page 47.

physical science (FIZ-i-kuhl SĪ-uhns) A science that studies nonliving matter and the energy associated with it. Physics, chemistry, and geology are physical sciences. ◘ Compare **life science.**

physics (FIZ-iks) The scientific study of matter and energy and the relations between them. Physics includes the studies of motion, light, sound, heat, electricity, magnetism, and the structure of atoms.

physiology (fiz-ē-OL-uh-jē) The scientific study of the processes in living things that are needed for survival, such as circulation, respiration, and digestion.

phytoplankton (fī-tō-PLANGK-tuhn) Tiny plants or plant-like organisms that float around in a body of water. Phytoplankton are a major source of food for animals that live or grow in the water.

pi (PĪ) A number that is necessary to figure out the circumference and area of a circle. Pi is equal to the circumference of any circle divided by its diameter. Pi is represented by the symbol π and its value is about 3.142.

Pickering (PIK-er-ing), **Edward Charles** Born 1846; died 1919. American scientist who improved the equipment used to observe stars and to measure how far stars are from Earth.

pie chart A graph that is a circle divided into pieces like a pie. The pieces are usually of different sizes to represent different amounts of the things that are being measured. ◘ See picture at **graph.**

pigment (PIG-muhnt) A chemical compound that gives a particular color to part of a plant or animal and that is needed for important life processes. Chlorophyll is a pigment that makes green plants green and is needed for photosynthesis. Hemoglobin is a pigment that makes red blood cells red and carries oxygen to other cells.

pincers (PIN-serz) A part in some invertebrates that is made of two sharp, curved parts that come together for grasping. The claws of lobsters and the mouthparts of spiders are pincers.

pine A kind of evergreen tree that has cones and clusters of needle-shaped leaves. Pines usually grow in cooler regions of the Northern Hemisphere.

pint **1.** A unit of volume used to measure liquids, equal to 16 fluid ounces. **2.** A unit of volume used to measure dry materials, equal to $\frac{1}{2}$ of a quart. ◘ See Table on page 148.

pipette (pī-PET) A narrow glass tube that is used in laboratories to measure and move liquids from one container to another.

pistil (PIS-tuhl) The female organ of reproduction of a flower. The pistil is made up of the ovary, style, and stigma. ◘ See picture at **flower.**

piston (PIS-tuhn) A solid cylinder or disk that fits snugly into a hollow cylinder and moves in and out of it, squeezing the fluid within it. Pistons are used in many engines and in some pumps. ◻ See picture at **engine.**

pith The soft, spongy tissue that is in the center of the stems of most flowering plants.

pituitary gland (pi-TOO-i-tair-ē gland) A small gland that is found underneath the brain in humans and other vertebrates. The pituitary gland produces hormones that control the body's growth and the actions of other glands in the body.

pivot (PIV-uht) A rod or pin on which something turns or swings.

pixel (PIK-suhl) One of the tiny squares or patches that light up in different colors to make up an image on a computer or television screen.

◻ **pixel**

Up close, you can see that each tiny pixel is a single color. From a distance, the thousands of pixels blend together to form natural-looking shapes and colors.

placebo (pluh-SĒ-bō) A substance that is made to look like a medicine but contains no medical ingredients. To research how well a medicine works, scientists give one group of people a real medicine and another group a placebo. Scientists then record the results from both groups of people and decide whether the group that took the real medicine did better than the group that took the placebo.

placenta (pluh-SEN-tuh) A sac that connects the developing young to the wall of the mother's womb in mammals. The placenta is attached to the developing young by the umbilical cord, which carries oxygen and nutrients to the young.

placer (PLAS-er) A layer of minerals laid down by flowing water. People who pan for gold search through placers.

plague (PLĀG) A serious disease that is caused by bacteria that enter the body through the bite of a flea that has bitten an infected rodent, especially a rat. The most common form of plague is **bubonic plague.**

plain **1.** A large area of flat land with few trees. **2.** A broad, flat area of the sea floor or on the surface of the Moon.

Planck (PLAHNGK), **Max Karl Ernst Ludwig** Born 1858; died 1947. German scientist who discovered that the energy of atoms and subatomic particles exists in units called **quanta.**

plane A flat surface on which any two points can be connected by a straight line.

planet (PLAN-it) An object in outer space that moves around a star, such as the Sun, and that is larger than an asteroid. A planet does not produce its own light but shines because it reflects the light of the star that it moves around. The nine planets of the Solar System are Mercury, Venus, Earth, Mars, Jupiter, Saturn, Uranus, Neptune, and Pluto. ◻ See Table on pages 184–185.

Planets of the Solar System

	Mercury	Venus	Earth	Mars
What is its order from the Sun?	1	2	3	4
How far is it from the Sun?	36 million miles or 58 million kilometers	67 million miles or 108 million kilometers	93 million miles or 150 million kilometers	142 million miles or 229 million kilometer
How long does it take for it to revolve around the Sun?	88 days	225 days	365 days	1 year and 322 days
How long does it take for it to rotate on its axis?	58 days and 15.5 hours	243 days	1 day	1 day and 0.5 hou
How big is it, and what is its size compared to the other planets?	Mercury has a diameter of 3,032 miles or 4,882 kilometers, and is the 2nd smallest planet. It is about one-third the size of Earth.	Venus has a diameter of 7,521 miles or 12,109 kilometers, and is the 4th smallest planet. It is very close in size to Earth.	Earth has a diameter of 7,926 miles or 12,761 kilometers, and is the 5th largest planet.	Mars has a diameter of 4,222 miles or 6,797 kilometers, an is the 3rd smallest planet. It is about on half the size of Earth
What is its average surface temperature?	354° Fahrenheit or 179° Celsius	847° Fahrenheit or 453° Celsius	46° Fahrenheit or 8° Celsius	−81° Fahrenheit o −63° Celsius
What is it like there?	Mercury is a hard, rocky planet covered all over with craters. It has almost no atmosphere and is both extremely hot and extremely cold. The side facing the Sun can reach 870° Fahrenheit (466° Celsius) and the side away from the Sun can fall to −300° Fahrenheit (−184° Celsius).	Venus has an atmosphere mainly of carbon dioxide, but it is covered by poisonous clouds of sulfuric acid. These clouds trap the Sun's heat and make Venus hotter even than Mercury. On its surface are mountains, valleys, and active volcanoes.	Earth has an atmosphere mainly of nitrogen and oxygen. It is the only planet that has water in liquid form. More than 70 percent of its surface is covered in water. Earth is also the only planet on which life is known to exist.	Mars has a thin atm phere mainly of carbon dioxide. Most o its surface is a vast desert, with mountains, craters, canyo and inactive volcanc There are ice caps o its northern and sou ern polar regions.

Jupiter	Saturn	Uranus	Neptune	Pluto
5	**6**	**7**	**8**	**9**
4 million miles or 9 million kilometers	887 million miles or 1.43 billion kilometers	1.78 billion miles or 2.87 billion kilometers	2.79 billion miles or 4.49 billion kilometers	3.68 billion miles or 5.92 billion kilometers
11 years and 318 days	29 years and 174 days	84 years and 25 days	164 years and 329 days	248 years and 260 days
10 hours	10.5 hours	17 hours	16.1 hours	6 days and 9 hours
iter has a diameter 88,846 miles or 3,042 kilometers. It is largest planet, and nore than 10 times ger than Earth.	Saturn has a diameter of 74,897 miles or 120,584 kilometers. It is the 2nd largest planet, and is almost 10 times bigger than Earth.	Uranus has a diameter of 31,763 miles or 51,138 kilometers. It is the 3rd largest planet, and is 4 times as big as Earth.	Neptune has a diameter of 30,775 miles or 49,548 kilometers. It is the 4th largest planet, and is almost 4 times as big as Earth.	Pluto has a diameter of 1,430 miles or 2,302 kilometers. It is the smallest of the planets, and is about one-sixth the size of Earth.
4° Fahrenheit or 3° Celsius	−301° Fahrenheit or −185° Celsius	−355° Fahrenheit or −215° Celsius	−373° Fahrenheit or −225° Celsius	−393° Fahrenheit or −236° Celsius
iter has no solid ace, only a vast an of cold, dense rogen. Its atmos- re is made up of ling clouds of rogen and helium, a giant, long-last- windstorm called Great Red Spot. as 40 moons, 4 of ch are larger than Earth's Moon.	Like Jupiter, there is no solid surface on Saturn, only very cold layers of hydrogen in the form of both liquid and gas. A brilliant disk that is made up of several hundred flat rings of ice and ice-covered particles encircles it. Saturn also has at least 30 small moons.	Uranus is similar to Jupiter and Saturn, though it is half their size. It is mostly made up of extremely cold hydrogen and helium. Although it has no solid surface, it may have a hard core of rock or metal. It has 21 small moons. Methane gas in the atmosphere gives it its blue-green color.	Neptune is even colder than Jupiter, Saturn, and Uranus, with a similar atmosphere of swirling clouds of hydrogen and other gases. Storms there can last hundreds of years, with winds of more than 600 miles (966 kilometers) per hour. It has 11 moons.	Pluto has a rocky core that is covered by a layer of ice. Its surface is a bright layer of frozen gases, and its atmosphere is mainly nitrogen gas. It is the darkest and coldest planet. Its one moon is about half the size of Pluto itself, and the Sun from Pluto looks like just a bright star.

planetarium (plan-i-TAIR-ē-uhm) A building in which special equipment projects an image of the night sky onto a domed ceiling. People go to planetariums to learn about the position and movement of the stars and other objects in outer space that can be seen at night.

planetary nebula (PLAN-i-tair-ē NEB-yuh-luh) An expanding ring of glowing gas that surrounds a smaller, older star. When the gas has moved off into space, the star that is left is called a **white dwarf star.** ☐ See picture at **star.**

plankton (PLANGK-tuhn) Tiny living things that float in great numbers in salt or fresh water. Plankton is the main source of food for many fish and other water animals, such as the blue whale. Plankton is made up of bacteria, protozoans, tiny crustaceans, and algae.

plant A member of a kingdom of living things that are made up of many cells and are usually able to make their own food through the process of **photosynthesis.** Plants are unable to move on their own and have no nervous system. The cells of plants have hard cell walls made mostly of cellulose.

plaque (PLAK) A film that coats the surface of the teeth. Plaque is made up of mucus and bacteria.

plasma (PLAZ-muh) **1.** The clear, liquid part of the blood. Plasma is made up mostly of water and proteins. The plasma in the blood of mammals also contains the platelets, tiny structures that control bleeding. **2.** A state of matter in which electrons have left their atoms and move about freely. Plasmas form at very high temperatures, as in the Sun and other stars. They also form when an electric current flows through certain substances, such as the gas in a fluorescent light bulb.

plastic (PLAS-tik) One of a large group of chemical compounds that are made by joining together simpler chemicals into long chains called **polymers.** Plastics are soft or liquid when they are heated, and they can be molded into solid objects, pressed into sheets, or drawn out into thin fibers.

Did You Know?

plastic
Plastics have taken the place of many different materials. They are used as alternatives to glass, wood, metal, cloth, rubber, leather, and countless other materials. Televisions, football helmets, furniture, lenses, jewelry, automobile parts, and many other things are made with plastics. Nearly every day, there is a new use discovered for this valuable group of chemicals.

plate **1.** A thin, flat sheet of metal or other material, especially one used as an electrode in a storage battery or capacitor. **2.** In the theory of plate tectonics, one of the sections of the upper layer of the Earth, known as the **lithosphere,** that move slowly over the Earth's inner layers. The continents ride piggy-back on the plates. The jostling and separation of the plates cause earthquakes and volcanoes.

plateau (pla-TŌ) A large area of raised land that is relatively flat. Plateaus make up 45 percent of the Earth's land surface.

platelet (PLĀT-lit) A tiny, round structure that is found in the blood of mammals. Platelets help to form the blood clots that stop cuts and bruises from bleeding.

A Closer Look

Plate tectonics

The hard, outer part of the Earth is made up of large sections called plates that move very slowly over the soft, inner part of the Earth. As the plates move, they come together, move apart, or slide past each other.

What happens when the plates come together?	• *They form mountains.* • *Or, one plate sinks below the other in a **subduction zone**. The sinking plate heats up and melts into **magma**. When the magma rises to the surface, it forms a chain of **volcanoes**.*
What happens when the plates move apart?	• *Magma rises up to the surface and spreads out as **lava** in a **spreading ridge**. As the lava cools, it hardens into rock and becomes part of the plates.* • *Or, a long, narrow valley known as a **rift valley** forms. This happens when the plates stop moving before magma reaches the surface.*
What happens when the plates slide past each other?	*The plates crack along their edges, forming **faults**.*
Do volcanoes only form where two plates come together?	*No, they can also form when a plate moves over an area of hot magma known as a **hot spot**, and magma burns through the moving plate to reach the surface. This is how the Hawaiian Islands formed.*

plate tectonics A theory in geology that states that the Earth's lithosphere (its crust and upper mantle) is divided into a number of large, plate-like sections that move very slowly over the softer inner part of the Earth. Plate tectonics explains how the continents slowly change their positions over thousands of years. It also shows that volcanoes and faults in the Earth's surface occur where the plates crash together or pull apart.

platinum (PLAT-i-nuhm) A silver-white chemical element that is a soft metal. Platinum has a high melting point and does not rust. It is used in jewelry and as a **catalyst**. ☐ See Table on pages 178–179.

platypus (PLAT-i-puhs) A mammal of Australia and Tasmania that spends much of its life in water and lays eggs. Platypuses have a broad flat tail, webbed feet, and a snout resembling a duck's bill. Platypuses are members of the group of mammals called **monotremes.**

Pleistocene Epoch (PLĪ-stuh-sēn EP-uhk) The period of time during the history of the Earth starting about 2 million years ago and ending about 10,000 years ago. During the Pleistocene Epoch, glaciers covered much of the Northern Hemisphere, and humans first appeared. ◻ See Table on pages 102–103.

Pliocene Epoch (PLĪ-uh-sēn EP-uhk) The period of time during the history of the Earth starting about 5 million years ago and ending about 2 million years ago. Many of the types of animals we know today first appeared during the Pliocene Epoch. ◻ See Table on pages 102–103.

plumage (PLOO-mij) The feathers on a bird.

plume **1.** A large feather. **2.** A pool of magma that rises from the Earth's mantle into the crust. Plumes sometimes erupt onto the surface as **lava. 3.** An area of air, water, or ground that contains pollutants. Plumes come from a single source, and the pollutants spread by way of wind, currents, or gravity.

plus sign **1.** The + sign, used to show addition, as in 4 + 5 = 9. It is also used to show that a number is positive (greater than zero), as in +32. **2.** The + sign, used to show that an atom, molecule, or substance has more protons than electrons, and therefore has a positive charge.

Pluto (PLOO-tō) The planet that is ninth in order from the Sun and usually the farthest in distance. Pluto is the smallest and the coldest planet in the Solar System, with a temperature on the surface of almost –400° Fahrenheit (about –240° Celsius). ◻ See Table on pages 184–185.

plutonium (ploo-TO-nē-uhm) A chemical element that is a silvery gray, radioactive metal. Plutonium is highly poisonous and is used in atomic bombs. ◻ See Table on pages 178–179.

pneumatic (noo-MAT-ik) Relating to or using air or another gas. A pneumatic tire is a tire filled with air. A pneumatic drill uses compressed air to make the tip move.

pneumonia (noo-MON-yuh) An infection of the lungs. Pneumonia is caused by bacteria or viruses.

pod The part of a flowering plant that contains the seeds and splits open to release them. Legumes such as peas have pods.

point An object that has a position but no length, width, or depth. A point is the most basic element in **geometry.** The intersection of two lines is a point.

poison (POY-zuhn) A substance that is harmful or fatal if it is breathed in, swallowed, or touched.

polar cap (PŌ-ler KAP) **1.** The mass of ice that surrounds the North Pole or the South Pole. The ice at the North Pole covers most of the Arctic Ocean, and the ice at the South Pole covers most of Antarctica. **2.** The

◻ **polar cap**

This photograph of Mars, taken by the Hubble Space Telescope, shows the southern polar cap. Icy clouds at the north pole are also visible.

mass of frozen carbon dioxide and water that surrounds the north or south pole on Mars.

Polaris (puh-LAIR-is) *See* **North Star.**

polarized light (PŌ-luh-rīzd LĪT) Light that is made up of electromagnetic waves that vibrate in only one direction, instead of many. Polarized light is used to prevent glare. Most sunglasses allow only polarized light to reach the eyes.

pole **1.** Either of the points on a sphere where the axis passes through the surface. **2.** Either of the two points where the Earth's axis passes through the Earth's surface. These points are called the **North Pole** and the **South Pole.** Other rotating bodies in space, such as the Sun and planets, also have poles. **3.** *See* **magnetic pole. 4.** One of the two ends of an electric device that connects to an electric circuit. Each pole has an electric charge. One pole is positive, and the other is negative. The ends of a battery are its poles.

polio (PŌ-lē-ō) A disease that is caused by a virus and can cause weakness or paralysis of the muscles. Polio is very contagious. ☐ Polio is short for *poliomyelitis* (pō-lē-ō-mī-uh-LĪ-tis).

pollen (POL-uhn) Powdery grains that contain the male sex cells of most plants. Pollen fertilizes the female sex cells to make seeds. Flowering plants and conifers produce pollen.

pollen tube The slender tube that is formed by a pollen grain after it lands on the stigma of a flower. The pollen tube grows down into the ovule, where it releases the male sex cell so fertilization can take place.

pollination (pol-i-NĀ-shuhn) The process that allows pollen to move from a male plant part to fertilize the sex cells in a female plant part. In most flowering plants, pollination takes place when wind, insects, or birds carry pollen from a stamen on one flower to a pistil on another. In plants that bear cones, wind carries pollen from male cones to female cones.

Did You Know?

pollination
Bees look as if they were designed to carry out pollination. They have hairy bodies for pollen to cling to, and some bees have long tongues to draw nectar and pollen—the bees' only source of food—from the flower. Petals with bright colors attract bees and often provide them with a good place to land to gather their food and to leave behind some of the pollen they picked up from other flowers.

☐ **pollination**

pollutant (puh-LOO-tuhnt) A substance, especially a waste material, that makes air, water, or soil unsafe for people or other living things.

pollute (puh-LOOT) To make the environment so dirty or unpleasant that it is harmful to living things.

pollution (puh-LOO-shuhn) The result of polluting the environment. Pollution

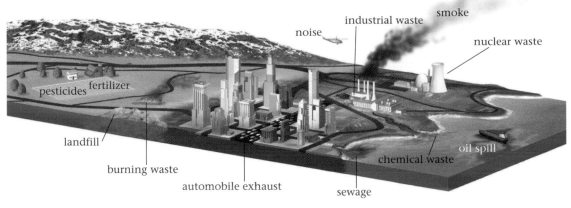

noise
industrial waste
smoke
nuclear waste
pesticides
fertilizer
landfill
burning waste
automobile exhaust
sewage
chemical waste
oil spill

◻ pollution

Pollution can affect air, water, or land and can threaten the health of humans, wildlife, and plants.

usually occurs when waste products, such as those produced by factories, dirty the land, air, or water. Too much noise or light can also cause pollution.

polyester (pol-ē-ES-ter) A substance that is created in a laboratory, usually from petroleum, and used to make plastics and fibers. Polyester is light and strong, and it is not affected by the weather.

polygon (POL-ē-gon) A flat figure that has three or more sides. Triangles, rectangles, and octagons are polygons.

polyhedron (pol-ē-HĒ-druhn) A three-dimensional object that has polygons for faces. A tetrahedron is a polyhedron with four triangular faces.

polymer (POL-i-mer) A chemical compound that is made up of a chain of smaller molecules. Cellulose is a polymer that occurs naturally in plants, and nylon and acrylic are polymers that scientists have created in the laboratory.

polyp (POL-ip) A stage in the life cycle of coral, jellyfish, and similar invertebrates. Polyps have hollow, tube-shaped bodies that attach to a surface at one end and at the other end have mouths that are

surrounded by tentacles. Some animals, such as coral and hydras, live their whole lives as polyps, while others, such as jellyfish, grow into a different form later in their life cycle.

pond A body of water that is smaller than a lake.

population (pop-yuh-LĀ-shuhn) A group of animals or plants of the same species that live in one place. Since New York's Central Park has many pigeons living in it, you can say that the park has a large pigeon population.

pore 1. A tiny opening that lets gases or liquids pass through it. The skin of animals and the leaves of plants have pores. 2. A space in soil, rock, or loose sediment that allows a liquid or gas, such as water, petroleum, or air, to pass through. Water that collects underground from rainfall and melting snow and ice moves through pores.

porous (POR-uhs) Having many small spaces or holes that let a liquid or gas pass through. Sponges are porous.

porpoise (POR-puhs) A small whale that is related to but smaller than a dolphin. Porpoises have blunt snouts and flat teeth.

Like dolphins, they are highly intelligent and communicate with each other using high-pitched whistling and squeaking sounds.

positive (POZ-i-tiv) **1.** Greater than zero. The plus sign is sometimes used to show that a number is positive, such as +2. Numbers written without a minus sign are assumed to be positive. **2.** Having the charge of a proton. The symbol for a positive charge is a plus sign. ◻ Compare **negative.**

postulate (POS-chuh-lit) A statement that is accepted as true without proof; an axiom.

potassium (puh-TAS-ē-uhm) A silvery-white chemical element that is a soft metal. Potassium is necessary for the growth of plants and animals, and it is used in fertilizers and soaps. ◻ See Table on pages 178–179

potential (puh-TEN-shuhl) The amount of energy needed to move an electric charge from one point to another in an electric field. Potential is measured in volts.

potential energy The energy that an object has stored up because of its position or condition. A ball on a 10-foot high shelf has more potential energy than one on a 5-foot high shelf, and a stretched rubber band has more potential energy than a rubber band that is not stretched. ◻ Compare **kinetic energy.**

pound A unit of weight equal to 16 ounces. ◻ See Table on page 148.

power **1.** Energy that is used to run machines. Steam is the power that runs a steam engine, and electricity is the power that runs pumps and washing machines. **2.** The rate at which work is done. Power is measured in units such as watts or horse-

◻ **potential energy**

top: *The unstretched exercise band has no potential energy.*
bottom: *The effort used to stretch the exercise band is stored as potential energy. This energy causes the exercise band to snap back to its normal shape when it is released.*

power. **3.** The number of times a number or an expression is multiplied by itself, as shown by an **exponent.** Thus ten to the sixth power, or 10^6, equals one million.

prairie (PRAIR-ē) A large area of flat or rolling grassland. The prairies of central North America extend from the Great Lakes to the Rocky Mountains.

Precambrian Eon (prē-KAM-brē-uhn Ē-on) The period of geologic time starting about 3.8 billion years ago and ending about 540 million years ago. During the Precambrian Eon, simple forms of life, including some types of algae, first appeared. ◻ See Table on pages 102–103.

precipitate (prē-SIP-i-tāt) A solid that is formed when a substance separates out from a solution.

precipitation (prē-sip-i-TĀ-shuhn) A form of water, such as rain, snow, sleet, or hail, that condenses from the atmosphere and falls to the Earth's surface.

predator (PRED-uh-ter) An animal that hunts another animal for food. Lions, eagles, frogs, and sharks are predators.

pregnant (PREG-nuhnt) Carrying developing young inside the body. A human female is pregnant for about nine months. A female elephant is pregnant for about 22 months.

prehensile (prē-HEN-suhl) Able to seize, grasp, or hold by wrapping around an object. Many birds have prehensile feet. Monkeys have prehensile tails.

premolar (prē-MŌ-ler) A tooth with two points, located between the canines and the molars. Premolars are used to tear and chew food. Most adult mammals have eight premolars, four on top and four on the bottom. ◻ A premolar is also called a *bicuspid.*

pressure (PRESH-er) Force that is applied against a gas, liquid, or solid. Pressure is described as the amount of force on an area, such as 10 pounds per square foot.

prey (PRĀ) An animal that is hunted by another animal for food. A zebra is prey to a lion.

Priestley (PRĒST-lē), **Joseph** Born 1733; died 1804. English scientist who in 1774 discovered a gas that made candles burn brighter. French scientist Antoine Lavoisier later showed that the gas was oxygen.

primary color (PRĪ-muh-rē KUHL-er) One of a group of colors that can be mixed together in different amounts to make other colors. ◻ See picture at **color.**

primate (PRĪ-māt) A type of mammal that is very intelligent and has eyes that face forward, a shortened nose, and oppos-

Biography

Joseph Priestley

Today we know that the air around us is made up of a mixture of different gases, but scientists used to believe that air was a single element. When Joseph Priestley discovered a gas that made a candle's flame burn brighter while other gases put the flame out, he did not fully understand the importance of what he had found. He assumed that it was a special type of air, different from the kind we breathe. After he told Antoine Lavoisier about his discovery, Lavoisier repeated Priestley's experiments and discovered that the gas was just one of the gases mixed in the air. It was Lavoisier who then named the mystery gas *oxygen.*

able thumbs. Most types of primates live together in groups and interact with each other in many ways. Monkeys, apes, and humans are primates.

prime meridian (PRĪM muh-RID-ē-uhn) The line of longitude that passes through the town of Greenwich, England, and that measures 0°. It is the line from which other longitude lines to the east and west are measured. A line of longitude that measures 15° East is located fifteen degrees east of the prime meridian.

prime number A positive whole number that cannot be divided by any whole number except itself and 1 without leaving a remainder. Examples of prime numbers are 7, 23, and 37. The only even prime number is 2.

printed circuit An electric circuit that is marked as a connected pattern on a surface, such as a chip or circuit board.

prism (PRIZ-uhm) A transparent object that breaks up the light passing through it into a spectrum of colors. A prism usually has triangular ends and rectangular sides.

probability (prob-uh-BIL-i-tē) The likelihood that something will happen. Probability can often be expressed as a fraction. The probability of rolling a particular side of a six-sided die is 1 in 6, or $\frac{1}{6}$.

□ prism

White light passing through a prism is split into the colors of the spectrum.

probe 1. A vehicle that is sent into outer space to collect information about objects in the universe. Space probes give astronomers information, such as pictures and temperature readings of planets, that they are unable to get from using a telescope. 2. A device that is used to examine the inside of a body part.

proboscis (prō-BOS-is) A long, tube-shaped part of an animal's body that is used for feeding. The trunk of an elephant is a proboscis. Butterflies and mosquitoes feed by means of a proboscis.

producer (pruh-DOO-ser) A living thing, especially a plant, that is a source of food for other living things in a **food chain.** Producers include green plants, which produce food through photosynthesis. Some bacteria are also producers.

product (PROD-uhkt) The number that is the result of multiplication. The product of 3 multiplied by 7 is 21.

program (PRŌ-gram) 1. The set of instructions that a computer needs to solve a problem or do a task. Programs direct the computer to collect and process data and to display results. 2. To provide a computer with a program.

projectile (pruh-JEK-tīl) An object that is shot or thrown forward through the air or through space. Bullets and rockets are projectiles.

prokaryote (prō-KAIR-ē-ōt) A member of a kingdom of living things that are made up of a single cell without a cell nucleus. Prokaryotes are the most ancient known forms of life. All bacteria are prokaryotes. □ A prokaryote is also called a *moneran.* □ Compare **eukaryote.**

propane (PRŌ-pān) A gas that is found in petroleum and is part of natural gas. Propane is used as a fuel.

propellant (pruh-PEL-uhnt) A substance that is used to push something forward with great power. Rocket fuel and the gas used in spray cans are both propellants.

propeller (pruh-PEL-er) A device that turns to cause an aircraft or a boat to move. A propeller is made of twisted blades mounted on a long shaft. When the shaft is spun by a motor, the blades push the surrounding water or air in a backward direction, and the aircraft or boat moves forward. □ See picture at **hovercraft.**

proper fraction (PROP-er FRAK-shuhn) A fraction in which the numerator is less than the denominator, such as $\frac{1}{2}$. □ Compare **improper fraction.**

prostate gland (PROS-tāt gland) A gland in male mammals that produces the fluid in which male sex cells travel during reproduction.

protein (PRŌ-tēn) A molecule that is made up of long chains of chemical compounds called **amino acids.** Living cells are made up largely of proteins. Proteins are an important part of the diet of many animals and are found in foods like meat, cheese, and beans.

protist (PRŌ-tist) A member of a kingdom of living things that are usually made up of a single cell, each with a cell nucleus. Many protists are able to move on their own and make their own food through the process of **photosynthesis.** Protozoans, most algae, and the slime molds are all protists.

proton (PRŌ-ton) One of the particles that make up an atom. Along with neutrons, protons make up the atom's nucleus. Protons have a positive electric charge.

protoplasm (PRŌ-tuh-plaz-uhm) A jelly-like substance that makes up the living material in all plant and animal cells. Protoplasm is made up of cytoplasm and the contents of the nucleus.

protozoan (prō-tuh-ZŌ-uhn) A member of a group of living things that are made up of a single cell. The amoeba is a kind of protozoan. Protozoans are members of the group of organisms known as **protists.**

psychology (sī-KOL-uh-jē) The scientific study of the mind, feelings, and behavior.

pterodactyl (tair-uh-DAK-tuhl) An extinct flying reptile that was about the size of a small bird. Pterodactyls lived during the time of the dinosaurs.

Ptolemaic system (tol-uh-MĀ-ik SIS-tuhm) The model of the universe that was thought of by Ptolemy. The Ptolemaic system has the Earth as its center, and the Sun, stars, and planets revolve around the Earth in circular orbits. The Ptolemaic system was thought to be correct until the 1500s, when Nicolaus Copernicus showed that the Earth moves around the Sun.

Ptolemy (TOL-uh-mē) Lived in the second century AD. Greek scientist who developed a model of the universe that has the Earth as its center.

puberty (PYOO-ber-tē) The stage in the life cycle of humans and other primates in which they become able to reproduce. The start of menstruation in females, and the ability to produce sperm in males, happen during puberty. Hormones that are produced during puberty cause physical changes in the body, such as the growth of facial hair in male humans.

pulley (PUL-ē) A simple machine that has a wheel over which a rope runs. The rope is attached to a load at one end, and a person pulls on the rope at the other end to lift the load. When two or more pulleys are attached in a **block and tackle,** it takes less work to lift a load. ◻ See picture at **machine.**

pulmonary (PUL-muh-nair-ē) Relating to the lungs.

pulp 1. The soft, moist part of a fruit. 2. The soft, spongy tissue of the stem of a plant; the pith. 3. The soft material that forms the inside of a tooth. 4. A mixture of materials that is used to make paper. Pulp is made of cellulose and can come from wood, rags, or recycled paper.

pulsar (PUHL-sar) A spinning star that gives off beams of radiation that sweep around like the beam of light sent out by a lighthouse.

pulse 1. The rhythmic movement of the arteries as blood is pushed through them by the beating of the heart. 2. A short burst of energy.

pumice (PUHM-is) A lightweight igneous rock that has holes like a sponge and is usually a light color. Pumice forms from hardened lava. The holes are called pores, and they form when water vapor and gases escape from the lava while it cools.

pump   A machine that is used to move fluids (liquids and gases) from one place to another, especially from a lower place to a higher place.

pupa   (PYŌŌ-puh) An insect in the stage of its life cycle between larva and adult. Insects in this stage do not feed and usually live in a protective case called a cocoon. Only some insects, such as moths, butterflies, ants, and beetles, develop as pupae during their life cycle. *Plural form*: **pupae** (PYŌŌ-pē).

pupil   (PYŌŌ-puhl) The opening in the center of the iris through which light enters the eye. ◻ See picture at **eye.**

pus   A thick, yellowish-white liquid that forms in an infected wound. Pus is made up of dead white blood cells.

pyrite   (PĪ-rīt) A silver or yellow mineral made of iron and sulfur. Because it is shiny, pyrite is often confused for gold. ◻ Pyrite is also called *fool's gold.*

Pythagoras   (pi THAG er uhs) Lived in the sixth century BC. Greek philosopher who believed that all things in nature could be understood through mathematics. He and his followers used mathematical principles to determine that the Sun, the Earth, and the other planets are round, and that the planets in the Solar System all revolve around the Sun.

Pythagorean theorem   (pi-thag-uh-RĒ-uhn THĒ-er-uhm *or* THEER-uhm) A theorem that states that the square of the length of the hypotenuse (the longest side) of a right triangle is equal to the sum of the squares of the lengths of the other sides. It is stated as the formula $c^2 = a^2 + b^2$, where c is the length of the hypotenuse and a and b are the lengths of the other two sides. The Pythagorean theorem is named after Pythagoras.

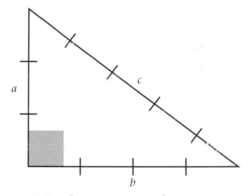

◻ **Pythagorean theorem**

*In this right triangle, **a** equals 3, **b** equals 4, and **c** equals 5. The formula for the Pythagorean theorem shows that $5^2 = 3^2 + 4^2$ (that is, 25 = 9 + 16).*

Qq

quadrant (KWAHD-ruhnt) Any of the four regions into which a plane is divided by the axes of the **Cartesian coordinate system.**

quadriceps (KWAHD-ri-seps) The group of muscles at the front of the thigh. The quadriceps straightens the knee.

quadrilateral (kwahd-ri-LAT-er-uhl) A flat shape that has four sides. Rectangles, squares, and rhombuses are all quadrilaterals.

quadruped (KWAHD-ruh-ped) An animal with four feet, such as most reptiles and mammals.

quantity (KWAHN-ti-tē) A number, or a symbol that represents a number. Addition, subtraction, multiplication, and division are performed on quantities.

quantum (KWAHN-tuhm) A unit that is used to measure energy, especially in the form of electromagnetic radiation. A quantum is the smallest amount of energy that can exist. The particle of energy that makes up light, called the **photon,** is a type of quantum. *Plural form*: **quanta** (KWAN-tuh).

quark (KWORK *or* KWARK) One of the subatomic particles that make up protons and neutrons.

quarry (KWOR-ē) An open pit from which stone is gotten by digging, cutting, or blasting. Quarry stone is usually used for building.

quart (KWORT) A unit of volume that is used to measure liquids, equal to $\frac{1}{4}$ of a gallon or 32 fluid ounces. ◻ See Table on page 148.

quartz (KWORTS) A hard, transparent mineral made of silica and oxygen. Quartz is the most common of all minerals and is found either by itself or as a part of rocks such as sandstone and granite. Flint, agate, and amethyst are all types of quartz.

◻ **quartz**

Quartz comes in many forms, including clear crystals (center) *and amethyst* (top right).

quasar (KWĀ-zar) A very bright, star-like object that is extremely far away from the Earth. A quasar produces several thousand times as much energy as the entire Milky Way galaxy. Many scientists believe that a quasar is actually a galaxy with a black hole at its center.

◻ **quadrilateral**

left to right: *square, rectangle, parallelogram, rhombus, and trapezoid*

Quaternary Period (KWAHT-er-nair-ē PEER-ē-uhd) The period of time during the history of the Earth starting about 2 million years ago and continuing until today. Humans first appeared during the Quaternary Period. ◻ See Table on pages 102–103.

queen   The fully developed female in a colony of bees, ants, or termites. The queen's only function is to lay eggs.

quicksand   A bed of loose sand that is mixed with water. This mixture forms a soft, shifting mass that swallows objects resting on its surface.

quill   **1.** The long, hollow, central part of a feather, the bottom of which attaches to the bird's skin. **2.** A sharp, hollow spine of a porcupine or hedgehog.

Did You Know?

quicksand

Quicksand does not deserve its bad reputation. These beds of sand and water are rarely deeper than a few feet. Even when quicksand is deeper, the human body is usually not pulled below the surface, because the body is less dense than quicksand. If a person who has fallen in stays still, the body will slowly rise to the surface.

quotient   (KWŌ-shuhnt) The number that results when one number is divided by another. If 6 is divided by 3, the quotient can be represented as 2.

Rr

rabies (RĀ-bēz) A disease that affects mammals, is caused by a virus, and causes damage to the brain and nerves. A person can get rabies if bitten by an animal that has the disease.

radar (RĀ-dar) A system that is used to locate distant objects and find their position, speed, and direction. Devices that use radar send out **radio waves** in all directions and receive the waves back after they bounce off an object. The reflected waves are then analyzed by a computer to provide information. Radar is used to control airplane traffic near airports and to keep track of satellites in space.

□ radar

An antenna sends out a short burst of radio waves (yellow). When these reach the airplane, they bounce off of it and send the reflected waves (blue) back to a receiver in the antenna. Special equipment is then used to calculate the distance and speed of the plane.

radial symmetry (RĀ-dē-uhl SIM-uh-trē) An arrangement of parts in a living thing that spread out from a central point. A line that is drawn through the central point will divide the body into equal parts.

The bodies of starfish show radial symmetry. □ Compare **bilateral symmetry**. □ See picture at **symmetry**.

radiant energy (RĀ-dē-uhnt EN-er-jē) Energy in the form of waves, especially electromagnetic waves. Radio waves, x-rays, and visible light are all forms of radiant energy.

radiation (rā-dē-Ā-shuhn) **1.** Energy in the form of **electromagnetic waves** or streams of particles, such as photons or electrons. Radiation is given off when the nuclei of radioactive atoms break down into smaller parts. **2.** The use of x-rays or other electromagnetic waves to treat diseases, especially cancer.

radiator (RĀ-dē-ā-ter) A type of heater that is often used in buildings. Radiators are usually made of a set of pipes that are connected to one another and that stand upright. Hot water or steam flows through the pipes, which then heat up the air around them.

radio (RĀ-dē-ō) The equipment used to send and receive radio waves that carry information, especially in the form of sound.

radioactive (rā-dē-ō-AK-tiv) Releasing energy in the form of radiation because of **radioactive decay.**

radioactive decay The natural breakdown of the nucleus of a radioactive chemical element. Radioactive decay releases energy in the form of **radiation** and results in a nucleus that has fewer protons and neutrons.

radioactivity (rā-dē-ō-ak-TIV-i-tē) The release of energy in the form of radiation from radioactive elements that are undergoing **radioactive decay.**

radiocarbon dating (rā-dē-ō-KAR-buhn DĀ-ting) A way of measuring how old the remains of living things are. Radiocarbon dating uses a radioactive form of carbon called carbon 14, which exists in small amounts in all living things.

Did You Know?

radiocarbon dating

All living things contain carbon, and a certain amount of the carbon is a radioactive form called carbon 14. Once a plant or animal dies, the carbon 14 starts to decay at a steady rate. By measuring how much carbon 14 is left in a piece of wood or a bone, scientists can figure out when the plant or animal died, and therefore how old it is.

radio frequency A range of frequencies that are used for sending and receiving radio waves through the air for broadcast on radios and televisions. Radio frequencies are measured in hertz.

radiometric dating (rā-dē-ō-MET-rik DĀ-ting) A way of figuring out the age of an object based on the amount of a particular radioactive material in it. Radiocarbon dating is one kind of radiometric dating.

radio telescope An instrument that is used to observe or study distant objects by gathering the radio waves that come from them. Because the wavelengths of radio waves are much longer than those of visible light, radio telescopes must be very large and can have a diameter of up to 1,000 feet (about 305 meters).

radio wave A wave of electromagnetic radiation that has wavelengths that are longer than any other form of electromagnetic radiation. Radio waves are used for sending and receiving radio and television broadcasting signals.

radium (RĀ-dē-uhm) A chemical element that is a radioactive metal and gives off its own light. It is found in very small amounts in rocks that contain uranium. Radium is used in scientific research and in the treatment of disease. ◻ See Table on pages 178–179.

radius (RĀ-dē-uhs) **1.** A line segment that goes from the center of a circle to any point on the circle, or that goes from the center of a sphere to any point on the surface of the sphere. The radius is half the length of the diameter. ◻ See picture at **circle. 2.** The shorter and thicker of the two bones of the forearm. ◻ See picture at **skeleton.** *Plural form:* **radii** (RĀ-dē-ī) or **radiuses.**

radon (RĀ-don) A radioactive chemical element that is a noble gas with no color or odor. Radon is made by the decay of **radium** and is found in very small amounts in soil, rocks, and the air near the ground. Radon is used in the treatment of cancer and other diseases. ◻ See Table on pages 178–179.

rain Water that falls to the Earth as separate drops from clouds. Rain condenses from water vapor in the atmosphere. It is a form of **precipitation.**

rainbow (RĀN-bō) An arc of colors that sometimes appears in the sky, usually after it rains. Rainbows appear when light from the Sun hits droplets of water that are floating in the air. The light is bent by the curved drops and separated into its different colors.

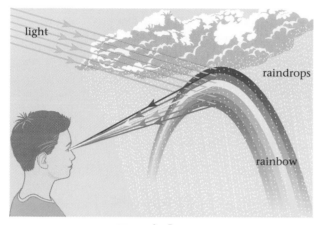

□ **rainbow**

Raindrops act like tiny mirrors that reflect sunlight back toward the observer. They also act like tiny prisms that refract (bend) the sunlight into the colors of the spectrum.

rainfall The amount of water that falls as rain, snow, hail, or sleet in a particular area over a set period of time. Rainfall is usually given in inches or centimeters

rain forest A thick evergreen forest that receives a high amount of rain. Most rain forests are found in the tropics along the equator. A rain forest is a kind of **biome.**

Ramsay (RAM-zē), **William** Born 1852; died 1916. British scientist who discovered the noble gases argon, neon, xenon, and krypton.

range 1. A chain of mountains, such as the Rockies or the Andes. 2. The distance over which something can travel or operate. A weak radio signal has a shorter range than a strong one. 3. The geographic area where an animal or plant is found. The range of the American alligator is limited to the southeastern United States. 4. The difference between the smallest and largest num-

Did You Know?

rain forest

The largest rain forest in the world is in the Amazon River basin in South America. It is home to millions of different plants, animals, insects, and other organisms, and scientists believe there are many more that have not yet been discovered! In recent years, the Amazon rain forest has been shrinking because of logging and agriculture. As farmers and ranchers cut down the forest, many species die out.

bers in a set of data. If the lowest test score of a group of students is 54 and the highest is 94, the range is 40.

raptor (RAP-ter) 1. A bird of prey, such as a hawk, eagle, or owl. 2. A type of small, meat-eating dinosaur whose back legs were good for leaping. Its claws were long and curved for seizing prey. Raptors were probably related to birds, and some even had feathers.

rare-earth element One of the chemical elements known as the **lanthanides.**

rate A quantity measured in relation to another quantity, usually a period of time. For example, a car that travels a distance of 50 miles (81 kilometers) in an hour travels at a rate of 50 miles (81 kilometers) per hour.

ratio (RĀ-shō) A relationship between two numbers. If a box has six red marbles and four blue marbles, the ratio of red marbles to blue marbles is 6 to 4. This is also written as 6:4.

rational number (RASH-uh-nuhl NUHM-ber) A number that is either an integer or a fraction made of integers. 2, –5, and $\frac{1}{2}$ are rational numbers.

ray 1. A narrow beam of light, heat, or other radiation. 2. The part of a line that is on one side of a point on that line. 3. A type of fish that has a wide, flat body and a long, pointed tail. In some species, such as the stingray, the tail is poisonous. Rays have skeletons made of cartilage rather than bone and are related to sharks.

react (rē-AKT) To undergo a chemical reaction. Acids and bases react to form salts.

reactant (rē-AK-tuhnt) A chemical element or a chemical compound that takes part in a chemical reaction, especially one that is present at the start of the reaction.

reaction (rē-AK-shuhn) 1. *See* **chemical reaction.** 2. *See* **nuclear reaction.** 3. An action that happens because of another action. When a ball is pushed, its reaction is to roll.

reactor (rē-AK-ter) *See* **nuclear reactor.**

reagent (rē-Ā-juhnt) A chemical element or a chemical compound that takes part in a chemical reaction, especially one that is used for testing and measuring another substance.

receiver (rē-SĒ-ver) A device that changes radio or microwave signals into sound or light. Radios and telephones have receivers in them.

Recent (RĒ-suhnt) *See* **Holocene Epoch.**

receptacle (ri-SEP-tuh-kuhl) The enlarged upper end of a flower stalk. Flowers or groups of flowers grow from the receptacle.

receptor (ri-SEP-ter) A cell or other tiny structure that is sensitive to something in the environment and sends a signal to the nervous system. Receptors in the skin are sensitive to touch and heat. Receptors in the nose detect smells.

recessive trait (ri-SES-iv TRĀT) A trait that does not appear in a living thing unless two genes for the same trait are inherited, one gene from the female parent and one gene from the male parent. Red hair in humans is a recessive trait. ◻ Compare **dominant trait.**

reciprocal (ri-SIP-ruh-kuhl) Either of two numbers that equal 1 when they are multiplied together. The number 3 is the reciprocal of $\frac{1}{3}$ because $3 \times \frac{1}{3} = 1$.

rectangle (REK-tang-guhl) A flat, four-sided figure that has four right angles. A rectangle with four equal sides is a square. ◻ See pictures at **geometry, quadrilateral.**

rectum (REK-tuhm) The lower part of the large intestine. The rectum is connected to the colon at its upper end. It is connected to the anus at its lower end. ◻ See picture at **digestive system.**

recycle (rē-SĪ-kuhl) To collect and reuse materials such as glass, paper, and plastic. Recycling helps protect the environment by preserving Earth's natural resources, creating less waste, and lessening pollution. For example, making cardboard out of old newspapers instead of from newly made paper means that fewer trees have to be cut down.

red blood cell A cell that is shaped like a disk and is found in the blood of humans and other vertebrates. Red blood cells contain **hemoglobin,** which carries oxygen to

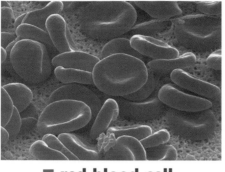

◻ **red blood cell**

all the cells of the body and gives red blood cells their red color. The red blood cells of mammals have no nucleus.

red giant   A very large, bright star that looks red because its surface is not as hot as the surface of most other stars. The Sun will become a red giant in several billion years. ◻ See picture at **star.**

red shift   An increase in the wavelength of radiation that is given off by an object in outer space as a result of the **Doppler effect.** Objects that are moving away from the Earth appear reddish.

red tide   A reddish-brown area in a body of water, such as an ocean or river. Red tides are caused by a sudden increase in dinoflag-ellates, a kind of protozoan. The dinoflag-ellates release a poison into the water that kills fish.

reduction   (ri-DUK-shuhn) **1.** A chemical reaction in which an atom gains one or more electrons. **2.** The changing of a fraction into a simpler form, especially by dividing the numerator and denominator by the same number. For example, the fraction $\frac{8}{12}$ can undergo reduction to $\frac{4}{6}$, and then to $\frac{2}{3}$, in each case by dividing both the numerator and denominator by 2. ◻ Compare **oxidation.**

redwood   A very tall evergreen tree that has cones and grows along the coast of northwest California and southern Oregon. Redwoods can grow to a height of 300 feet (91.4 meters).

Reed, Walter   Born 1851; died 1902. American army doctor who proved that yellow fever is spread to humans through the bite of a mosquito rather than by direct contact between people.

reef   An underwater ridge of rock or coral that rises up to or near the surface. Reefs are important ecosystems that provide a home for a great variety of sea life.

◻ **reef**

a coral reef in the Fiji Islands

refinery (ri-FĪ-nuh-rē) A place where certain substances, such as petroleum or sugar, are made pure or turned into other, more useful substances. Petroleum that was pumped out of the ground is turned into gasoline, kerosene, and other products in a refinery.

reflecting telescope (ri-FLEK-ting TEL-uh-skōp) A telescope that uses a bowl-shaped mirror to gather and focus light from distant objects.

reflection (ri-FLEK-shuhn) The throwing back of a wave, such as a wave of light or a sound wave, when it runs into an obstacle, such as a mirror or wall. ◻ Compare **refraction**.

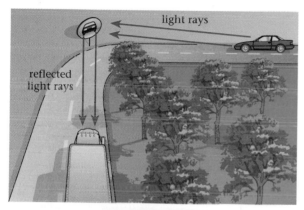

light rays

reflected light rays

◻ **reflection**

The mirror at the bend in the road allows the driver of the yellow truck to see the red car before it turns the corner. Mirrors reflect light and can be used to see objects around corners.

reflex (RĒ-fleks) An automatic response by a living thing to a stimulus. Pulling your hand away from a burning hot surface is a reflex.

refracting telescope (ri-FRAK-ting TEL-uh-skōp) A telescope that uses two lenses to gather and focus light from distant objects.

refraction (ri-FRAK-shuhn) The bending or turning of a wave, such as a wave of light, when it passes through one substance into another. ◻ Compare **reflection**.

◻ **refraction**

Light waves bend as they pass from one substance into another. This pencil appears to be bent at various angles as the light passes through air only; through air and glass; through water, air, and glass; and through water and glass.

refrigerant (ri-FRIJ-er-uhnt) A substance that is used to cool something down by absorbing heat from it. Refrigerants usually evaporate quickly, and the process of evaporation draws heat from anything nearby. Ice and ammonia are refrigerants.

regenerate (ri-JEN-uh-rāt) To regrow body parts that have been lost or destroyed. Some lizards regenerate their tails. Many plants and some invertebrates, such as starfish, can regenerate completely from a single cutting or body part.

region (RĒ-juhn) 1. A part of the Earth that contains a particular kind of plant or animal life. 2. A particular area of the body.

regular polygon (REG-yuh-ler POL-ē-gon) A polygon whose sides are all equal in length. A square is a regular polygon.

regurgitate (rē-GER-ji-tāt) To return partly digested food from the stomach to the mouth.

Did You Know?

regurgitate

When an animal regurgitates, it is not always sick. Birds feed their young by regurgitating food directly into their mouths. The parent bird can carry a lot of food in its stomach back to the nest, and the regurgitated food is easier for the baby birds to get nutrients from. Birds also regurgitate food in order to attract a mate. The regurgitated food is considered an offering.

relative humidity (REL-uh-tiv hyōō-MID-i-tē) The amount of water vapor in the air at a given temperature compared to the maximum amount that the air can hold at that temperature. Relative humidity is a ratio that is given as a percentage. If a mass of air has a relative humidity of 50 percent, it contains half of the water vapor that it can actually hold at its present temperature. ◻ Compare **absolute humidity**.

relativity (rel-uh-TIV-i-tē) A two-part theory of physics developed by Albert Einstein. The first part states that the laws of physics are the same for all objects, even if they are moving, and that the speed of light is the same everywhere. The second part states that gravity is not a force but a bending of space.

relay (RĒ-lā) An electric switch that is operated by a magnet with a wire coiled around it. When an electric current passes through the wire, it causes a small iron bar to move, which either opens or closes the switch.

Did You Know?

relativity

Einstein made many strange predictions in his theory of relativity. He stated that time will actually slow down as one travels at high speeds, and that an object's mass will increase enormously as it travels close to the speed of light. With his famous formula $E = mc^2$, Einstein stated that even a small amount of mass contains a large amount of energy.

REM Short for **rapid eye movement**. A stage of normal sleep in which the muscles of the eyes and face twitch, the heart beats faster, and more blood flows to the brain. Dreaming takes place during REM sleep.

remainder (ri-MĀN-der) The number that is left over when one number is divided by another number. When 20 is divided by 3, the remainder is 2, because 3×6 is 18, and $20 - 18$ is 2. Numbers that can be divided evenly have a remainder of 0.

remission (ri-MISH-uhn) A period of time when the signs of a disease, such as cancer, go away.

remote control (ri-MŌT kuhn-TRŌL) The control of an activity or machine from a distance, especially by radio or electricity.

renal (RĒ-nuhl) Relating to the kidneys.

renewable (ri-NŌŌ-uh-buhl) Relating to a natural resource that is either never used up or that can be replaced by new growth. Sunlight is an example of a renewable resource that can never be used up, and wood is an example of one that can be replaced by new growth. ◻ Compare **nonrenewable**.

reproduce (rē-pruh-DŌOS) To produce offspring. Many animals reproduce by mating. Other organisms, such as fungi and some plants, reproduce by producing spores.

reproduction (rē-pruh-DUHK-shuhn) The process by which living things produce offspring. Reproduction that takes place when the sex cell from the male parent joins together with the sex cell of the female parent is called **sexual reproduction.** Humans and all other vertebrates reproduce in this way. In **asexual reproduction,** offspring are produced by only one parent, without the joining together of sex cells. Bacteria reproduce in this way.

reproductive cell (rē-pruh-DUHK-tiv SEL) *See* **sex cell.**

reproductive system The parts or organs that are involved in **reproduction.** In flowering plants, the reproductive system is made up of pistils and stamens. The reproductive system in mammals is mainly made up of the ovaries, uterus, and vagina in females and of the testes and penis in males.

reptile (REP-tīl) A kind of animal that is cold-blooded, breathes air with lungs, and

□ reptile

A Nile crocodile carries and protects her young in her mouth.

has skin covered with scales or hard plates. Reptiles are vertebrates. Crocodiles, snakes, turtles, and lizards are reptiles.

repulsion (ri-PUHL-shuhn) The electric or magnetic force that pushes apart particles that have the same charge. Protons push each other apart by repulsion.

reservoir (REZ-er-vwar) A natural or man-made pond or lake that is used for the storage of water.

resin (REZ-in) **1.** A clear, yellowish or brownish substance that oozes from certain trees and plants. Resins are used to make varnishes, plastics, and medicines. **2.** A substance made in the laboratory that is like a natural resin. Like natural resins, artificial resins are also used to make plastics.

resistance (ri-ZIS-tuhns) **1.** A force, such as friction, that prevents or slows down motion. Many cars are designed with sleek shapes in order to cut down wind resistance. **2.** The ability of a material or an object to slow down the flow of an electric current through it. Good conductors, such as copper, have low resistance. Good insulators, such as rubber, have high resistance. Resistance is measured in ohms. **3.** The ability of a living thing to fight off germs and disease.

resistor (ri-ZIS-ter) A device that controls the electric current in an electric circuit by providing **resistance.**

respiration (res-puh-RĀ-shuhn) The process by which living things exchange gases, especially oxygen and carbon dioxide, with the environment. In animals that breathe air, oxygen is breathed in and carbon dioxide is breathed out using the lungs. In fish, respiration takes place in the gills. Respiration in green plants takes place during **photosynthesis.**

respiratory system (RES-per-ruh-tor-ē SIS-tuhm) The parts of the body that are needed for respiration. In humans and other vertebrates that breathe air, the mouth, nose, bronchial tubes, and lungs are the main parts of the respiratory system. In fish and many invertebrates, gills are the main parts of the respiratory system.

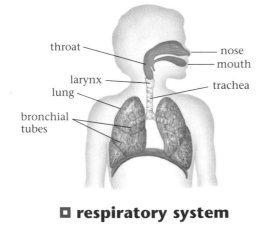

throat
nose
mouth
larynx
lung
trachea
bronchial
tubes

◻ **respiratory system**

retina (RET-i-nuh) The lining on the inside of the back of the eyeball that is sensitive to light. The retina is connected to the brain by the optic nerve. The cells of the retina are called rods and cones. ◻ See picture at **eye.**

revolution (rev-uh-LOO-shuhn) The act of revolving around a central point or object. The Earth makes one complete revolution around the Sun in about 365 days.

revolve (ri-VOLV) To move in a circle around a central point or object. The Moon revolves around the Earth in about 28 days. ◻ Compare **rotate.**

rheostat (RĒ-uh-stat) A resistor that can be adjusted to control the flow of current in an electric circuit. A thermostat is a rheostat that is adjusted to control the temperature in a room.

Rh factor (AR-ĀCH FAK-ter) A protein in red blood cells that is found in most people and is used to determine which kind of blood to use when a blood transfusion is necessary. Blood that contains the Rh factor works best when it is given to a person whose own blood also contains the Rh factor.

rhombus (ROM-buhs) A parallelogram with four equal sides. A square is a rhombus with four right angles. ◻ See pictures at **geometry, quadrilateral.**

rib A long, curved bone that goes from the spine to the sternum in the middle of the chest. The ribs form a bony cage that protects the heart and lungs. Ribs grow in pairs. Humans have 12 pairs of ribs. ◻ See picture at **skeleton.**

ribosome (RĪ-buh-sōm) A tiny part in a cell that is the place where proteins are made.

Richards (RICH-erdz), **Ellen Swallow** Born 1842; died 1911. American scientist who investigated the quality of the water supply in Massachusetts.

Biography

Ellen Swallow Richards

Ellen Swallow Richards first became interested in science when she attended Vassar College. She went on to become the first woman to attend, graduate from, and teach at MIT. Her research on pollution in rivers and streams helped to set up the first standards of water quality, and led to the first modern sewage treatment plant.

Richter scale (RIK-ter skāl) A scale that is used to rate the strength of earthquakes. The Richter scale ranges from 1 to 9. Each increase of 1 on the scale means an increase of 10 times the strength. An earthquake rated at 6 is 10 times more powerful than one rated at 5, and 100 times more powerful than one rated at 4.

rickets (RIK-its) A disease that is caused by too little vitamin D in the diet. Rickets usually affects children. The bones of a child with rickets are soft and do not grow properly.

rift valley A narrow area of low-lying land between two faults in the Earth's crust. The faults form when the forces of **plate tectonics** pull two plates apart. When this happens, the land that lies between the faults sinks. ◻ See picture at **plate tectonics.**

right angle An angle that measures 90°. Two lines that are perpendicular to each other form a right angle. ◻ See picture at **angle.**

right triangle A triangle that has a right angle for one of its angles.

rip current A sudden, strong current of water that flows rapidly away from the shore. Rip currents return water to the sea that the wind and waves have built up along the shore. The currents are strong enough to pull a swimmer away from shore, but they are narrow enough to swim out of. ◻ A rip current is also called a *rip tide.*

rip tide See **rip current.**

river (RIV-er) A natural flow of fresh water. Rivers empty into a body of water, like an ocean, a lake, or another river. They are often fed by smaller rivers or streams that flow into them.

◻ **river**

Rivers flow as a single stream (left) *or as many connected channels* (right).

RNA Short for **ribonucleic acid.** The material in the cell that carries the instructions for making proteins from one part of the cell to another. RNA first copies the information contained in a segment of DNA. RNA then carries this information to the part of the cell where proteins are made. ◻ Compare **DNA.**

robot (RŌ-bot) A machine that can perform a variety of tasks either on command or by being programmed in advance. Robots can move about on their own and often have sensors so they can react to things around them. Robots can be used in factories and in scientific research.

◻ **robot**

In this factory, robots are used to assemble cars.

robotics (ruh-BOT-iks) The scientific study of the design, building, and operation of robots.

rock The hard, solid mass of minerals that makes up the Earth's crust. Rock can be

Rock Types

IGNEOUS ROCKS

- form from cooling of **magma** (underground) and **lava** (at the Earth's surface).
- often form deep down in the Earth and are later pushed to the Earth's surface by the forces of **plate tectonics.**

EXAMPLES: granite, pahoehoe, basalt, obsidian

cliffs of igneous rocks

close-up photograph of granite

pahoehoe from a volcano

SEDIMENTARY ROCKS

- form when sediment, such as sand and mud, becomes hard.
- form from the broken-down fragments of other rocks that are carried and later laid down by water, wind, glaciers, and other forces.
- often contain fossils of animals and plants that died when the rocks were forming.

EXAMPLES: sandstone, shale, limestone, conglomerate

sandstone dunes

shale

shrimp fossil in limestone

METAMORPHIC ROCKS

- form when igneous or sedimentary rocks get heated, squeezed, or stretched by the processes of **plate tectonics.**
- often contain **folds** and sometimes contain precious minerals.

EXAMPLES: gneiss, schist, marble, slate

gneiss with folds

schist

marble

made of a single mineral or of several different minerals. The three main types of rock are **igneous rock, sedimentary rock,** and **metamorphic rock.** ☐ See Table on page 208.

rocket (ROK-it) A vehicle that has one or more engines that burn fuel without taking oxygen from the air. The burning of the fuel releases hot gases that push the body of the rocket forward. Because they do not need oxygen from the atmosphere, rockets can be used in outer space.

rod A rod-shaped cell in the retina of the eye. Rods make vision in dim light possible. ☐ Compare **cone.**

rodent (RŌ-dint) A usually small mammal with front teeth that are used for gnawing. The front teeth of rodents grow throughout the animal's life, and gnawing keeps them from getting too long. Rats, mice, beavers, squirrels, shrews, and hamsters are all rodents.

roe The eggs of a fish, together with the membrane in which they are held.

Roentgen (RENT-gen or RENT-jen), **Wilhelm Konrad** Born 1845; died 1923. German scientist who discovered x-rays in 1895.

root 1. A part of a plant that usually grows underground. Roots keep the plant in place, absorb minerals and water, and store the food that is made by the leaves and other plant parts. In certain plants, additional roots grow out from the stem above ground and bend down into the soil to provide more support. 2. The part of a tooth that is embedded in the jaw and not covered by enamel.

root hair A fine, hair-like growth on a plant root that absorbs water and minerals from the soil. ☐ See picture at **root.**

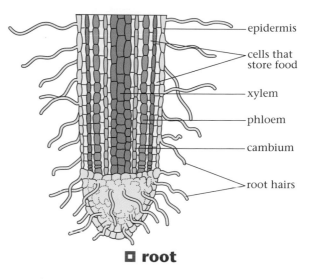

epidermis
cells that store food
xylem
phloem
cambium
root hairs

☐ **root**

a buttercup root showing inside structures

rot To decay by being broken down into simple chemical compounds, especially by bacteria or fungi. Dead plants that rot on the forest floor enrich the soil with nutrients.

rotate (RŌ-tāt) To spin on an axis. The Earth rotates once every 24 hours. ☐ Compare **revolve.**

rotation (rō-TĀ-shuhn) The act of spinning on an axis. The Earth makes one complete rotation every 24 hours.

rotor (RŌ-ter) A part of a machine that spins in a circle.

Roux (RŌO), **Pierre Paul Émile** Born 1853; died 1933. French scientist who, with Alexandre Yersin in 1888, identified the toxin that is produced by the bacteria that cause diphtheria. This discovery led to the development of a treatment for the disease.

rubber (RUHB-er) A material that bends easily and returns to its original shape after being stretched. Rubber is used to make tires, electrical insulation, and other products. It is made from the milky sap of certain tropical plants and can also be made from petroleum in a laboratory.

rubella (roo-BEL-uh) *See* **German measles.**

ruby (ROO-bē) A deep-red form of the mineral corundum that is valued as a precious stone.

rudder (RUHD-er) A part at the back of a boat or on the tail of a plane that is used for steering. A rudder is long and flat and swings left or right on a hinge.

ruminant (ROO-muh-nuhnt) A kind of mammal with a stomach that is divided into four parts. Ruminants have hooves, an even number of toes, and usually horns. Cattle, sheep, and goats are ruminants.

runoff Rainfall or melted snow that reaches a stream or lake because it is not absorbed by the soil.

Russell (RUHS-uhl), **Henry** Born 1877; died 1957. American scientist who studied binary stars and developed methods to calculate their mass and distances from the Earth. He also developed a theory explaining how stars change over millions of years.

rust A reddish-brown substance that forms on things made of iron when they are exposed to oxygen and moisture. Rust is an oxide of iron.

Did You Know?

rust

Rust is the result of a chemical reaction called oxidation, which is the combination of a substance with oxygen. Rust forms when iron combines with oxygen. When a substance burns, it is undergoing a very rapid form of oxidation. So rust can be thought of as burning that happens very slowly.

Rutherford (RUH*TH*-er-ferd), **Ernest** Born 1871; died 1937. British scientist who was a leader in the study of the structure of atoms. He discovered the atom's nucleus, and he discovered the electromagnetic radiation that is given off by the nuclei of radioactive atoms during radioactive decay. He named the proton, and he also made up the word *half-life* to measure the rate of radioactive decay.

saber-toothed tiger (SĀ-ber-tōōtht TĪ-ger) A large, extinct cat that had two very long upper teeth. The largest saber-toothed tigers were about 4 to 5 feet (1.2 to 1.5 meters) long and 3 feet (0.9 meter) tall. They died out during the Pleistocene Epoch.

Sabin (SĀ-bin), **Albert Bruce** Born 1906; died 1993. Russian-born American scientist who developed a vaccine against polio that contained a weak form of the polio virus.

sac A bag-shaped structure that acts as a container. Spiders lay their eggs in sacs. The bladder in humans is a sac.

saline (SĀ-lēn) Containing dissolved salt. The water in the ocean is saline.

saliva (suh-LI-vuh) The watery fluid in the mouth that is produced by glands under the tongue and in the jaw. Saliva moistens food and contains **enzymes** that help in digestion.

Salk (SAWLK), **Jonas Edward** Born 1914; died 1995. American scientist who developed the first effective vaccine against polio in 1955.

salt **1.** A white or clear mineral found naturally in all animal fluids, in seawater, and in underground deposits. It is used to season food and to keep food from spoiling. As a chemical compound, salt is called **sodium chloride.** When salt is found in the ground, it is often called **halite. 2.** A chemical compound that forms when an acid and a base are combined, or when a metal is mixed with an acid. Salts have an electric charge, conduct electricity, and dissolve in water.

Biography

Jonas Edward Salk

It took eight years for Jonas Salk to develop his vaccine for polio, a disease that every year left thousands of children with physical disabilities. Injections with the Salk vaccine greatly reduced the number of  polio cases throughout the world. Salk's vaccine was used until 1963, when Albert Sabin introduced a vaccine that could be swallowed and provided longer-lasting protection.

saltwater (SAWLT-wah-ter) Containing water that is very salty. Oceans are saltwater bodies that are fed mainly by rivers, which pick up dissolved salts from the ground as they flow.

sand Small grains or particles of broken-down rock. Sand is coarser than silt and finer than gravel. It is often made of quartz.

sandbar A low ridge of sand that is built up in the water along a seashore or riverbank. The sand in a sandbar is piled up by the action of waves or currents.

sandstone A sedimentary rock made of grains of sand that have been joined together. Sometimes the grains of sand are pressed together by pressure from rocks above them, and sometimes they are joined together by particles of silt or clay that act like glue. Sandstones are yellow, red, gray, or brown, and their grains of sand are usually made of the mineral **quartz.** ◻ See Table on page 208.

Sanger (SANG-er), **Frederick** Born 1918. British scientist who explained the structure of the hormone insulin in 1955. It then became possible to make insulin in laboratories and use it to treat diabetes.

sap The liquid that flows through plant tissues and carries water, minerals, and food.

sapphire (SAF-īr) One of several forms of the mineral corundum, especially a blue form that is valued as a gem.

saprophyte (SAP-ruh-fīt) An organism that lives on and feeds off dead organisms or decaying matter. A mushroom that grows on a rotting log is a saprophyte.

satellite (SAT-uh-līt) **1.** An object that moves around a larger object in outer space. The Moon is a satellite of the Earth. **2.** An object that is made by people and sent into outer space to move around the Earth or another object such as a planet or the Sun. Satellites carry special equipment and are used for research, communications, weather information, and navigation.

satellite dish An antenna that is shaped like a dish and is used to receive signals from and send signals to a satellite.

saturated (SACH-er-ā-tid) **1.** Containing as much water vapor as possible. Air that is saturated has a relative humidity of 100 percent. **2.** Relating to a solution that is unable to dissolve any more of a particular dissolved substance. Saltwater is saturated with salt when it cannot dissolve any more salt.

saturated fat A fat that is found in some oils and in meat and other foods that are made from animal products, such as butter and cheese. Eating too many foods with high levels of saturated fats can lead to heart disease. ◻ Compare **unsaturated fat.**

Saturn (SAT-ern) The planet that is sixth in distance from the Sun and is the second largest planet in the Solar System. Saturn is

◻ **satellite**

A satellite used for telecommunications receives information, such as television signals, from a station on the ground. The satellite sends these signals back to other parts of the Earth.

encircled by a large, flat system of rings that are made up mostly of tiny particles of ice. ◻ See Table on pages 184–185.

savanna (suh-VAN-uh) A flat, treeless grassland located in hot, dry regions. Savannas cover nearly half of Africa and are home to such wildlife as lions, zebras, and hyenas. A savanna is a kind of **biome.**

scale **1.** One of the small, thin, plate-like parts that form the outer covering of fish, reptiles, and some other animals. **2.** A small, thin, usually dry plant part. The protective leaves that cover a tree bud are scales. The flat structures on the cones of a conifer are scales. **3.** A series of marks or numbers that are placed at regular distances to measure size, volume, or degree. **4.** A device that is used for weighing. **5.** The relationship between the size of a drawing or model and the actual size of the thing that is represented by it. Maps are drawn to a specific scale, with one inch or centimeter equal to a certain number of miles or kilometers.

scalene triangle (SKĀ-lēn TRI-ang-guhl) A triangle that has three sides of different lengths. ◻ See picture at **triangle.**

scanner (SKAN-er) A device that turns printed pictures and text into digital information that can be stored or changed by a computer.

scanning electron microscope An electron microscope that makes a three-dimensional image by shooting a stream of electrons at an object and moving the stream across it.

scapula (SKAP-yuh-luh) Either of two flat, triangle-shaped bones on the upper part of the back on either side of the spine. The scapula is part of the shoulder. ◻ The scapula is also called the *shoulder blade.* ◻ See picture at **skeleton.**

scavenger (SKAV-uhn-jer) An animal that eats dead plants or animals. Most scavengers are meat-eating animals that eat dead animals rather than hunt live prey. Vultures and hyenas are scavengers.

Scheele (SHĀ-luh), **Karl Wilhelm** Born 1742; died 1786. Swedish scientist who discovered nitrogen, chlorine, and several chemical compounds. Scheele discovered oxygen around 1772, but because the results of his experiments were not published until 1777, Joseph Priestley is usually credited with its discovery.

schist (SHIST) A shiny metamorphic rock that can be easily split into flakes or slabs. Schist has a silvery appearance because it has crystals of the mineral mica that reflect light. ◻ See Table on page 208.

Schoolcraft (SKOOL-kraft), **Henry Rowe** Born 1793; died 1864. American scientist who was the first explorer to locate the source of the Mississippi River in 1832.

science (SĪ-uhns) The study of how the world works and how living things live and grow, from the smallest units of matter and energy to the stars and galaxies. The work of science is based on observation, hypothesis, and experiment, which make up what is known as the **scientific method.**

scientific (sī-uhn-TIF-ik) Relating to science.

scientific method The process of observing and measuring things that happen, making a hypothesis to explain these things, and performing experiments to see if the hypothesis is correct. By using the scientific method, scientists learn how the world works.

scientific name A name that is used by scientists for a living thing. Most scientific names have two parts, the name of the **genus** followed by the name of the **species,** and are usually Latin or Greek. *Homo sapiens,* which means "wise human" in Latin, is the scientific name for humans.

scientific notation   A method of expressing numbers in terms of a decimal number between 1 and 10 that is multiplied by a power of 10. For the number 10,492, the scientific notation is 1.0492×10^4.

scientist   (SĪ-uhn-tist) A person who is an expert in science. Most scientists study or do research in a branch of science, such as physics or biology.

sclera   (SKLAIR-uh) The strong, white, outer coating that covers all of the eyeball except the cornea.

screw   A pin that has a spiral ridge going around it along most of its length. Screws are used to hold or fasten things together. A screw is considered a simple machine because it is really an **inclined plane** that is wrapped around a central shaft or pole. ◘ See picture at **machine.**

scrotum   (SKRŌ-tuhm) The sac of skin that encloses the testes in most mammals.

scurvy   (SKUR-vē) A disease that is caused by too little vitamin C in the diet. Scurvy leads to weakness, bleeding gums, and loose teeth.

sea   1. The ocean. 2. A large area of an ocean that is partly enclosed by land, such as the Caribbean Sea. 3. A large body of either fresh water or salt water that is completely enclosed by land, such as the Caspian Sea.

sea anemone   (SĒ uh-NEM-uh-nē) A type of sea animal that looks like a flower and is related to jellyfish and corals. Sea anemones have a tube-shaped body that is attached to a surface at one end, and they have a mouth with tentacles around it at the other. Sea anemones are invertebrates.

seal   A type of sea mammal that has a streamlined body, thick fur or hair, and flippers. Seals eat meat and are related to walruses but smaller.

sea level   The level of the surface of the ocean, which is the same all over the Earth. This measurement is used as a standard to determine land elevation or sea depth. If a mountain is 3,500 feet high, that means that it rises 3,500 feet above sea level.

search engine   A software program that searches websites for information about particular words and phrases.

season   (SĒ-zuhn) 1. In the Temperate Zones, one of the four natural periods into which the year is divided: spring, summer, autumn, and winter. Each period has a different range of temperature and weather. The North and South Temperate Zones have opposite seasons, so when it is summer in the Northern Hemisphere, it is winter in the Southern Hemisphere, and the other way around. 2. In the Torrid Zone, either of the two periods, rainy and dry, into which the year is divided.

seaweed   One of the many kinds of algae or plants that live in the ocean. Some kinds of seaweed are attached to the ocean bottom, while others float freely in the water. Seaweed range from the size of a pinhead to 100 feet (30.5 meters) long.

sebum   (SĒ-buhm) An oily substance in the skin of mammals that keeps the skin and hair from drying out. Sebum is produced by glands that lie beneath the hair follicles.

second   (SEK-uhnd) 1. A unit of time equal to $\frac{1}{60}$ of a minute. 2. In geography, a

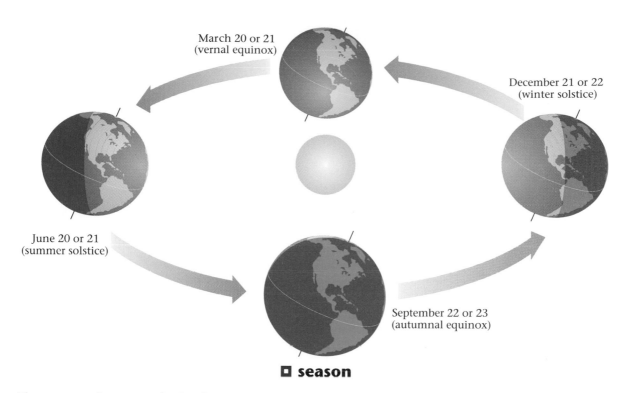

■ **season**

The seasons change as the Earth moves around the Sun during the year. From mid-March to mid-September, the Northern Hemisphere is tilted toward the Sun, causing the warm seasons of spring and summer. From mid-September to mid-March, the Northern Hemisphere is tilted away from the Sun, causing the cool seasons of autumn and winter. The seasons are just the opposite in the Southern Hemisphere.

unit used to measure longitude and latitude that is equal to $\frac{1}{60}$ of a minute.

secondary color (SEK-uhn-dair-ē KUHL-er) A color that is produced by mixing two **primary colors** in equal amounts. ■ See picture at **color**.

secondary sex characteristic A change in the appearance of an animal that takes place as the animal matures. Secondary sex characteristics are controlled by the **sex hormones**. The growth of facial hair in men, the growth of antlers in antelopes, and the colorful feathers in male birds are secondary sex characteristics.

secrete (si-KRĒT) To give off or release a substance, such as saliva, that is produced by a gland or organ in the body.

sediment (SED-uh-muhnt) **1.** Material

such as silt, sand, or rock that has been moved from one place to another by water, wind, or a glacier. Over time, sediment can harden into **sedimentary rock. 2.** Particles of solid matter that settle to the bottom of a liquid.

sedimentary rock (sed-uh-MEN-tuh-rē ROK) A rock that is formed when sediment, such as sand or mud, becomes hard. Sedimentary rocks form when sediments are collected in one place by the action of water, wind, glaciers, or other forces, and are then pressed together. Limestone and shale are sedimentary rocks. ■ See Table on page 208.

seed A plant part that contains an embryo and the food that it will need to grow into a new plant. Seeds are **ovules** that have ripened after **fertilization**. ■ See picture at **germination**.

215

seed leaf   *See* **cotyledon.**

seedling   (SĒD-ling) A young plant that is grown from a seed.

segment   (SEG-muhnt) **1.** *See* **line segment. 2.** A part of a circle that is made of an arc on that circle and the straight line that connects the two endpoints of the arc. ◘ See picture at **circle.**

seismic   (SĪZ-mik) Relating to earthquakes.

seismograph   (SĪZ-muh-graf) An instrument that detects and records vibrations and movements in the Earth during an earthquake. By comparing the records that are produced by seismographs in three or more locations, scientists can figure out where an earthquake occurred and how strong it was.

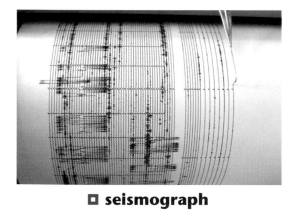

◘ **seismograph**

seismology   (sīz-MOL-uh-jē) The scientific study of earthquakes, including their causes and effects.

self-pollination   (self-pol-i-NĀ-shuhn) A kind of pollination that takes place in plants with flowers that have both male and female parts in a single flower. ◘ Compare **cross-pollination.**

semen   (SĒ-muhn) A whitish fluid in male mammals that contains the sperm. Semen is produced in the testes.

semiarid   (sem-ē-AIR-id) Fairly dry because of low rainfall. Semiarid regions, such as a prairie, usually have enough water for grasses and some bushes to grow but not enough for most trees.

semicircular canal   (sem-i-SER-kyuh-ler kuh-NAL) One of the three loop-shaped tubes of the inner ear. The semicircular canals help humans and many other animals keep their sense of balance. ◘ See picture at **ear.**

semiconductor   (sem-ē-kuhn-DUHK-ter) A material that is used in making circuits for computers. Semiconductors conduct electricity more easily than insulators but less easily than conductors. Semiconductors are often made of **silicon.**

Semmelweis   (ZEM-uhl-vīs), **Ignaz Phillipp** Born 1818; died 1865. Hungarian doctor who showed that it was important to keep the area around a patient free of germs during surgery. He proved that many fewer people died of infection when doctors and nurses washed their hands.

sense   A particular body function that takes place when a **sense organ** is stimulated by something in the environment. Living things rely on their senses to survive and respond to changes in their surroundings. Sight, hearing, taste, smell, touch, and the ability to feel heat and cold are senses.

sense organ   An organ, part, or cell in a living thing that is sensitive to something in the environment, such as sound, touch, or light. The ear and nose are sense organs in mammals.

sensor   (SEN-ser) A device that produces an electric signal in response to something in its environment. The signal is sent to another device or to a machine. A sensor in a printer detects that the paper tray is empty

Did You Know?

sensor

Sensors are similar to your body's sense organs. Both sense organs and sensors react to a physical stimulus, like motion, sound, light, or heat. Sensors inform machines and computers in the same way that your sense organs inform your brain of the surrounding environment—by sending impulses of electricity.

and sends a signal for the printer to indicate that the tray is out of paper.

sensory (SEN-suh-rē) Relating to the senses or sense organs. Nerves carry sensory information to the brain from the rest of the body.

sepal (SĒ-puhl) One of the usually green parts of a plant that look like leaves and grow out from the base of a flower. Together, the sepals form the calyx, which surrounds and protects the flower bud.

septic system (SEP-tik SIS-tuhm) A system used to get rid of waste from a house that is not connected to a **sewer system.** Water that contains waste from toilets and sinks flows into an underground tank, called a septic tank. There, the waste is broken down by bacteria into water, gases, and other harmless substances that are let out into the air or the soil.

series circuit (SEER-ēz SER-kuht) An electric circuit in which the source of electricity is connected to two or more devices that follow one after the other on the same wire. If the flow of current is interrupted anywhere in the circuit, all of the devices will stop working. ◻ Compare **parallel circuit.** ◻ See picture at **circuit.**

serum (SEER-uhm) **1.** The clear, liquid part of the blood. Serum is plasma from which platelets, which cause blood clots to form, have been removed. **2.** A liquid that contains antibodies that can protect a person or animal from infection.

server (SER-ver) A computer that stores and controls data for another computer to download, use, or change.

set A group of elements that have something in common. In mathematics, sets are written using curly braces. For example, the set of all positive integers from 1 to 5 is written {1, 2, 3, 4, 5}.

sewage (SOO-ij) Liquid and solid waste that is produced by humans and carried away by drains and sewer pipes. Sewage is treated with chemical compounds to get rid of substances that pollute the environment and to kill off germs that can cause disease.

sewer system (SOO-er SIS-tuhm) A system of underground pipes that carry wastewater away from a town or city. Sewer systems are usually connected to industrial plants that clean wastewater so it does not pollute the environment.

sex **1.** The condition of being male or female. **2.** See **sexual intercourse.**

sex cell A cell that unites with a cell of the opposite sex to form a new organism. In animals, eggs and sperm are sex cells. In plants, eggs and grains of pollen are sex cells. ◻ Sex cells are also called *gametes* or *reproductive cells.*

sex chromosome Either of two chromosomes, the X-chromosome or the Y-chromosome. The sex of humans, many animals, and some plants is determined by the types of sex chromosomes in the **sex cells.** The sex cells of females have two X-chromosomes, and the sex cells of males have

217

one X-chromosome and one Y-chromosome.

sex hormone   A hormone that controls the ability of an animal to mature, mate, and reproduce. Estrogen is the main sex hormone in females. Testosterone is the main sex hormone in males.

sex-linked trait   A trait that is passed from parent to offspring through a gene on a sex chromosome. Color blindness in humans is a sex-linked trait.

sextant   (SEK-stuhnt) An instrument that is used to figure out the location of a ship. A sextant measures the angle between the horizon and certain stars. This information is then used to calculate latitude and longitude.

sexual intercourse   (SEK-shoo-uhl IN-ter-kors) The act of reproducing in humans and many other vertebrates. In sexual intercourse, sperm from the male is deposited in the female, where it can fertilize an egg.

sexual reproduction   A kind of reproduction in which the sex cell from the male parent joins with the sex cell of the female parent to produce a new organism. Most many-celled animals create offspring by sexual reproduction. ◘ Compare **asexual reproduction.**

shadow   (SHAD-ō) A dark or shaded area that appears when light is blocked.

shale   A sedimentary rock that is made of hardened clay, silt, or mud. Shale has many layers and splits easily into thin sheets or slabs. It is usually gray or brownish red. ◘ See Table on page 208.

shark   A type of fish that has a long, streamlined body, five to seven slits for the gills, and a skeleton made of cartilage rather

◘ **shadow**

When the sun is low in the sky, shadows are long (top). When the sun is high, shadows are short (bottom).

than bone. Sharks eat meat and have tooth-shaped scales. One species, the whale shark, is the largest fish in the world.

shell   **1.** The hard outer covering of an animal, such as a clam, snail, turtle, or insect. **2.** The hard outer covering of a bird's egg. **3.** The hard outer covering of a seed, nut, or fruit. **4.** One of the levels that electrons move in as they travel around the nucleus of an **atom.** Depending on the number of protons in the nucleus, an atom can have up to seven shells for its electrons. The electrons in the shells that are farthest from the nucleus have more energy than those in the shells that are closer to the nucleus.

shoal   A shallow place in a body of water near the shore.

shock   **1.** The passing of an electric current through the body. The amount of damage that is caused by a shock depends on how strong the current is and how long it lasts. **2.** A strong reaction of the body to a serious injury or illness. Shock can lead to a drop in blood pressure that can be severe enough to cause death.

shock wave   A large wave that forms when a substance or an object moves through a fluid so fast that the waves in the fluid pile up on each other. Shock waves can be caused by explosions or by objects moving through a fluid at a speed greater than the speed of sound. Airplanes traveling at supersonic speeds create shock waves.

shooting star   *See* **meteor.**

short circuit   An accidental connection between two wires in an electric circuit. Short circuits can let too much current flow through one part of the circuit and cause the circuit to break or a fire to start.

short ton   *See* **ton** (sense 1).

shoulder blade   (SHŌL-der blād) *See* **scapula.**

shrub   A woody plant that is smaller than a tree. A shrub usually has several stems rather than a single trunk. ◻ A shrub is also called a *bush.*

sierra   (sē-AIR-uh) A high, rugged group of mountains that has an irregular outline somewhat like the teeth of a saw.

signal   (SIG-nuhl) A pattern of electromagnetic waves or electric impulses that carries information. Radio transmitters broadcast radio signals.

silica   (SIL-i-kuh) A chemical compound that is made of the elements silicon and oxygen. Silica is found in most kinds of rocks and is the main chemical compound in sand. Silica is used to make glass, concrete, and other materials.

silicon   (SIL-i-kon) A chemical element that makes up about one-fourth of the Earth's crust. Silicon is found in sand, quartz, and flint and is the second most common element in the Earth's crust. It is used in glass, semiconductors, concrete, ceramics, and computer chips. ◻ See Table on pages 178–179.

silk   A strong fiber that is made by spiders and some insect larvae, especially silkworms. Spiders spin webs from silk. Silkworms are the larvae of a type of Asian moth that use silk to spin their cocoons.

silt   Small grains or particles of broken-down rock. Silt particles are smaller than grains of sand but larger than the particles in clay. Silt is often found at the bottom of bodies of water, such as lakes, where it piles up slowly by settling gradually through the water.

siltstone   A sedimentary rock that is made of hardened silt.

Silurian Period   (si-LUR-ē-uhn PEER-ē-uhd) The period of time during the history of the Earth starting about 438 million years ago and ending about 408 million years ago. During the Silurian Period, the first land plants and invertebrate land animals appeared. The first fish with jaws also appeared during the Silurian Period. ◻ See Table on pages 102–103.

silver   (SIL-ver) A chemical element that is a shiny, grayish-white metal. It conducts heat and electricity better than any other metal. It is used to make jewelry, photographic paper, and electric circuits and conductors. ◻ See Table on pages 178–179.

simulation   (sim-yōō-LĀ-shuhn)   An activity or process that is used to imitate something real. Simulations are often controlled by computers, which can be programmed to see what will happen under different conditions. Simulations are used to study earthquakes and weather patterns and to train airplane pilots.

A Closer Look

Skeleton

All vertebrates (animals with backbones) have an internal skeleton made of bone or cartilage, which supports the body and gives it shape. Bones meet at flexible joints, which move by the action of muscles. Nerves, muscles, and a strong skeleton make it possible for animals to move around.

<u>human</u>

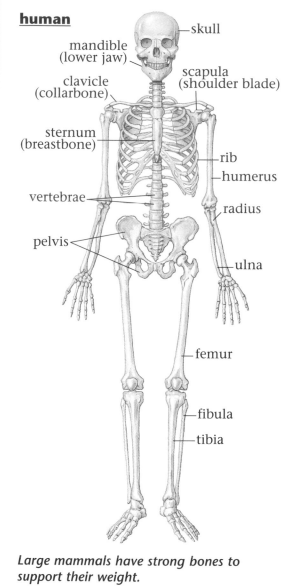

- skull
- mandible (lower jaw)
- scapula (shoulder blade)
- clavicle (collarbone)
- sternum (breastbone)
- rib
- humerus
- vertebrae
- radius
- pelvis
- ulna
- femur
- fibula
- tibia

Large mammals have strong bones to support their weight.

<u>fish</u>

Fish have lightweight, streamlined skeletons. Their bones are thin because they do not have to support much weight.

<u>snake</u>

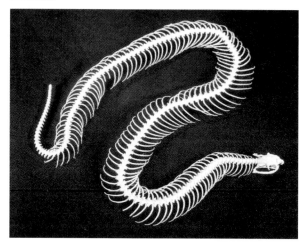

Snakes have long spines that curve easily from side to side. Their ribs give their bodies the shape of a flexible tube.

sinus (SĪ-nuhs) A hollow space in a bone of the skull. The sinuses of the skull are filled with air and connect with the nose.

siphon (SĪ-fuhn) A tube that looks like an upside-down U. It is used to make liquid flow upward through it from one container and down into a lower container.

SI unit Short for **Système International**, which is French for **International System.** A unit of the International System, the formal name for the most modern version of the **metric system.** The meter, kilogram, and second are SI units.

skeleton   (SKEL-i-tuhn) The framework of bones that supports the body and protects the organs in humans and other vertebrates. In sharks and some other fish, the skeleton is made of cartilage instead of bone. The human skeleton has 206 bones.

skin   **1.** The outer covering of humans and other vertebrates. Skin protects the inside of the body from infection and from the Sun's rays, and it also helps control heat loss from the body. Hair, scales, feathers, fat, and many glands and sense organs are contained in the skin. **2.** The outer covering of some invertebrates. The skin of a clam or snail is called the **mantle.**

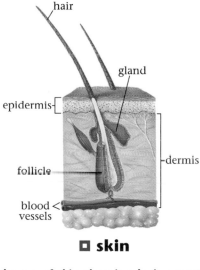

hair

gland

epidermis

dermis

follicle

blood vessels

◻ skin

layers of skin showing hair growth

skull   The part of the skeleton that is made up of the bones of the head and face. The skull encloses and protects the brain. ◻ The skull is also called the *cranium.* ◻ See picture at **skeleton.**

sky   The region above or beyond the Earth, as it is seen looking up from the ground. During the day the sky looks blue, because the atmosphere scatters all the col-

ors that make up sunlight except for blue. During the night the sky looks black, because you can see through the atmosphere into the darkness of outer space.

slate   A metamorphic rock made from shale that is put under great pressure underground. Slate splits easily into thin layers with smooth surfaces. It is usually gray, red, or green. ◻ See Table on page 208.

sleep   A natural state of rest that occurs at regular times. During sleep, growth is thought to take place, and energy is conserved and stored away. Dreams take place during a stage of sleep called **REM.**

Did You Know?

sleep
Sleep is very important for the brain. During sleep, the brain sorts through experiences and stores important new information for later use. Without enough sleep, the brain has difficulty learning and remembering.

sleet   Water that falls to the Earth in the form of frozen or partly frozen raindrops. Sleet is a form of **precipitation.**

slime   A slippery or sticky substance that is produced by the skin of slugs, snails, and some other animals.

small intestine   The long, narrow part of the intestine, in which nutrients are taken up from food during digestion. The small intestine is found between the stomach and the large intestine. ◻ See picture at **digestive system.**

smallpox   A serious disease that causes high fever and pimples that scar as they heal. Smallpox is caused by a virus and is very contagious. Vaccines have led to the disappearance of the disease, but some laboratories still have samples of the virus.

smelt   To melt ores in order to separate out the metals they contain.

smog   **1.** A form of air pollution that is produced when sunlight reacts with poisonous gases from factories and automobiles. Smog is common in many large cities, especially during hot, sunny weather. It appears as a thin brown haze. **2.** Fog that has been mixed with smoke. This kind of smog appears as a thick gray mist.

smoke   A mixture of carbon dioxide, water vapor, gases, and often soot that is produced by the burning of a material that contains carbon.

snake   A kind of reptile that has a long, thin body and no legs. Some snakes have sharp fangs that can give a poisonous bite. The jaws of a snake come apart, making it possible for the snake to swallow prey that is thicker than itself. Rattlesnakes, cobras, pythons, and boa constrictors are snakes.

snow   Water that falls to the Earth as crystals of ice, called snowflakes. The crystals form in a cloud when water vapor freezes suddenly, without first condensing into a raindrop. Snow is a form of **precipitation.**

snowfall   The amount of snow that falls in a particular area over a set period of time. Snowfall is usually given in inches or centimeters.

snow line   The border of an area that is always covered with snow. The snow line on a mountain is the lowest point where the snow never melts.

soap   A substance that is used for washing and cleaning. Soaps are made by combining something containing sodium or potassium (such as lye) with vegetable or animal fat. Soaps work by surrounding particles of dirt or grease, making it easier for water to carry them away.

sodium   (SŌ-dē-uhm) A chemical element that is a silvery, soft, and lightweight metal. Sodium is very easily shaped, and it reacts explosively with water. It combines

□ **smog**

smog over the city of Denver, Colorado

with chlorine to make the salt that is used to season food. ■ See Table on pages 178–179.

sodium carbonate (SŌ-dē-uhm KAR-buh-nāt) A powdery chemical compound that is used to make baking soda, glass, ceramics, detergents, and soap.

sodium chloride (SŌ-dē-uhm KLOR-īd) The chemical compound that is used as table salt. When sodium chloride is found in the ground, it is called **halite.**

software The computer programs that control the way a computer works. The programs that allow people to write documents on a computer or play video games are software. ■ Compare **hardware.**

soft water Water that has very few or no salts dissolved in it. ■ Compare **hard water.**

soil The loose top layer of the Earth's sur-

■ soil

Soil usually has several layers. The top layer is usually darkest because it contains decayed leaves and twigs and other organic matter. The middle layer is rich in minerals and has some organic matter. The third layer has many rock fragments and lies directly over bedrock.

face. Soil is made of broken-down pieces of rock and minerals mixed with decayed bark, dead leaves, and other materials. Soil provides the support and nutrients that many plants need to grow.

solar (SŌ-ler) **1.** Relating to the Sun. **2.** Using or operated by energy from the Sun.

solar cell A device that changes sunlight into electricity. Solar cells are used to supply power to satellites, calculators, and other devices. They are also used as a source of electricity in areas that have no system of wires to deliver electricity. ■ Solar cells are also called *photovoltaic cells.*

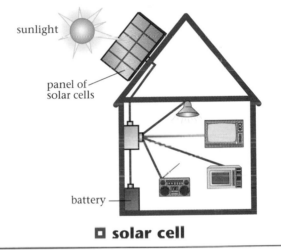

■ solar cell

solar eclipse An eclipse of the Sun that happens when the Moon is between the Sun and the Earth. During a solar eclipse, the Moon blocks our view of the Sun.

solar energy Energy that comes from the Sun's radiation. Solar energy can be used to heat up rooms that have windows facing the Sun. It can also be used to make electricity in **solar cells.**

solar flare A sudden throwing off of burning gases from a small part of the surface of the Sun. Solar flares happen near sunspots and cause a sudden increase in brightness. ■ See picture at **sun.**

Solar System The Sun and all the objects in space that orbit it, including the nine planets and their moons, along with numerous comets, asteroids, and meteoroids. The Solar System is part of the **Milky Way** galaxy. ◻ See Table on pages 184–185.

solar wind A stream of high-speed, charged atomic particles that flow outward from the Sun.

solder (SOD-er) A mixture of tin and another metal that can be melted and used to join or repair metal parts. Solder has a lower melting point than the metal parts it is applied to.

soldier (SŌL-jer) An ant or termite that is built for fighting but unable to reproduce.

solenoid (SŌ-luh-noyd) A coil of wire that acts as a magnet when an electric current passes through it. Solenoids are used in the devices that start engines and in automatic door locks.

solid (SOL-id) **1.** One of the three basic forms of matter. Solids are made up of molecules that can vibrate back and forth but can't move to change places with other molecules. Solids have both a set volume and a set shape. **2.** A shape that has three dimensions. Cubes and spheres are solids.

solstice (SOL-stis) Either of the two times during the year when the Sun is farthest north or south of the equator. The two solstices are known as the **summer solstice** and the **winter solstice.** ◻ See picture at **season.**

soluble (SOL-yuh-buhl) Able to be dissolved. Salt is soluble in water. Metal is soluble in acid.

solute (SOL-yoot) A substance that is dissolved in another substance, forming a **solution.** Salt is a solute in salt water.

solution (suh-LOO-shuhn) **1.** A mixture in which atoms or molecules of one substance, called the **solute,** are spread out evenly among the atoms or molecules of another substance, called the **solvent. 2.** The answer to a problem in mathematics that makes an equation true. The solution to the equation $x + 2 = 3$ is 1, because $1 + 2 = 3$.

solvent (SOL-vuhnt) A substance that can dissolve another substance to form a **solution.** Water is the solvent in salt water.

◻ **solution**

The pale blue solution in the beaker is a mixture of powdered copper sulfate (the solute) in water (the solvent).

Somerville (SUM-er-vil), **Mary Fairfax Greig** Born 1780; died 1872. Scottish scientist whose books on science were written in everyday English, using simple experiments and illustrations to explain scientific concepts. At a time when most textbooks were very complex, Somerville made science easier to understand for the general public.

sonar (SŌ-nar) A system that is used to locate underwater objects such as submarines or schools of fish. Sonar equipment sends out **sound waves** in all directions and receives the waves back after they bounce off an object. Because the speed of sound in water always stays the same (about 4,800 feet, or 1,463 meters, per second), the time it takes for a sound wave to reach an object and bounce back can be used to calculate the object's distance.

sonic boom (SON-ik BOOM) A loud, explosive sound that is caused by an aircraft traveling faster than the speed of sound (faster than 1,070 feet, or 326 meters, per

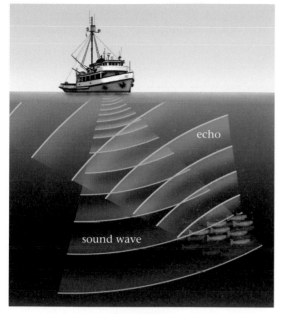

■ **sonar**

Sonar equipment on the ship sends out sound waves underwater. The sound waves reflect off a school of fish and return to the ship, where the sonar equipment calculates how far away the fish are.

second). The sound waves that the aircraft makes cannot move away from it fast enough, and the front of the aircraft pushes against the sound waves, creating a booming sound.

soot   A black powder that forms when fuel, such as wood, coal, or oil, burns incompletely. Soot is made up mainly of **carbon.** The inside of a chimney is usually covered with soot.

sound   1. A type of energy that travels as waves and can often be detected by the ears. Sound starts out as a vibration of something, such as a guitar string. The vibration causes **sound waves** to move through another substance, such as air, water, or a piece of wood. Sound waves move through air at a speed of about 1,070 feet (326 meters) per second. 2. The sensation that is produced in the organs of hearing by sound waves. 3. A long body of

water, wider than a strait, that connects two larger bodies of water. 4. A large arm, or extension, of the ocean that often runs parallel to the coast.

Did You Know?

sound

Sound is measured in decibels. A normal conversation has a loudness of about 60 decibels, and thunder at very close range has a loudness of about 140 decibels. Sound greater than 85 decibels can cause damage to the ear, and sound with intensity above 120 decibels can cause pain.

sound barrier   A force that makes it difficult for an object to move faster through the air as it gets close to the speed of sound (1,070 feet, or 326 meters, per second). An airplane traveling at supersonic speeds feels this force because the pressure and sound waves in the air around it can't move fast enough to get out of its way, so they push against the airplane.

sound wave   A kind of wave that moves as changes in pressure and density through a substance and carries sound. How loud a sound is depends on the **amplitude** of the sound wave. How high a sound is depends on its **frequency.**

south   The direction to your left when you face a sunset.

Southern Hemisphere   The half of the Earth that is south of the equator.

southern lights   *See* **aurora australis.**

South Frigid Zone   The region of the Earth that extends from the Antarctic Circle to the South Pole. ■ *See* picture at **zone.**

South Pole   The most southern point of the Earth. The South Pole is the southern end of the axis on which the Earth rotates. It is located in Antarctica.

South Temperate Zone   The region of the Earth that is located between the Antarctic Circle and the Tropic of Capricorn. ◻ See picture at **zone.**

space   **1.** The three dimensions of length, width, and depth, in which objects exist. **2.** The entire area in which Earth, the Solar System, and all the stars and galaxies exist; the universe. **3.** The part of the universe that is outside the Earth's atmosphere; outer space.

space-time   The three dimensions of length, width, and depth that are used to describe space, together with the fourth dimension of time. All objects in the universe can be described as occupying a specific space at a specific point in time.

spark   A tiny, hot glowing particle that is thrown off from a burning substance or produced when objects rub against each other.

spark plug   A device that is used to create an electric spark in engines that run on gasoline. The spark causes the fuel and air mixture to burn in the cylinder. ◻ See picture at **engine.**

spawn   To lay eggs, usually in large numbers and in the water. Fish, frogs, and mollusks spawn.

species   (SPĒ-shēz *or* SPĒ-sēz) One of the major groups in the classification of living things. A species is below a genus. Only organisms that belong to the same species are able to breed with each other. ◻ See Table on page 47.

specific gravity   (spi-SIF-ik GRAV-i-tē) A number that shows how dense a substance is by comparing it with the density of water at 39° Fahrenheit (4° Celsius). The specific gravity of gold is around 19, meaning that a given volume of gold is about 19 times denser than the same volume of water.

specific heat   A number that shows how much heat it takes to raise the temperature of a substance 1 degree by comparing it with the amount of heat needed to raise water by 1 degree. The specific heat of vinegar is about 0.5, meaning it takes around half as much heat to raise a given amount of vinegar by 1 degree as it does to raise the same amount of water by 1 degree.

specimen   (SPES-uh-muhn) A sample of something that is taken for the purpose of scientific study. Scientists can compare the body structure of different insects by examining insect specimens. Laboratory workers study blood specimens.

spectrometer   (spek-TROM-i-ter) An instrument that measures the wavelengths and power of radiation by splitting the radiation up into a **spectrum.** In a spectrometer that measures light (visible radiation), light enters a slit, is focused by a lens, and passes through a prism that splits it up into a spectrum.

spectrum   (SPEK-truhm) **1.** An arrangement of all electromagnetic radiation according to its **frequencies** and **wavelengths.** Radiation with low frequencies and long wavelengths is at one end of the spectrum, and radiation with high frequencies and short wavelengths is at the other end. The whole spectrum ranges from radio waves to gamma rays, with visible light in the middle. **2.** A band of colors that is seen when white light is broken up according to its different **wavelengths.** When white light passes through a prism, it produces a spectrum. A rainbow is also a spectrum.

speed The rate at which an object moves. Speed is measured as the distance traveled divided by the amount of time it takes to travel the distance. A car that travels 100 miles in two hours has an average speed of 50 miles per hour.

sperm **1.** The sex cell of male animals that is able to fertilize an egg. An egg that has been fertilized by a sperm can grow into a new animal. Sperm are produced in the **testes. 2.** The male sex cell of plants, algae, and some fungi that is able to fertilize an egg. An egg that is fertilized by a sperm grows into a new organism.

spermatozoa (sper-mat-uh-ZŌ-uh) Sex cells that are produced by a male animal; sperm. *Singular form*: **spermatozoon** (sper-mat-uh-ZŌ-ahn).

Sperry (SPAIR-ē), **Roger Wolcott** Born 1913; died 1994. American scientist who proved that the right and left sides of the brain each control different functions of the body.

sphere (SFEER) A three-dimensional object shaped like a ball. All the points on the surface of a sphere are the same distance from a point in the sphere's center. ◻ See picture at **geometry.**

spider (SPĪ-der) A type of small animal that has eight legs and a body that is divided into two parts. Spiders produce silk, which they often use to spin webs for catching prey, especially insects. Spiders, together with ticks and mites, are members of the group of animals called **arachnids.**

spinal column (SPĪ-nuhl KOL-uhm) *See* **spine.**

spinal cord The part of the nervous system in vertebrates that begins at the lower end of the brain and is enclosed by the bones of the spine. The spinal cord is made of bundles of nerves, which branch out to connect with other nerves in the limbs and trunk.

spindle (SPIN-duhl) A bundle of fibers that forms in the nucleus of a cell during **cell division.** The chromosomes of the dividing cell attach to the spindle before moving to opposite ends of the cell.

spine **1.** The column of bones in a vertebrate that runs down the center of the back. The spine supports the body and encloses and protects the **spinal cord.** ◻ The spine is also called the *backbone* or *spinal column.* **2.** A sharp-pointed part on a plant. Spines protect plants from being eaten. The spines of a cactus are hard, narrow leaves. ◻ See picture at **leaf.**

spinneret (spin-uh-RET) One of the small openings in the back part of spiders and some insect larvae. The spinnerets release a sticky fluid that dries into silk.

spiral (SPĪ-ruhl) **1.** A two-dimensional curve that winds around a central point. **2.** A three-dimensional curve that winds around a central axis. A spiral can be imagined as winding around a cylinder or cone.

spleen An organ in humans and other vertebrates that is near the stomach. The spleen stores red blood cells, produces some white blood cells, and filters dead cells from the blood.

sponge A type of sea animal that attaches to rocks or other objects. Sponges are invertebrates with only one kind of body tissue and no organs. Their

◻ **sponge**

a basket sponge growing on coral

bodies have many holes and passages that are used to filter food out of the water.

spontaneous combustion   (spon-TĀ-nē-uhs kuhm-BUHS-chuhn) The bursting into flame of a material that has not been heated by something else. Spontaneous combustion is caused by chemical reactions that take place inside the material itself. Oily rags and damp hay can undergo spontaneous combustion.

spore   **1.** A single cell that can grow into a new living thing without being fertilized by another cell. Fungi, algae, some protozoans, and plants that do not bear seeds reproduce by means of spores. **2.** A form of some bacteria that can become active after a long period of being inactive. Bacteria become spores as a way of surviving extreme conditions, such as dryness and cold.

spreading ridge   An area where two of the Earth's plates are moving away from each other. As the plates move apart, magma rises up through the space between them and spreads out, forming new rock. ◻ See picture at **plate tectonics.**

spring   **1.** A device, such as a coil of wire, that returns to its original shape after it is stretched or pressed together. Springs are used to store energy, as in clocks, and to absorb energy, as from the wheels of a car when they go over a bump. **2.** A small stream of water that flows naturally from the Earth. **3.** The season of the year between winter and summer, when plants begin to grow. In the Northern Hemisphere, it lasts from the vernal equinox, in late March, to the summer solstice, in late June.

spring tide   A tide in which the difference between the high and low tide is the greatest. Spring tides happen when the

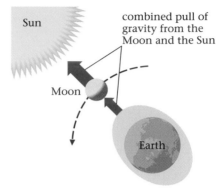

◻ **spring tide**

Spring tides occur when the Sun and Moon are directly in line with the Earth. When this happens, the pull of gravity on the Earth and its waters is strongest.

Moon is either new or full. During this time, the Sun, the Moon, and the Earth are lined up, causing the pull of gravity on the Earth's water to be stronger. ◻ Compare **neap tide.**

square   **1.** A rectangle that has four equal sides. **2.** The result of multiplying a number by itself. 16 is the square of 4 because $4 \times 4 = 16$. **3.** To multiply a number by itself. 5 squared is 5×5, or 25. **4.** Relating to a unit of measurement that measures area. Square units, such as square miles and square meters, are one unit long and one unit wide.

square root   A number that yields a given number when it is squared. Since $5 \times 5 = 25$, the square root of 25, which is written $\sqrt{25}$, is 5.

stable   **1.** Relating to an atom that is not radioactive and will not change on its own into a smaller atom. The most common form of carbon, carbon 12, is stable. **2.** Relating to a chemical compound that does not easily break down or change into other chemical compounds or into chemical elements. Water is a stable compound.

stainless steel   A mixture of steel and chromium or nickel. The chromium or nickel keeps the steel from rusting.

stalactite   (stuh-LAK-tīt) A long, thin structure that is made of minerals and hangs downward from the roof of a cave. Stalactites form slowly, as water that is saturated with minerals drips from a cave's roof. They are usually made of the mineral calcite, but they can also be made of other minerals.

stalagmite   (stuh-LAG-mīt) A cone-shaped structure that is made of minerals and sticks up from the floor of a cave. Stalagmites form slowly, as water that is saturated with minerals drips from a cave's roof onto the floor. Stalagmites are usually made of the mineral calcite, but they can also be made of other minerals.

stalk   **1.** The main stem of a plant, such as a flower. **2.** A slender plant part that supports or attaches another plant part, such as a leaf.

stamen   (STĀ-muhn) The male organ of reproduction of a flower. The stamen has a slender stalk called the filament that ends in a pollen-bearing tip called the anther. ❏ See picture at **flower.**

standard time   (STAN-derd TĪM) The time in any of the 24 time zones into which the Earth's surface is divided. Standard time is usually measured at the meridian that runs down the center of a given zone. The continental United States has four standard time zones: Eastern (75th meridian), Central (90th meridian), Mountain (105th meridian), and Pacific (120th meridian).

star   An object in outer space that is made up of very hot gas and is held together by its own gravity. Nuclear fusion at the center of a star is the source of its energy. The release of this nuclear energy is what makes stars shine. ❏ See picture on page 230.

starch   A chemical compound that is used by plants to store energy. Starch is a carbohydrate and in its pure form is a white powder. It is found especially in wheat, corn, rice, and potatoes.

starfish   A type of sea animal that has a body shaped like a star. The arms of a starfish, usually five in number, have

❏ **stalactite/stalagmite**

Blanchard Springs Caverns in Ozark National Forest, Arkansas

small suckers on the bottom that are used for moving around and for holding on to prey. Starfish are invertebrates.

state of matter   One of the conditions in which matter exists. The three states of matter are solid, liquid, and gas. Some scientists consider plasma to be a fourth state of matter.

static   (STAT-ik) **1.** Relating to objects or systems that are not moving or changing. ☐ Compare **dynamic. 2.** An interruption of a radio or television signal that causes a crackling or hissing sound or specks to appear on a television screen. Static is a form of **interference** and is caused by electricity in the atmosphere.

static electricity   **1.** Electric charge that piles up on an object instead of flowing through it as a current. Static electricity forms when two objects that are not good conductors of electricity are rubbed together, so that electrons from one of the objects rub off onto the other. Combing

A Closer Look

Star

A star is a ball of very hot gas. Stars form when a giant cloud of dust and hydrogen gas, called a **nebula**, *clumps into a dense mass. As the atoms in the nebula get packed tightly together, the temperature of the newly formed star rises. When the star gets hot enough, the hydrogen atoms join together to form heavier atoms in a process called* nuclear fusion. *The energy that is released during nuclear fusion gives the star its light. Stars go through various "life stages" over millions or billions of years, as shown below. Smaller stars cool down gradually and end up as* **white dwarf stars.** *Larger stars explode as* **supernovas** *and end up as either* **neutron stars** *or* **black holes.**

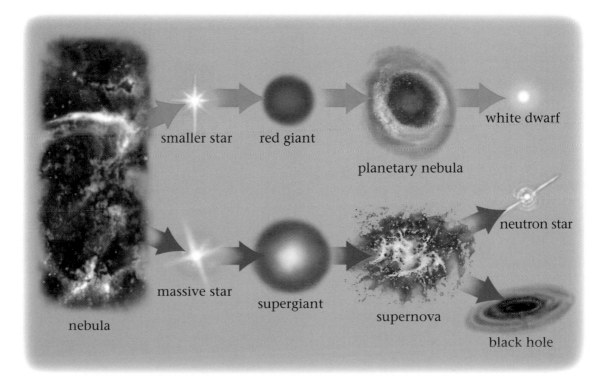

nebula

smaller star   red giant

planetary nebula

white dwarf

massive star   supergiant   supernova

neutron star

black hole

the hair or taking off a sweater can create static electricity. **2.** A brief flow of electricity, in the form of a **spark,** that takes place after static electricity has built up in a place and there is a path for the electricity to follow.

◻ static electricity

A balloon rubbed on the head picks up electrons from the hair and takes on a negative charge. The hair is then more positively charged and the two surfaces attract each other.

statistics (stuh-TIS-tiks) The branch of mathematics that studies how to collect, organize, and analyze data. Statistics can be used to study health problems in large populations.

steam Water that exists as a gas because it is above its boiling point of 212° Fahrenheit (100° Celsius).

steam engine An engine that changes the energy of hot steam into motion. In most steam engines, steam from a boiler is fed into

Did You Know?

steam engine

A major difference between a steam engine and an internal-combustion engine is where the fuel is burned. A steam engine burns its fuel—coal, oil, or natural gas—outside the engine, where it heats a boiler of water to produce steam. This steam runs through pipes to power the engine. The internal-combustion engine, however, burns its fuel inside the engine. This burning releases hot gases like those that drive the pistons in a car.

a cylinder, where it expands. The expanded steam then pushes on a piston, which is connected to a rod that turns a wheel.

steel A metal that is made of iron and carbon. The carbon makes the iron stronger, harder, and able to be bent without breaking. Steel is used to make many tools and to hold up tall buildings.

stegosaurus (steg-uh-SOR-uhs) A large plant-eating dinosaur that had a very small head and a double row of plates down the middle of its back. Its tail had large spikes used to defend itself.

stellar (STEL-er) Relating to or made up of stars.

stem A plant part that grows above ground and supports or attaches other plant parts, such as branches, leaves, or flowers.

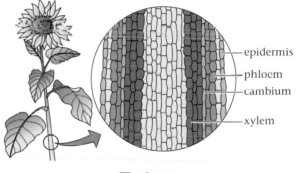

epidermis
phloem
cambium
xylem

◻ stem

a portion of stem from a sunflower plant, showing xylem, phloem, and other structures

steppe (STEP) A vast, semiarid, grassy plain. Steppes are found in southeast Europe and Asia.

sterile (STAIR-uhl) **1.** Not able to reproduce. A sterile animal cannot produce offspring. Sterile plants do not produce seeds or fruit. **2.** Free from bacteria or other germs that can cause disease.

sterilize (STAIR-uh-līz) **1.** To make something free of germs that can cause disease.

Dentists sterilize their instruments before using them. **2.** To make a living thing unable to reproduce.

sternum (STER-nuhm) The long flat bone in the middle of the chest. The ribs attach to the sternum. ◻ The sternum is also called the *breastbone.* ◻ See picture at **skeleton.**

steroid (STAIR-oyd) A type of chemical compound that is found in living things and has many actions in the body. Sex hormones, cholesterol, and bile are kinds of steroids. Some steroids are used as medicines and can be made in a laboratory.

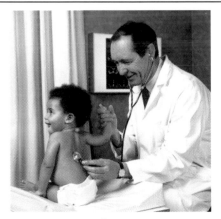

◻ **stethoscope**

stethoscope (STETH-uh-skōp) A medical instrument that is used to listen to sounds made in the body, such as those of the heart or lungs.

Stevens (STĒ-vuhns), **Nettie Marie** Born 1861; died 1912. American scientist who demonstrated in 1905 that the sex of a living thing is determined by the sex chromosomes, the X-chromosome and the Y-chromosome. Working independently of Stevens, Edmund Beecher Wilson announced similar findings in the same year.

stigma (STIG-muh) The sticky tip of the pistil of a flower. Pollination begins when pollen lands or is left on the stigma. ◻ See picture at **flower.**

stimulant (STIM-yuh-luhnt) A substance, such as a medicine or caffeine, that makes the heart beat faster and speeds up the action of other body organs.

stimulus (STIM-yuh-luhs) Something that causes an automatic response in a body part or living thing. Sense organs, such as those in the skin, are sensitive to stimuli. A person who accidentally touches a hot surface automatically moves away from the stimulus to keep from getting burned. *Plural form:* **stimuli** (STIM-yuh-lī).

stinger A sharp stinging part that usually contains venom. Bees, scorpions, and stingrays have stingers.

stoma (STŌ-muh) A tiny opening or pore in the surface of a plant leaf. A stoma allows gases and water vapor to pass into and out of a plant. Most stomata are on the underside of the leaf. *Plural form:* **stomata** (STŌ-muh-tuh).

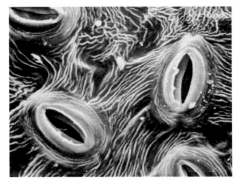

◻ **stoma**

A stoma opens when the guard cells surrounding it fill with water. The photograph of these open stomata was taken using an electron microscope.

stomach (STUHM-ik) **1.** The sac-shaped part of the body in humans and other vertebrates that stores food during **digestion.**

Fluids in the stomach help break down food into simpler chemical compounds. Food from the stomach then passes into the small intestine, where nutrients are taken up by the blood. ◻ See picture at **digestive system**. **2.** Any of the four compartments into which the stomach of a ruminant is divided.

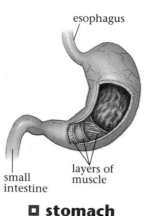

esophagus

layers of muscle

small intestine

◻ **stomach**

stone **1.** A general term for rock, especially as used in construction. **2.** A hard clump of minerals that forms in an organ or part of the body. Stones sometimes form in the kidneys or other part of the **urinary system.**

Stone Age The earliest period of prehistoric human development when people first used stone tools. The tools were made by chipping stones until they had sharp edges for cutting, scraping, and chopping. The Stone Age is divided into the **Paleolithic Period,** the **Mesolithic Period,** and the **Neolithic Period.**

straight angle An angle that measures 180°. A straight angle is a straight line.

strain **1.** The degree to which an object's shape and size change as a result of being stretched or squeezed. **2.** A group of living things, such as bacteria, that belong to the same species but that differ in some way from other members of the species. There are many different strains of viruses that cause the common cold.

strait A narrow passage of water that joins two larger bodies of water. The Strait of Gibraltar connects the Mediterranean Sea with the Atlantic Ocean.

stratified rock (STRAT-uh-fīd ROK) Rock that is arranged in layers. The Grand Canyon is made of stratified rock.

stratocumulus cloud (strat-ō-KYOOM-yuh-luhs KLOWD) A low-lying, fairly flat cloud that often spreads across the sky in streaks or patches. Stratocumulus clouds usually have gray bottoms and white, rounded tops. ◻ See picture at **cloud.**

stratosphere (STRAT-uh-sfeer) The layer of the Earth's atmosphere lying above the troposphere and below the mesosphere. Jet airplanes often fly in the lower parts of the stratosphere, and the **ozone layer** is found in the upper parts.

stratum (STRĀ-tuhm *or* STRAT-uhm) A layer of rock or other material. A rock stratum looks different from the rock strata above and below it. *Plural form:* **strata** (STRĀtuh *or* STRAT-uh) or **stratums.**

stratus cloud (STRAT-uhs KLOWD) A low-lying, grayish cloud layer that covers the whole sky and sometimes produces light rain or drizzle. A stratus cloud that is close to the ground or water is called fog. ◻ See picture at **cloud.**

stream **1.** A body of water that flows. Rivers, brooks, and creeks are streams. **2.** A steady flow of liquid or gas.

streamlined (STRĒM-līnd) Having a rounded or narrow shape that passes easily through water or air. The bodies of most fish are streamlined, and so are airplanes, rockets, and many cars.

strep throat An infection of the throat that is caused by streptococcus bacteria. A person with strep throat has fever and a red, painful throat.

streptococcus (strep-tuh-KOK-uhs) A germ that can cause serious infections in humans, such as strep throat and pneumonia. Streptococci are bacteria. *Plural form:* **streptococci** (strep-tuh-KOK-ī).

stress **1.** A force that changes the shape and size of something by squeezing or stretching it. When you squeeze a rubber ball, the stress causes the ball to change shape. **2.** A response by a living thing to danger or something that is highly unusual or unpleasant. In humans and many other animals, stress causes the heart to beat faster, the blood pressure to rise, and the mind to become more alert. Too much stress can lead to poor health.

striation (strī-Ā-shuhn) One of a number of parallel lines or grooves on the surface of a rock. Striations are formed when a **glacier** moves over a rock or when different rocks scrape against each other in an **earthquake.**

strip mine A mine that is dug in strips at the surface of the Earth, rather than being dug deep underground. Coal mines are often strip mines because the layers of coal are close to the surface, and the coal can be found by removing the dirt above it.

☐ **strip mine**

a large coal mine in central Germany

style The slender part of the pistil of a flower. The style extends from the ovary to the stigma. ☐ See picture at **flower.**

subatomic particle (sub-uh-TOM-ik PAR-ti-kuhl) One of the basic units that make up atoms. Protons, neutrons and electrons are subatomic particles.

subduction zone (suhb-DUHK-shuhn zōn) A place where two of the Earth's plates meet, and one sinks beneath the other. Earthquakes often occur in the plate that does not sink, and volcanoes form on its surface. The western coast of South America is along a subduction zone. ☐ See picture at **plate tectonics.**

sublimation (suhb-li-MĀ-shuhn) The process of changing from a solid to a gas, or from a gas to a solid, without turning into a liquid first. Frost sometimes evaporates by sublimation.

Did You Know?

sublimation
Solid carbon dioxide, known as dry ice, seems to give off smoke at room temperature. This "smoke" is actually the solid carbon dioxide turning directly into a gas in the process known as sublimation. Dry ice is useful for packing certain materials that need to stay cold, since it doesn't melt and get everything wet.

subset (SUHB-set) A set whose members are all contained in another set. The set {3, 4, 5} is a subset of {1, 2, 3, 4, 5, 6, 7, 8}.

subtract (suhb-TRAKT) To perform subtraction on one number by another number.

subtraction (suhb-TRAK-shuhn) The process of taking away one number from another to figure out their difference.

subtrahend (SUHB-truh-hend) A number that is subtracted from another number. In the equation 7 – 2 = 5, 2 is the subtrahend.

subtropical (suhb-TROP-i-kuhl) Relating to the warmest regions of the Temperate Zones that border on the Torrid Zone. The subtropical regions lie just north of the Tropic of Cancer and just south of the Tropic of Capricorn.

succulent (SUHK-yuh-luhnt) A plant that has thick leaves or stems that store water. A cactus is a succulent.

sucker 1. A part in an animal that uses suction to cling to a surface. Octopuses have suckers on their tentacles. Leeches use suckers to draw blood from other animals. 2. A shoot that grows from the bottom or root of a tree or shrub and becomes a new plant.

sucrose (SOO-krōs) A sugar that is found in many plants, especially sugar cane and the sugar maple. Sucrose is purified in factories and sold as sugar for sweetening food.

suction (SUHK-shuhn) A force that causes fluids or solids to flow from one area into another. Suction works by lowering the air pressure in the area into which the fluid or solid flows, so that the higher pressure in the first area pushes the fluid or solid into it. Drinking straws work by suction.

Suess (ZOOS), **Eduard** Born 1831; died 1914. Austrian scientist who proposed the idea that South America, Africa, Antarctica, India, and Australia were once joined together in a landmass called Gondwana-land.

sugar (SHUG-er) 1. A type of carbohydrate that forms crystals that taste sweet and can dissolve in water. Glucose and sucrose are sugars. 2. Sucrose that is purified and used to sweeten food.

sulfur (SUHL-fer) A pale-yellow chemical element that burns easily and can have a strong smell. Sulfur is very common and is found in many minerals, natural gas, and petroleum. It is used to make gunpowder, fireworks, matches, and fertilizer. ◘ See Table on pages 178–179.

sulfuric acid (suhl-FYUR-ik AS-id) A strong acid that contains sulfur, hydrogen, and oxygen. It is used in industry more than any other acid.

sum The result of adding numbers. The sum of 6 and 9 is 15.

summer (SUHM-er) The warmest season of the year, between spring and autumn. In the Northern Hemisphere, it lasts from the summer solstice, in late June, to the autumnal equinox, in late September.

summer solstice The moment of the year when the Sun is farthest north of the equator. This happens on June 20 or 21. In the Northern Hemisphere, the summer solstice marks the beginning of summer and is the day of the year with the longest period of sunlight. ◘ Compare **winter solstice**. ◘ See picture at **season**.

sun 1. The star that is orbited by all of the planets and other objects of the Solar System and that supplies the heat and light that sustain life on Earth. The Sun has a diameter of about 864,000 miles (1,390,000

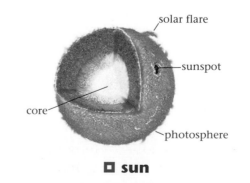

◘ **sun**

kilometers), an average distance from Earth of about 93 million miles (150 million kilometers), and a mass about 330,000 times that of Earth. ◨ The Earth's Sun is often spelled with a capital *S*. **2.** A star that is the center of a system of planets.

sunspots The dark spots that appear in groups on the Sun's surface. Sunspots appear dark because they are somewhat cooler than the rest of the Sun's surface. Sunspots have strong magnetic fields. ◨ See picture at **sun**.

superconductor (soo-per-kuhn-DUHK-ter) A metal, alloy, ceramic, or other material that can conduct an electric current with almost no **resistance**. Most superconductors work only at very low temperatures, such as –459° Fahrenheit (–273° Celsius), but a few alloys work at temperatures around –200° Fahrenheit (–128° Celsius). Scientists hope to find materials that become superconductors closer to room temperature, so they can make electronic devices that use less energy.

supergiant (SOO-per-jī-uhnt) A star that is larger, brighter, and more massive than a **giant star**. Some supergiants are thousands of times brighter than the Sun. ◨ See picture at **star**.

supernova (SOO-per-nō-vuh) A gigantic explosion of a star. Supernovas occur when the inner part of a star collapses because the star has so much mass that its gravity pulls this material into its center. The energy released by the collapse of the star's core causes its outer layers to explode. Supernovas can be 100 million times brighter than the Sun. ◨ See picture at **star**.

supersonic (soo-per-SON-ik) Traveling at a speed greater than the speed of sound (greater than 1,070 feet, or 326 meters, per second). Some aircraft are supersonic.

supplementary angles (suhp-luh-MEN-tuh-rē ANG-guhlz) Two angles whose sum is 180°. ◨ See picture at **angle**.

surface (SER-fuhs) One of the sides of an object that has length, width, and depth. A cube has six flat surfaces. A sphere has one curved surface.

surface tension A property of liquids that makes their surfaces behave as if they were covered by a thin, elastic film. Surface tension is caused by the uneven attraction that molecules at or near the surface of a liquid have for each other.

Did You Know?

surface tension
Surface tension allows small objects to be supported by the surface of a liquid without sinking. Thanks to the surface tension of water, insects can walk across the surface of a pond. Surface tension is also responsible for water droplets, because the tension causes the bits of water to take the shape of a sphere.

suspension (suh-SPEN-shuhn) A mixture in which small particles of a substance are spread out in a gas or liquid. If a suspension is left alone, sooner or later the particles will settle down to the bottom. Muddy water is a suspension.

swamp A low-lying area that is either filled with water most of the time or is flooded at certain seasons. Trees and shrubs are the main plants that grow in a swamp.

sweat A liquid that is produced by glands in the skin of mammals and is made of water and salts. Sweat that evaporates from the skin causes cooling of the body. ☐ Sweat is also called *perspiration*.

swim bladder *See* **air bladder.**

switch A device that allows or shuts off the flow of electricity in a circuit. A switch is made of a movable piece of metal that completes the circuit when it closes, or interrupts the circuit when it opens.

symbiosis (sim-bē-Ō-sis) The relationship between two or more different organisms that live in close association. Symbiosis is often, but not always, to the advantage of both organisms. **Commensalism, mutualism,** and **parasitism** are kinds of symbiosis.

symbol (SIM-buhl) A written sign that stands for something else. H is the symbol for the element hydrogen, and + is the symbol for addition.

symmetry (SIM-uh-trē) An exact matching of parts on opposite sides of a dividing line or around a central point.

symptom (SIM-tuhm) A physical change in the body that is a sign of illness or infection. Symptoms usually affect how a person looks or feels. Fever and headache are common symptoms of illness.

synapse (SIN-aps) The gap between two

☐ **symmetry**

In bilateral symmetry (left), a central line divides the body into two equal parts. In radial symmetry (right), a line drawn anywhere through a central point will show an equal arrangement of parts.

nerve cells. Signals in the form of electric impulses pass from one nerve cell to another across a synapse.

synthesis (SIN-thi-sis) The formation of a chemical compound by combining chemical elements or simpler chemical compounds.

synthetic (sin-THET-ik) Relating to a substance that has been made by scientists in a laboratory. Nylon and polyester are synthetic fabrics. Many car tires are made of synthetic rubber.

system (SIS-tuhm) A group of parts that work together to form something that is more complex. The different masses of warm and cool air in a particular area, along with any wind, clouds, rain, or snow that they produce, make up a weather system. The computer, keyboard, screen, and other parts make up a computer system.

Tt

tactile (TAK-tuhl *or* TAK-tīl) Relating to touch.

tadpole (TAD-pōl) The larva of a frog or toad. A tadpole lives in the water, has a tail and gills, and has no limbs. As the tadpole grows into an adult, legs and lungs develop and the tail and gills disappear.

taiga (TĪ-guh) A forest located in the far northern regions, just south of the tundra. This forest is made up mainly of evergreen trees, such as firs, pines, and spruces, and its wildlife includes wolves, bears, foxes, and elk. The taiga is a kind of **biome.**

Did You Know?

tail

Many animals, like cats and dogs, use their tails for balance while they run. But tails have other uses too. Wolves communicate by the position of their tails. Monkeys sometimes hang from their tails. Birds change their flight direction with their tails. And the large lizards known as Komodo dragons even fight with their tails.

tail 1. A usually slender body part that sticks out from the rear of an animal's body. 2. A long, bright stream of gas or dust that is forced from a comet when it is close to the Sun. A comet's tail always points away from the Sun.

talc A very soft, white or green mineral found in igneous and metamorphic rocks. Talc feels soapy to the touch and is used to make face powder and talcum powder.

talon (TAL-uhn) A sharp, curved claw on the foot of a bird or other animal such as a lizard. Talons are used for seizing and tearing prey.

talus (TĀ-luhs) A sloping pile of small pieces of rock that is at the base of a cliff. A talus is formed by the erosion of the rocks above it.

tapeworm A long, flat worm that lives as a parasite in the intestines of many animals. The body of a tapeworm is made of a chain of small, flat segments and can grow to be several yards long.

tar A thick, oily, dark substance made by heating wood, coal, or peat in the absence of air. Tar is made mostly of **hydrocarbons.**

taste bud A sense organ on the tongue that is sensitive to taste. Taste buds can detect four types of taste: sweet, sour, salty, and bitter.

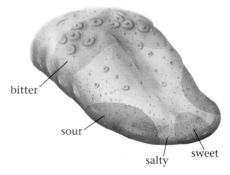

bitter

sour

salty

sweet

□ **taste bud**

A human tongue can detect four different tastes.

taxonomy (tak-SON-uh-mē) The scientific classification of living things into groups. In taxonomy, living things are placed into groups based on their similari-

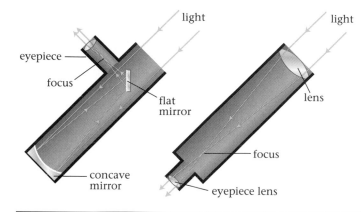

□ telescope

left: *A reflecting telescope uses a concave mirror to focus the light that enters it. A second, smaller mirror directs the focused light to the eyepiece.*
right: *A refracting telescope uses a lens to focus the light. The focused light passes straight through the telescope to the eyepiece.*

ties and how they are related to each other.
□ See Table on page 47.

tear (TEER) A drop of clear, salty liquid that is produced by glands in the eye. Tears keep the eyes moist and help get rid of substances that can irritate the eye.

teat The part near the center of the mammary gland, from which milk can be drawn to the surface.

technology (tek-NOL-uh-jē) The use of scientific knowledge to make new and better products and to find new and better ways of making things. Technology affects almost all aspects of our lives, from computers to cars to laundry detergents.

telecommunications (tel-i-kuh-myōō-ni-KĀ-shuhnz) The science and business of sending messages as electric impulses, pulses of light, or electromagnetic waves. Through advances in telecommunications, people are able to make telephone calls, send data between computers, and send and receive radio and television signals.

telegraph (TEL-uh-graf) A system for sending messages in the form of electric impulses, either by wire or radio, to a receiving station. The telegraph has been mostly replaced by the telephone and by computer networks.

telephone (TEL-uh-fōn) A device that sends and receives sound, especially speech, over a distance. Telephones change the sound waves of human speech into electric signals and then change those signals back into sound waves on the receiving end. The signals are sent by wires or radio waves.

telescope (TEL-uh-skōp) An instrument that is used to observe or study distant

Did You Know?

telescope

Many telescopes do not gather visible light, but instead record energy that we cannot see, such as infrared waves, ultraviolet light, or gamma rays. These other kinds of electromagnetic radiation are usually blocked by the Earth's atmosphere, so telescopes must be placed in orbit around the Earth to be of any use. Computers can form visible images from the data that these telescopes collect.

objects by gathering the electromagnetic radiation that comes from them. Most telescopes gather and focus visible light by using lenses or mirrors. Other kinds of telescopes may gather radiation that is not visible, such as radio waves, infrared waves, or x-rays.

television　(TEL-uh-vizh-uhn) **1.** A system that sends and receives pictures of objects and actions and the sounds that go with them. Television sends the pictures and sounds through the air as radio waves or through special cables as electric signals. **2.** The device that receives these radio waves or electric signals and changes them back into pictures and sound.

temper　(TEM-per) To make glass or metal harder by heating it and then cooling it.

temperate　(TEM-per-it) Having a climate that does not get extremely hot or extremely cold, as in the Temperate Zone.

Temperate Zone　Either of two regions of the Earth, the **North Temperate Zone** and the **South Temperate Zone,** that lie in the middle latitudes. The Temperate Zones have four distinct seasons: spring, summer, autumn, and winter.

temperature　(TEM-per-uh-chur) **1.** A measure of the hotness or coldness of a substance. Temperature is measured in units of a standard scale, such as the Celsius and Fahrenheit scales. Unlike heat, temperature does not depend on how much of the substance there is, but on how fast the molecules of a substance are moving. **2.** A body temperature that is higher than normal; a fever.

tendon　(TEN-duhn) A tough band of body tissue that connects a muscle to a bone.

tendril　(TEN-druhl) A slender, coiling plant part that helps support the stem of a climbing plant by clinging to or winding around an object, such as a stake or fence. Peas, squash, and grapes have tendrils. A tendril is usually a kind of leaf that has evolved to take a special shape.

tensile strength　(TEN-suhl STRENGKTH) The ability of a material to resist a force that tends to pull it apart. A steel wire has much greater tensile strength than a piece of sewing thread.

tension　(TEN-shuhn) A force that tends to stretch or pull something. When there is tension on a rope, the rope is pulled tight so that there is no slack.

tentacle　(TEN-tuh-kuhl) A narrow, flexible body part that sticks out from the bodies of some animals. Tentacles are used for feeling, grasping, or moving. The octopus, jellyfish, and sea anemone all have tentacles around their mouths.

terabyte　(TAIR-uh-bīt) A unit of information that can be stored in a computer memory and is equal to 1,024 gigabytes or more

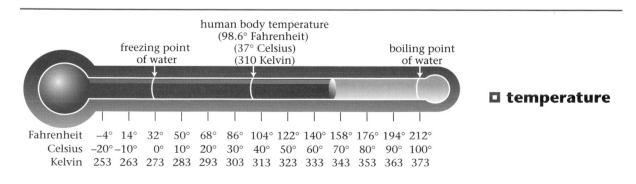

human body temperature
(98.6° Fahrenheit)
(37° Celsius)
(310 Kelvin)

freezing point
of water

boiling point
of water

◻ **temperature**

Fahrenheit	−4°	14°	32°	50°	68°	86°	104°	122°	140°	158°	176°	194°	212°
Celsius	−20°	−10°	0°	10°	20°	30°	40°	50°	60°	70°	80°	90°	100°
Kelvin	253	263	273	283	293	303	313	323	333	343	353	363	373

than a trillion bytes. A terabyte is equal to 2 multiplied by 2 forty times.

terminal   (TER-muh-nuhl) The negatively or positively charged pole of an electric device, such as a battery.

termite   (TER-mīt) A type of insect that is pale-colored, lives in large colonies, and feeds on wood. Termites look like ants but belong to a different group of insects.

terrarium   (tuh-RAIR-ē-uhm) A glass bowl or box that is filled with a layer of soil and rocks. It is used for growing plants or keeping small animals.

terrestrial   (tuh-RES-trē-uhl) **1.** Relating to the planet Earth or to the organisms that live on it. **2.** Relating to or living on land.

territory   (TAIR-uh-tor-ē) An area of land that is occupied by an animal or a group of animals. Many animals defend their territory against intruders. Some animals mark off territory by leaving traces of their scent along the boundaries or by making certain calls or sounds when an intruder approaches.

Tertiary Period   (TER-shē-air-ē PEER-ē-uhd) The period of time during the history of the Earth starting about 65 million years ago and ending about 2 million years ago. Most of the animals and plants we know today first appeared during the Tertiary Period. ◻ See Table on pages 102–103.

Tesla   (TES-luh), **Nikola** Born 1856; died 1943. Serbian-born American scientist who invented alternating current and developed the first motors and generators that used it. Tesla also invented fluorescent lighting and made important contributions to the development of radio.

testes   (TES-tēz) The organs of reproduction in male humans and other vertebrates. Sperm and sex hormones are produced in

Biography

Nikola Tesla

Nikola Tesla's system of alternating current is used today to bring electricity to homes and buildings all over the world. Tesla also invented a metal coil that made it possible to transmit electric energy through the air and led to the invention of radio. He imagined a global system of wireless communication, which was far beyond human knowledge at the time, but which has since become a reality.

the testes. In most animals, the testes are inside the body, but in mammals, the testes lie outside the body and are contained within the scrotum. *Singular form*: **testis** (TES-tis).

testicle   (TES-ti-kuhl) Either of the two testes of a male mammal.

testosterone   (tes-TOS-tuh-rōn) A hormone that controls the growth and development of the reproductive system in male vertebrates.

test tube   A glass tube that is open at one end and rounded and closed at the other. Test tubes are used to hold small amounts of a substance during experiments in a laboratory.

tetanus   (TET-uhn-uhs) A serious disease that is caused by bacteria that usually enter the body through a wound. Tetanus leads to painful tightening of the muscles, especially of the jaw, and can be fatal.

tetrahedron   (tet-ruh-HĒ-druhn) A three-dimensional object that has four faces, each one a triangle.

thaw   To change from a frozen solid to a liquid by gradual warming.

theorem (THĒ-er-uhm *or* THEER-uhm) A mathematical statement that can be proved to be true by reasoning from a set of assumptions or **axioms.**

theory (THĒ-uh-rē *or* THEER-ē) A set of statements that explain how something works in the natural world. Most theories that are accepted by scientists have been tested by experiments and can be used to make predictions about what will happen under a given set of conditions. Many theories, such as the theory that germs cause disease, are so widely accepted that they are no longer referred to as theories.

thermal (THER-muhl) **1.** Relating to heat. Thermal energy is the energy produced by heat. Thermal underwear keeps your body heat from escaping to the air outside. **2.** A current of air that rises because it is warmer than the air around it. Thermals are created when the Sun heats one part of the ground, such as a flat valley, more than it heats the surrounding parts, such as a steep mountainside.

thermal vent An opening in the Earth's surface that gives off hot water and dissolved minerals. Thermal vents are usually on the ocean floor.

thermocouple (THER-muh-kuhp-uhl) A device that is used to measure the temperature of very hot substances by converting heat into electricity. A thermocouple is made of an electric circuit that has two wires of different metals. When one of the metals is dipped into something hot, such as lava, an electric current starts to flow through the circuit. The strength of the current can be used to determine the temperature.

thermodynamics (ther-mō-dī-NAM-iks) The scientific study of the relationships between **heat** and other forms of **energy.**

The three laws of thermodynamics state that energy cannot be created or destroyed, that heat always flows from hotter areas to cooler areas, and that nothing can ever be cooled to **absolute zero.**

thermometer (ther-MOM-i-ter) An instrument that is used to measure temperature. One kind of thermometer is made of a sealed glass tube that has marks on its side to show the temperature and a liquid on the inside that expands or contracts as the temperature goes up or down. Electronic thermometers work by sensing changes in the resistance of a material to the flow of electricity at different temperatures.

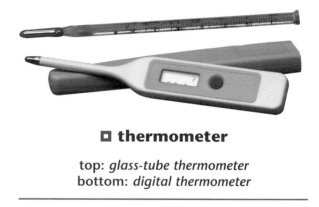

◻ **thermometer**

top: *glass-tube thermometer*
bottom: *digital thermometer*

thermonuclear reaction (ther-mō-NOO-klē-er rē-AK-shuhn) A reaction in which the nuclei of different atoms are joined together through the process of **fusion.** Thermonuclear reactions occur naturally in the Sun and in other stars, where there is enough heat to make the nuclei crash into each other.

thermosphere (THER-muh-sfeer) The outermost layer of the Earth's atmosphere, lying above the mesosphere and reaching hundreds of miles into outer space. Auroras take place in the lower part of the thermosphere, and satellites orbit the Earth in the upper part.

thermostat (THER-muh-stat) A device that controls equipment for heating or cooling in a way that keeps an area at the same temperature. Thermostats are used in buildings, ovens, and refrigerators.

Thompson (TOMP-suhn *or* TOM-suhn), **Benjamin.** Also known as **Count Rumford** Born 1753; died 1814. American-born British scientist who proved that heat was not a substance, as was commonly believed at the time, but was produced by the movement of particles. He used his research to make improvements in lighting, cooking, and heating.

Thomson (TOM-suhn), **Joseph John** Born 1856; died 1940. British scientist who is one of the founders of modern physics. He studied the conduction of electricity in gases, and in 1897 discovered the electron.

thorax (THOR-aks) **1.** The part of the trunk of the body between the neck and abdomen. The thorax contains the rib cage, which encloses the heart and lungs. **2.** The middle part of the body of an insect, to which the wings and legs are attached. The thorax lies between the head and the abdomen. ◻ See picture at **insect.**

thorn A short, hard, pointed part on a stem or branch of a woody plant.

throat The passageway that leads from the nose and mouth to the windpipe (trachea) and esophagus. The throat contains the **larynx** and the **pharynx.**

thrust The force that causes an object to move forward. The thrust of a jet engine or rocket comes from the hot gases that go rushing out from the back end. The thrust of a propeller comes from the spinning of the propeller blades that pushes air or water behind the plane or boat.

thunder (THUN-der) The explosive noise that follows a bolt of lightning. The lightning heats the surrounding air and makes it expand very rapidly. This creates sound waves that travel outward from the lightning and that we hear as thunder.

thunderstorm (THUN-der-storm) A storm that has lightning and thunder along with heavy rains and strong winds. Thunderstorms sometimes produce **hail.**

thymus (THĪ-muhs) A gland in humans and other vertebrates that helps the body fight disease by producing white blood cells called **lymphocytes.** The thymus stops growing in early childhood and gets smaller with age.

thyroid gland (THĪ-royd gland) A gland in humans and other vertebrates that produces hormones that are important for the body's growth and metabolism. The thyroid gland is at the base of the neck.

tibia (TIB-ē-uh) The larger of the two bones of the lower leg. ◻ See picture at **skeleton.**

tick A tiny animal that attaches itself to the skin of mammals and feeds by sucking their blood. Ticks often carry microorganisms that cause disease. Ticks, like mites and spiders, are members of the group of animals known as **arachnids.**

tidal pool (TĪ-duhl pool) An area of water that remains after a tide has retreated. Many sea animals, such as starfish, crabs, and barnacles, live in tidal pools. ◻ A tidal pool is also called a *tide pool.*

tidal wave **1.** The bulge of ocean water that travels around the Earth as a result of the pull of gravity from the Moon and the Sun. When the tidal wave reaches a shore, it causes a **high tide. 2.** *See* **tsunami.**

tide The regular rise and fall in the surface level of the Earth's oceans. Tides are caused by the force of gravity of the Moon and the Sun pulling on the Earth's water.

◻ tide

top: *high tide*
bottom: *low tide*

High tide and **low tide** occur twice each day, with just over six hours in between.

tide pool   *See* **tidal pool.**

timberline   (TIM-ber-līn) A limit that trees do not grow beyond. On mountains, a timberline is the highest elevation at which trees can grow. A timberline can also be the most northern or most southern latitude at which trees can grow. ◻ A timberline is also called a *tree line.*

time   The past, the present, and the future. Time is a quantity that can be measured by counting the number of occurrences of a regular event, like a complete rotation of the Earth on its axis (a day) or a complete revolution of the Earth around the Sun (a year).

time zone   A region in which the same time is used. The Earth has 24 time zones, and local time moves ahead one hour as you travel east from one time zone to another. So when it is noon in Los Angeles, it is 1:00 P.M. in Denver, 2:00 P.M. in Chicago, and 3:00 P.M. in New York City.

tin   A silvery chemical element that is an easily shaped metal. Tin is used to coat other metals, such as steel, to prevent rust. Once used to make cans, it has been replaced by aluminum. ◻ See Table on pages 178–179.

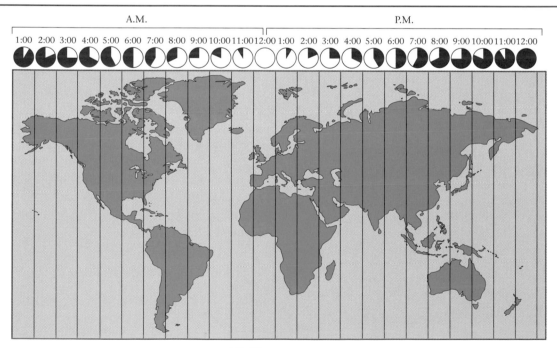

◻ time zone

tissue (TISH-ōō) A large group of cells that together form a particular part of a living thing. Skin, bone, muscle, and nerves are kinds of tissues in animals. Cambium, xylem, and phloem are tissues in plants.

titanium (tī-TĀ-nē-uhm) A shiny, white chemical element that is a lightweight, strong metal. Titanium can withstand high temperatures and does not rust easily. It is combined with other elements to make parts for aircraft and ships. ◻ See Table on pages 178–179.

TNT Short for **trinitrotoluene**. A yellow chemical compound that is used as an explosive.

toad A kind of amphibian that is related to the frog but has a broader body, shorter legs, and rougher skin. Adult toads usually live on land rather than in the water.

ton 1. A unit of weight equal to 2,000 pounds. ◻ This kind of ton is also called a *short ton*. 2. A unit of weight equal to 2,240 pounds. ◻ This kind of ton is also called a *long ton*. 3. *See* **metric ton**. ◻ See Table on page 148.

Did You Know?

tongue

For mammals, the tongue is the organ of taste that helps in the chewing and swallowing of food, but for many animals, it is something entirely different. Snakes flick their tongues to sense what is around them. Frogs, toads, and lizards use their tongues as sticky weapons to stun and capture prey. Humans use their tongues to make the different sounds we call syllables and words.

tongue A muscle in humans and other vertebrates that is usually attached to the bottom of the mouth. In humans, the tongue is important for digestion and speech.

tonsils (TON-suhlz) The two small, oval parts that are found at the back of the throat. The tonsils often become infected by viruses or bacteria.

tooth 1. One of a set of hard, bony parts in the mouth that are used to chew and bite. In mammals, the teeth grow in sockets in the jaw. In many fish and amphibians, the teeth grow all over the roof of the mouth. 2. One of the bumps on the rim of a gear. *Plural form*: **teeth**.

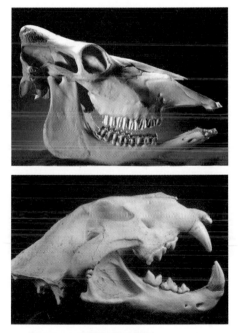

◻ **tooth**

top: *skull of a cow showing flat back teeth used to grind and chew plants*
bottom: *skull of a lion showing sharp teeth used to kill prey and to tear the meat into smaller pieces for swallowing*

topography (tuh-POG-ruh-fē) The physical features of the Earth's surface in a place or region. The topography of an area includes natural features, such as moun-

▫ topography

mountains, sloping hills, and level ground

tains and rivers, and features such as roads and railroads.

topsoil The upper part of the soil. Topsoil is usually dark brown in color and contains **humus.**

tornado (tor-NĀ-dō) A whirling, funnel-shaped cloud that sometimes develops during a violent thunderstorm.

torque (TORK) The force that causes an object to turn about an axis. Torque causes the axles of a car to turn, making the wheels spin.

Torricelli (tō-ruh-CHEL-ē), **Evangelista** Born 1608; died 1647. Italian scientist who discovered that atmospheric pressure exists and in 1643 invented the first barometer to prove it. He also built a simple microscope and improved the telescope to make observations clearer and more accurate.

Torrid Zone (TOR-id zōn) The region of the Earth that lies between the Tropic of Cancer and the Tropic of Capricorn. This area of central latitude has hot and humid weather all year. ▫ See picture at **zone.**

torsion (TOR-shuhn) The twisting force that turns or tries to turn the two ends of an object in opposite directions.

Did You Know?

tornado

Each tornado's funnel of whirling air is different in size and strength. Some tornadoes appear in the air for a few seconds and then are gone; others can cause enormous damage when they move over the ground. The funnels can measure just a few yards or meters across to more than a mile (1.61 kilometers), and the wind in funnels can spin as fast as 300 miles (483 kilometers) per hour.

tortoise (TOR-tis) A turtle that lives on land.

▫ tortoise

a plowshare tortoise from the island of Madagascar

toxic (TOK-sik) Poisonous.

toxin (TOK-sin) **1.** A poison that is made

by a living thing. Toxins in snake or spider venom are used to kill prey. Toxins produced by bacteria can cause disease. **2.** A substance that is harmful or poisonous to living things. Toxins from car exhaust cause air pollution.

trachea (TRĀ-kē-uh) A tube with tough bands of cartilage that goes from the throat to the lungs. The trachea carries air to the lungs. ◻ The trachea is also called the *windpipe.* ◻ See picture at **respiratory system.**

trade winds Winds that blow steadily from east to west over most of the **Torrid Zone.** During the days of sailing ships, the trade winds provided steady power for ships traveling westward in tropical waters.

trait Something in the appearance, activity, or behavior of a living thing that is determined by the **genes.** The color of an animal's coat and the shape of a plant's leaves are physical traits. Nest-building in birds is a behavior trait.

trajectory (truh-JEK-tuh-rē) The path of an object, such as an arrow or a rocket, that is moving above the Earth's surface. Trajectories are usually curved because gravity pulls the object down.

transducer (trans-DŌŌ-ser) A device that changes one type of energy into another. The transducer in a microphone changes sound waves into electric impulses. The transducer in a loudspeaker changes electric impulses into sound waves.

transformer (trans-FOR-mer) A device that is used to increase or decrease the **voltage** of an electric current. Transformers are made of a frame of iron that has a wire wound around each end. When a current enters the transformer through one of the wires, the magnetic field it produces causes a current to flow in the other wire. The volt-

age in the other wire changes according to the number of times each wire is wound around the frame.

transfusion (trans-FYŌŌ-zhuhn) The transfer of blood from one person to another.

transistor (tran-ZIS-ter) An electronic device that controls the flow of an electric current and is used as an **amplifier** or **switch.** Transistors are made of three layers of semiconductor material that are connected to an electric circuit. Transistors work like gates, allowing or closing off the flow of electrons.

transition element (tran-ZISH-uhn EL-uh-muhnt) One of the chemical elements in the middle of the Periodic Table. The transition elements are metals that combine easily with other elements to form **alloys.** Iron, copper, zinc, and silver are transition elements. ◻ See Table on pages 178–179.

translucent (trans-LŌŌ-suhnt) Letting some but not all light through so that objects appear blurry. Frosted glass is translucent.

transmission (trans-MISH-uhn) **1.** The sending of signals in the form of waves or impulses, as in radio. **2.** The part of a car or other vehicle that sends power from the engine to the wheels.

transmitter (TRANS-mit-er) A device that sends information in a communications system. A transmitter creates radio waves, changes their amplitude or frequency to make different signals, and sends these signals out from an antenna. Radio and television signals are broadcast by transmitters.

transparent (trans-PAIR-uhnt) Allowing light to pass through so that objects on the other side can be seen clearly. The glass in windows is usually transparent.

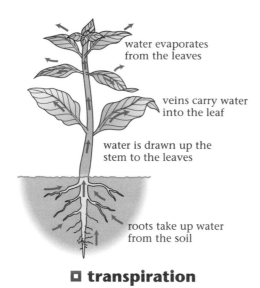

water evaporates from the leaves

veins carry water into the leaf

water is drawn up the stem to the leaves

roots take up water from the soil

◻ transpiration

Water vapor carrying oxygen evaporates from leaves. This makes it easier for water to be drawn into the plant at the roots.

transpiration (tran-spuh-RĀ-shuhn) The release of water vapor into the air by green plants, usually through small pores called stomata on the underside of leaves. Transpiration allows the plant to get rid of the oxygen it produces as a waste product of **photosynthesis.** Transpiration also draws up water that contains nutrients from the roots to the stems and leaves.

transplant (trans-PLANT) **1.** To transfer an organ or other tissue of the body from one person or body part to another. **2.** To move a growing plant from soil in one place to soil in another place.

trapezoid (TRAP-uh-zoyd) A four-sided figure that has two sides that are parallel to each other. **◻** See pictures at **geometry, quadrilateral.**

tree A woody plant that has a single stem, produces seeds, and has branches and leaves. Trees are usually tall. Most trees are either **flowering plants,** such as maples and oaks, or **conifers,** such as pines and firs.

tree line *See* **timberline.**

tremor (TREM-er) A shaking or vibrating movement, as from a small earthquake.

trench A long steep-sided valley on the ocean floor. **◻** See picture at **plate tectonics.**

triangle (TRI-ang-guhl) A flat figure that has three sides. There are three main types of triangles: **equilateral triangles, isosceles triangles,** and **scalene triangles.**

Triassic Period (trī-AS-ik PEER-ē-uhd) The period of time during the history of the Earth starting about 245 million years ago and ending about 208 million years ago.

◻ tree

left to right: *balsam fir, coconut palm, Coulter pine, and red oak. Firs, palms, and pines are evergreen trees. The oak is a deciduous tree. The cones of the fir and pine contain the organs of reproduction. The coconut of the palm and the acorn of the oak contain the trees' seeds.*

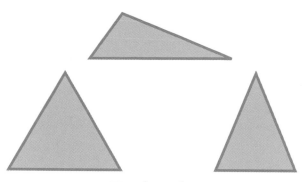

□ triangle

top: *scalene triangle*
bottom: *equilateral triangle* (left) *and isosceles triangle* (right)

□ trilobite

fossil from the Cambrian Period

During the Triassic Period, the number of species that lived on land increased, and dinosaurs and mammals first appeared. □ See Table on pages 102–103.

tributary   (TRIB-yuh-tair-ē) A stream that flows into a river or larger stream.

triceps   (TRĪ-seps) The muscle at the back of the upper arm that straightens the elbow.

triceratops   (trī-SAIR-uh-tops) A large, plant-eating dinosaur that measured up to 25 feet (7.6 meters) long. The triceratops had a long horn over each eye and a short horn over its mouth, which was shaped like a beak. A wide, bony plate covered the back of its neck for protection.

trilobite   (TRĪ-luh-bīt) A type of extinct animal that lived in the ocean during most of the Paleozoic Era. Most trilobites were small and had a hard outer covering that was divided into several sections. Trilobites belonged to the group of invertebrates called **arthropods.** Their closest living relatives are horseshoe crabs.

tropic   (TROP-ik) Either of the two lines of latitude that represent the points farthest north and south at which the Sun can shine directly overhead. The northern tropic is the **Tropic of Cancer,** and the southern one is the **Tropic of Capricorn.** The hot and humid region that lies between these two lines of latitude is the **Torrid Zone.**

tropical   (TROP-i-kuhl) Relating to the hot and humid regions of the Earth that are in the **Torrid Zone.**

Tropic of Cancer   The line of latitude that forms the boundary between the Torrid Zone and the North Temperate Zone. The Tropic of Cancer lies north of the equator and has a latitude of 23 degrees, 27 minutes. □ See picture at **equator.**

Tropic of Capricorn   The line of latitude that forms the boundary between the Torrid Zone and the South Temperate Zone. The Tropic of Capricorn lies south of the equator and has a latitude of 23 degrees, 27 minutes. □ See picture at **equator.**

tropism   (TRŌ-piz-uhm) Growth or turning of a plant or animal toward or away from a source of light or heat.

troposphere   (TRŌ-puh-sfeer *or* TROP-uh-sfeer) The lowest region of the atmosphere, lying between the Earth's surface and the stratosphere. Most of what we can see in the daytime sky, including birds, clouds, and airplanes, is found in the troposphere.

trough   (TRAWF) The lowest part of a wave. □ See picture at **wave.**

true north The direction from any point on the Earth toward the North Pole. ☐ True north is also called *geographic north.* ☐ Compare **magnetic north.**

trunk **1.** The main stem of a tree. Trunks are often tall and thick. **2.** The main part of the body of a human or other vertebrate, apart from the arms, legs, and head. **3.** The long, flexible snout of an elephant or related animal, such as a mammoth.

Did You Know?

trunk

An elephant's trunk is a combination of the upper lip and the nose. There is not one bone in the trunk, but there are an estimated 40,000 muscles! That's a lot of muscles, especially compared to the roughly 600 muscles of the human body. Muscles at the end of an elephant's trunk serve as fingers that allow them to pick up small objects like peanuts.

tsunami (tsoo-NAH-me) A very large ocean wave that is caused by an underwater earthquake or volcanic eruption. A tsunami often causes great destruction when it strikes land.

tuber (TOO-ber) The thick part of an underground stem of a plant, such as the potato. Tubers have buds from which new plant shoots grow.

tuberculosis (tu-ber-kyuh-LO-sis) A disease that damages the organs of the body, especially the lungs. Tuberculosis is caused by bacteria and is very contagious.

tumor (TOO-mer) An abnormal growth in the body that is caused by cells that multiply without stopping. Tumors are found in different kinds of **cancers.**

tundra (TUN-druh) A cold, treeless area of the Arctic region. It lies between the taiga and the polar cap, and it is frozen for much of the year. A tundra is a kind of **biome.**

tuner (TOO-ner) A device that allows a person to select radio signals at a particular **frequency.** On a radio, a tuner lets a person select a particular radio station.

tungsten (TUHNG-stuhn) A grayish-white chemical element that is a hard metal. Tungsten does not rust easily and has the highest melting point of all the elements. It is used to strengthen steel and to

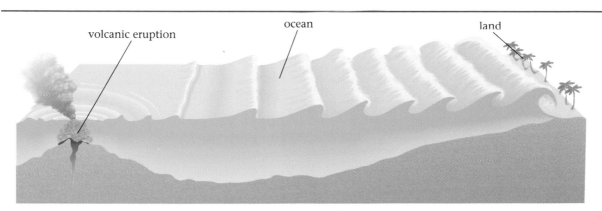

☐ **tsunami**

Waves created by an underwater earthquake or volcanic eruption lose speed as they reach shallower water, but they gain height and get closer together.

make the wires that glow in light bulbs. ◘ Tungsten is also called *wolfram*. ◘ See Table on pages 178–179.

turbine (TER-bin *or* TER-bīn) A machine that uses the energy of a moving fluid, such as water, steam, or gas, to make something turn in a circular motion. Windmills and jet engines are types of turbines. ◘ See pictures at **jet engine, nuclear reactor.**

turbojet engine (TER-bō-jet EN-jin) A type of jet engine that creates more power by directing the gases from burned fuel over the blades of a **turbine.** The spinning turbine drives a fan-like device that forces more air into the engine.

Turing (TUR-ing), **Alan Mathison** Born 1912; died 1954. British mathematician who developed an idea for a machine that solved complex problems by imitating the way the human mind works. Turing's idea became the basis for the modern electronic computer.

turpentine (TER-puhn-tīn) A light oil that is made from certain pine trees and is used as a paint thinner.

turtle (TER-tuhl) A type of reptile that has a hard shell over most of its body. A turtle's head, legs, and tail can be pulled into the shell for protection. Turtles live both in water and on land.

tusk A long, pointed tooth that sticks out of the mouth of some animals, such as elephants, walruses, and wild pigs. Tusks usually grow in pairs.

twin One of two children that are born to the same mother at the same time. Twins that develop from the same fertilized egg look alike, always belong to the same sex, and are said to be *identical*. Twins that develop from two different eggs can belong to different sexes, do not always look alike, and are called *fraternal*.

typhoon (tī-FOON) A hurricane that occurs in the western Pacific Ocean.

typhus (TĪ-fuhs) A serious disease that causes a high fever and a rash on the skin. Lice, fleas, and mites carry typhus from one person to another.

Tyrannosaurus rex (ti-ran-uh-SOR-uhs REKS) A very large, meat-eating dinosaur that grew to 47 feet (14.3 meters) long or longer. Tyrannosaurus rex walked on two legs and had very small front limbs and a large head with sharp teeth.

Uu

udder (UHD-er) A bag-shaped part of a cow and some other female mammals, in which milk is made and stored.

UFO Short for **unidentified flying object.** An object or light that is seen in the sky but cannot be identified on sight. UFOs usually turn out to be planets, bright stars, meteors, satellites, or some other common object.

ulcer (UHL-ser) A sore or wound on the surface of a body part. Ulcers are often caused by infection. They can be painful because of **inflammation.**

ulna (UHL-nuh) The longer of the two bones of the forearm. ◻ See picture at **skeleton.**

ultrasound (UL-truh-sownd) Sound that has a wave frequency that is too high (over 20,000 hertz) to be heard by humans. The vibrations in ultrasound waves can be used to clean machine parts. Devices that use ultrasound can make images of things inside the body, such as the organs or a developing fetus.

ultraviolet light (ul-truh-VĪ-uh-let LĪT) Electromagnetic radiation that has wavelengths shorter than those of visible light but longer than those of x-rays. Ultraviolet light is given off by the Sun but is invisible. Too much ultraviolet light can cause sunburn and skin diseases. Ultraviolet light is used in hospitals to sterilize medical equipment.

umbilical cord (um-BIL-i-kuhl kord) The long cord that connects the placenta in the mother's womb to the developing young. The umbilical cord carries oxygen and nutrients to the young and removes its wastes. The belly button is the place where the umbilical cord once grew.

umbra (UHM-bruh) The darkest part of a shadow. The dark, central part of the shadow that is cast by the Moon onto the Earth during a solar eclipse is the umbra. ◻ Compare **penumbra.** ◻ See picture at **eclipse.**

understory (UHN-der-stor-ē) Shrubs, plants, and young trees that grow beneath the canopy of a forest.

undertow (UHN-der-tō) An underwater current that flows away from shore. After a wave breaks on the shore, the undertow returns the water to the sea.

ungulate (UHNG-gyuh-lit) A mammal with hooves at the ends of its toes. Some ungulates, such as pigs, deer, sheep, and giraffes, have an even number of toes on each foot. Horses and rhinoceroses are ungulates with an odd number of toes on each foot.

◻ **ungulate**

the foot of a hippopotamus **(left)** *and a giraffe* **(right)**

unicellular (yōo-ni-SEL-yuh-ler) Made of a single cell; one-celled. Bacteria and protozoans are unicellular organisms. ◻ Compare **multicellular.**

unidentified flying object (uhn-ī-DEN-ti-fīd FLĪ-ing OB-jekt) *See* **UFO.**

union (YOO-yuhn) A set whose members belong to at least one of a group of two or more given sets. The union of the sets {1,2,3} and {3,4,5} is the set {1,2,3,4,5}, and the union of the sets {6,7} and {11,12,13} is the set {6,7,11,12,13}.

United States Customary System A system of measuring in which the yard, the pound, and the gallon are the basic units. The United States Customary System is used in the United States and a few other countries. ◻ See Table on page 148.

univalve (YOO-ni-valv) A mollusk with a single shell that is usually twisted into the shape of a coil. Snails and conchs are univalves. Univalves belong to the group of mollusks called **gastropods.** ◻ Compare **bivalve.**

universal time (YOO-nuh-ver-suhl TIM) The time of day as measured at the prime meridian, which is 0° longitude. Universal time is used as a basis to calculate time throughout most of the world. ◻ Universal time is also called *Greenwich Time,* because the prime meridian runs through the town of Greenwich, England.

universe (YOO-nuh-vers) Everything that exists, including the Earth, the Solar System, and all the stars and galaxies. Scientists believe that the universe is between 12 and 18 billion years old and that it began with the explosion called the **big bang.**

unsaturated fat (un-SACH-uh-rā-tid FAT) A fat that is found in oils that are made from plants and in some fish. Eating foods with high levels of unsaturated fats can help protect against heart disease. ◻ Compare **saturated fat.**

unstable (uhn-STA-buhl) **1.** Relating to an atom that is **radioactive** and that will change on its own into a smaller atom. All uranium atoms are unstable. **2.** Relating to a chemical compound that easily breaks down or changes into other compounds or into chemical elements.

uranium (yu-RA-nē-uhm) A chemical element that is a silvery white, radioactive metal. Uranium is heavy and very poisonous. It is used as a fuel for nuclear reactors and nuclear weapons. ◻ See Table on pages 178–179.

Uranus (YUR-uh-nuhs *or* yu-RA-nuhs) The planet that is seventh in distance from the Sun. Uranus is the third largest planet in the Solar System. It is made up mostly of gas and is surrounded by a group of thin, dark rings made mostly of carbon. ◻ See Table on pages 184–185.

urea (yu-RE-uh) A chemical compound that is the main waste product in the urine of mammals and some fish. Urea is produced in the liver and is rich in **nitrogen.** Urea can also be made in the laboratory for use in fertilizers and medicines.

ureter (yu-RE-ter) Either of the two long, narrow tubes that carry urine from the kidney to the bladder. ◻ See picture at **kidney.**

Did You Know?

universe
Many scientists believe that the universe is expanding. In the 1920s, astronomers observed that distant galaxies were moving away from the Earth. By calculating the speed of these galaxies, and the distance from the Earth, scientists were able to estimate when the big bang occurred.

urethra   (yu-RĒ-thruh) The tube through which urine passes from the bladder to the outside of the body. In most male mammals, the urethra also carries sperm during **reproduction.**

urinary system   (YUR-uh-nair-ē SIS-tuhm) The group of organs in the body that produce, store, and release urine. The urinary system helps control the amount of fluid in the body. The kidneys, ureters, and bladder are the main parts of this system.

urine   (YUR-in) A clear or yellow fluid that is made in the kidneys and stored in the bladder before leaving the body as waste. The kidneys make urine by filtering waste products from the blood.

uterus   (YŌO-ter-uhs) The sac-shaped part of the body in most female mammals in which the young develop before being born. The walls of the uterus are made of muscle, which contracts to push the young out of the body during birth. ◘ The uterus is also called the *womb*.

UV index   A scale that is used to tell the risk for sunburn at midday, when the Sun's **ultraviolet light** is the strongest. The UV index ranges from 0 to 10, with 10 being the greatest risk.

Vv

vaccination (vak-si-NĀ-shuhn) **1.** The placement of a vaccine into the body, either by injection or by swallowing. Vaccination gives a person **immunity** to a particular disease, such as smallpox, measles, or mumps. **2.** A vaccine for a particular disease. ◻ Vaccination is also called *inoculation*.

vaccine (vak-SĒN) A substance that prevents a person from getting a disease that is caused by a particular virus or other germ. Vaccines work by strengthening a person's **immunity**. Most vaccines are given by injection or are swallowed as liquids.

Did You Know?

vaccine

Scientists often make vaccines by taking some of the germs that cause a disease and weakening them with heat or chemical compounds. The germs lose their ability to make us sick, but they still provoke the body to make antibodies that can fight off full-strength germs. Today, scientists can also change the DNA of viruses and bacteria by removing the most harmful parts and then using what is left in vaccines.

vacuole (VAK-yoo-ōl) A tiny part of a cell that is surrounded by a membrane and filled with a watery fluid. Vacuoles help cells store food and get rid of waste products. Plant cells often have larger vacuoles than animal cells. ◻ See picture at **cell.**

vacuum (VAK-yoom) A space in which there is no matter or almost no matter.

vagina (vuh-JĪ-nuh) The part in female mammals that goes from the bottom of the uterus to the outside of the body. Young pass through the vagina during birth.

valence (VĀ-luhns) A number that tells how many electrons an atom or group of atoms can lose, add, or share when it combines with other atoms. A carbon atom can share four electrons with other atoms, and so its valence is 4.

valley (VAL-e) **1.** A long, narrow area of low land between mountains or hills, often with a river or stream that runs along the bottom. Most valleys are made by rivers or glaciers that gradually wear away the land. **2.** A large area of land that is drained by a river and the streams that empty into it.

value (VAL-yoo) A number that is used in place of a symbol or as an answer to an equation in mathematics. For example, in the equation $4 + 3 = x$, the value of x is 7.

valve **1.** A device that controls the flow of liquids, gases, or loose material through a pipe or channel by narrowing or widening an opening. **2.** A structure that keeps a fluid in the body from flowing backward. The body has valves in the veins and between the chambers of the heart. **3.** One of the two shells of a clam, oyster, or similar mollusk. The valves are connected by a hinge for opening and shutting.

Van Allen belt (van AL-uhn belt) Either of two zones of powerful radiation that surround the Earth, one inside the other. In the Van Allen belts, a large number of charged atomic particles move at high speeds but are trapped by the Earth's magnetic field.

Van de Graaff (VAN duh graf), **Robert Jemison** Born 1901; died 1967. American scientist who invented the Van de Graaff generator in 1929.

Van de Graaff generator A device that is used to build up an electric charge by moving positively charged particles from a power supply, up along a moving rubber belt, to a metal sphere. When the sphere has collected enough charge, it can make the hair of a person touching the sphere stand up on end. The Van de Graaff generator is named after Robert Van de Graaff.

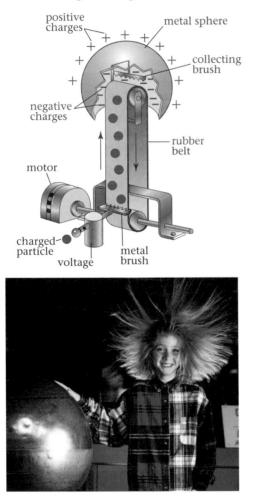

▫ Van de Graaff generator

top: *A moving rubber belt carries charged particles from a metal brush up to a metal sphere, where they separate into positive and negative charges.*
bottom: *Touching the metal sphere makes a person's hair stand straight up. Positive charges race to the tips of the hair and then push each other apart.*

vapor (VĀ-per) A gas that contains molecules of a substance that is liquid at room temperature. Unlike substances that exist as gases at room temperature, vapors can be turned back into a liquid if they are subjected to pressure.

variable (VAIR-ē-uh-buhl) A part of a scientific experiment that is allowed to change in order to test a **hypothesis.**

variable star A star that sometimes changes in brightness. A variable star becomes brighter or dimmer because of changes inside it or because another, darker star gets between it and the Earth.

vascular (VAS-kyuh-ler) **1.** Relating to the parts that carry fluid, such as blood or water, in the body of an animal. Arteries and veins make up the vascular systems of many animals. **2.** Relating to the parts of a plant that carry water or sap from one part of the plant to another. Xylem and phloem are the vascular tissues of plants such as trees and shrubs.

VCR Short for **videocassette recorder.** A device that records television programs onto magnetic tapes and then plays them back on the screen.

vector (VEK-ter) A living thing, such as an insect or a tick, that carries and spreads germs that cause disease. Mosquitoes that carry the microorganism that causes malaria are vectors.

vegetable (VEJ-tuh-buhl) **1.** A plant that is grown for its edible parts. **2.** An edible part of one of these plants. The leaf of spinach, the root of a carrot, and the flower of broccoli are all vegetables.

vegetation (vej-uh-TĀ-shuhn) The plant life that grows in an area or region.

vein **1.** A blood vessel that carries blood toward the heart. Veins have flaps called valves that prevent blood from flowing backward. Most veins contain blood with low levels of oxygen. **2.** A small branching tube that forms a supporting part in a leaf or an insect's wing. In plants, veins carry nutrients to leaves. **3.** A long, narrow section of one type of mineral or rock that is found in a second type of rock. Veins usually form when magma flows into cracks in rocks and then cools and hardens.

veldt (VELT *or* FELT) A large, treeless grassland of southern Africa.

velociraptor (vuh-LOS-uh-rap-ter) A small, fast dinosaur that ate meat and grew to about 6 feet (2 meters) long. It had long, curved claws, walked on two legs, and was good at leaping.

velocity (vuh-LOS-i-tē) The rate at which an object moves in a particular direction. A change in an object's velocity is called **acceleration.**

Did You Know?

velocity

To scientists, speed is the rate at which an object moves—the distance traveled divided by the time needed to travel it. Velocity is the same thing as speed, but it also refers to the direction in which an object moves—velocity is speed in a certain direction. Imagine two cars traveling at 50 miles (81 kilometers) per hour. If one is going north and the other west, the two cars are moving at the same speed with different velocities.

Venn diagram A diagram that uses circles to represent **sets.** Relationships between the sets can be shown by the arrangement of the circles. For example, drawing one circle within another shows that the set represented by the smaller circle is a subset of the set represented by the larger circle.

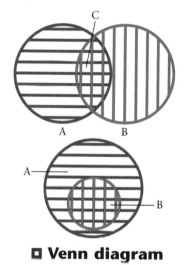

■ **Venn diagram**

top: *Sets A and B intersect to form set C. All members of C are also members of A and B.* bottom: *Set B is a subset of set A. All members of B are also members of A.*

venom (VEN-uhm) A poison that some snakes, spiders, scorpions, and insects produce for killing prey or for defending themselves. Venom flows into a victim through a bite or a sting.

vent **1.** A tube-like hole in a volcano that releases lava, ashes, and gases in an eruption. Vents can either be at the top of a volcano or along its sides. ■ See picture at **volcano. 2.** An opening on the ocean floor from which hot water that is full of minerals comes out.

ventral (VEN-truhl) Located on the front or bottom side of an animal.

ventricle (VEN-tri-kuhl) A chamber of the heart that receives blood from an atrium and pumps it into the arteries. Mammals, birds, and reptiles have two ventricles; amphibians and fish have one.

Venus (VĒ-nuhs) The planet that is second in distance from the Sun and the fourth smallest in the Solar System. Venus is the hottest planet, with a temperature on the surface of almost 850° Fahrenheit (about 450° Celsius). It is the brightest object in the night sky except for the Moon. ◻ See Table on pages 184–185.

vernal equinox (VER-nuhl Ē-kwi-noks) The moment of the year when the Sun crosses the equator while moving from south to north. This happens on March 20 or 21. In the Northern Hemisphere, the vernal equinox marks the beginning of spring. ◻ Compare **autumnal equinox.** ◻ See picture at **season.**

Vernier (ver-NYĀ), **Pierre** Born 1580; died 1637. French mathematician who invented a measuring scale that is used to make other scales more precise. A Vernier scale is marked on a bar as a series of lines that are very closely spaced. The bar is placed up against another scale, such as a ruler or thermometer, to make it easier to judge very small, partial units of the first scale.

vertebra (VER-tuh-bruh) One of the small bones that form the spine. *Plural form:* **vertebrae** (VER-tuh-brā) or **vertebras.** ◻ See picture at **skeleton.**

vertebrate (VER-tuh-brit) An animal that has a spine. Vertebrates have a nervous system that is divided into a brain and a spinal cord, and they have no more than two pairs of limbs. Fish, amphibians, reptiles, birds, and mammals are vertebrates. ◻ Compare **invertebrate.**

vertex (VER-teks) **1.** The point where the sides of an angle meet. **2.** The point of a tri-

angle, cone, or pyramid that is farthest away from its base; the apex. *Plural form:* **vertices** (VER-ti-sēz) or **vertexes.**

Vesalius (vi-SĀ-lē-uhs), **Andreas** Born 1514; died 1564. Flemish doctor who was one of the first people to dissect the human body in order to study its anatomy.

Biography

Andreas Vesalius

Andreas Vesalius did something daring. He examined the insides of the human body by dissecting dead bodies, and he recorded his observations in drawings. In doing this, Vesalius proved that the teachings of Galen, a doctor from ancient Rome whose ideas had been followed for more than 1,000 years, were based on the body structures of dogs and other animals, not humans.

vestigial (ve-STIJ-ē-uhl) Relating to a body part that has evolved so that it no longer has a practical use or function. Vestigial body parts are small and often don't look like the parts they evolved from. Some snakes have vestigial legs on the underside of the body.

vibration (vī-BRĀ-shuhn) A fast backward and forward movement along a straight line. The vibration of a plucked guitar string causes sound waves to form in the air.

vine A plant with long, thin stems that climbs on, creeps along, or wraps around something for support. Grapes, pumpkins, and cucumbers grow on vines.

vinegar (VIN-i-ger) A sour chemical compound that is made by the fermentation of a liquid that contains sugars, such as apple cider. Vinegar is made mostly of water and **acetic acid.**

vinyl (VĪ-nuhl) One of a group of chemical compounds that contain carbon and hydrogen and are used to make plastics, fabrics, and paints.

virology (vī-ROL-uh-jē) The scientific study of viruses and the diseases that are caused by viruses.

virtual reality (VIR-choo-uhl rē-AL-uh-tē) A computer simulation of something real that allows a person to feel like he or she is part of the simulation. To participate in virtual reality, a person usually wears goggles or a helmet that show an image of a space. The person can then perform actions within that space, and the effects of those actions appear on the inside of the goggles or helmet as they happen.

virus (VĪ-ruhs) **1.** A microscopic structure that can grow and reproduce only by invading a living cell. Once a virus enters a cell, it can multiply and cause infection in a person or other living thing. Viruses are not cells themselves but instead are made up of a tiny bit of DNA or RNA that is covered by a coating of protein. Polio and measles are caused by viruses. **2.** A computer program that causes damage to a computer's memory or to the programs that are on the computer. Viruses usually spread from one computer to another over computer networks.

viscosity (vi-SKOS-i-tē) A measure of how hard it is for a liquid or gas to flow. The viscosity of a fluid depends on its **resistance** to flow. Water flows very easily and has a low viscosity. Molasses does not flow very easily and has a high viscosity.

viscous (VIS-kuhs) Relating to a thick liquid that flows slowly. Honey is viscous.

visible light (VIZ-i-buhl LĪT) Electromagnetic waves that can be seen by the human eye. Other forms of electromagnetic radiation, such as infrared light and ultraviolet light, have longer or shorter wavelengths than visible light and cannot be seen.

vitamin (VĪ-tuh-min) A chemical compound that is found in nature and needed by living things for good health. Most vitamins cannot be made by the body and must be taken in as food. Plants get vitamins by absorbing them from the soil. ☐ See Table on page 260.

Did You Know?

vitamin
Most of us know that vitamins are good for us, but what exactly do they do? Vitamins help the body break down fats, carbohydrates, and proteins and convert them into energy that our cells can use to grow and divide.

vocal cords (VŌ-kuhl kordz) Either of two pairs of bands or folds of tissue in the part of the throat called the **larynx.** Sound is produced when air that is breathed out passes through the vocal cords and causes them to vibrate.

voice box *See* **larynx.**

volatile (VOL-uh-tuhl) Evaporating easily at room temperature. Gasoline and turpentine are volatile liquids.

volcanic (vol-KAN-ik) Relating to volcanoes.

Vitamins

Name of Vitamin	Found in	Important for
Vitamin A	fortified milk • green leafy vegetables such as broccoli and spinach • fish	healthy skin and eyes
Vitamin B$_1$ (thiamine)	whole grains • meat • beans	cell metabolism • healthy nervous system
Vitamin B$_2$ (riboflavin)	milk • cheese • eggs • fortified cereals	cell growth • healthy skin
Vitamin B$_6$	whole grains • meat • fish • nuts and seeds	metabolism of proteins and fats • healthy nervous system
Vitamin B$_{12}$	meat • eggs • milk	healthy blood cells and nervous system
Vitamin C	citrus fruits such as oranges and grapefruit • tomatoes • potatoes • green pepper	healthy bones and teeth
Vitamin D	fortified milk • fish • eggs • formed in skin on exposure to sunlight	normal bone growth
Vitamin E	vegetable oil • egg yolks • beans • green vegetables such as avocados • nuts	cell metabolism
Vitamin K	green leafy vegetables such as spinach • meat • vegetable oil	normal blood clotting

volcano (vol-KĀ-nō) An opening in the Earth's crust from which lava, ash, and hot gases come out during an **eruption**. In some volcanoes, the materials are thrown out in a powerful explosion, and in others, they come out slowly. Many volcanoes are mountains, but they can also be cracks in the Earth's surface called **fissures**. When a volcano no longer has eruptions, it is said to be **dormant**.

volt (VŌLT) A unit that is used to measure voltage. One volt is equal to the force that carries one ampere of electric current through a conductor that has a resistance of one ohm.

The volt is named after Alessandro Volta.

Volta (VŌL-tuh), **Alessandro** Born 1745; died 1827. Italian scientist who invented the electric battery in 1800. Called a *voltaic pile,* it was the first device to produce a steady flow of electric current.

voltage (VŌL-tij) **1.** The amount of force that an electric current carries through a circuit. Voltage is measured in volts. **2.** The difference in electric potential between two points in a circuit.

voltmeter (VŌLT-mē-ter) An instrument that is used to measure the difference in volt-

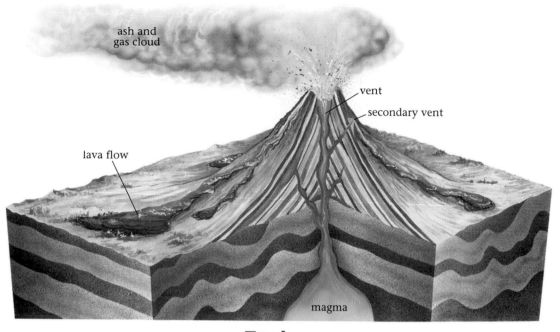

ash and
gas cloud

vent

secondary vent

lava flow

magma

□ **volcano**

---

age between two points in an electric circuit. Voltmeters measure the voltage of both alternating and direct currents.

volume (VOL-yoōm) **1.** The amount of space that is filled by an object. Volume is measured in cubic units, such as cubic feet or cubic meters, and includes the number of feet or meters that make up the length, the height, and the depth of an object. **2.** The loudness of a sound. The higher the volume is, the louder the sound is.

vortex (VOR-teks) A whirling mass of water or air that sucks everything near it toward its center. Tornadoes and whirlpools are vortexes. *Plural form*: **vortexes** or **vortices** (VOR-ti-sēz).

vulcanize (VUHL-kuh-nīz) To harden rubber by heating it and combining it with sulfur. Vulcanizing makes rubber strong and elastic.

Ww

Waksman (WAKS-muhn), **Selman Abraham** Born 1888; died 1973. American scientist who in 1944 discovered the first drug for treating tuberculosis. Waksman invented the word *antibiotic* to describe this drug and the several other drugs he discovered.

Wallace (WAHL-is), **Alfred Russel** Born 1823; died 1913. British scientist who was a leader in the development of the theory of evolution by natural selection.

Biography

Alfred Russel Wallace

Alfred Wallace spent eight years traveling in Malaysia, where he developed a theory of natural selection. He sent his ideas to the English scientist Charles Darwin, who had been working on a similar theory himself. Wallace and Darwin's ideas were so similar that they decided to present their findings to the public together in 1858.

Walton (WAHL-tuhn), **Ernest Thomas Sinton** Born 1903; died 1995. British scientist who, with John Cockcroft, performed the first successful splitting of an atom in 1932.

warm-blooded Having a warm body temperature that stays about the same even if the temperature of the environment changes. Birds and mammals are warm-blooded.

warm front The advancing edge of a mass of warm air that rises over a mass of

Did You Know?

warm-blooded

Warm-blooded animals keep their bodies at a steady temperature by making and storing energy from the food they eat. Being warm-blooded allows an animal to move around, find food, and defend itself even when the temperature outside is much lower than the animal's body temperature. On hot days, warm-blooded animals cool down by getting wet, finding shade, or, in the case of mammals, sweating or panting.

cold air. A warm front often brings a long period of steady rain. ◻ See picture at **front**.

wasp A type of insect that is related to bees and ants. Wasps have two pairs of wings, and females often have a stinger. Wasps live alone or in colonies.

waste **1.** A substance that is left over from a particular process, such as digestion. Living things discharge wastes or waste products such as urine and carbon dioxide. **2.** *See* **hazardous waste**.

waste product Something that is left over or discharged as waste. The lungs give off carbon dioxide as a waste product. Wood chips and sawdust are waste products of the timber industry.

wastewater (WĀST-wah-ter) Water that contains waste products because it has been used for washing, flushing, or some other process; sewage.

water (WAH-ter) A colorless liquid that falls to Earth as rain, is a very important part of all living things, and is necessary for most of life's processes. Water covers three-quarters of the Earth's surface and also occurs as a solid (in the form of ice) and as a gas (in the form of vapor). Water contains two atoms of hydrogen for every one atom of oxygen; its chemical formula is H_2O. ◻ See picture at **molecule.**

water cycle The continuous movement of water throughout the Earth and its atmosphere. Energy from the Sun evaporates water from the Earth's surface. The water vapor rises into the atmosphere, where it condenses to form **clouds.** Water returns to the Earth as rain or another form of **precipitation,** and the cycle begins again. ◻ The water cycle is also called the *hydrologic cycle.*

watershed (WAH-ter-shed) **1.** A region that includes a river and all its tributaries. Rain or snow that falls anywhere in the same watershed will eventually flow to the same river. **2.** A ridge of land that forms a dividing line between two river systems.

water table The level at which the ground is soaked with water. The water table is usually higher after heavy rainfall and after the melting of snow, and lower during drier periods. When a well is built into the ground to collect water, its base must be lower than the top of the water table in order to draw water.

water vapor Water that exists naturally as a gas, especially in the atmosphere. When water vapor condenses in the atmosphere, it forms clouds. When it condenses close to the Earth's surface, it forms dew or frost.

Watson (WAHT-suhn), **James Dewey** Born 1928. American scientist who, with Francis Crick, explained the structure of DNA in 1953.

Watson-Watt (WAHT-suhn-WAHT), **Robert Alexander** Born 1892; died 1973. British scientist who invented radar in 1935.

watt (WAHT) A unit that is used to measure power. One watt is equal to one joule of work per second. In electricity, a watt is equal to the amount of current in a circuit (in amperes) multiplied by the force that is needed to make it flow (in volts). The watt is named after James Watt.

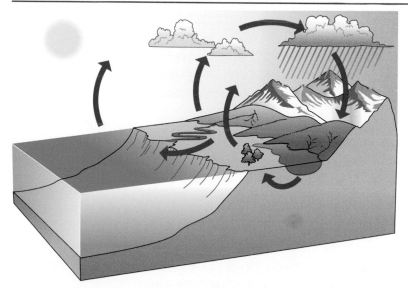

◻ water cycle

Water that evaporates from the Earth's surface forms clouds and returns to the Earth as rain or snow.

A Closer Look

Wave

*Sound, light, x-rays, and other types of energy spread outward in the form of waves. Waves travel through what is known as a **medium**. A rock dropped in a pool creates waves that travel through the medium of water. Sound waves usually travel through the medium of air. The lines on the oscilloscope screen below are an image of the sound waves from a bird's song.*

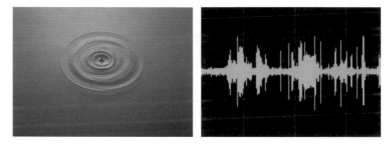

*Waves that travel up and down are measured by two things: their **amplitude** (how high and low they go from a line through their center) and their **wavelength** (how far it is from one crest to another):*

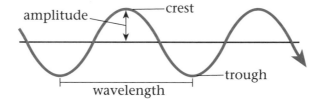

*Waves that travel back and forth are measured by their **frequency** (how close each wave is to the next one):*

high   low

Watt, James Born 1736; died 1819. Scottish inventor who made the steam engine more efficient. Watt also introduced the unit of horsepower to measure the power of engines and motors.

wattage (WAHT-ij) An amount of electric power, such as the amount of power that is needed to light a bulb or run a dishwasher. Wattage is measured in watts or kilowatts.

wave A motion back and forth or up and down that passes energy from one point to another. Light, sound, and heat travel as waves of energy. In ocean waves, energy passes through the water even though the water molecules do not have any overall forward movement.

wavelength The distance between the crest of a wave and the crest that comes before or after it in a series of waves. ☐ See picture at **wave**.

wax A sticky solid substance that quickly softens or melts when it is heated. Waxes in nature are made by various animals and plants. Waxes can also be made in the laboratory from petroleum.

weather (WE*TH*-er) The state of the atmosphere at a particular time and place. Weather is described by changing conditions such as the temperature and humidity of the air, the speed and direction of the wind, and the presence of rain, snow, or other **precipitation.**

weather map A map that shows the weather conditions for a particular area. A weather map gives local temperatures throughout the area and shows whether there are any clouds or **precipitation.** It also shows the position of any warm fronts or cold fronts that might be present, which is useful in predicting how the weather is likely to change.

weather satellite A satellite that has special instruments for observing conditions in the Earth's atmosphere. Weather satellites send photographs, infrared images, and other information back to Earth for use in tracking storms and forecasting the weather.

web 1. A network of fine, silky threads that is spun by a spider or the larvae of some insects. Spiders use webs to catch insects for food. 2. A fold of skin between the toes of some animals, such as water birds and otters, that helps them swim. 3. *See* **World Wide Web.**

wedge An object that is thick at one end and very thin at the other. Wedges are used for splitting, tightening, or holding things in place. A wedge is a kind of **inclined plane** that is moved to perform work. ◻ See picture at **machine.**

Wegener (VĀ-guh-ner), **Alfred Lothar** Born 1880; died 1930. German scientist who introduced the theory of continental drift in 1915.

weight (WĀT) A measure of the force with which gravity pulls an object toward the center of the Earth or another object in

Biography
Alfred Lothar Wegener
Alfred Wegener was not the first to notice that the coasts of eastern South America and western Africa were shaped as if they were once joined together, like two pieces of a puzzle. But he was the first to investigate this, and he found that rocks and fossils on the two coasts matched up. This led him to the idea that the continents had once been part of a giant land mass that had split into large pieces—an idea that is accepted today as correct.

space. An object's weight depends on its **mass** and the strength of the pull of gravity. An object's weight can vary, depending on the pull of gravity. A rocket that weighs many tons on the surface of the Earth will have no weight in outer space.

well A hole dug into the Earth to collect water, oil, or natural gas. The wells used to collect drinking water are usually made of pipes that have a section made of screen to let in water from the **water table.** The water in the pipe is then pumped up to the surface.

west The direction in which the Sun sets.

Western Hemisphere The half of the Earth that includes North America, Central America, and South America.

Westinghouse (WES-ting-hows), **George** Born 1846; died 1914. American inventor who introduced the system of electricity that uses alternating current to the United States.

wet cell An electric cell in which the chemical compounds that produce the current are in the form of a liquid. Car batteries are made of a series of wet cells.

◘ wetland

left to right: *a marsh in Florida, a swamp in Louisiana, and a bog in Argentina*

wetland　A low-lying area of land that is either soaked or covered with water. Marshes, swamps, and bogs are wetlands. A wetland is a kind of **biome.**

whale　A type of sea mammal that often grows very large. Whales have a flat, horizontal tail and nostrils on the top of their heads. Some whales, like the sperm whale, have teeth in their jaws, while others, like the blue whale and humpback whale, have **baleen.**

wheel　A round, flat object that can turn on a point at its center. Wheels can be used to move vehicles or to drive machines. ◘ See picture at **machine.**

whirlpool　(WERI-pool) A current of water that spins rapidly. Whirlpools can swirl with great force and often can pull objects beneath the surface of the water. They are caused by the meeting of two tides or currents, by the shape of the shoreline, or by the wind.

white blood cell　A colorless cell that is found in the blood of humans and other vertebrates and helps protect the body from infection by fighting germs. White blood cells have a nucleus, unlike red blood cells. **Lymphocytes** are a kind of white blood cell.

white dwarf star　A whitish star that is very dense and small, about the size of Earth. A white dwarf star is the last stage in the life of a star. It will eventually cool and dim to become a **black dwarf star.** ◘ See picture at **star.**

Whitney　(WIT-ne), **Eli** Born 1765; died 1825. American inventor who developed the cotton gin, a machine that removes the seeds from cotton fiber. Whitney later opened the first factory to manufacture large quantities of products with parts that would fit any product of the same design.

whole number　A positive integer or zero. 0, 1, 2, 3, and 452 are all whole numbers. 16.1 and $\frac{2}{5}$ are not whole numbers.

whooping cough　(HOOP-ing KAWF *or* HUP-ing KAWF) A disease in which a person has periods of coughing that can't be stopped and the cough is followed by a series of loud gasps. Whooping cough mostly affects young children, is caused by bacteria, and is very contagious. ◘ Whooping cough is also called *pertussis.*

width　The distance of a thing measured from side to side.

wildlife　Animals that live in their natural surroundings without the influence or control of humans.

Wilkins (WIL-kinz), **Maurice Hugh Frederick** Born 1916. British scientist who helped discover the structure of DNA.

Wilson (WIL-suhn), **Edmund Beecher** Born 1856; died 1939. American scientist who studied the role that genes play in the development of cells. In 1905 he demonstrated that the sex of an organism is determined by chromosomes, a discovery independently reached by Nettie Stevens in the same year.

wind A flow of air, especially a natural flow that moves along the surface of the Earth. Winds are named according to the direction they come from. For example, a west wind is a wind that blows from west to east.

wind chill The effect that wind has in making bare skin feel colder. Wind causes skin to lose heat, even though it doesn't change the temperature of the air. If the air temperature is 20° Fahrenheit (7° Celsius) and the wind is blowing at 40 miles (64 kilometers) per hour, the wind chill would make it feel like –1° Fahrenheit (–18° Celsius).

windmill A tower with a set of sails or wide blades at its top that are spun by the wind. The moving sails or blades give power to machines on the ground that can pump water, crush grain into flour, or make electricity.

windpipe *See* **trachea.**

wind tunnel A room or structure that is equipped with a large fan that blows air at set speeds. Scientists use wind tunnels to study the effect of air on a moving object, such as an aircraft.

wing 1. One of a pair of movable parts that allow a bird, bat, or insect to fly. 2. A part that sticks out from the side of an aircraft and allows it to fly. Wings have a curved upper surface that causes the pressure of the air rushing over it to decrease. The greater air pressure below pushes the wing upward and causes the aircraft to lift. 3. A thin part that sticks out on certain plant seeds and allows them to be carried by the wind. Ash, elm, and maple tree seeds have wings.

◻ **wing**

Wings allow birds, bats, and insects to glide and soar: (top) a screech owl, (bottom left) a brown bat, and (bottom right) a dragonfly.

winter (WIN-ter) The coldest season of the year, between autumn and spring. In the Northern Hemisphere, it lasts from the winter solstice, in late December, to the vernal equinox, in late March.

winter solstice (WIN-ter SOL-stis) The moment of the year when the Sun is farthest south of the equator. This happens on December 21 or 22. In the Northern Hemisphere, the winter solstice marks the beginning of winter and is the day of the year with the shortest period of sunlight. ◻ Compare **summer solstice.** ◻ See picture at **season.**

wire A usually flexible, thin strand or rod that is made of metal. Wires that carry electricity are usually made of copper or aluminum and are often bundled together and covered with **insulation.** Wires made of steel can be twisted together to form thick, rope-like cables and used to hang extremely heavy objects.

wisdom tooth (WIZ-duhm TŌOTH) One of four molars in humans, the last on each side of both jaws. The wisdom teeth are the last molars to grow in and usually appear in young adulthood.

womb (WŌOM) *See* **uterus.**

wood The hard material beneath the bark of trees and shrubs that makes up the trunk. Wood consists of the tissue known as **xylem** and is mainly made of cellulose and lignin. Wood is used for fuel and for building.

woodland *See* **forest.**

Woods, Granville Born 1856; died 1910. American inventor who developed electric and mechanical devices to make railroad transportation safer and more efficient. He invented an electric rail system that is today used to power subway trains.

woody plant A plant that contains wood in its trunk, stem, or roots. Trees, shrubs, and some vines are woody plants.

work The transfer of energy from one object to another, especially in order to make the second object move. Work is equal to the amount of force multiplied by the distance over which it is applied. If a force of 10 newtons is applied over a distance of 3 meters, the work is equal to 30 newtons per meter (or 30 joules).

worker An ant or bee that builds the nest and does other work in a colony. Workers are usually females that do not have the ability to reproduce.

World Wide Web An enormous collection of electronic documents that are stored on computers connected over the **Internet.** Documents on the World Wide Web require the use of HTTP (short for Hypertext Transfer Protocol) and have "http" as the start of their website names.

worm **1.** An animal with a soft, long body and usually no limbs. Some worms, such as the earthworm, live in soil, while others live in water or as parasites in other animals. Worms are invertebrates. **2.** A destructive computer program that copies itself over and over until it fills up all of the computer's space for storing information.

wound (WŌOND) An injury to a part of the body in which tissue, such as skin or bone, is cut or broken.

Xx

x-axis (EXS-AK-sis) The horizontal axis of a graph. ◘ See picture at **Cartesian coordinate system.**

X-chromosome (EKS-KRŌ-muh-sōm) The sex chromosome that is combined with another X-chromosome in the sex cells of females and with a **Y-chromosome** in the sex cells of males. ◘ See picture at **chromosome.**

x-ray A stream of electromagnetic radiation that has wavelengths shorter than those of ultraviolet light but longer than those of a gamma ray. X-rays are taken in and absorbed by many

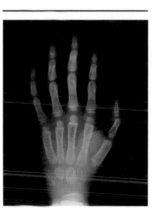

◘ **x-ray**

of a human hand

forms of matter, including body tissues, and are used to take pictures of the inside of things, such as parts of the body. Doctors use x-rays to determine the health of bones.

x-ray astronomy The branch of astronomy that studies objects in space by collecting and analyzing the x-rays they give off. In x-ray astronomy, scientists locate and learn about objects that don't give off **visible light,** such as black holes.

x-ray telescope An instrument that is used to observe or study distant objects by gathering the x-rays that come from them.

xylem (ZĪ-luhm) A tissue in plants that carries water and minerals up from the roots, through the stem, and to the leaves. ◘ Compare **phloem.** ◘ See pictures at **root, stem.**

Yy

Yalow (YAL-ō), **Rosalyn Sussman** Born 1921. American scientist who invented a way to measure very small amounts of substances, such as hormones, that are found in blood. Her discovery made it easier for doctors to tell if a person has a particular disease and if the medicines used to treat it are working.

yard A unit of length equal to 3 feet or 36 inches (0.91 meter). ❑ See Table on page 148.

y-axis (WĪ-AK-sis) The vertical axis of a graph. ❑ See picture at **Cartesian coordinate system**.

Y-chromosome (WĪ-KRŌ-muh-sōm) The sex chromosome that is combined with an **X-chromosome** in the sex cells of males. Females do not have a Y-chromosome. ❑ See picture at **chromosome**.

year The period of time that it takes for a planet to make one complete orbit around the Sun. A year on Earth lasts 365 days; a year on Mars lasts as long as 687 days on Earth.

Did You Know?

year

A year is actually 365 days and 6 hours long. After 4 years, those extra 6 hours add up to a whole day. We see that extra day every 4 years, when there is a leap year. The extra day is February 29.

yeast A tiny living thing that is made up of one cell and turns sugar into alcohol and carbon dioxide in the process called **fermentation**. Yeast is a kind of fungus. When yeast is used to make bread, the carbon dioxide bubbles that form make the dough rise.

yellow fever (YEL-ō FĒ-ver) A serious disease in which a person has fever and the skin and eyes turn yellowish in color. Yellow fever is caused by a virus and is carried by mosquitoes. Yellow fever is most often seen in tropical climates.

yellow jacket A small wasp that has black and yellow bands on its body and lives in colonies. The females sting and are fiercely protective of their nests.

Yersin (yer-SAHN), **Alexandre Émile John** Born 1863; died 1943. French scientist who, with Émile Roux in 1888, discovered the toxin produced by the bacteria that cause diphtheria. Their discovery led to the development of a treatment for the disease. In 1894, Yersin discovered the bacteria that cause bubonic plague and developed a serum to prevent the disease.

yolk (YŌK) The yellow part of the egg of a bird or reptile. The yolk supplies nutrients to the developing animal before it hatches.

young An animal that is in an early stage of development; offspring. The young of a frog is called a tadpole. The young of most mammals first develop inside the mother's womb.

Yukawa (yōō-KAH-wuh), **Hideki** Born 1907; died 1981. Japanese scientist who studied the forces that hold the nucleus of an atom together.

Zz

zenith (ZĒ-nith) The point in the sky that is directly overhead.

zero (ZEER-ō) The number 0. When zero is added to a number, that number remains unchanged. When a number is multiplied by zero, the result is zero.

zero gravity A condition in which an object appears to have no weight because it is moving in such a way that it balances out the pull of gravity.

Did You Know?

zero gravity

Astronauts in orbit around the Earth experience zero gravity and float around inside their spacecraft. This happens not because the astronauts no longer have any weight, but because the spacecraft undergoes just enough acceleration as it moves around the Earth to counterbalance the pull of gravity. If the spacecraft and its astronauts actually had no weight, they would drift away from Earth into space.

zinc A chemical element that is a soft, shiny, bluish-white metal. Zinc is an important ingredient of brass and bronze, and it is used as a coating for iron and steel to prevent rust. Zinc is necessary in small amounts for the growth of humans and animals. ◻ See Table on pages 178–179.

zirconium (zer-KŌ-nē-uhm) A chemical element that is a shiny, grayish-white metal. Zirconium is used to build nuclear reactors, because it is not damaged by the high temperatures and the **nuclear reaction.** ◻ See Table on pages 178–179.

zone **1.** One of the five regions into which the surface of the Earth is divided according to climate and latitude. The five zones are the **Torrid Zone,** the **North Temperate Zone,** the **South Temperate Zone,** the **North Frigid Zone,** and the **South Frigid Zone. 2.** *See* **time zone.**

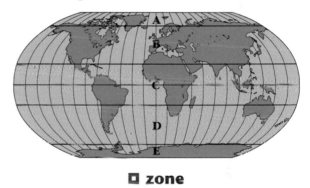

◻ **zone**

A. *North Frigid Zone;* B. *North Temperate Zone;*
C. *Torrid Zone;* D. *South Temperate Zone;*
E. *South Frigid Zone*

zoology (zō-OL-uh-jē *or* zōō-OL-uh-jē) The scientific study of animals.

zooplankton (zō-uh-PLANGK-tuhn) Plankton that is made up of tiny animals and some microscopic organisms.

zygote (ZĪ-gōt) The fertilized egg of an animal or plant. A zygote is formed when two **sex cells,** one from the male parent and one from the female parent, join together.

Scientific Abbreviations

Measurements

Length in the Metric System

km kilometer
m   meter
cm centimeter
mm millimeter

Length in the United States Customary System

mi. mile
yd. yard
ft. foot
in. inch

Weight in the Metric System

kg kilogram
g   gram
mg milligram

Weight in the United States Customary System

lb. pound
oz. ounce

Volume in the Metric System

l   liter
ml milliliter

Volume in the United States Customary System

gal. gallon
qt.   quart
pt.   pint

Temperature in the Metric System

C Celsius
K Kelvin

Temperature in the United States Customary System

F Fahrenheit

Geometry

A area
c circumference
d diameter
h height
l length
r radius
V volume
w width

Physics

c speed of light
g acceleration of gravity
m mass

Time

s second
m minute
h hour
D day
M month
Y year

Timeline of Scientific Discovery

6th century BC **Pythagoras** proposes that nature can be understood through mathematics

5th–4th century BC **Hippocrates** takes steps to make medicine scientific by basing treatment on observation and logic rather than superstition

4th century BC **Aristotle** founds a school that teaches the importance of observation, logic, and theory

3rd century BC **—Euclid** writes a book on geometry that is used until the 19th century

—Eratosthenes estimates the circumference of the Sun and the distance to the Sun and Moon

2nd century BC **Hipparchus** creates the first chart of stars and planets

2nd century AD **—Galen** describes the parts and functions of the human body

—Ptolemy develops a model of the universe that has the Earth as the center of the Solar System ◻

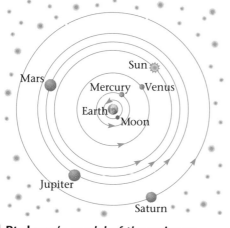

◻ Ptolemy's *model of the universe*

1202 Fibonacci popularizes the decimal system that is still in use today

1506–1513 Leonardo da Vinci creates drawings in astronomy, mechanics, and anatomy and draws up plans for machines that are not built until centuries later

1543 —Copernicus proposes that the planets revolve around the Sun

—Vesalius publishes books on human anatomy learned from dissection

1572 Brahe observes a supernova (later called Tycho's star) before the invention of the telescope

1600 Gilbert introduces the words *electricity* and *magnetic pole* in the first major scientific book published in England

1609 —Galileo studies stars and planets using a telescope

—Kepler publishes his discovery that planets orbit around the Sun in the shape of an ellipse

1628 Harvey publishes a book that shows how the heart pumps blood through the body

1637 Descartes publishes a group of writings in which he uses algebra to solve geometry problems

1643 Torricelli invents the barometer

1659 Huygens discovers the rings of the planet Saturn

1662 Boyle and **Hooke** publish findings on the behavior of gases

1665 Hooke publishes his observations of plants under a microscope and invents the word *cell*

274

□ **Newton's** *reflecting telescope*

1668 Newton invents the first reflecting telescope □

1674 Leeuwenhoek studies bacteria and protozoans under a microscope

1687 Newton publishes works on mathematics and explains gravitation

1714 Fahrenheit invents the mercury thermometer

1724 Fahrenheit develops the Fahrenheit scale

1742 Celsius develops the Celsius scale

1753 Linnaeus publishes a book containing scientific names for plants

1756 Black discovers carbon dioxide

1766 Cavendish discovers hydrogen

1769 Watt invents the modern steam engine

1774 Priestley discovers oxygen

1781 Herschel discovers the planet Uranus

1785 Hutton proposes the theory that the history of the Earth can be explained by the study of its rocks

1789 Lavoisier publishes the *Elementary Treatise of Chemistry*

1796 Jenner performs the first smallpox vaccination

1800 Volta invents the first electric battery

1805 Dalton describes how matter is made up of small particles called *atoms*

1807 Fulton invents the steamboat □

1808 Gay-Lussac describes how gases behave when they combine

1812 Mohs develops a scale for determining hardness in rocks

1819 Oersted observes that electric current produces a magnetic force and founds the study of electromagnetism

1831 Faraday develops the first electric generator and transformer

1833 Lyell finishes his book *Principles of Geology,* which popularizes the field of geology

mid-1830s Babbage draws up plans for a machine that performs mathematical calculations, the forerunner of the modern computer

1844 Morse develops the telegraph

1847 Helmholtz proposes the law of conservation of energy

□ *painting of* **Fulton's** *steamboat*

Timeline of Scientific Discovery

◻ **Foucault** *pendulum*

1848 Kelvin develops the Kelvin scale

1850 Foucault measures the velocity of light

1851 Foucault uses a pendulum to show that the Earth rotates on its axis ◻

1858 Darwin and **Wallace** together present the theory of evolution by natural selection to the public

1859 Lenoir designs the first practical internal-combustion engine

1862–1877 Pasteur's study of microorganisms leads to theory that germs cause disease

1865 —Maxwell shows that light is a form of electromagnetic radiation

—**Lister** introduces antiseptics to the practice of surgery

1865–1866 Mendel proposes theories about heredity in plants

1869 Mendeleev develops the Periodic Table of the elements

1876 Bell invents the telephone

1879 Edison invents the incandescent lamp ◻

1882–1887 Tesla invents alternating current and devices for using it

1888 Roux and **Yersin** discover the toxin that causes diphtheria

1894–1910 Ramsay discovers the noble gases

1895 Roentgen discovers x-rays

1896 Becquerel's studies of uranium show that it is radioactive

1897 Thomson discovers the electron

1898 Marie and **Pierre Curie** discover the elements polonium and radium

1900 —Ehrlich describes how antibodies form

—**Planck** discovers units of energy called *quanta*

1901 Marconi sends radio waves across the Atlantic

1905 Einstein introduces the first part of his theory of relativity

1911 Rutherford discovers the nucleus of the atom and describes the basic structure of the atom

1913 Bohr develops a new theory of the structure of the atom, based on the work of Rutherford and Planck

1915 Wegener introduces the theory of continental drift

◻ **Edison's** *incandescent lamp*

1916 Einstein introduces the second part of his theory of relativity

1919 Eddington proves the second part of Einstein's theory of relativity

1921 Banting and **Best** discover the hormone insulin

1924 Hubble presents proof of the existence of other galaxies

1926 Goddard builds the first rocket

1928 Fleming discovers penicillin

1930 Alexanderson builds the first practical television

1932 —**Chadwick** discovers the neutron

—**Cockroft** and **Walton** perform the first successful splitting of an atom

1935 Watson-Watt invents radar

1937 Krebs shows how cells store energy and make food

1938 Work by **Hahn** and colleagues on uranium leads to the discovery of nuclear fission

1942 Fermi creates the first man-made nuclear chain reaction

1942–1949 Hodgkin discovers the structure of penicillin and vitamin B_{12}

1944 Waksman and colleagues discover the first antibiotic for treating tuberculosis

1951 Rosalind Franklin uses x-rays to study the structure of DNA

1953 Watson and **Crick** explain the structure of DNA, based in part on studies by Rosalind Franklin and Maurice Wilkins

1955 —**Salk** introduces the first polio vaccine

—**Sanger** explains the structure of the hormone insulin

late 1950s Sperry discovers that the two sides of the brain control different body functions

1959 Louis and **Mary Leakey** discover early human fossils in Africa

1960 —**Maiman** invents the first working laser

—**Goodall** begins her study of chipanzees in Tanzania

1962 Carson publishes a book that details the effects of pesticides on the environment

1964 Gell-Mann introduces the idea of quarks

1967 Barnard performs the first successful human heart transplant

1974 Hawking describes the energy in a black hole using mathematics

1980 Luis and **Walter Alvarez** introduce the theory that an asteroid caused extinction of the dinosaurs

1990 Hubble Space Telescope is launched

1991 World Wide Web becomes widely available

1997 Handheld computers become popular ◻

2000-2003 Hundreds of millions of people worldwide use cell phones

◻ *handheld computer*

277

Picture Credits (continued)

Sugar **lens** EM **Leonardo da Vinci** Art Resource, New York/Alinari; Art Resource, New York/Réunion des Musées Nationaux **life cycle** EM **ligament** CI **lightning** PDI-GI/R. Morley, PhotoLink **litmus paper** Image Finders/Jim Baron **liver** CI **longitude** Raquel Sousa **magnet** CMSP/T. Bannor **mammal** PR/Gerald C. Kelley; COR/Douglas Faulkner **marsupial** PR/Tom McHugh **matter** EM **Mendeleev** PR/Science Photo Library **metamorphosis** EM **microscope** PDI-GI/E. Pollard, PhotoLink; PR/Meckes-Ottawa **Milky Way** PR/SPL, Dr. Fred Espenak **mimicry** Grant Heilman Photography, Inc./Eric Heyer **mineral** AA-ES/Color Pic; CMSP/D. Weinstein; PR/Biophoto Associates **mirage** PDI-GI/Jeremy Woodhouse **molecule** RS **moon** PDI-GI/StockTrek; David Mackay Ballard **Morse code** Academy Artworks **moss** COR/Richard Hamilton Smith **muscle** CI **mutualism** COR/Kennan Ward **neap tide** PG **nebula** COR/AFP **neon** COR/Paul A. Souders **Newton** Art Resource, New York/Erich Lessing **nitrogen cycle** EM **nuclear reactor** PG **observatory** COR/Roger Ressmeyer **oscillation** PG **ozone** PR/SPL, NOAA **Pangaea** EM **parasite** PR/Larry West; COR/Frank Blackburn, Ecoscene **Pasteur** Art Resource, New York/Réunion des Musées Nationaux **peninsula** PR/SPL, NOAA, NSIDC **petri dish** PR/SPL, Simon Fraser **photosynthesis** EM **pixel** UG/GGS Information Services **polar cap** NASA and the Hubble Heritage Team (STScI/AURA) **pollination** COR/Tony Hamblin, Frank Lane Picture Agency **pollution** David Mackay Ballard **potential energy** EM **prism** PR/SPL, David Parker **Pythagorean theorem** RS **quadrilateral** RS **quartz** FP/Paul Silverman **radar** UG/GGS **rain forest** COR/Yann Arthus-Bertrand **rainbow** PG **red blood cell** PR/SPL, Andrew Syred **reef** PR/F. Westmoreland **reflection** PG **refraction** Jerry Malone **reptile** AA-ES/Roger De La Harpe **respiratory system** CI **Richards** MIT Museum **river** Image Finders/Joanne Williams; Getty Images-Stone/David Hiser **robot** COR/Zuma Press, Inc. **root** EM **rust** FP/Sylvester Allred **Salk** Corbis-Bettmann **satellite** Jerry Malone **season** RS **seismograph** COR/Roger Ressmeyer **shadow** COR/Phil Schermeister; AA-ES/Peter Baumann **skin** CI **smog** COR/Ted Spiegel **soil** PG **solar cell** UG/GGS Information Services **solution** Image Finders/Jim Baron **sonar** PG **sponge** FP/David & Doris Krumholz **spring tide** PG **stalactite** PR/Farrell Grehan **star** PG **static electricity** COR/Roy McMahon **stem** EM **stethoscope** PR/SPL, CC Studio **stoma** PR/SPL, Andrew Syred **stomach** CI **strip mine** PR/Georg Gerster **sun** Academy Artworks **surface tension** COR/Robert Pickett **symmetry** PG **taste bud** CI **telescope** PG; NASA, Marshall Space Flight Center **temperature** EM **thermometer** Corbis Royalty-free; Corbis Royalty-free **tide** PR/Jeffrey Greenberg; PR/Jeffrey Greenberg **time zone** UG/GGS Information Services **tooth** Grant Heilman Photography, Inc./Runk & Schoenberger; Peter Arnold, Inc./Martin Harvey **topography** Digital Vision-Getty Images **tornado** COR/Jim Zuckerman **tortoise** AA-ES/Patti Murray **transformer** RS **transpiration** EM

tree Wendy Smith **triangle** RS **trilobite** COR/James L. Amos **tsunami** Jerry Malone **ungulate** EM **Van de Graaff generator** Academy Artworks; COR/Paul A. Souders **Venn diagram** EM **Vesalius** PR/Science Photo Library **volcano** Patrice Rossi Calkin **water cycle** EM **wetland** AA-ES/Lightwave Photography; AA-ES/Manfred Gottschalk; AA-ES/Brian K. Miller **wing** COR/Joe McDonald; AA-ES/McDonald Wildlife Photography; PR/Art Wolfe **x-ray** PDI-GI/Jim Wehtje **zero gravity** PR/SPL, NASA **zone** UG/GGS Information Services

Parts of the Dictionary
bacteria PT/Dennis Kunkel; PT/Microworks; PT/Dennis Kunkel **bond** RS **bone** CI **bony fish** COR/Kennan Ward

Charts, Tables, and Other Features
Cell: animal cell PG plant cell PG cell division PT/Dennis Kunkel
Classification of Life: EM
Color: EM
Flower: EM
Geologic Time: roadway PG spot illustrations EM
Greenhouse Effect: PG
Leaf: broad AA-ES/Gordon & Cathie Sullivan grass AA-ES/Robert Comport needle COR/Lowell Georgia spine PDI-GI
Machines: EM
Plate Tectonics: PG
Periodic Table: Cathy Hawkes, Cat & Mouse
Planets of the Solar System: Mercury PDI-GI Venus Courtesy of NASA/JPL/Caltech Earth PDI-GI Mars PDI-GI Jupiter PDI-GI Saturn PDI-GI Uranus NASA Neptune PDI-GI Pluto Courtesy of Dr. R. Albrecht, ESA/ESO Space Telescope, European Coordinating Facility and NASA
Rock Types: igneous AA-ES/Boyle & Boyle granite PDI-GI lava AA-ES/C.C. Lockwood sandstone COR/Pat O'Hara shale COR/Tom Bean limestone COR/Layne Kennedy gneiss COR/Steve Austin, Papilio schist COR/Gary Braasch marble Index Stock Imagery/Dale Chinn
Skeleton: human CI fish COR/Enzo & Paolo Ragazzini snake Grant Heilman Photography, Inc./Runk & Schoenberger
Star: PG
Wave: liquid Grant Heilman Photography, Inc./Runk & Schoenberger oscillogram Courtesy of Mr. Andreas Nieder structure RS frequency EM

Timeline of Scientific Discovery
Ptolemy: RS
Newton: COR/James A. Sugar
Fulton: Corbis-Bettmann
Foucault: Corbis-Bettmann
Edison: COR/Schenectady Museum, Hall of Electrical History Foundation
handheld computer: Digital Vision-Getty Images